Socia...
Physical Education
Learning to Teach

Editors
THOMAS J. TEMPLIN, Ph.D.
Purdue University
PAUL G. SCHEMPP, Ed.D.
University of Oregon

Brown &
Benchmark

Library of Congress Cataloging in Publication Data:
TEMPLIN, THOMAS J., 1950 -

SOCIALIZATION INTO PHYSICAL EDUCATION: LEARNING TO TEACH

Cover Design: Gary Schmitt
Copy Editors: Lynn Hendershot; Becky Claxton

Library of Congress Catalog Card number: 87-72234
ISBN: 0-697-14831-9

Printed in the United States of America by Brown & Benchmark, 2460 Kerper Boulevard, Dubuque, IA 52001.

10 9 8 7 6 5 4 3 2

The Publisher and Author disclaim responsibility for any adverse effects or consequences from the misapplication or injudicious use of the information contained within this text.

Contents

DEDICATION

This book is dedicated:
  to Sarah, Kate, and Andrew
  T.J.T.
  to Sandy, Adam, and Peter
  P.G.S.
  to those public school physical educators, physical education
teacher educators, and all others who strive to make school physical education a positive experience for students and teachers alike.
  T.J.T. and P.G.S.

Contributors

Linda Bain, Ph.D.
California State University-Northridge
Northridge, CA

Alison Dewar, Ph.D.
Miami University
Oxford, Ohio

Patt Dodds, Ph.D.
University of Massachusetts
Amherst, MA

Sarah Doolittle, Ed.D.
University of Massachusetts
Amherst, MA

John Evans, Ph.D.
University of Southampton
Southampton, England

Kim C. Graber, Ph.D.
University of Oregon
Eugene, OR

Pat Griffin, Ph.D.
University of Massachusetts
Amherst, MA

Marian E. Kneer, Ph.D.
University of Illinois-Chicago
Chicago, IL

Colin Lacey, Ph.D.
University of Sussex
Falmer, Sussex, England

Hal A. Lawson, Ph.D.
Miami University
Oxford, Ohio

Thomas J. Martinek, Ed.D.
University of North Carolina-Greensboro
Greensboro, NC

Bernard Oliver, Ph.D.
St. Cloud State University
St. Cloud, MN

George H. Sage, Ph.D.
University of Northern Colorado
Greeley, CO

Paul Schempp, Ed.D.
University of Oregon
Eugene, OR

Susan Schwager, Ed.D.
Montclair State College
Upper Montclair, NJ

Andrew Sparkes, Ph.D.
Exeter University
Exeter, Devonshire, England

Thomas J. Templin, Ph.D.
Purdue University
West Lafayette, IN

Trefor Williams
University of Southampton
Southampton, England

Foreword

Studies into the socialization and selection of teachers have a relatively long tradition within the social sciences. Willard Waller's classic study *The Sociology of Teaching* (1932) began an analysis of the role of the teacher and its effects on personality and social status, which has continued in many modern studies. Waller pointed to the uncertain authority of the teacher, which he described as a 'despotism resting upon children'. He saw their authority as being constantly threatened by the pupils in the classroom and by parents, the school board, other groups in the community, the alumni, and more disturbingly, each other. The fragility of their authority and status was seen by Waller as a major factor in shaping the social and classroom persona of the teacher. Waller describes the granite-like expressions on the faces of teachers in the study hall as the result of being forced to pose as symbols of authority.

Later researchers have shifted the focus of study according to the more fashionable preoccupations of the period. During the 1950s the social class origins of teachers became an important issue. Later in the same decade and in the 1960s, the progress made within psychology on the study of personality and attitudes gave rise to a large number of studies using personality and attendant innovations. The best of these studies endeavored to discover what makes a person decide to take up teaching and what attitudes characterize different groups of teachers. Despite Waller's emphasis on authority, teachers emerged from these studies as high on person-centeredness and with a substantial number of them emphasizing the welfare of the child above interest in their subject.

The application of case study and participant observation to the socialization of teachers in the 1970s gave rise to studies that had two important characteristics. First, they were able to utilize the methodological and theoretical advances of earlier studies. In drawing on these strengths, they were able to study a range of issues from the precocious nature of teacher authority, through the family and social class origins of teachers, to attitudes and personality indicators. The price that had to be paid for this eclecticism was the relatively small sample of teachers it was possible to include in such detailed research. However, this gave rise to the second important characteristic of this approach. By choosing the cohort of teachers carefully it was possible to minimize the effects of a small sample. On the other hand the rich description of the course, the response of teachers in training to their course and teaching practice, and the descriptions of early adjustments of new entrants to their first job meant that these studies were far more accessible and interesting to the students themselves. They were less specialized and less closed and could be used reflexive in the training of new teachers.

This development has made it possible to link research and the training of teachers in new and exciting ways. Lortie (1975) pointed out that social workers, clinical psychologists, and psychotherapists are trained to take their own personalities into account in their work with people. Their professional stance needs to be open and analytical, and to achieve this, their education needs to include exercises in reflexivity and openness. It is clear from Waller's early writings and subsequent research that teachers are placed in universally stressful situations. One of the steps that can be taken to minimize the effects of this stress is for the teacher to understand its causes and realize that other teachers are similarly affected. The need for analytical openness has never been greater.

One of the inhibitions of communication and openness among teachers has been their heterogeneity. They are drawn from a wide variety of backgrounds and subject disciplines. These disciplines have shaped their world view and contributed to the skills and knowledge from which they teach. The effects are, therefore, ongoing and reproduce themselves within schools as teacher groups form around subject departments. It is of particular importance that teachers get to know themselves and understand each other in this process.

Teachers of physical education have in the past been neglected as an area of study. The reasons for this are not difficult to search out. Teachers of physical education are frequently trained in specialist institutions or in groups separate from other disciplines. Teachers in these institutions or departments are themselves frequently removed from the research traditions that make these studies possible. The present volume of essays is an important break with past neglect. The authors have put together the results of their study and produced some insightful and important contributions. Teachers of physical education face particular problems and stresses. Many of these problems are not recognized by other teachers or the organizations in which they work. For example, recruits to the teaching of physical education frequently join the profession because they enjoy or are good at sport. Yet within 15 years many find that their ability or enjoyment in participation has passed them by and they need to gain satisfaction solely from organizing, teaching, and coaching. Some make this transition successfully, but others will wish to 'move up or get out'. Those that stay may well find the world of coaching more open to the stresses from 'other groups in the community' as pointed out by Waller.

The essays in this volume examine these and other issues. Templin and Schempp are to be congratulated for collecting them together.

Colin Lacey
The University of Sussex
Falmer, Sussex, England
October, 1988

1

Socialization into Physical Education: Its Heritage and Hope

THOMAS J. TEMPLIN
Purdue University

PAUL G. SCHEMPP
University of Oregon

Why does one become a teacher of physical education? How does one acquire the skills, knowledge, values, and attitudes so essential in performing the role of the physical educator? What socialization processes are involved in the development of one's teaching perspective?

These questions and others have been of interest to the editors for some time. We have been engaged in the study of teacher socialization for more than a decade and, with the help of others, this text represents our desire to examine the socialization of physical education teachers more closely. Although one can go back to Waller's (1932) classic work, *The Sociology of Teaching*, it has only been in the last four decades where a significant conceptual and empirical thrust in research on teacher socialization has taken place (Becker, 1952; Edgar & Warren, 1969; Feiman-Nemser & Floden, 1986; Hoy & Rees, 1977; Lacey, 1977, 1988; Lortie, 1975; Sikes, Measor, & Woods, 1985; Tabachnik & Zeichner, 1985; Wright &

Tuska, 1968; Zeichner & Tabachnick, 1981, 1983). Research related to the socialization of physical educators has a much shorter history, yet here, too, significant progress has been made over the last decade (Dewar & Lawson, 1984; Earls, 1981; Evans, 1986, 1988; Hendry, 1975; Lawson, 1983a, 1983b, 1986, 1988; Locke, 1974, 1984; Locke & Massengale, 1978; Locke & Dodds, 1984; Locke, Griffin, & Templin, 1986; Marrs & Templin, 1983; Pooley, 1971, 1972; Schempp, 1983, 1985, 1986; Steen, 1985; Templin, 1979, 1981, 1988; Templin, Woodford, & Mulling, 1982; Templin, Savage, & Hagge, 1986; Woodford, 1977).

This book is designed to illustrate this progress by presenting empirical and conceptual pieces on teacher socialization in physical education. The chapters make a statement about what is known about various socialization processes such as recruitment into the field, the impact of teacher preparation and the influence of the world of work. We hope to identify gaps in our knowledge base and thereby continue the search related to why teachers do what they do. Finally, it is our hope that this knowledge will be useful in enabling others, both school teachers and teacher educators alike, to examine both the heritage and conditions that shape the teaching perspectives of those who teach physical education.

SOCIALIZATION DEFINED: A DIALECTICAL PERSPECTIVE

Although the formal study of teacher socialization is in its infancy, the study of socialization as it relates to adults dates back nearly a century. With this study numerous definitions of socialization have evolved over the years. For example, definitions range from socialization as the moral obligation to uphold societal norms *to* socialization as a Freudian conception *to* socialization as a training phenomenon *to* socialization as learning whereby an individual moves into behavioral alignment with societal norms or the expectations of a given social system (Wenworth, 1980).

Robert Merton and his associates (1957) defined socialization as

. . . the process by which people selectively acquire the values and attitudes, the interests, skills and knowledge—in short, the culture—current in groups to which they are, or seek to become, a member (pp. 278).

This definition, characterized as functionalist (Lacey, 1987; Wentworth, 1980) is representative of the socialization as learning conception and has its roots in the seminal work of Parsons (1951). Wentworth (1980) describes this perspective in the following way:

. . . all that is needed is to learn proper role expectations to become a functioning element in a social system. Such role learning is what

Parsons calls socialization, but it is more. Just as the cog exists for the machine after it has been put in place, the actor only exists in the Parsonian system's framework as a properly functioning element. Socialization brings actors into existence, or that is constitutes them according to socially sanctioned expectations and need dispositions. . . . (pp. 33-34)

Hence, the Parsonian perspective as well as that of Merton appears to be one of order and compliance—it is functionalist. This view resides in a framework that suggests "individuals are products of society; that is, historical social structures" (Wentworth, 1980, p. 2). Such a perspective does not address failure, deviance, or nonconformity and has created "the oversocialized conception of man" (Wrong, 1961).

In contrast, a dialectical perspective of socialization represents man as an active agent in determining one's own behavioral destiny. It suggests that man can produce and create versus simply reproducing the expected and familiar. Within the teaching context, Dewar said (personal communication):

Becoming socialized involves more than learning the appropriate scripts, it is an active process whereby individuals negotiate not only what they learn but how they interpret what is necessary to be a successfully socialized teacher.

Negotiation and interpretation are linked to the influence of one's life history and to the demands of the different social settings in which one resides. Therefore, socialization focuses on the constant interplay between individuals, societal influences, and the institutions into which they are socialized. According to this view, "while social structures are compelling in the construction of identity, the concept of socialization should define people as both recipients and creators of values" (Popkewitz, 1976, p. 4). Thus, the argument is made that while people are constrained by social structural limitations, they at the same time play an active part in shaping their identities, often acting in ways that contradict the norms and values that prevade a social setting. As Apple (1979, p. 102) stated, "the institutions of our society are characterized by contradiction as well as simple reproduction."

Hence, socialization is a dynamic process involving pressure to change from various directions as individuals assume roles and learn and attempt to influence the role expectations within a given social setting. It is a process "in which an individual is taught and learns what behaviors and perspectives are customary and desirable within a professional role" (Van Maanen & Schein, 1979, p. 212).

SOCIALIZATION INTO PHYSICAL EDUCATION

With the above theoretical and definitional overview in mind, let us turn to the contents of the text and the socialization of PE teachers. The research that has been conducted over the last two decades illustrates a shift from a functionalist to dialectical perspective. It shows how teachers can play an active role in the formulation of their beliefs, attitudes, and behavior. This research has focused on three primary socialization phases: recruitment into teaching, professional preparation, and the influence of the school setting and related educational agencies. The first two phases of socialization are often classified as preservice socialization, for they represent important socializing experiences that occur before one actually enters the service of teaching. The latter phase is classified as inservice, for it represents socializing experiences that occur after one enters the teaching ranks.

PRETRAINING SOCIALIZATION AND RECRUITMENT

Why does one enter physical education and what is the influence of one's pretraining—childhood experiences? Does one's childhood—public school experiences—influence one's decision to enter teaching and the way in which one teaches during and after one's professional training? These questions have been of interest to researchers within physical education beginning with the dissertation research of Pooley (1971) and Woodford (1977) and followed more recently in the research of Dewar (1983). Both Schempp (Chapter 2) and Dewar (Chapter 3) examine pretraining influences and recruitment in this text.

Paul Schempp opens this text with his analysis of the apprenticeship-of-observation theory as it applies to the development of physical education teachers. Schempp explores the impact of being a student on learning teaching tasks, identification with teachers, teaching assessment, and the development of teachers' professional perspective. While he cautions the reader about the "cumulative" nature of the socialization process, he concludes that the apprenticeship-of-observation does, in fact, serve as a significant socializing experience in the development of teachers.

In Chapter 3, Alison Dewar provides a stimulating look at recruitment and entry into physical education teaching. Dewar reviews research in the area, implications of the research, and the relationship between recruitment into teaching and the teachers' work. Dewar argues "that in order to fully understand who enters physical education teaching and why, it is important that we take seriously the ways in which physical education is defined in schools" and that we examine one's entry in relation to the broader socio-historical contexts to which one's decision may be linked.

PROFESSIONAL TRAINING

While teachers learn much from their apprenticeship and recruitment patterns select the potential teacher corps, the first formal process in becoming a teacher occurs in university teacher education programs. Teacher training extends from coursework, through preservice field experiences, and into inservice education programs.

This section of the text addresses the influence of preservice and inservice education. Certainly, the structure and impact of teacher education has received a great deal of attention in the United States in the last decade. Equally, a great deal has been written about the nature and significance of teacher education processes in the preparation of physical education teachers (Lawson, 1986; Locke, 1984; Locke & Dodds, 1984; Locke, Mand, & Siedentop, 1981). With the reform movement in education, widespread change has resulted in state policies related to preservice and inservice requirements for teacher licensure. In essence, the discussion and reform of teacher education over the past five years has created a period of reflection and change that is unprecedented. The chapters within this section illustrate this period and analyze those processes whereby preservice and inservice teachers may be socialized.

Kim Graber (Chapter 4) opens this section by examining the preparation of university undergraduates. The purpose of this chapter is to "address how preservice education is impacted by personal biographies that recruits bring into the training program; students' expectations for preservice training; students reactions to the force of socialization; and the overall influence of the training program on the recruits development." Graber concludes that although teacher education is generally a low-impact enterprise, students do, to varying degrees, learn some teaching skills from both the formal or intended curriculum and from the hidden or unintended curriculum. Graber suggests that the "apprenticeship-of-observation" is a significant socializing agency—a lasting effect that lessens the impact of professional training. She concludes with thought-provoking recommendations that call for teacher educators to become more analytical about the nature of the students with whom they work.

Although many of the processes related to preservice training are considered by some to be insignificant, one dimension of teacher education is acknowledged to be of great influence—namely, those field or clinical experiences in which preservice students teach. In Chapter 5, Patt Dodds analyzes the influence of field experiences by examining various socialization constructs related to field experiences. Dodds presents a framework that examines teaching perspectives, socializing agents, and various socializing strategies. She discusses the implications of her analysis and focuses on the importance of reflection and choice making by preservice trainees and teacher educators alike.

The education and socialization of teachers does not end with an undergraduate degree. Teachers continue to learn about teaching for as long as they teach. In Chapter 6, Sarah Doolittle and Susan Schwager share their experience and expertise related to inservice education. The authors state that "inservice teacher education is intended to counteract the negative effects of teacher socialization in the schools" and to challenge the status quo promoted by teachers and schools in relation to physical education. They cite those characteristics needed for successful inservice programs and provide illustrations of programs that have served as powerful socializing agents in the education of inservice physical educators.

Marian Kneer provides a unique examination of the influence of professional organizations in the education of preservice and inservice physical educators in Chapter 7. Kneer discusses the socializing power of both direct and indirect services offered through professional organizations, the problems that affect the socialization process, and a look toward the future relative to the potential influence of professional organizations. Kneer illustrates her analysis by examining the American Alliance of Health, Physical Education, Recreation, and Dance and its various sub-structures such as the National Association of Sport and Physical Education.

THE INFLUENCE OF THE SCHOOL SETTING

This section is comprised of chapters that address the agents of socialization that impact the inservice teacher on a regular basis. It addresses the construct of organizational socialization referred to earlier; that is, it refers to the process whereby the neophyte is molded into a mature practitioner as a result of learning and employing the cultural perspective of a given setting. Hal Lawson provides the "tactical dimensions" and features of organizational socialization in Chapter 8. Hence, these chapters focus upon the work life of the physical educator. They address the influence of the teacher's colleagues, students, administrators, curriculum, school policy, rewards, and the culture of teaching physical education in our schools. These chapters should be of particular interest to those training to become teachers as well as those who already teach. The chapters may provide insight into the future for the preservice teacher and a source of comparison for inservice teachers. The messages of these chapters are clear for both groups however, and that is that many school physical education teachers work under difficult circumstances and, as Andrew Sparkes points out in Chapter 16, that the culture of teaching physical education is not characterized by change and innovation. The culture of teaching physical education in the future may look very much like that of the past and today.

Hal Lawson begins the examination of the work setting in Chapter 8 and points out "that schools double as work places that process teachers as well as students." He focuses on the influence of two stages of profes-sional induction—teacher education and the practice of one's teaching role. Lawson provides a conceptual insight into the process of organiza-tional socialization and organizational cultures and their relationship to work place conditions. The author provides case studies of the influence of organizational culture on a teacher and a discussion of political and economic, organizational, situational, and personal-social factors affect-ing the teacher. Also examined is the concept of "occupational commun-ities," revealing the power of this concept in the study of teacher socialization.

Thomas Templin (Chapter 9) provides further illustration of Lawson's model by presenting a case study of a female, mid-career physical educa-tor frustrated by the constraints of her work setting. Templin presents a life history of the teacher and examines the influence of various agents of socialization: administrators, colleagues, students, parents, curriculum, school policy, and rewards, among others. Although the case provides a rather negative example of socialization, it points out the need for more and more examples of research on positive work place socialization (Feiman-Nemser & Floden, 1986).

Students serve as powerful socializing agents as pointed out in the next two chapters by Martinek (Chapter 10) and Griffin (Chapter 11). Tom Martinek's research on the self-fulfilling prophecy over the last decade has provided great insight into how this phenomenon has operated in physical education. In this chapter, Martinek reviews the research that has been conducted and presents a model that examines how teacher expectations are formed and communicated and the extent to which they influence student behavior and performance. Martinek concludes that "Pygmalion" must become a positive force in the teaching-learning process.

Related to Martinek's chapter on teacher expectancy is the work of Pat Griffin in her examination of the influence of gender within physical education (Chapter 11). Griffin questions the sexist structure of sport and physical education. She calls for an end to the superficial and mechanistic strategies used to promote gender equity within our school through an understanding of the socio-historical roots of sexism in our society and its embeddedness in our schools and in the attitudes and behavior of physi-cal educators and teacher educators. Griffin concludes by presenting ex-amples of how sexism could be reduced, if not eliminated, within our schools and physical education programs. Her words challenge physical educators to reflect on the attitudes and practices of their gymnasia that perpetuate social injustice.

The rewards of teaching most certainly influence one's attitudes and behavior within the school setting. In Chapter 12, John Evans and Trefor Williams present an occupational analysis of the system of rewards that physical education teachers from England must endure. Evans and Williams explain how English physical educators, particularly female teachers, are victimized by a meritocratic system that views PE teachers as lacking academic credibility and as a consequence are not subject to significant rewards related to job mobility. The authors provide between and within subject area analyses related to the rewards of teaching so readers can make their own cross cultural comparisons.

Grounded in the work of organizational and occupational theory, George Sage explores the multiple role demands of those who teach and coach in public schools within Chapter 13. Based on formal interviews with 50 teacher/coaches as well as informal observations and discussion with other teacher/coaches, non-coaching teachers, and school administrators, Sage qualitatively examines the daily experience and demands placed on teacher/coaches. Sage describes inter-role conflicts and supports previous research that concludes that one's teaching role is negatively impacted by multiple role responsibilities. Sage offers solutions to this role conflict, but acknowledges that change is unlikely in most situations given the inflexibility of role structures and expectations in many schools.

School and program policy is the focus of Chapter 14 by Bernard Oliver. Oliver examines models of educational policy and historical impact of federal policy and education. In addition, the role of educational policy in teaching and physical education is discussed.

Chapter 15, written by Linda Bain, examines the hidden curriculum in physical education as a agent of teacher socialization. The hidden curriculum refer to the implicit values taught and learned through the process of schooling and through an extensive review of literature, Bain analyzes "the extent to which these values, even though unstated, are recognized or intended by teachers." Bain discusses "life in the gym" and suggests that teacher behavior and perceptions that project compliance and control, rather than learning, are of value to many physical educators. Bain explains the origins of these values relative to the characteristics of those who enter physical education, the nature of teacher education programs, and school factors that influence one's teaching perspectives. Bain discusses many dimensions of the hidden curriculum and concludes that the "initial step in evaluating and changing the hidden curriculum is a careful analysis of our programs." She suggests awareness is only the first step from which an examination of the explicit messages presented in our schools must be analyzed relative to the intended outcome of these messages. Such a process is important if we are to uphold the ideals of educational practice.

In the final chapter, Andrew Sparkes returns us to an examination of the culture of physical education and its implications for change and innovation. The author questions whether or not change or innovation is possible in physical education given the entrenched nature of various norms within culture, schools, and physical education settings. This very thesis seems to be present in many of the chapters throughout this text. Sparkes cleverly uses a "tool kit" metaphor to point out the static nature of physical education and its teachers due to cultural and ideological constraints placed upon the subject and its teachers.

SUMMARY

This book is intended to bring together research and theory on teacher socialization in physical education to better enable teachers and teacher educators to make informed and constructive changes in the way they carry out their work. The collective efforts of the authors of this text make an important statement regarding what is presently known about physical education teachers and their practices. Understanding what physical educators do and why they do it is a precursor to improving physical education in schools.

The chapters presented in this book make a statement about what remains to be known. In this regard, we hope the book stimulates an agenda for future research. Our limitations to understanding the socialization of teachers comes from many directions. Our research has not enjoyed a long tradition, and thus the body of knowledge is limited even though it appears to address various socialization issues such as those within this text. The methodologies used to generate knowledge have been mixed, inconsistent, and seem to cut across both quantitative and qualitative traditions. Most certainly, their application with research on teacher socialization in physical education has yet to stand the test of time. However, work such as that included within this book leads one to be optimistic. As more teachers and teacher educators pursue trustworthy answers to important questions about teacher socialization, the quality and number of studies in this area will increase. Equally, expanded theory related to teacher socialization will give scholarly inquiry a cleaner and more comprehensive fit to target questions. Finally, physical education faces the limitation that all professions face, and that is applicability. As those most capable of providing the best professional answers pursue academic and scientific respectability, an increased need to serve the needs of practitioners must be met. Research on teacher socialization must be concerned with application—it must be concerned with the ways in which the lives of physical educators might be enhanced.

As the reader turns to the following chapter, we sense that there is much to celebrate in the publication of this book, for it provides a substantial and useful body of knowledge. At the same time, we acknowledge that this effort does not represent an end, but merely a beginning, and, at best, the continuation of inquiry into the socialization of the physical education teacher. There is much left undone in our lives as teachers, learners, and researchers.

REFERENCES

Apple, M. (1979). What correspondence theories of the hidden curriculum miss. *The Review of Education, 5*, 101-112.

Becker, H. (1952). Career of the Chicago public schoolteacher. *American Journal of Sociology, 57*, 470-477.

Dewar, A. & Lawson, H. (1984). The subjective warrant and recruitment into physical education. *Quest, 36*, 15-25.

Edgar, D. & Warren, R. (1969). Power and autonomy in teacher socialization. *Sociology of Education, 42*, 386-399.

Earls, N. (1981). Distinctive teachers' personal qualities, perceptions of teacher education and the realities of teaching. *Journal of Teaching in Physical Education, 1*, 59-70.

Evans, J. (1986). *Physical education, sport, and schooling: Studies in the sociology of physical education.* Lewes: Falmer Press.

Evans, J. (1988). *Teachers, training, and control in physical education.* Lewes: Falmer Press.

Feiman-Nemser, S. & Floden, R. (1986). The cultures of teaching. In M. Wittrock (Ed.) *Handbook of research on teaching* (505-526). New York, Macmillan Publishing Co.

Hendry, L. (1975). Survival in a marginal role: The professional identity of the physical education teacher. *British Journal of Sociology, 26*, 465-4776.

Hoy, W. & Rees, R. (1977). Bureaucratic socialization of student students. *Journal of Teacher Education, 28*, 23-26.

Lacey, C. (1977). *The socialization of teachers.* London: Metheun.

Lacey, C. (1987). Professional socialization of teachers. In M. Dunkin (Ed.) *The international encyclopedia of teaching and teacher education* (634-644). Oxford: Pergamon Press.

Lawson, H. (1983a). Toward a model of teacher socialization in physical education: The subjective warrant, recruitment, and teacher education. *Journal of Teaching in Physical Education, 2*(3), 3-16.

Lawson, H. (1983b). Toward a model of teacher socialization in physical education: Entry into schools, teachers' role orientations and longevity in teaching. *Journal of Teaching in Physical Education, 3*(1), 3-15.

Lawson, H. (1986). Occupational socialization and the design of teacher education programs. *Journal of Teaching in Physical Education, 5*, 107-116.

Lawson, H. (1988). Occupational socialization, cultural studies, and the physical education curriculum. *Journal of Teaching in Physical Education, 7*(4), 265-288.

Locke, L. (1984). Research on teaching teachers: Where are we now? [Special issue]. *Journal of Teaching in Physical Education, 3*(Summer).

Locke, L. & Dodds, P. (1984). Is physical education teacher education in American colleges worth saving? Evidence, alternatives, judgment. In N. Struna (Ed.) *NAPEHE Proceedings* (v.5, 91-107). Champaign, Il: Human Kinetics.

Locke, L., Griffin, P., & Templin, T. (Eds.) (1986). Profiles in struggles. *Journal of Physical Education, Recreation, and Dance, 57*(4), 32-63.

Locke, L., Mand, C., & Siedentop, D. (1981). The preparation of physical education teachers: A subject matter centered model. In H. Lawson (Ed.) *Undergraduate physical education programs: Issues and approaches, 33-54*). Reston, VA: AAHPERD.

Locke, L. & Massengale, J. (1978) Role conflict in teacher/coaches. *Research Quarterly, 49*(2), 162-174.

Lortie, D. (1975). *Schoolteacher: A sociological study.* Chicago: The University of Chicago Press.

Marrs, L. & Templin, T. (1983). Student teacher as social strategist. In T. Templin and J. Olson (Eds.) *Teaching physical education* (118-127). Champaign, IL.: Human Kinetics.

Merton, R., Reader, G., & Kendall, P. (1957). *The student-physician: Introductory studies in the sociology of medical education.* Cambridge: Harvard University Press.

Parsons, T. (1951). *The social system.* Glencoe, IL.: The Free Press.

Pooley, J. (1971). The professional socialization of physical education students in the United States and England. (Doctoral dissertation, University of Wisconsin, 1971), *Dissertation Abstracts International, 32*, 07-A. University Microfilm No. DA 71-29008.

Pooley, J. (1972). Professional socialization: A model of the pretraining phase application to physical education students. *Quest, 18*, 57-66.

Popkewitz, T. (1976). *Teacher education as a process of socialization: The social distribution of knowledge.* Madison, WI: U.S.O.E./Teacher Corps Technical Report No. 17, 1976.

Schempp, P. (1983). Learning the role: The transformation from student to teacher. In T. Templin and J. Olson (Eds.) *Teaching in Physical Education* (109-117). Champaign, Il.: Human Kinetics.

Schempp, P. (1985). Becoming a better teacher: An analysis of the student teaching experience. *Journal of Teaching in Physical Education, 4*, 158-166.

Schempp, P. (1986). Physical education student teachers' beliefs in their control over student learning. *Journal of Teaching in Physical Education, 5*, 198-203.

Sikes, P., Measor, L., & Woods, P. (1985). *Teacher careers: Crisis and continuities*. Lewes: Falmer Press.

Steen, T. (1985). Teacher socialization in physical education settings during early training experiences: A qualitative study. Paper presented at the annual meeting of the AAHPERD, Atlanta, GA.

Tabachnick, R. & Zeichner, K. (1985). *The teacher perspectives project: Final report*. Madison, WI: Center for Educational Research.

Templin, T. (1979). Occupational socialization and the physical education student teacher. *Research Quarterly, 50*, 482-493.

Templin, T. (1981). Student as socializing agent. *Journal of Teaching in Physical Education, Introductory issue*, 71-79.

Templin, T., Woodford, R., & Mulling, C. (1982). On becoming a physical educator: Occupational choice and the anticipatory socialization process. *Quest, 34*(2), 119-133.

Templin, T., Savage, M., & Hagge, M. (1986). Deprofessionalization and the physical educator. In *Trends and developments in physical education: Proceedings of the VIII Commonwealth and International Conference on Sport, Physical Education, Dance, Recreation, and Health* (322-327). London: E. & F.N. Spon Ltd.

Templin, T. (1988). Settling down: An examination of two women physical education teachers. In J. Evans (Ed.) *Teachers, teaching, and control in physical education*. 57-81. Lewes: Falmer Press.

Van Maanen, J. & Schein, E. (1979). Toward a theory of organizational socialization. *Research on Organizational Behavior, 1*, 209-264.

Waller, W. (1932). *The sociology of teaching*. New York: John Wiley & Sons.

Wenworth, W. (1980). *Context and understanding: An inquiry into socialization theory*. New York: Elsevier.

Woodford, R. (1977). *The socialization of freshmen physical education majors into role orientations in physical education*. Unpublished doctoral dissertation, University of New Mexico at Albuquerque.

Wright, B. & Tuska, S. (1968). From dreams to life in the psychology of becoming a teacher. *School Review, 76*, 253-293.

Wrong, D. (1961). The oversocialized conception of man in modern sociology. *American Sociological Review, 26*, 183-193.

Zeichner, K. (1979, February). *The dialetics of teacher socialization*. Paper presented at the annual meeting of the Association of Teacher Educators. Orlando, FL.

Zeichner, K. (1980). Myths and realities: Field-based experiences in preservice teacher education. *Journal of Teacher Education, 31*, 44-55.

Zeichner, K. & Tabachnick, R. (1981). Are the effects of university teacher education "washed out" by school experience? *Journal of Teacher Education, 32*, 7-11.

2

Apprenticeship-of-Observation and the Development of Physical Education Teachers

PAUL G. SCHEMPP
University of Oregon

The mind of the education student is not a blank awaiting inscription.
-D. C. Lortie

The education of a teacher is most often attributed to a university. However, contemporary educational theory and recent research have begun to reconceptualize that notion. There is growing recognition of a powerful, informal educational process occurring long before a teaching candidate enters a university. The years spent as a student in physical education and sport programs have been theorized to provide influential social contacts for potential physical education teachers (Lawson, 1983; Pooley, 1972). In the course of their careers as students, prospective teachers are given the opportunity to observe many physical education teachers plying their trade. While in the role of student, these future teachers witness the everyday tasks of teaching and come to know well the attitudes, skills and responsibilities of those who teach. Lortie (1975) described this early socialization period as an "apprenticeship-of-observation." This chapter examines the apprenticeship-of-observation served by physical educators and the influence this apprenticeship holds over the development of physical education teachers.

APPRENTICESHIP AS METAPHOR FOR EARLY SOCIALIZATION

Equating an early segment of teacher socialization with an apprenticeship conjures visions of a young person acquiring the rudimentary skills and attitudes necessary to practice a valued craft, while under the instruction of a master craftsperson. While the apprenticeship metaphor serves well in providing a perspective from which to view the socialization of teachers prior to formal training, it also has limitations.

Although teaching holds similarities to crafts (Tom, 1984), teaching is not a craft. Teachers do not engage a particular set of skills to mold raw materials into finished products, but rather their "efforts must coincide with those of the students to engage in critical thinking and the quest for mutual humanization" (Freire, 1970, p. 62). The socialization of a teacher extends beyond the restricted vision of an apprentice subserviently acquiring a trade from a demanding and watchful master. Lortie (1975) recognized the limits of the apprenticeship metaphor when he stated:

> the student's learning about teaching, gained from a limited vantage point and relying heavily on imagination, is not like that of an apprentice and does not represent acquisition of the occupation's technical knowledge. It is more a matter of imitation, which, being generalized across individuals, becomes tradition. (p. 63)

Teachers do not view their students as the next generation of professional educators, and thus do not see themselves as master craftspeople training their successors. They view the people in their classes as students, not future teachers. Thus, they offer few explanations for the decisions they make, and provide little opportunity for the apprentice to undertake measured and selected occupational tasks or discuss the technical demands and requisites of their work. Any influence stemming from the apprenticeship can be little more than recollected imitation. The work of the student and the work of the teacher are seen as interrelated only to the degree they depend and interact with one another. The work of students does not progress to become the work of teachers (Anyon, 1981). Students do not learn the underlying requirements and conditions which shape either the teacher's world of work or their role in that world. A student's learning of the teaching profession is restricted to that which is seen, and is strongly skewed to the requirements of a student.

The occupational demands of teaching require teachers to make judgments regarding their practice based on an array of competing factors including, but not limited to, personal interpretation, experience and educational background, and the conditions of the workplace. The work of teachers does not allow them to simply fall back on the recollections of their own experiences as teachers. The "apprenticeship-of-observation" does not, therefore, perform a reproductive function, at least not a directly corresponding one. The changing social relationships in which teachers continually find themselves prohibit such direct correspondence between observations made as students and their practice as professional educators. The professional practices of teachers are therefore influenced, but not determined, by the apprenticeship they served as students. Teachers do not simply imitate the practices of their predecessors. Rather the apprenticeship provides a first look at the work of teachers. Because the apprenticeship is the first introduction to teaching and because the exposure is long (up to 14 years), it is hypothesized to be a formidable and detectable thread in the socializing fabric of a teacher.

THE APPRENTICESHIP-OF-OBSERVATION THEORY

Despite its limitations, the apprenticeship metaphor provides a useful perspective for gaining insight into the social dynamics of the early school experience of teachers. Lortie (1975) identified the early socialization phase of teachers as an "apprenticeship" period because his research with public school teachers led him to conclude that much of what is learned about teaching is learned while in the role of student. Further, these early learning experiences provide an evaluation screen through which all subsequent experiences pass.

The "apprenticeship-of-observation" is comprised in the experiences gained while a student in public schools which have a discernible and traceable influence on the future decisions, practices, and ideologies of a teacher. The results of his study led Lortie (1975) to set forth several propositions regarding the dynamics and functions of an apprenticeship-of-observation. Four of those propositions will provide the theoretical underpinnings of this chapter. These propositions are:

a. teachers become acquainted with the tasks of teaching during their apprenticeship-of-observation,
b. teachers begin their identification as teachers during their apprenticeship,
c. assessments of teaching technique are similar both prior to and after entry into the role of teacher, and
d. because the apprenticeship represents the analysis of personal experience, a teacher's analytic orientations toward the work of teaching are individualistic in nature.

AN ANALYSIS OF THE 'APPRENTICESHIP-OF-OBSERVATION' IN PHYSICAL EDUCATION

The discussion that follows stems from an analysis of critical teaching incidents reported by 49 physical education student teachers. The four propositions previously cited formed the analytic themes used to summarize these experiences. Data were collected using the critical incident technique (Flanagan, 1954). This technique was used because Lortie found extended reports of incidents from the apprenticeship period and incidents of teaching practice most useful in deriving his theory. Therefore, in examining the tenability of the apprenticeship-of-observation theory for physical education, it seemed most appropriate to use these data forms and Lortie's theoretical framework.

Two sets of teaching events were reported by the student teachers. The first set recalled incidents of good and poor teaching from the days when the student teachers were public school students. The second set of events were recollections of good and poor teaching by the teachers themselves during their 10-week student teaching experiences. The incidents were synthesized and compared in order to determine which influences carried forward from the student role into the teaching role.

It is important to remember that the apprenticeship is an influential experience, not a deterministic one. Therefore, themes were sought in the sets of descriptions rather than in the individual descriptions from each teacher. If themes were evident in both sets of reports, then identifiable influences could be traced from the apprenticeship period into the teaching role. Support then could be given to the apprenticeship-of-observation theory. If no such evidence was available the applicability of the theory for physical education teachers would be questionable.

Proposition one: Teachers become acquainted with the tasks of teaching during their apprenticeship-of-observation

The apprenticeship period offers prospective teachers an opportunity to witness an extensive array of teaching tasks. In describing the competence of their predecessors, the student teachers identified a variety of tasks ranging from class preparation to student evaluation. Four major categories of teaching tasks were described in both the apprenticeship and student teaching reports. These tasks were related to: (a) student learning, (b) class operation, (c) teacher/student interpersonal relationships, and (d) the exhibition of a teacher's personal qualities.

Student learning. Tasks relative to student learning witnessed in the apprenticeship period included motivating students, selecting content, using a variety of teaching styles, providing feedback, demonstrating and explaining skills or concepts, and utilizing student evaluation procedures. A greater attention appeared to focus on the ability of task performance to motivate, include, and stimulate the interest of the students rather than on the actual acquisition of specific knowledge or skills. The ability to interest and motivate students was a consistent theme in both the apprentice period and the teaching period. The following apprentice reports revealed student preference and enjoyment as primary criteria in evaluating the learning experience.

"(the) teacher had a definite understanding of each student and their capabilities and skill level was attended to according to capability. Students' preference of activity was always taken into consideration. In gymnastics, we were graded on the task we were most efficient at. We moved progressively from one lesson to another and never became bored."

"Another reason I enjoyed the class was that the teacher was working out right along with us which proved the idea was not to all be at the same level of condition, but to improve."

Similarly, the incidents reported in the teaching role demonstrated a strong concern for evoking student interest. Student interest was not absent from the criteria for student learning, but rather than being associated with motivating students to learn, it was linked with keeping students on task and enjoying themselves. This finding was similar to Placek's (1983) observation that "they (teachers) provided activities for the students to participate in, and did their best to ensure that the students had a good time and kept active" (p.49). It was interesting to note that student "fun" was used as a criterion in the teaching period, but not in the apprenticeship period. This seems to imply that teachers use students' fun as an important measure of teaching success, but students do not view their own enjoyment as a critical factor in the evaluation of a teacher.

"I think I did a good job with New Games, especially with the 5th graders. They had fun and so did I."

"stations (were) set up for between, under, through, over, and around for the 1st and 2nd grades. (The students) rode scooters at the stations—the kids loved it."

"at the elementary school level I can remember a lesson using mats where the children were shown a picture of figures and they had to create that figure with two others using their bodies. Those who could do it best got to show the class their figure. Children were spending almost all of their time on task being physically and socially active. You could almost feel the creativity and energy in the air. When the time was up many children asked when they were coming to gym again so they could have more fun like that, most of all their bubbling excitement as they left my room told me I was successful."

Teaching specific skills or concepts was viewed by the apprentices as an essential task of a teacher. Teachers held in the highest regard by the apprentices were those who taught the greatest amount of content. In fact, the teaching of specific concepts and skills appeared to be the single most important factor in an apprentice's determination of good teaching.

"she expected some degree of perfection in the performance of each gymnastic skill."

"the teacher introduced the paddleball skills and rules of the game very effectively."

"they (teachers) were very demanding and expected high achievement."

As in the apprenticeship period, teachers believed teaching specific skills or concepts were an important part of the teaching enterprise. Unfortunately, this belief did not seem to hold a strong or consistent conviction among the teachers. Nonetheless, it was present. This finding is congruent with previous research on teachers' perceptions of their role tasks (Placek, 1983; Schempp, 1983). There appeared different ways of articulating the concern for student learning ranging from process-product achievement

"Students exhibited excellent skill techniques in both sports (basketball and volleyball) after my demonstrations."

to a focus on student time-on-task

"while teaching badminton to a class of 37 students, I feel I did a good job of setting up the unit so all students would get as much participation time as possible."

to the use of feedback to stimulate learning

"(I) gave proper feedback for students to know how they were doing."

Selecting content as a teaching skill appeared to be linked to the notion that good teachers offer a variety of content. Apprentices paid particular attention to the variety of activities offered by their teachers (e.g. "we covered a wide variety of activities such as golf, bowling, swimming, etc., which many other students in other schools did not" or "we did not have a variety of activities throughout the year; we played 'killerball' most of the time"). A teacher's knowledge of the content or his ability to select content appropriate to the needs and requirements of the students did not appear to be skills recognized by the apprentice. The task of content selection, or more specifically the task of selecting a wide-variety of activities, seems well formed in the apprentice period as it was strongly evident in the teaching period as well (e.g., "I believe I provided the students with a variety of activities during class periods which kept them interested and active").

Using a variety of teaching styles or methods was another teaching task identified in both the apprentice and teacher reports. (As will be noted later, caution should be used in interpreting the results on teaching style as the language of the reports indicates an influence from the university preparation program.) It seems that the task was recognized during the apprenticeship period, but the label (i.e., specific teaching style) was culled from latter experiences.

"His teaching methods varied with the content."

"Mr. Q. was a hard-nosed command style teacher."

Reports of teaching experiences indicated that the recognition of the task of selecting teaching styles was carried from the apprenticeship into the teaching assignment. However, a difference was noted in that apprentice reports described teaching styles in either a general manner or dependent upon personality traits. In the teaching reports, however, teaching styles were viewed more as a tool of a teacher.

"I used the reciprocal style of teaching for the pass in basketball."

"I feel I used various media material appropriately to reinforce points I wanted stressed."

The ability to clearly communicate information through demonstrations and explanations of skills and concepts was another teaching task prospective teachers became acquainted with during their apprenticeships:

"in self-defense class in high school, the physical education teacher would demonstrate and take time to teach us specific skills. She was always prepared for class. We worked a lot on skills in a lot of different content areas."

"in 11th grade the teacher would teach skills about a certain sport in the beginning of class. The students would then be drilled in the skill. (During) the last 20 minutes of class we would play the game."

Although demonstrations and explanations are tasks identified in the apprenticeship period, mastery of these tasks does not begin until the teaching role is assumed. The student teachers in this study were self-critical as to their expertise in these tasks. The abilities to demonstrate and explain were considered by these teachers to be important criteria in assessing their own competence as teachers:

"my explanation of how to do (the gymnastic) skills needed to be more detailed. For example, when working on tasks at different stations, the students were unsure of how to execute the skills."

"one incident which I believe was good teaching was during one of my 4th grade classes. I was describing the start, running form, and the finish of a sprint in track. Throughout my explanation and demonstration the students watched without moving around or making any noise. All eyes were focused on me. The students were asking some very good questions and showing a lot of interest in the subject. When practicing the skills the students did extremely well."

"my cooperating teacher said I was doing fine in skill explanation and had thorough knowledge of the subject matter. Many good experiences came when they performed the skill incorrectly, then I would re-explain and they grasped the concepts."

Providing feedback to students was another teaching task prospective teachers became acquainted with during the apprenticeship.

"she was always reinforcing people about their ability and how they were playing."

"I had a conditioning unit during my 9th grade physical education class where we worked in stations doing various exercises. We were asked to do our best and give a good effort. Those of us who did were reinforced by the instructor."

When these students became teachers, the task of giving feedback was recognized as an important skill in promoting student learning.

"in one of my classes I had only 12 students so I got to know all of them pretty well. When the students were playing a volleyball game (which was what my unit was) I was frequently able to make comments such as 'that was a nice floater serve Art, the ball moved erratically,' or 'Jason hit an excellent forearm pass because he was directly under the ball and used his legs for power and control.' Being able to call all the kids by name was good reinforcement and the size of the class allowed me to qualify my reinforcements most of the time."

"during a balancing and jumping lesson the students all participated at the same time. While they were doing the activities I walked around and offered positive feedback to the students."

The task of evaluating students was still another teaching skill recognized during the apprenticeship-of-observation. As one would expect, students considered this an important pedagogical practice. They were annoyed at unfair practices and showed appreciation for competence and effort in this area.

"everyone got A's. For what? As far as I know we were never graded on anything."

"he had a progressive program and kept records on students performance each year to see how far they came along. I feel that a teacher who spends that much time keeping records deserves a lot of credit."

"we were graded on the number and degree of difficulty of the gymnastic skills."

The same level of importance was not attached to the evaluation practices once the teaching role was assumed. In many cases, the process of grading was associated more with student discipline and school policy than with the assessment of student learning. It seemed that the teachers simply forgot how important evaluation was to students.

"The students worked well in partners and carried on the responsibility of evaluating well."

"Some of the students tried to get away with not doing an assignment. I called them down to my office and talked with them. I had them do extra reports and take home a note to their parents telling them why they were getting an F in gym."

Perhaps most disturbing was the apprentices witnessing neglected pedagogical practice. A significant number of incidents were reported which would support Locke's (1977) contention that "it is not inadequate teaching that bedevils us, it is mindless teaching; the non-teaching teacher" (p. 13). If the apprenticeship period acquaints teachers with the important tasks leading to student learning, many physical education teachers have a debilitating heritage.

"I remember in my junior year of high school, the athletic director was the p.e. teacher and he did not do one single thing to help us with the sport. He would call roll and tell us what we could do. Then he would go back in the office and smoke a cigarette. More than half the students just sat around the gym and did nothing. He would come out of the office 20 minutes later and check up on us. The people who got A's in the class were students who were participating or students who were on an athletic team."

"When I was in 5th grade my physical education teacher would just have different games that we would play. He didn't really teach us anything, we would just play games everyday like it was recess."

"All he did was throw out 10-12 basketballs, take attendance, and then go back and sit in his office."

Not all the pedagogical practice was poor, in fact several accounts appear to demonstrate an admiration for a superb teacher who faced difficult professional obstacles. One student teacher reported the heroics of one teacher this way:

"I had many p.e. teachers, but this one lady was very well organized. She helped all the students in the class, not just the good ones. She used the equipment very well and she used all kinds of equipment in which we learned a great deal. I went to a very small private school in which the school did not put much money in the p.e. program. But Mrs. Johns used everything she could to make us become better skilled at some sports. And she did!"

Reports of this type represented a very small minority.

Students in physical education classes appear to become acquainted with the teaching tasks and seem to carry the recognition of those tasks into their role as physical education teachers. Although the tasks of motivating students, selecting content, using a variety of teaching styles, providing feedback, demonstrating and explaining skills or concepts, and utilizing student evaluation procedures appear to be identified during the apprenticeship period, they take on a more technical appearance when implemented by teachers. In the apprenticeship period, a link appeared between the tasks of student learning and student interest and motivation. In the teaching role a stronger association between student learning appears forged with class operation.

Class operation. During their apprenticeship period, teachers become familiar with a variety of tasks necessary for orchestrating the operation of a class. The specific tasks identified in both the apprenticeship and teaching reports included rule setting and enforcement, establishing classroom order, lesson planning, activity transition, administration, and safety. While the greater majority of the reports stemming from the apprenticeship period were categorized under student learning, the majority of reports from the student teaching experience were concerned with class operation. This finding was consistent with previously completed research (Boggess, McBride, & Griffey, 1985; Schempp, 1985, 1986).

The beliefs of these teachers regarding class operation was perhaps summed up best by the teacher who said a "lack of discipline is not conducive to a good learning situation." Establishing the order of the classroom seemed to be first and foremost in the minds of the teachers. They showed a sharp concern for the rules and their enforcement and found these tasks to be of critical importance in evaluating their skill as teachers. Classroom operation tasks were consistently identified in the apprenticeship period and they assumed even greater importance in the teaching role. The apprenticeship reports described rule setting and enforcement in general terms and appeared to relate them more to a teacher's personality than professional competence.

"The head football coach was our physical education teacher in 7th grade. The students had a great amount of respect for him. If he gave a command you would listen or pay the consequences, but he was fair."

"We had two very strict disciplinarian-type physical education teachers, every student either feared or respected (them)."

"In high school, a young new teacher out of State U. came to town. Uniforms were thrown out, co-ed classes began, and an elective program was started. Above all, discipline with respect was achieved right from the start."

Prospective teachers learn from their apprenticeship that the task of setting and enforcing rules is ultimately a teacher's responsibility. They may even learn a few techniques for carrying out this task. But once in the teaching role, they quickly come to believe that setting and enforcing class rules is crucial to life as a teacher.

"I established general class rules the first day of class and enforced them immediately to establish a rapport."

"In a game called angleball, I was having problems with boys getting the ball to girls on the same team. The girls became angry so I made a rule that before a goal could be scored, the ball had to hit, or be in possession of a girl at least once."

"I started off teaching by being too nice and I did not discipline strongly enough. After awhile it was very difficult for me to discipline. So I learned that it is better to be very strict at discipline at first and then soften up instead of the other way around."

Although closely related, establishing classroom order transcends the task of setting and enforcing rules. Establishing classroom order focuses more broadly on the general boundaries of the classroom in addition to specifying cogent rules. Classroom order comprises the patterns of living in the class. Establishing classroom order means defining the routines and rituals of everyday life for both the students and teacher. Routines and rituals are used by the participants in a given social setting as a basis for understanding and interacting with one another. The apprenticeship period acquaints students with the teacher's task of establishing these patterns of social order.

"In junior high, we were required to be out and in our uniform, on the line, at a specific time."

"In high school physical education classes there was no structure at all. Every class period was spent playing basketball, very often unsupervised. There were no units, no variety, and little organization. The classes in elementary school were very much the same."

The establishment of classroom order was a high priority for the teachers and they considered it a critical dimension of their teaching role.

"I came into an elementary setting in which the students were used to sitting always in squads, lining up, taking turns, and basically moving only on command. The second week I was there I started a gymnastics apparatus unit, in which there were five different stations at which students had specific tasks to perform. At first they were very hesitant to work in such a setting—they'd ask me what to do next, or what to do if they'd already gone once. But in a very short amount of time, with coaching, they were checking their task sheets, taking as many turns as was fair and time allowed, and spotted each other (this was just charming in K & 1st grade). I guess I feel that it was good teaching in that I could get what were once phys. ed. 'robots' and turn them into more independent, responsible, decision making students."

"I think I expected too much out of the 9th grade in terms of letting them work on their own because I felt they would be more responsible. Well, needless to say, it didn't work quite as I expected and the classroom seemed more like a circus."

The teachers realized that establishing classroom order was more than establishing and enforcing rules; it was establishing gymnasium routines that both the teacher and students could live with. At times, this required the teachers to alter previously held perceptions of teaching and/or themselves as teachers.

"Once in awhile I saw some behavior I did not like and I did not jump on it right away. Sometimes I'd compromise my standards to get through my lesson. An example is when I'd start my lesson when there were still several students talking."

"I wanted to be a strict, traditional teacher. I told the students that when I talked no one else talks. It almost became a personal challenge to some students. They attempted to see how much they could get away with (horseplay). My biggest mistake was to accept their challenge. What I eventually did was to say 'we'll start class when we have complete silence' and that worked. Students made other students be quiet."

Although teachers become acquainted with the task of establishing classroom order during their apprenticeship, it appears that it is not until the teaching role is assumed that an actual understanding of both the mechanics of the task and its importance to conducting a class are recognized.

An important element in the establishment of classroom order appeared to be a related task: lesson planning. The task of planning a lesson was one in which these teachers were acquainted with in the apprenticeship. Lesson planning was a task also identified in reports from the teaching experience. When lesson planning is discussed in university classes, the assumed purpose of the lesson plan is to act as a flexible guide for stimulating student learning and achievement. However, the teachers in this study did not equate planning with student learning. Lesson planning was associated with organization and class operation. Planning was necessary so that the students were kept active (not necessarily learning anything) and classroom time was not "wasted." This definition appears to form in the apprenticeship period and holds through the teaching experience. The following is an excerpt from an apprentice report:

"(The teachers) lacked organization and preparation in their lesson plans; there was a lot of wasted class time."

The above excerpt is similar to reports of teaching experiences:

"During gymnastics, I didn't plan for enough things (so that) the students could stay busy. There were far too many students standing around. I should have had some partner or group work preplanned for the tumbling mats."

"(I) had to repeat directions too many times when explaining the day's events. Sometimes I wasn't flexible enough with the lesson plan for a specific day. I didn't have alternatives at first to the daily activity."

Activity transitions was another teaching task in which wasted time was the price paid for incompetence. A precise definition of wasted time was never given, but it was most often linked to student activity time (i.e., students were either active or time was being wasted). The task of activity transitions and its consequences were seemingly learned in the apprenticeship period (e.g., "too much time was wasted between activities."). The definition and consequences appear to carry forward into the teaching role (e.g., "explanations of some games and activities were often not clear to the students which resulted in too much wasted time in transition from one activity to another."). Both apprentices and teachers believed that the task of activity transition was one which was to be completed with expedience.

The apprenticeship-of-observation is also a time in which prospective teachers became acquainted with the administrative demands placed upon a teacher. Administrative tasks recognized by apprentices included taking attendance, managing and maintaining equipment, and performing grading procedures:

"warm-ups and roll call took too much time."

"the p.e. teacher of the junior high was very organized; equipment was set up and enough time was spent on each skill."

"the teacher was not organized, (he) had no control of the class, there was no motivation, and nothing was learned. Most of the period was spent making sure everyone had a uniform and took a shower."

Administrative tasks were not allocated much attention in the teaching reports. These tasks seemed to be taken more for granted as an extraneous duty and not central to the classroom operation. However, several teachers viewed the ability to organize and manage equipment and resources as a functional task in their teaching repertoire.

"while teaching badminton to a class of 37 students, I feel I did a good job of setting up the unit so all students would get as much participation time as possible. I set up four nets on the floor and one extra net up on the balcony, which had never been used before. I was without badminton lines, so I had to use shoe polish as a substitute. While practicing the skills I had taught, I had them practice in groups of seven each, with only four practicing at a time. When it came time for the tournament, I had them play doubles games up to only seven points so the games would go faster."

Gymnasium safety was another task which did not hold strong attention, but was present in both apprentice and teacher reports. Gymnasium safety is a responsibility of the teacher; teachers become acquainted with this responsibility during their apprenticeship periods. One apprentice reported the following:

"Some of the tasks that concerned throwing with balls were not well supervised and balls were thrown at unprepared students leading to injury."

As can be noted from the following, teachers recognize their responsibility for safety, but this task did not appear to require much effort:

"during my track unit I was using relays around the gym with two teams against each other. At first, the team that got to the turn first was getting pushed out of the way by the other teams. So after the first two people ran I stopped the race and told all of the teams that whoever got to the turn first the other team had to give that team room without touching them (sic). This made the races better in safety and competition. After class many of the students came into my office and told me how much they enjoyed the lesson and the change I made."

It was interesting to note that a majority of incidents relative to class operation were reported as events indicative of poor teaching, while many incidents relative to student learning were reported under events characteristic of good teaching. This implies that teachers believe they should be able to operate and manage a classroom, and failure to do so is a failure to meet the fundamental priority of a teacher: management. It also implies that student learning is a nice addition, but not critical, to the teaching act. Failure to stimulate student learning is not seen as a dereliction of duty. The teachers appeared to have become acquainted with the tasks of student learning and class operation in the apprenticeship period, however there is a shift in the importance attributed to those tasks as one moves from student to teacher in physical education. This finding appears to lend support to the notion that teachers are expected to operate and manage a classroom, but student learning is a secondary concern in physical education (Schempp, 1985).

Teacher/student interpersonal relationships. Tasks relative to teacher/student interpersonal relationships were considered more the manner in which the teacher interacted with the students than actual teaching duties. These interactions were hypothesized to form the professional demeanor of the teacher by observing how "good" teachers interacted with students in contrast to the interactions of "poor" teachers. These tasks included being fair and just, establishing relationships based on trust and/or respect, and serving as a counselor, friend or confidant. Some descriptions of apprentice relationships are given below.

"He was not only a teacher but he was also a friend. He was on our level, understanding our problems and helping us with them."

"It was around the 1st or 2nd grade. There was always one boy that the class picked on, especially in dodgeball. He'd always end up crying every period and the teacher would really lay into him and call him a baby. It was a real down-grading situation and I think the attitude of the teacher in this situation was very poor and cruel."

"The teacher was not fair in dealing with the athletes during class. Since he was head basketball coach, all his players got preferential treatment throughout the year. He was not very helpful to the poor performer or the impaired individual."

The interpersonal relationships continue to be a strong concern once teachers begin their teaching role. Similarities can be noted between apprenticeship and teaching descriptions.

"On my last day of class I had an 8th grade boy come up to me and wrap his arms around me and cry. He told me he was glad I cared.

This boy was a little slow and so I just gave him some reinforcement which helped his performance and attitude toward the class."

"I've relaxed much more and can joke around and laugh and still present the lesson in a serious manner."

One difference was detected between apprentice and teaching reports regarding interpersonal relationships. The apprentice reports were drawn from the perspective of one student (apprentice) interacting with one selected teacher. The teacher reports were drawn from the perspective of one teacher interacting with large groups of students. It would be natural to expect the apprentice reports to reflect a deeper personal meaning while the teacher reports reflected a more general description of the relationships.

"I feel the rapport between the students and myself was quite good which provided a good learning atmosphere."

"Slowly I became more comfortable and enjoyed myself and classes more, particularly the student-teacher interaction."

Although the apprenticeship period appears to influence, it does not determine the interpersonal relationships a teacher will forge with their students. The relationships that the student teachers developed with their students was based on human considerations, not professional ones. That is, teachers interact with students based on their familiarity and understanding of the students as people. The teachers in this study appear to agree with Barzun (1929) that "teaching is not a process, it is a developing emotional situation" (p.43). The personalities of the individuals involved will determine, in large part, the relationships established between a teacher and a student. The apprenticeship allows prospective teachers to understand the importance and role of such relationships in the classroom.

Exhibition of personal qualities. Tasks related to the exhibition of the teacher's personal qualities were actually personal characteristics that manifested during the teaching experience. These tasks included serving as a role model, displaying attitudes regarding occupational duties and individuals, demonstrating leadership characteristics, and being assertive, knowledgeable, and enthusiastic. These characteristics were diverse and represented a broad spectrum of human attributes. Thus, it would be difficult to identify specific characteristics apprentices associated with teachers or teachers' personal characteristics which apprentices adopted and carried into their teaching role. However, the apprenticeship does appear to acquaint prospective teachers with the reality that teachers are people and their personal characteristics influence their classroom behavior and professional attitudes.

Apprentice reports described the personal qualities of teachers in the following ways:

"Miss R. was a short, hateful lady who taught health & p.e. at my junior high. She was argumentative and distrustful, even when unwarranted. But the worst thing of all: she stood in the lockerroom, grade book in hand, checking off whether or not we took showers."

"(He was) very physically fit. (He was) also stern, but cared; you felt a caring attitude."

"He was a good motivator and looked upon as a role model and leader. His teaching methods varied with the content but he was always calm and assured."

"My junior high PE teacher was a very personable teacher. She wasn't *too* friendly, but all the students enjoyed her classes."

"The instructor did not make an impression on me that he was too knowledgeable on the subject matter."

"They (teachers) were in perfect health and physical shape. They were also very knowledgeable in first aid and athletic training. They were enthusiastic about p.e."

The exhibition of personal characteristics was also recognized by the teachers as influencing their classroom behavior. Teaching descriptions included:

"My tinikiling lesson was a disaster mainly because I lost my patience with them when they couldn't even get the rhythm down."

"I did an action story play and one of the important things to do was to get enthusiastic and into it. The children really loved it when the teacher got into it."

". . . A lack of motivation, self-confidence, and enthusiasm in the beginning of my experience. I was too tense. I needed more confidence so my personality could come across to the students."

Summary. The data in this study supports Lortie's (1975) theory that the apprenticeship-of-observation acquaints prospective teachers with an extensive array of teaching tasks. However, the apprenticeship does not appear to offer an opportunity to practice, analyze or master those skills in any detail. Given the familiarity from protracted exposure, the apprenticeship offers a powerful source of influence for teachers in learning the tasks of teaching.

Proposition two: Teachers begin their identification as teachers during their apprenticeship

Contrary to Lortie's (1975) apprenticeship theory, the teachers in this study did not appear to form an identification with teachers while they were students in physical education. There appears, in many cases, to be teachers that were admired. But, many of the student teachers did not consider their physical education teachers to be outstanding teachers. Several student teachers identified their physical education teachers as exhibiting both excellent and poor teaching qualities.

"(He chose) very poor content. We played a lot of battleball. When he did teach, he was an excellent teacher."

Physical education teachers do not appear to serve as the professional role models for the next generation of teachers. Many apprentices are left to form their own opinions and beliefs about what a teacher should do and be. One teacher summarized her high school experience this way:

"Overall my experience in p.e. in high school was a bad experience. I ended up hating the class even though I was good at it, simply because my teacher showed that she didn't enjoy her job. She never demonstrated or participated and would spend a lot of time in the lounge smoking. I feel all this led to my idea of poor teaching. First, I believe a p.e. teacher should care enough to believe in a philosophy of 'physical education'. How can a p.e. teacher stress physical importance when ruining their own body with cigarettes, etc.? Secondly, my idea of teaching is exactly that; to teach new skills or broaden and expand previous ones. Teaching involves so much more than just a classroom, it involves your whole life—in school and out. I feel a good teacher can make a subject interesting enough so students want to learn; and they will."

Another teacher described her high school physical education experience like this:

"The teacher never showed us how to dribble, shoot, block or play defense. None of the rules were explained until one was broken, but the teacher mainly let everything go. So while the teacher sat on the bleachers reading or eating, the class as a whole was trying to play basketball. The teacher left the teaching and the rules of the game up to those who knew how to play. Instead of being a fun activity in which everyone participated, it turned out to be just a game of clowning around, goofing off, and fighting. I love basketball, but I hated playing it in gym class."

Given these dour experiences, it seems amazing that these people chose to become physical education teachers. It is less surprising that their teachers were not seen as role models, nor was their identification as teachers formed while they were students in these classes.

Why don't physical educators begin their identification as teachers during their apprenticeship? Several reasons seem plausible. But regardless, these speculations all need further exploration. The first explanation is offered by Lortie (1975). Critical to developing an identification with one's teachers in the apprenticeship period is the time of decision to enter teaching. The earlier one makes the decision to enter teaching, the stronger the identification with teachers encountered during the apprenticeship. Data on time of decision was, unfortunately, not gathered in the course of this study. However, the findings indicate that physical educators are late deciders in their career choice.

A second reason for the lack of identification with teachers may reside in the determinant of career choice. Bain and Wendt (1983) found that the primary determinant for entering physical education was not teaching, but rather coaching. In these cases the coach would be the more likely role model and the identification of the prospective teacher would be to the coaching profession and not teaching. Lortie (personal communication, July 7, 1986) questioned the influence of agencies outside the school (e.g., camps, YMCAs, athletic teams) on the developing physical education teacher. Such influences are unique to physical education teachers over classroom teachers.

A third potential explanation was identified by several of the studied teachers who reported limited experience in physical education. Only in a very few schools does time in physical education rival time spent in other subject matter areas. Many of the elementary physical education classes experienced by the people of this study were not taught by physical education teachers, but rather classroom teachers. Given these limitations, the apprenticeship-of-observation in physical education would be a lesser influence on its teachers in comparison to classroom teachers.

Proposition three: Assessments of teaching technique are similar both prior to and after entry into the role of teacher

The assessments of good and poor teaching technique by the teachers of this study were similar across experience. Incidents recalled from the apprenticeship period used assessment criteria which also was used in the teaching role. Assessment criteria, both pre- and postentry, appeared based on personal appeal and emotion rather than professional knowledge. The teachers based their judgments on feelings, beliefs, and uninformed, simplistic observations.

"I believe I provided the students with a variety of activities during class periods which kept them interested and active."

"I think I did a good job with New Games, especially with the 5th graders. They had fun and so did I."

Beliefs held as a student appeared to carry the same validity after the teaching role was assumed. The criteria upon which these early judgments were made did not change. This finding is consistent with a previous finding that accumulated teaching experience appears to hold little influence over beliefs of good teaching (Schempp, 1985). The examples below indicate that the teachers consider judgments they made as students are just as valid today:

"A new female 3rd grade teacher was, I feel, being challenged by the popularity of one of her students. After being reprimanded for laughing, I was sent to the principal for a smile during our next activity. I feel that a mere smile shouldn't result in punishment."

"He had a progressive program and kept records on students performance each year to see how far they came along. I feel that a teacher who spends that much time keeping records deserves a lot of credit."

There were two noticeable differences between pre- and postteaching reports. First, as previously noted, the teachers evaluated their own practice from a more technical perspective with class management serving as the major assessment criterion. Students used a more personal perspective in assessing their teachers. Second, the teachers evidenced a greater sophistication in analyzing their own behavior by looking to multiple feedback sources in assessing their performance as teachers.

"Dance routines (were) performed by each class for my cooperating teacher, principal, and other teachers. The children learned the dance, were eager to learn, and had fun doing it. The principal and cooperating teacher were very impressed."

"(The) fourth grade students were able to put together, practice and perform a quality routine in three weeks, with two classes per week. Their performances were indicative of good teaching and hard work on their part. I feel the visual aids and handout that I had made for them helped tremendously."

"It was evident from the wrestling tournament that all the boys gained knowledge about wrestling and the different moves they were taught. Also, after this unit was over some boys said they were going to go out for the team next year."

Generally, however, it was difficult to separate assessments made as students from assessments made as teachers. The assessments, both pre and postentry, were random and practical rather than systematic and problematic. They lacked a connection to the teacher's pedagogical purpose or the students' life situation. The social or political ramifications of the teacher's actions were never scrutinized. Also absent was a connection of the teacher's actions to a wider school context or the society at large. The assessments focused on the teacher as an independent entity faced only with the immediate concerns of the class. The findings of this study offer support to Lortie's (1975) contention that the apprenticeship-of-observation does not "lay the basis for informed assessment of teaching technique or encourage the development of analytic orientations toward the work (of teaching)" (p. 67). And that which

> constituted good teaching then constitutes good teaching now; there is no great divide between preentry and postentry evaluations. Training (and even subsequent experience) is not a dramatic watershed separating the perceptions of naive laymen from later judgments by knowing professionals (p. 66).

Proposition four: Because the apprenticeship represents the analysis of personal experience, a teacher's analytic orientations toward the work of teaching are individualistic in nature

> "I had one P.E. teacher that was teaching a volleyball unit and we were in a practice-game type lesson. I was serving underhand and she helped me learn an overhand serve which was never taught to me. It was a very individualized type of lesson. I think it happened before the start of class but I remember it because she took the time to help me learn a new skill that I'm glad someone taught me after all that time. It was very reinforcing and very personal. I think because it was so individualized I remember it."

Both the pre- and postteaching reports were descriptions of selected moments in each teacher's life. In the preteaching reports, those people were students. In the postteaching reports those same people were teachers. Being a student in public schools is a personal experience and as the move is made from student to teacher, the school experience as personal experience appears to remain intact. As students become teachers the struggles they face are viewed as personal achievements and failures, not professional ones. The analytic orientations these teachers held appeared to be personal and individualistic; not professional and collective.

The teachers of this study depicted teaching as an activity performed by an individual in the presence of a group of students. Responsibility for in-class activity rested entirely with the teacher. The resources used by the teacher to orchestrate the actions necessary to meet these responsibilities were primarily internal, individual, personal characteristics. No reports were made of teachers who were respected by their peers or demonstrated the ability to draw upon professional or external resources to better perform their work as teachers. No apprentices reported teachers who used extensive outside resources or peer help to teach more effectively. In some cases these student teachers were even discouraged from drawing upon outside resources:

> "During my lecture on badminton I pulled out a 3x5 note card to make sure I didn't leave anything out. Steve Sommers (cooperating teacher) said that that should never be done because the students look to the teacher as an expert and by pulling out a note card I lessened their view of me as a teacher/expert."

Other teachers and administrators were mentioned in a few post-entry reports, but these incidents recounted those individuals confirming or disputing individual decisions made by the teacher. Collegiality was not viewed as an essential element in a teacher's work:

> "Staff members told me I had 'great control' over my classes."

> "My supervising teacher said that he was glad to see that I was tough with the 8th grade boys and didn't let them get the best of me."

> "Specific comments from the principal after he observed me teach (indicated that) he was impressed with how I handled discipline in class. He also liked the positive reinforcement given to the students."

Although personal, individual characteristics framed the analytic orientation in both the pre- and postentry reports, a change in the nature of those characteristics was found in this study. A shift from empathetic characteristics (caring, friendly, encouraging, fair) to more technical characteristics (flexible, organized, concise) was noted. This finding supports Lortie's (1975) conclusion that the apprenticeship is formed from the perspective of a student, which may differ from the perspective and concerns of a teacher. It appears the orientation toward the work of teachers is formed with sufficient strength and flexibility during the apprenticeship to incorporate shifting concerns as one leaves the world of student and enters the occupation of teacher.

What is learned in the apprenticeship?

The apprenticeship period acquaints the prospective teacher with a host of demonstrable teaching tasks as they are practiced in the everyday classroom life of the teacher. But those tasks are inactive until a teaching role provides an opportunity to engage them. "What students learn about teaching, then, is intuitive and imitative rather than explicit and analytical; it is based on individual personalities rather than pedagogical principles" (Lortie, 1975, p. 62).

The skills, attitudes, and professional orientation carried into the teaching role are shaped by recollections of the past. Teachers draw upon their past experiences as students to meet present responsibilities. Those recollections are further mediated by both the teacher's personality and occupational demands of the gymnasium. They are selected based on personal likes and dislikes and represent pleasant memories and disturbing nightmares. The apprenticeship-of-observation does not represent a professional or systematic introductory framework. The apprenticeship-of-observation represents collected and recollected experiences from days as a student. And those experiences provide a continuing influence over the pedagogical practices and orientations of physical education teachers.

Disconfirming Evidence

Analyzing these data revealed an influence on teaching role perceptions stemming from the undergraduate experience. This influence did not appear to overpower the apprenticeship reports; but, even its minor presence should signal a note of caution. Apprentice data were collected during a five-week teaching methods course that was taught the same semester in which the student teaching experience occurred. The data were collected over a two-year period and it was not always possible to collect data on the first day of class. The influence from the course was evident in cases were data were collected after the second or third class meeting. These particular reports appeared to focus more closely on teaching methods and used language specifically referred to in the undergraduate program. For example, the technical language used by one student teacher betrays the influence of the university program on their perceptions of past public school teachers:

> "There was no movement education nor was there any vertical or horizontal development."

The socialization process is a cumulative one. Unless one can identify those who will be teachers while they are still students and then follow those people from student to the undergraduate major to public school teacher, socialization research will have data tainted by the accumulated socializing influences. Therefore, the reader is cautioned that the perceptions of teaching described in this study were under the influence of preservice socialization. The reader is further advised that the findings offered in this chapter are limited by two additional factors: a) the theoretical posture taken in analyzing the data, and b) the data available for analysis. Surely other theories would reveal different dimensions of the apprenticeship period, as would other data forms.

PROPHECY OR PROFIT?: IMPLICATIONS FOR TEACHERS AND TEACHER EDUCATORS

Physical education teachers, as most teachers, appear to serve an apprenticeship-of-observation while students in public schools. The apprenticeship period informs the prospective physical educator of the tasks of teaching, influences assessment strategies for determining the quality of teaching, and helps shape the analytic orientation toward each teacher's professional work. The perspectives toward teaching formed during this apprenticeship are personal and individualistic, which mitigates against collective and reflective change in the current practices of physical education teachers. Lortie (1975) said, "the apprenticeship-of-observation is an ally of continuity rather than of change" (p. 67). Drawing this conclusion appears to condemn attempts by those committed to improving the practice of teachers; for if the apprenticeship is indeed a formidable force, what hope is there that 16 years of impressionable observation can be undone by a few years at a university or with inservice education? Will the past determine the future for physical education teachers?

I think not—at least not completely. Those assuming teaching roles are not the same people as those who were students, nor are the schools they enter to teach the same they left as students. Although tradition stands strong in the process of schooling, time washes anew the circumstances of the educational experience. Teachers will, most certainly, carry with them the lessons learned from their apprenticeship and these lessons will inform their practice as professionals. But herein lies the potential for profit. Teachers and teacher educators can root collective and constructive improvement in physical education teaching in the apprenticeship-of-observation.

Both teachers and teacher educators must recognize and work with the power of the apprenticeship. Understanding the powerful influences residing in the sedimented experiences of teachers will enable teachers to profit from their early school experiences by critically reflecting on their apprenticeship. This reflection allows teachers to separate useful perspectives and practices from those that are dysfunctional and debilitating. Reflection permits teachers to consciously chart their future professional activities and reject the reflexive practices imposed by an unconscious past. Teachers often work in professional isolation and cannot observe the practices of their peers. Reflection on their apprenticeship presents teachers with a rich pool of observed teachers for ideas on improving their own practices (McEvoy, 1986).

Teacher educators who recognize the futility of ignoring the handprint of history will treat preservice teachers not as naive to the ways of schools, but rather as those intimately familiar with life in public schools.

These teacher educators will use the apprenticeship-of-observation as a point of departure in the preparation of future generations of physical educators. Grounding the professional preparation program in influential past experiences will not only recognize the validity of those experiences, but allow the preservice teacher a greater consciousness of the influence of his own history. "By helping our students become aware of their own former experiences we can provide them with that 'perception of practice' that is so often necessary to validate the theory we teach" (McEvoy, 1986, p.15). As teacher educators struggle to make the knowledge they teach both personally and professionally relevant for prospective teachers, there appears no better place to start than with the knowledge and experiences students already hold.

Physical education may have something unique to offer the larger field of education. The study discussed in this chapter revealed that the power of the apprenticeship may be less for the physical educator than their classroom counterparts. The length of time in physical education as a student and the lack of identification with other physical education teachers indicates the foundation upon which apprenticeship perspectives are based may not be as formidable as they are for other teachers. Therefore, the likelihood of altering apprenticeship perspectives in favor of a more informed perspective is greater. To profit from this potential, future research must uncover more thoroughly the physical education teacher's sources of occupational perspective. Stronger connections between the experiences of the past and the behavior and ideology of the present need to be forged. These links can then be used as a guide in understanding the perspective and, ultimately, improving the practice of physical education teachers.

REFERENCES

Anyon, J. (1981). Social class and school knowledge. *Curriculum Inquiry, 11*, 3-14.
Bain, L. L., & Wendt, J. C. (1983). Undergraduate physical education majors' perceptions of the roles of teacher and coach. *Research Quarterly for Exercise and Sport, 54*, 112-118.
Barzun, J. (1929). *Teacher in America.* Garden City, NY: Doubleday & Company.
Boggess, T. E., McBride, R. E., & Griffey, D. C. (1985). The concerns of physical education student teachers: A developmental view. *Journal of Teaching in Physical Education, 4*, 202-211.
Flanagan, J. C. (1954). The critical incident technique. *Psychological Bulletin, 4*, 327-358.
Freire, P. (1970). *Pedagogy of the oppressed.* New York: Seabury.
Lawson, H. A. (1983). Toward a model of teacher socialization in physical education: The subjective warrant, recruitment, and teacher education (Part I). *Journal of Teaching in Physical Education, 2*, 3-16.
Locke, L. F. (1977). Research on teaching physical education: New hope for a dismal science. *Quest, 28*, 2-16.
Lortie, D. C. (1975). *Schoolteacher.* Chicago: University of Chicago Press.
McEvoy, B. (1986, April). *"She is still with me": Influences of former teachers on teacher practice.* Paper presented at the American Educational Research Association, San Francisco, CA.
Placek, J. (1983). Conceptions of success in teaching: Happy, busy and good? In T. Templin & J. Olson (Eds.), *Teaching in Physical Education*, (pp. 46-56). Champaign, IL: Human Kinetics.
Pooley, J. C. (1972). Professional socialization: A model of the pre-training phase applicable to physical education students. *Quest, 18*, 57-66.

Schempp, P. G. (1983). Learning the role: The transformation from student to teacher. In T. Templin & J. Olson (Eds.), *Teaching in Physical Education*. Champaign, IL: Human Kinetics.

Schempp, P. G. (1985). Becoming a better teacher: An analysis of the student teaching experience. *Journal of Teaching in Physical Education, 4*, 158-166.

Schempp, P. G. (1986). Physical education student teachers' beliefs in their control over student learning. *Journal of Teaching in Physical Education, 5*, 198-203.

Tom, A. (1984). *Teaching as a moral craft*, New York: London.

3

Recruitment in Physical Education Teaching: Toward a Critical Approach

ALISON M. DEWAR
Miami University

Socialization into physical education is a complex process. This chapter presents one aspect of this process, examining the issues of recruitment and entry into physical education teaching. Questions to be addressed include: Which students become teachers of physical education? For what reasons? What are these individuals' perceptions of physical education teachers and teaching? Do these perceptions influence the career choices of potential teachers? If so, in what ways?

The purpose of this chapter is to provide a framework for discussing recruitment and entry into physical education teaching. The discussion starts with an exploration of the recruitment process in physical education. Following this is a review of the research on recruitment and entry into physical education, which answers the questions raised at the beginning of the chapter. The first section concludes with a discussion of the gaps that exist in our knowledge about this aspect of the socialization process and provides suggestions for future work.

I would like to thank Jennifer Gore and Hal Lawson for their helpful comments and criticisms on earlier drafts of this paper.

The chapter continues with a discussion of the implications of research and scholarship on recruitment into physical education for teachers and teaching. This section examines the relationship between recruitment into physical education and teachers' work. It suggests that the ways in which teachers negotiate and define their work in physical education has an important impact on recruitment. The argument is made that in order to fully understand who enters physical education and why, it is important that we take seriously the ways in which physical education is defined and taught in schools. In addition, it is suggested that it is important to view the decision to become a physical education teacher in a broader social and political context. The intent here is to raise a set of questions about recruitment into physical education which place physical educators and their work at the center of the research and scholarly enterprise. These questions are intended to present a different perspective on socialization and are designed to provide the stimulus for discussion and debate about teachers' work in physical education. The last part of the chapter presents conclusions and suggestions for future consideration in this work.

RECRUITMENT AND THE SOCIALIZATION PROCESS

Recruitment is a common term, typically understood as the process of actively seeking out and attracting new members for a group. It is also a term frequently associated with sport. We often hear about new recruits, potential recruits, and the recruiting process in relation to high school, college, and professional sports. We all know and understand, at least at a basic level, what these terms mean and their importance in the sporting world.

Recruiting and recruitment are also important when discussing physical education teaching. Unfortunately, this is not reflected in either our common sense views or the research and scholarship in physical education. Rarely do we ask: Who enters physical education programs? Why did they choose physical education? What are their perceptions about physical education teachers and teaching? How are these perceptions produced and developed? What are the implications of these perceptions for school programs and practices? How do these perceptions help to reproduce or challenge the dominant practices and belief systems that exist in physical education, schools, and society? These questions are important because they help us to conceptualize recruitment into physical education teaching within the socialization process and contextualize it in terms of broader social relations.

Recruitment, much like socialization, is defined many different ways. How recruitment is defined depends on the theoretical perspective being used to study it. For example, individuals working within a functionalist perspective on socialization see recruitment as the process whereby individuals make decisions to enter physical education teaching. For these individuals the empirical task is to identify and define the factors that influence this decision. Once this has been achieved the next task is measuring the relative impact of different factors or variables on individuals' choices to become teachers of physical education. Functionalists consider this task important because it allows researchers to predict not only who enters physical education programs but also the values, attitudes, skills, and behaviors they bring with them. This knowledge is considered important because the assumption is that a clear understanding of recruitment will allow for greater control of individuals' socialization once they enter physical education programs and schools.

Thus, recruitment is conceptualized by functionalist researchers as the first part of the process of socialization into teaching. It is seen as important because it allows for an understanding of what recruits bring with them to teacher education programs in physical education. This creates the potential for greater uniformity in the control over their subsequent socialization and increases the chances that recruits will be "successfully" socialized by the program and their teaching experiences.

Recruitment takes on a different set of definitions for individuals working within an interpretative perspective. Recruitment is still seen as the processes involved in making the choice to become a teacher of physical education. The difference between an interpretive perspective of recruitment and a functionalist one is in the conceptualization of this process. Recruitment is interesting to interpretative researchers because it allows for a greater understanding of the ways in which potential teachers of physical education create and negotiate their personal and professional identities. The processes involved in creating and developing identities as physical educators are seen as important because they allow for an understanding of the ways in which individuals interpret and define their professional practices. It is assumed that recruitment cannot be reduced to a set of clearly identifiable beliefs and behaviors, but that it needs to be located within the specific contexts in which it is occurring.

The challenge for individuals studying recruitment using an interpretive framework is to describe and explain in considerable detail the processes involved in individuals' decisions to become physical education teachers. The assumption is that recruitment is context dependent; individuals' choices and decisions to enter physical education teaching are assumed to be unique to the specific situations and contexts in which they are being made. The in-depth study or "thick description" (Geertz, 1973) of the contexts in which individuals develop perceptions and perspectives about physical education are seen as extremely important. Recruitment is not viewed as a fixed process, rather one that is developed and changed in different ways by different people in different situations.

Despite the differences that exist in the ways recruitment is defined by functionalist and interpretive frameworks, it is defined as important by both. Researchers working within an interpretative framework study recruitment because it allows them to examine the processes involved in the development and negotiation of recruits' professional and personal identities. Recruitment is defined in this perspective as one aspect of a complex process of negotiation over professional beliefs and practices. An understanding of the complexities and subtleties of recruitment allows for a greater understanding of the ways in which recruits respond to and interpret the socialization experiences they encounter in professional education and schools.

There is a third perspective for viewing recruitment. When recruitment is viewed from a critical perspective it is seen as a process by which individuals are selected for and allocated to careers in physical education. This perspective views the selection and allocation process as problematic because it questions the criteria used in decision making about the kinds of individuals deemed to be suitable recruits for physical education careers. Recruitment serves as a means of ensuring the maintenance of the physical education profession as it is most commonly defined and practiced. The argument made by critical researchers is that physical education is defined in ways that protect and privilege the interests and needs of a powerful few (in American physical education this can be translated to mean the interests and needs of white, middle class males). One way to maintain and secure the continued existence of this dominance is to select recruits of like minds and like kind. Thus, recruitment is seen as extremely important to critical researchers because it is one way that dominant groups can maintain and secure continued control over the nature of physical education in schools and colleges.

Much like the interpretive perspective, the critical perspective examines recruitment within the context it occurs. However, this is done in a different way. Individuals working within a critical perspective view recruitment practices as historically produced and socially constructed. What this means is that recruitment is not viewed as a neutral process. Rather, it is seen as a set of cultural, social, and educational practices in which dominant meanings and values are negotiated and contested. This is important because individuals' perspectives are examined and interpreted within the social, political, and cultural contexts in which they occur. Recruitment is defined as more than a set of values, attitudes and behaviors. It is seen as a process of selection that can be used to maintain or transform the relations of power and dominance that characterize physical education teaching.

My position on both socialization and recruitment into physical education teaching is that we must view these processes from a critical perspective. I am in agreement with the work of Connell (1985), Stanworth (1983), Walker and Barton (1987), and Weiner (1985) who view teachers and teaching in terms of the social relations of class, race, and gender.

This chapter does not deal with socialization into teaching or recruitment, per se. However, it provides examples of the kinds of questions critical analyses of physical education might produce, and shows clearly the importance of understanding the ways in which physical education teachers are involved in reproducing and challenging the dominant social relations that exist in society. This recognition is extremely important for our understanding of recruitment because it is through recruitment that an occupation is able to recreate itself or change.

RESEARCH ON RECRUITMENT IN PHYSICAL EDUCATION TEACHING

Reviews of research are typically lengthy discussions which are used to catalog a wide array of research studies and their findings for the reader. However, in this chapter, there is no vast body of research and scholarship to draw on about recruitment into physical education teaching. Relatively speaking, there are few studies of socialization into physical education teaching and even fewer on recruitment into the field. This may be because socialization has only recently captured the imagination of scholars and researchers in physical education. Most of the work that has been done on socialization has focused on sport and athletes.[1]

This review will examine only the research on recruitment into physical education teaching. The purposes of this review are to locate the research within the appropriate theoretical perspective, and to discuss and critically analyze what we know about recruitment from this work.

The few examples of work that exist on recruitment into physical education (e.g., Dewar, 1983, 1984; Dewar and Lawson, 1984; Lawson, 1983a; 1983b; Mulling 1981; Pooley, 1972, 1975; Templin, Woodford and Mulling, 1982; Woodford, 1977) are similar in a number of important ways. First, they all begin with the assumption that recruitment is the first of a three stage process of socialization into physical education teaching. The first stage is one of anticipatory socialization in which individuals develop perceptions about a profession before entering programs of professional education. The second stage is defined as professional education. The final stage in the process is the socialization individuals receive when they leave professional education programs and enter the working world. This three stage model for professional socialization is borrowed from the literature on socialization into medicine and law (Becker, Geer and Hughes, 1961; Merton, Reader and Kendal, 1957).

---

[1] See Fishwick and Greendorfer (1987) for a critical analysis of the sport socialization literature.

Recruitment (the first stage of the socialization process), or the process of anticipatory socialization, is assumed to be important because of its relationship to the rest of the socialization process. That is, its relationship to the impact of professional education (the second stage of the process) and entry into the workplace (the final stage) on individuals' professional identities and practices. Although this work adopts a functionalist model of socialization, in which the process is reduced to three distinct stages, it does differ in the ways in which the processes involved in the recruitment phase of the model are operationalized.

For example, some of the earlier work on recruitment (Pooley, 1970; 1975; Mulling, 1981; Woodford, 1977) studied the attitudes and values of individuals who had already entered physical education programs. These studies used psychological inventories and questionnaires to describe and explain the nature of students' socialization experiences prior to entering physical education teaching programs.

Templin, Woodford and Mulling (1982) and Dewar and Lawson (1984) provide summaries of the research on recruitment in physical education. Both reviews remark on the paucity of research in this area. Unfortunately little has changed since these reviews were written.

These articles used a schema developed by Lortie (1975) to organize and link the research findings in physical education. This schema was taken from Lortie's work on schoolteachers in which he argued that occupations are involved in a "silent" competition for recruits. Part of this silent competition involves what Lortie calls recruitment resources. These are "the properties which assist an occupation in competing for manpower (sic) and talent" (Lortie, 1975, p. 26). He breaks down these recruitment resources further into attractors and facilitators. Attractors are the benefits offered to potential recruits. They include things such as money, job security, mobility opportunities, power, prestige, enjoyment and satisfaction. Facilitators, on the other hand, are the mechanisms, including socialization, that are implicated in recruits' choices of specific occupations. These include the factors such as the influence of significant others, the range of realistic choices available to recruits (the difference between what occupations individuals are attracted to and the ones that they are actually qualified for), and recruits' perceptions of the requirements necessary for entry into an occupation.

The data from the earlier studies on recruitment (Pooley, 1970; Mulling, 1981; Woodford, 1977) show that individuals are attracted to careers in physical education teaching because the occupation is one that is perceived as providing opportunities to work with and help others, to serve society, and to continue associations with sport and physical activity which are viewed as rewarding and enjoyable.

The data also suggest that physical education teaching may be one of the few alternatives open to recruits. The relatively low entrance requirements of many physical education programs and the generally mediocre records of high school academic achievement of many physical education teacher education students suggest that physical education may be one of the few university programs to which these individuals may realistically be able to gain access. When this is viewed in relation to the relatively low status and prestige associated with teaching, and the even lower status of physical education in schools, it is unlikely that a career in physical education will be attractive to individuals who believe they have other more prestigious options available to them.

In terms of the facilitators that exist for a career in physical education teaching the data suggest that both success and interest in sport and physical activity are important factors in recruits' decisions to enter the field. In addition, there is evidence to suggest that teachers, coaches, parents, siblings (especially brothers), and peers are significant influences in recruits' socialization prior to their entry into physical education teacher education programs.

For example, Pooley (1975), Woodford (1977), and Templin, Woodford and Mulling (1982) suggest that coaches, rather than teachers of physical education, are more influential in male recruits' decisions to teach physical education. The opposite trend appears to be true for female physical educators; physical education teachers rather than coaches are more important in female recruits' decisions to enter the field.

Lawson's (1983a, 1983b) work represents a different approach to recruitment. He developed the foundation for a model of teacher socialization in physical education that moved beyond the measurement of traits and behaviors of individuals who had already made their career choices. He suggested that,

> People choose a career such as physical education. When attention is directed only to people who have already entered teacher education programs, the dynamics of the choice remain largely undetected. Important antecedents—events, experiences, people, processes—that act and interact to influence career choice beginning early in childhood remain unexplored. (Lawson, 1983a, p. 6)

He also argued that recruits' subjective meanings and interpretations of their experiences must be examined if we are to understand how and why individuals make the choice to become physical education teachers. Lawson developed his argument by suggesting that a potential avenue for research is the study of recruits' "subjective warrants". This construct is defined as "each person's perceptions of the requirements for teacher education and for actual teaching in schools" (Lawson, 1983a, (p. 6).

The subjective warrant is important in Lawson's analysis because it attempts to locate recruitment within a large social context. This is illustrated, as he develops the subjective warrant more fully:

Constructed on the basis of personal biography, the effects of significant others, societal influences, and direct experiences in schools, it is as important to the understanding of identity formation as it is to a career choice. (Lawson, 1983a, p. 7)

This analysis of the subjective warrant and its importance in recruitment into physical education teaching marks a step forward in this area of research and scholarship. Lawson's (1983a) work provides a critique of Lortie's (1975) and Templin, Woodford and Mulling's (1982) narrow definitions of the subjective warrant. He calls for research that does more than identify and measure the subjective warrant as a psychological construct and suggests that recruitment needs to be reconceptualized in ways that place recruits and their experiences at the center of the research enterprise.

Lawson's (1983a) work was a call for a broadening of research on recruitment to include different kinds of methodologies and data collection techniques. This call represents the first attempt to introduce an interpretive framework into physical education recruitment research. His challenge suggested that researchers move away from functionalist studies that identify and measure psychological variables and move toward more interpretive studies that enable thick description and analysis of the processes involved in the development of individuals' professional and personal identities, and their perceptions of physical education teachers and teaching.

Lawson's (1983a) work formed the basis for Dewar's (1983, 1984) research on the subjective warrant and recruitment into physical education. This work differed from prior studies of recruitment, which had examined college students already enrolled in physical education programs, because it focused on high school students' subjective warrants for physical education. This work is the first example of research on recruitment in physical education that examined students' subjective warrants *prior* to their entry into physical education programs. By focusing on high school students, this work was able to examine the subjective warrants of individuals who were attracted to careers in physical education as well as those who, despite success in sport and physical education, were not interested in entering the profession. The inclusion of individuals who had decided against careers in physical education allowed for an examination of the reasons why physical education is seen as unattractive by students who theoretically might be expected (from the profiles developed in earlier studies) to be attracted to a career in physical education.

Dewar's (1983, 1984) work had two main purposes. First, a theoretical framework for the subjective warrant was developed from a synthesis of the occupational choice and professionalization literature. Secondly, this framework was used to examine high school students' subjective warrants for physical education and career choices.

There were three categories of subjects in the study. The first category was males and females who were attracted to careers in physical education. The second category was males and females who had decided upon careers in physical education. The final category were males and females who were highly successful in sport and physical education but had decided against careers in the field.

The students in the study were all in grades 10-12 in high school and were identified by physical education teachers and career counseling staff. Each student was given a questionnaire, consisting of open and closed questions, which had been derived from the theoretical framework developed for the study.

The results of the study showed that the majority of students in all three categories had extensive involvements in sport and physical activity, and saw these activities to be the main focus of their lives. Despite having similar background experiences in sport and physical activity there were differences in the students' subjective warrants for physical education.

Subjective Warrants of Students Attracted to And Decided Upon Careers in Physical Education

The dominant view, held by the majority of students who were attracted to or decided upon careers in physical education, was one in which physical education was seen as being primarily skill oriented, involving learning how to play games and how to teach them to others. This view was held by both male and female students who were attracted to physical education teaching because it was viewed as a job that would provide a continuous association with sport, opportunities to work with children, and a good working atmosphere. These individuals also were influenced by physical education teachers, coaches, family members, and peers and made their decisions to enter programs because they felt comfortable with the systems they had come through and wanted to reproduce, as teachers, the kinds of experiences they had as students.

There were also four non-dominant subjective warrants held by the students attracted to and decided upon careers in physical education. The first of these was one held by students who were oriented to coaching rather than teaching. These individuals viewed teaching as a means of gaining access to a coaching position. They saw physical education as an area primarily concerned with high levels of skilled performance and were attracted to the profession because of their desire to maintain participation in high levels of sport. Coaches and teachers of physical education were important influences in the development of these students' perspectives. These perspectives were largely conservative in that the students expressed the desire to teach and coach in the same ways they had been taught and coached.

The second non-dominant subjective warrant was one held by students who were oriented to careers in sports medicine. These individuals viewed knowledge about physical education as a prerequisite to a career in sports medicine. They were influenced by teachers or physical education, coaches, and physicians specializing in sports medicine. These individuals did not see physical education as primarily experiential and skill oriented. They suggested that if they were to teach they would develop programs in which scientific knowledge was used as the foundation for their teaching content and practices.

The third non-dominant subjective warrant was one in which students viewed physical education as more than teaching and coaching. These individuals wanted careers involving the administration and planning of sport programs. They suggested that an education preparing them to teach would be useful for their careers as sport planners, and that by becoming involved in planning they could change the ways in which sport was organized and delivered. They expressed reservations about skill oriented, elitist physical education programs and wanted to develop programs primarily committed to participation.

The final non-dominant subjective warrant was held by one subject who can be described as an early decider but late entrant to a career in physical education. This individual shared a similar perception of the profession as those who held the dominant view. However, he differed from this group in one important way. He believed teaching opportunities in physical education to be limited in both availability and salary. Thus, he believed that entry into the profession would be best after achieving a secure income in a business career.

Subjective Warrant of Students Decided Against Careers in Physical Education

The perceptions of the individuals who had decided against careers in physical education were similar to the dominant view held by those students who were attracted to or decided upon careers in physical education. They saw physical education as restricted to careers in teaching and coaching, and having low pay and a limited life span. It was because of these perceptions that they chose to pursue alternative careers outside of physical education.

Although Dewar's (1984) research examined recruitment into physical education teaching in a different way than earlier work in this area, these differences were in degree rather than kind. Because this work focused on high school students' rather than college students'; perceptions of physical education, it simply provided descriptions of a different stage of the recruitment process. Much like earlier work, this research was exploratory and descriptive in nature. Its intent was to describe and begin to explain the ways in which high school students developed perceptions about physical education and the impact of these perceptions on their career choices.

THEORETICAL ASSUMPTIONS OF THE RECRUITMENT RESEARCH

The recruitment research in physical education discussed thus far provides clear examples of how ideas and concepts are developed and refined in the beginning stages of inquiry. It would be easy to focus only on the weaknesses of this work without acknowledging the important contribution it has made to our understanding of recruitment into physical education teaching. Before discussing the weaknesses in this research it is important that it is located within the theoretical perspective from which it stems.

First, the vast majority of the research and scholarship on recruitment into physical education teaching adopts a functionalist perspective on socialization (Pooley, 1972, 1975; Woodford, 1977; Templin, Woodford and Mulling, 1982). This work begins with the assumption that an understanding of recruitment or the anticipatory socialization process is important because it provides an insight into the ways in which students are socialized into their potential roles as teachers of physical education. This insight is important because it is assumed that an understanding of socialization will eventually result in the design and control of professional education programs and practices that socialize students appropriately and successfully. As Templin, Woodford and Mulling (1982) suggest:

> Several practical implications from the entry studies discussed may be generated and related to the major themes of the paper. This is particularly true in relation to the professional preparation process. Specifically, there seem to be implications for the entrants' plan of study in relation to their pretraining experiences and implications in terms of admission standards in physical education. (p. 129)

This statement shows that recruitment research is seen as a way of providing professional educators with baseline information on entering students. The assumption is that if we know about students' knowledge, skills, attitudes, and behaviors when they enter professional education programs we can ensure that they are all successfully socialized in the same ways before they leave. In addition, the assumption is that by understanding how the socialization process works, physical education programs can develop standards for the selective recruitment of appropriate students. This in turn is seen as a way of gaining more control over the definition and enforcement of a standard for "appropriate and successful" socialization.

Lawson's (1983a), Dewar and Lawson's (1984) and Dewar's (1983, 1984) work on recruitment into physical education is more difficult to locate. This work is critical of functionalist work that defines socialization and recruitment too narrowly. This is especially true of Lawson's (1983a) work, which presented an argument for interpretive research on recruitment. Yet, if individuals look at the ways in which they define and examine recruitment into physical education, there are a number of contradictions that appear to make this work fit more easily into a functionalist perspective than an interpretative one.

The reasons for placing this work within a functionalist perspective are as follows. First, the recognition within this work that recruitment is a complex process whereby recruits develop their professional and individual identities as a result of the interaction of a number of individual, situational, and societal factors is not enough to make it interpretive or critical. The frameworks used in this work were developed in ways that make them well articulated and refined models for examining the effects of a number of different variables on individuals' subjective warrants. Although they provide a different perspective, the work remains essentially functionalist in its translation.

For example, despite arguing for alternative methodologies for studying recruitment, Lawson (1983a) and Dewar and Lawson (1984) essentially refine and elaborate upon the three stage model for socialization that was used in the earlier work. Their continued use of a three stage model implied a view of socialization that was linear and progressive which could be studied by breaking down the progression into a number of constitutive parts. The difference in these later models seems to be that there is more sophistication in the number and kinds of factors that are assumed to impact on recruitment and socialization.

Another reason these models can be defined as functionalist is the ways in which the underlying theoretical frameworks have been translated into research. A case in point is that despite the fact that Lawson's (1983a) recognition of the importance of human action in the decision making processes created an atmosphere for debate and discussion about an alternative (interpretative) perspective for teacher socialization. This led to research studies that were essentially descriptive, and functionalist rather than interpretative, critical, and analytical.

This leads to the second argument. This work, like earlier work in the field, is based on the assumption that an understanding of recruitment will lead to a better understanding of teacher socialization. The justification for this work and the underlying assumptions are what make it functionalist.

In essence, the often unwritten but clearly understood position in all of the work on recruitment is the belief that if physical education is to survive and thrive as a profession, professional education programs must have the same kinds of impact on recruits and provide them with the requisite knowledge, sensitivities and skills to be good professionals. The assumption is that in order to gain control over the socialization of recruits, all professional education programs must develop a "shared technical culture" (Lawson, 1983b). This means that physical educators must identify what is meant by "good teaching" and develop programs that produce students to meet these standards.

What this means is that professional education programs are seen as being pivotal in achieving standardization in the socialization of recruits. The important point is that, despite differences in the levels of sophistication of the analyses of recruitment in physical education, they all share the same goal. They are concerned about producing "better" physical education teachers. This is an important concern. However, the ways in which this concern has been translated has important consequences for physical education teachers and teaching, which appear to be unquestioned and unexamined in this work.

The questions that remain unasked in this work are the questions that are characteristic of interpretative and critical work. For example, interpretative work on recruitment would ask questions such as:

- What are students interpretations of their experiences in sport and physical education classes?
- How do students respond to these experiences?
- What do they select and interpret as important for careers in physical education, and why?
- What do they see as unimportant and why?
- How do different programs in different settings influence individuals' perceptions of physical education?

These questions are aimed at describing the responses of individuals to their experiences in particular settings. They are questions aimed at "thick" description rather than at the identification and measurement of the impact of structural, situational, and individual variables on recruitment.

Critical work on recruitment would ask a set of different questions. Examples might be:

- What is the dominant view of successful socialization in physical education?

- How has this view been contested and negotiated at different historical moments in the field?
- Whose interests are served by this dominant view of teachers and teaching?
- How has this definition been challenged and opposed?
- How is this view able to present itself as the most appropriate and legitimate view of socialization in physical education?
- What impact does this view of the field have on the recruitment and selection of potential recruits?
- What kinds of individuals are deemed appropriate for careers in physical education?
- What kinds of individuals are deemed inappropriate for careers in physical education?
- Does recruitment serve to reproduce the profession in its existing form or does it help to challenge existing power relations in physical education?

These examples of interpretative and critical questions represent some of the key differences between research from a functionalist perspective and research from interpretative and critical perspectives.

LIMITATIONS OF EXISTING RESEARCH

Despite the contribution recruitment research has made to our knowledge about socialization into physical education, there are problems with this work. It is silent on a number of important issues and does not recognize the contradictions in its conceptualization results and application. For example, the selection of subjects in the earlier studies on recruitment (Pooley, 1970; Mulling, 1981; Woodford, 1977) meant that the results were limited to those individuals who already had chosen physical education careers. The problem is that an understanding of recruitment developed from the narrow perspectives of individuals who were largely similar in their values, attitudes, and background experiences. Consequently, these studies provided descriptions of the conservatism of the field. Recruits who have been successful in sport and who want to reproduce the systems that led to their success are the individuals who are successful in the recruitment process in physical education. The implications of this conservative recruitment are never discussed, yet one gets a clear sense from this research that something is wrong with the socialization of prospective physical educators.

The problem is that the early research defines the recruitment as important because it is seen as a necessary first step. The contradiction is that this stems from a concern by researchers about creating programs and recruitment strategies that have more impact on potential recruits, when in fact it appears as the recruitment process is having an extremely large impact because it selects individuals committed to the preservation of the status quo. The problem may be that recruitment and socialization are too successful, and because of this physical education attracts individuals who do not want to change. Understanding how this kind of recruitment operates and its implications for the maintenance of a dominant set of beliefs, practices, and power relations in the field is simply not explored.

The research which examined high school students' subjective warrants for physical education (Dewar 1983, 1984) shares many of the same problems. Although there was an attempt in this work to broaden the scope of the subject pool and investigate why students who were apparently suited to careers in physical education had chosen to pursue other options, it did not examine the broader social and political implications of these decisions. It is clear from the descriptions of students' subjective warrants in this work that physical education is attractive to those students who typically do not question its dominant structure and practices and is unattractive to others who may not be comfortable working within them. Because this work did not adopt a critical perspective, one can only speculate about the ways in which the recruitment process in physical education selects and allocates rewards. It seems as if this process is extremely conservative and acts to select out those individuals who are accepting of and who are privileged by the continuation of the system as it is currently defined and structured. The missing link in all of this work is what happens to individuals who are critical of the dominant structures and practices in physical education and continue in physical education in order to try to challenge and change them.

There is no critical research on recruitment in physical education. No one has studied socialization in relation to the social relations of class, race, and gender that exist in our society. We have been slow to ask questions such as:

- Whose interests are served by professional education programs in physical education?
- How do potential recruits develop their identities as physical educators?
- How do they respond to their experiences in sport and physical education programs that may be sexist, racist, ageist, and classist?
- Who decides what constitutes appropriate socialization into physical education teaching?
- Do the definitions of appropriate socialization into physical education challenge or reproduce the dominant relations in society?

These are only a few examples of the kinds of questions that have not been asked in our research and scholarship on recruitment into physical education teaching. These questions suggest that socialization is a highly complex process that must be seen within the contexts in which it is negotiated and experienced. They are examples of the kinds of research that needs to be completed if we are to fill the gaps that exist in the current work.

Research that begins, through the use of critical, ethnographic case studies, to document how students of different social classes, ethnic and racial groups and sexes, develop their personal and professional identities as physical educators would help fill the gap. This work would allow us to understand how recruitment is used as a mechanism for the selection and allocation of recruits, which would help in our understanding of the ways in which potential recruits negotiate their ways through this selection and allocation process. In addition, critical research of this type would facilitate an understanding of the ways in which the social relations of class, race, and gender are reproduced or challenged by actions of students and teachers of physical education.

IMPLICATIONS FOR TEACHERS AND TEACHING

It is clear that it is difficult to isolate and discuss the process of recruitment into physical education teaching as a separate entity in and of itself. In this section I will briefly allude to some of the relationships that exist between recruitment and physical education teachers' work. (This discussion is short because this relationship is discussed in much greater detail in other chapters in this book).

The first and perhaps most obvious point that needs to be made is that it is clear from the research findings on recruitment that physical education teachers are extremely important in the socialization of potential recruits. Students' experiences in physical education programs and their exposure to the teachers and teaching associated with these programs are influential in their early socialization. Students get very clear messages from their experiences with physical education teachers about what a career in physical education is all about. It is no accident that research shows there are many similarities between teachers of physical education and recruits. It may be that teachers, through their programs and practices, are used as a standard against which students evaluate their interests in and suitability for a career as a physical educator. Therefore, the ways in which physical education teachers think about and execute their work is extremely important in the process of socialization into physical education teaching. Given this, it is unlikely that students who are unsuccessful in their school physical education or sport programs will select careers in physical education despite the fact that the programs may be ones that are designed to advantage only a relatively few highly skilled individuals in a narrow range of activities.

It is likely, because of the differences that exist in physical education programs and practices and the students involved in them, that teachers may be serving the interests and needs of only a few students. For example, we know that physical education programs and practices are often sexist (Dewar, 1987; Griffin, 1983, 1984; Scraton, 1987), racist (Carrington, 1986) and classist (Mangan, 1983). This appears to be the case when the curriculum places a strong emphasis on sport. What this means is that teachers may be teaching programs that have been constructed in ways that reflect a white, middle class, androcentric bias. The result of this may be that students who do not see the value of these programs and feel they are not being treated equally may either drop out or try to challenge these practices only to discover that they are defined as "problems" and unsuitable for careers in physical education. Either way there is a risk that they are selected out of the recruitment process. The problem then is that individuals who perceive physical education as a suitable career may be the ones who have been successful in and are privileged by the system. It is these individuals who are most likely to be committed to and have a vested interest in the preservation of the system[2].

Another point is that in order to fully understand who enters physical education programs and why, we have to take seriously the ways in which teachers are able to define and control the work they do in schools. It is important that we understand not only how physical education teachers articulate their identities, but also how their work is affected by the social and structural relations that exist in schools, and the communities of which the schools are a part. Teachers working in inner city schools where facilities and opportunities for sport are limited by a lack of funding and space will face very different challenges and problems than teachers working in more affluent communities and school districts that provide considerable support for physical education and sport programs. These challenges and teachers' responses to them need to be considered. It is only through this kind of analysis that we will be able to understand the ways in which the social relations of class, race, and gender impact on teachers' work and the consequences of this for recruitment into physical education.

If we begin to see recruitment and socialization into physical education within broader contexts, we may be able to understand the dynamics of these highly complicated processes. This means it is important that we do critical research on recruitment into physical education teaching rather than simply trying to describe and explain the variables that influence career choices. By engaging in critical research we will gain a

---

[2] This is not to say that individuals who are committed to challenging the system do not choose physical education careers. They do. I am simply suggesting that we need to understand the complex and often contradictory ways in which the recruitment process works in physical education, which necessitates locating it within the social, historical, and political contexts in which it occurs.

greater understanding of how the recruitment process works and its impact on the definition and structure of the field.

It is inappropriate to continue to argue for the development of universal criteria for judging "good" and "adequate" teachers of physical education when these standards are often ones that contribute to the reproduction of the social relations of class, race, and gender that exist in society. By challenging the ways in which these relations of power and domination are produced and reproduced by the actions of physical educators we may begin to understand how to create programs and practices that challenge the legitimacy of views of physical education that serve the interests and needs of a select few. If this were to happen then recruitment into physical education teaching might begin to look very different. This is the promise of critical work and one that is both necessary and exciting.

CONCLUSIONS

This chapter shows that the issues concerned with recruitment into physical education teaching are broader than the ways in which functionalist researchers have conceptualized it. If recruitment is reduced to a set of variables that influence individuals' career choices, it is separated from the historical, social, and political contexts in which it is occurring. This separation of processes of recruitment from their contexts ensures that issues about who controls and defines "good" and "appropriate" physical education teaching are never raised. This means that the dominant power relations within physical education and the structures associated with them are justified and legitimated in functionalist work.

Physical education teaching cannot adequately be reduced to a set of role requirements. It is much more. What physical educators do, and how they do it is important because the events that occur in the gymnasium, playing field, or swimming pool are not isolated. They are intricately bound in the social relations of the school, community, and society. This means that students in physical education classes (as in other subjects in the curriculum) are given strong messages about what is appropriate and necessary to survive and thrive in the class. These messages are important because they often reflect and reproduce the dominant social relations of power that exist in our society.

For example, the unskilled, uncompetitive, weak, and sensitive get very different messages from many physical education programs than do the skilled, competitive, and strong. The result is that this bias may have an enormous impact on the ways in which recruitment selects and allocates rewards to potential teachers.

The critiques of the research on recruitment in physical education presented in this chapter suggest that more interpretative and critical research is long overdue. Examples of the kind of work that is needed is research and scholarship that explores the ways in which teachers of physical education develop their personal and professional identities. We need to locate teachers' work in physical education more broadly and examine how teachers are able to negotiate and contest their professional identities within work settings that may be both enabling and constraining. Understanding how teachers are able to define and control what and how they teach, and to whom they teach it, will allow for a greater understanding of the selection processes involved in recruitment.

This chapter has set the stage for such critical work. By building on the insights that have been gained from previous work on recruitment we are in a strong position to be able to articulate a new set of questions and research agenda. This agenda must be one that places teachers, teaching, and students at the center of the research enterprise. In so doing we will move away from functionalist research that is driven by attempts to achieve greater uniformity in the standarization and control over socialization into physical education teaching towards critical research that is committed to the creation of physical education programs and practices that foster opportunities for students to question and challenge and recreate a variety of forms of physical education that are inclusive rather than exclusive of the needs of all human beings. The achievement of this critical consciousness in physical education may enable the attraction of different kinds of recruits to the profession and start the move away from the highly conservative images in which we seem entrenched. This is the promise of critical research and scholarship on recruitment into physical education.

REFERENCES

Becker, H. S., Geer, B & Hughes, E. (1961) *Boys in white.* Chicago, Il: University of Chicago Press.
Carrington, B. (1986). Social mobility, ethnicity and sport. *British Journal of Sociology of Education, 7,* 3-18.
Connell, R. W. (1985). *Teachers' work.* Sydney: George Allen & Unwin.
Dewar, A. M. (1983). The subjective warrant and recruitment into physical education. Unpublished master's thesis: University of British Columbia.
Dewar, A. M. (1984). High school students subjective warrants for physical education. Paper presented at the Olympic Scientific Congress, Eugene, Oregon.
Dewar, A. M. (1987). The social construction of gender in physical education. *Women's Studies International Forum, 10,* 453-466.
Dewar, A. M. & Lawson, H. A. (1984). The subjective warrant and recruitment into physical education. *Quest, 36,* 15-25.
Fishwick L., & Greendorfer, S. (1987). Socialization revisited. A critique of the sport-related literature. *Quest, 39,* 1-8.
Geertz, C. (1973). Thick description: Toward an interpretative theory of culture. In C. Geertz (Ed.). *The interpretation of cultures.* New York: Basic Books.
Griffin, P. S. (1983). Gymnastics is a girls thing: Student participation and interaction patterns in a middle school gymnastics unit. In T. Templin and J. Olson (Eds.). *Teaching in physical education.* Champaign, Il: Human Kinetics.
Griffin, P. S. (1984). Girls' participation patterns in a middle school team sports unit. *Journal of Teaching in Physical Education, 4,* 30-38.

Lawson, H. A. (1983a). Toward a model of teacher socialization in physical education: The subjective warrant, recruitment and teacher education. *Journal of Teaching in Physical Education, 2* (3), 3-16.

Lawson, H. A. (1983b). Toward a model of teacher socialization in physical education: Entry into schools, teachers' role orientations and longevity. *Journal of Teaching in Physical Education, 3* (1), 3-15.

Lortie, D. C. (1975). *Schoolteacher: A sociological study.* Chicago: The University of Chicago Press.

Mangan, J. A. (1983). *Athleticism in the Victorian and Edwardian public school.* Cambridge, England: Cambridge University Press.

Merton, R. K., Reader, G. G., & Kendal, P. L. (1957). (Eds). *The student physician.* Boston, Mass: Harvard University Press.

Mulling, C. (1981). An investigation of selected factors contributing to the desocialization of the physical education major. Unpublished Master's Thesis: Purdue University.

Pooley, J. (1970). The professional socialization of physical education students in the United States and England. Unpublished doctoral dissertation: University of Wisconsin.

Pooley, J. (1972) Professional socialization: A model of the pre-training phase application to physical education students. *Quest, 18,* 57-66.

Pooley, J. (1975). The professional socialization of physical education students in the United State and England. *International Review of Sport Sociology, 3-4,* 97-107.

Scraton, S. (1987). Gender and physical education: Ideologies of the physical and the politics of sexuality. In S. Walker & L. Barton (Eds.). *Changing policies, changing teachers: New directions of schooling?* Milton Keynes, England: Open University Press.

Stanworth, M. (1983). *Gender and schooling: A study of sexual division in the classroom.* London: Hutchinson.

Templin, T. J., Woodford, R., & Mulling, C. (1982). On becoming a physical educator: Occupational choice and the anticipatory socialization process. *Quest, 34*(2), 119-133.

Walker, S., & Barton, L. (1987). (Eds.). *Changing policies, changing teachers: New directions for schooling?* Milton Keynes, England: Open University Press.

Weiner, G. (1985). (Ed.). *Just a bunch of girls: Feminist approaches to schooling.* Milton Keynes, England: Open University Press.

Woodford, R. (1977). The socialization of freshman physical education majors into role orientations in physical education. Unpublished doctoral dissertation: University of New Mexico.

4

Teaching Tomorrow's Teachers: Professional Preparation as an Agent of Socialization

KIM C. GRABER
University of Oregon

Each year a cohort of students enters teacher training programs at colleges and universities across the nation. These recruits expect to become certified professionals capable of assuming a teacher's role upon graduation. Teacher educators expect the undergraduate to become socialized during that period of time, internalizing the dispositions of the teaching role and becoming committed to maintaining a professional orientation in their work. It is astonishing, therefore, to discover that little is known about what happens to students as they progress through training programs.

Fortunately, both educators and researchers have shown a recent and growing interest in professional socialization. The search has begun for answers that may help to explain why recruits elect to become teachers, how they determine the legitimacy of training, how they react to the demands of the preservice environment, and what elements of training they will bring into the field once they become certified teachers. Study in this area, however, is in the preliminary stage of development, and definitive information simply is not available.

While it is possible to synthesize the small amount of literature regarding preservice physical education teacher preparation programs, it is worthwhile to explore the greater body of available literature regarding professional socialization. The related field of general education and more ancillary field of medicine have something to offer in the search for useful constructs and relevant theory that may apply to preservice socialization in physical education.

The purpose of this chapter is to review what is known about how students acquire skills, knowledge, and the dispositions for belief and action which form the orientation of the training program. Specifically, this chapter will address how preservice education is impacted by the personal biographies that recruits bring into the training program, students' expectations for preservice training, students' reactions to the forces of socialization, and the overall influence of the training program on the recruits' development. Finally, a discussion will address possible directions teacher education may take to become more responsive in the socialization of tomorrow's physical education teachers.

ENTRY INTO PRESERVICE

Locke (1984) suggests that little is known about the biographies of physical education recruits. "Social class, personal and career aspiration, motivation, and experiential background are all relatively unexplored. We do not even know if physical education is a secondary or a primary career choice, why so many students drop out of our training programs, or how many transfer in after attempting and abandoning other areas of study" (p. 23). The field of physical education, therefore, is at a disadvantage in attempting to understand why recruits enter and exit from preservice training programs. It is particularly difficult to resolve the seeming paradox of students maintaining dispositions which are contrary to those encouraged during training.

Researchers investigating biographies of recruits in the more general field of education have suggested that dispositions, past experiences, and reasons for entering the field of teaching may influence what recruits learn during preservice preparation and later believe when they become certified teachers. When recruits enter training programs with strong preconceived beliefs based upon personal experience, it is not surprising to discover conflicts between students' expectations and the intentions of the teacher education faculty. These conflicts, if unresolved, will affect what students come to learn about teaching and which aspects of training will be internalized while in the program.

Unlike students enrolled in the fields of business, law, or medicine, students who have selected teaching as their vocation have been in contact with the profession for much of their lives. Students interact more closely with teachers than any other occupational group; they have spent an average of 13,000 hours in direct association with teachers prior to formal training (Lortie, 1975). This period of anticipatory socialization is a process of beginning to acquire some of the more visible professional values (Western & Anderson, 1968). Students observe what teachers do and say, how they feel about their subject matter, how they treat pupils, and how they evaluate achievement. At a very early age, students have acquired considerable information about the teaching role and many have even speculated about how they would act as a teacher.

Naturally, students select characteristics of their favorite teachers and coaches for the type of person they hope to emulate. Unfortunately, this presents a problem because, as Lortie (1975) indicates, a student's viewpoint is imaginary. That is, students are like observers at a play who watch the performance but never go backstage. "What students learn about teaching, then, is intuitive and imitative rather than explicit and analytical; it is based on individual personalities rather than pedagogical principles" (p. 62). Students think they know what it is like to teach, but have no basis for their knowledge other than what they have observed while being active participants in the classroom. Fantasy or not, it has been argued that the influences exerted during this period of anticipatory socialization are so powerful that formal training cannot alter the beliefs about teaching already developed (Feiman-Nemser, 1983).

In addition to the beliefs students carry forward from the period of pretraining, recruits also choose to enter teaching for many reasons. At some point these reasons may fit the dimensions of the role, at other points, however, there may be a dysfunctional fit which will negatively affect socialization during preservice. The following fictional vignette provides an illustration of two individuals enrolled in a physical education teacher training program.

Jane is a senior in the physical education teacher preparation program at Fitchmore University. She elected to become a physical educator after her sophomore year in college when she realized that she wanted to work with children, and after being denied entrance into the school of business because of a low grade point average.

Now that she is a senior, Jane is pleased with the decision she has made. Both of her parents are teachers and she believes that she has the ability to make physical education a more enjoyable experience than when she was a student in the public schools. Jane acknowledges, "When I was going through school it seems like all we ever did was relay races, play dodgeball, or participate in physical fitness tests which we had not been properly prepared to take. Now that I have decided to become a physical educator I am happier in college and have even raised my grade point average considerably."

Jane's classmate, Steve, also is a senior at Fitchmore. He had decided to become a physical education instructor while he was a student in the public schools. Steve indicates, "I can't ever remember wanting to do anything except becoming a coach and gym teacher. I had great coaches in high school, and they told me that if I majored in physical education I'd definitely be guaranteed a coaching position. I realize that the field doesn't pay very well, however, you sure can't beat the vacations or job security. I'm looking to teach at the high school level because that's where I want to coach, and I think it will be more fun than teaching fundamental movement skills to little kids."

This illustration describes why two individuals may have elected to enter physical education. Jane and Steve, while unique, also represent characteristics of other students who enter physical education teacher education programs every year. Jane decided to become a physical educator because she wasn't successful in the business training program and because she believed she would find happiness working with children. Steve's primary reason for becoming a physical educator was that he believed the profession would enable him to coach. His enjoyment for sport and desire to teach at the high school level seemed to fit the dimensions of the role quite nicely.

Unfortunately, Jane and Steve's rationale for becoming teachers may at some point conflict with the intentions of the training program. Lortie (1975), when discussing education majors, suggests that individuals are frequently attracted to the teaching profession because, among others, they want to work with children, can't imagine leaving schools, hope to reap material benefits, or desire lengthy vacations. Some of these reasons for entering teaching may negatively affect socialization during preservice. Recruits who select teaching because of ancillary rewards like length of vacations or job security, for example, are not likely to be highly committed to a service orientation. Accordingly, they may be particularly resistant to some values espoused within the preservice program.

Current conditions guarantee the presence of such problems in every new class of undergraduates. A career in teaching cannot promise to offer benefits which are comparable to the fields of government, business, law, medicine, engineering, or even careers in service industries. Recruits can expect to find, among others, modest financial rewards, limited upward mobility, students who aren't interested in the basic service which teachers provide, and long, tough work days. Because a career in teaching cannot provide many tangible rewards, potentially good teachers will be lost to other fields. As a result, the pool of prospective teaching candidates is reduced and recruits must be accepted who have characteristics which clearly mark them as poor candidates for the socializing influence of the training program.

Common examples include accepting recruits into teacher training programs who are unlikely to have strong career commitment, or recruits who are not likely to identify with the goals of the training program. Templin, Woodford, and Mulling (1982) discuss the ease of entrance into teaching. Some students will enter because they can't meet requirements for entrance into other fields. Other students enter teaching as a secondary career option when other options have fallen through. Some enter because of long vacations and short work days (Lortie, 1975). Still, others choose to teach because, as Geer (1968) discovered, education majors have less difficult and less time consuming coursework. In consequence, the combination of beliefs brought forward from previous school experience and motivations for entering teaching can cause difficulties for the teacher education faculty attempting to mold recruits into dedicated professionals.

STUDENTS' EXPECTATIONS FOR PRESERVICE TRAINING

If recruits enter training programs with many preconceived beliefs about teaching, it is not surprising that they also enter with expectations for what their training should offer. On the one hand, teacher educators tend to view these recruits as ignorant laypeople, enthusiastically waiting to be filled with professional ideology. On the other hand, recruits believe they already know what teaching is about and have expectations of training programs and teacher educators which are not necessarily congruent with the aims or capabilities of preservice training. When the expectations of the two groups differ markedly, socialization is not likely to occur in a predictable or idealized fashion.

Students have *program expectations*. At entry, students believe preparation programs offer valuable experiences and expect to be provided with the necessities they will require as teachers. Their expectations range from certification through graduation to the desire for exclusive attention to practical content in coursework and extensive opportunity to develop teaching skills in clinical practice. While some expectations may be highly individual, most are held in common by all recruits, and thus form a powerful and shared reality in the student sub-culture. For example, while few students may expect to become accomplished in planning curricula, all students expect to receive ample practice time in what they regard as "real" teaching.

In some areas, educators may hold beliefs that are quite similar to those held by students and, accordingly, will comfortably meet student expectations. They may, however, hold sharply dissimilar beliefs, and conflicts will occur. Some conflict is positive, especially if it helps students begin to examine their beliefs more critically. If, however, conflicts of belief are too threatening to students or faculty and thus are ignored or unresolved, the end effect may be destructive for the growth of students and the goals of the program.

Preservice students also hold *training experience and curriculum expectations.* At one extreme are those students who expect to be educated about broad issues related to teaching and learning. These individuals have expectations about professional preparation which are close to those of their teacher education professors. At the other extreme are the students who expect training to be limited to specific skills they will be able to put into use in the classroom (Western & Anderson, 1968). They want prescriptions for doing the work of teaching (Lanier & Little, 1986), and see no relevant use for foundational knowledge (Feiman-Nemser, 1983). These students are similar to those in law who seek simple rules which will allow them to become accomplished attorneys upon graduation (Lortie, 1959), or those in medicine who expect to be given the "know how" to perform delicate surgery without the need for lengthy study and training (Becker, Geer, Hughes, & Strauss, 1961).

Students in the latter group also want extensive opportunities for practical experiences which will help them become confident in the smooth routines they identify with the teaching role (Book, Byers, & Freeman, 1983). Practical experiences are, of course, essential in learning to teach, but too often discrepancies emerge between what teacher educators want recruits to learn and what actually is learned. For example, recruits may enter a practicum experience with a specific set of skills learned in the training program, skills they will later abandon because they either are insufficiently practiced or because they don't provide the reinforcement of immediate success. These recruits will have been given the clinical opportunities they expected, but not the adequate supervisory support required to transfer what was learned in training. Instead of implementing what is learned in the training program classroom, recruits may resort to teaching in ways which are immediately successful in gaining pupil compliance or are familiar models from their schooldays, but which are not necessarily effective for promoting student learning.

Many students also have *role training expectations,* the belief that training should enable them to assume a particular role upon graduation. For example, students may enter physical education teacher training programs so they may later assume a coaching position (Chu, 1984; Lawson, 1983a, 1983b; Templin, Woodford, & Mulling, 1982; Woodford, 1977). Students such as these are similar to Steve (in the earlier vignette), individuals who assume coaching is the same as teaching. Locke and Massengale (1978), however, have demonstrated great differences between the two roles. Students expect to be trained as coaches, but instead encounter an almost exclusive emphasis on preparation for teaching. When such a sharp violation of expectations exists, it is certain to interfere with acquisition of program values and role related skills.

Students have various *teacher expectations* which dictate their reactions to professors. Among many, students have expectations for how professors should act, how they should grade, what types of assignments are reasonable, and how much work an instructor can expect from students in any given course. In turn, students realize teachers have expectations of them which, in part, will determine how they will be graded, evaluated, and regarded. When congruence of expectations exists between professors and students, socialization is supported. When expectations differ, socialization is impeded.

Students also have *college expectations*, beliefs about their lives as students outside of the training program. Becker, Geer, and Hughes (1968) have divided college life into three areas: academic coursework, campus organizations, and personal relationships. Each can have a direct relationship to an individual's performance and commitment to the training program. For example, teacher educators can be insensitive about the degree to which coursework intrudes on students' social life, being quite happy to soak up virtually every moment of their free time (Locke & Jensen, 1970). Perhaps this is because professors can't remember their own college lives (Becker et al., 1968). When academic demands make a personal life impossible, students may rebel by doing only enough work to get by and giving little serious attention to the work they are doing.

Unfortunately, educators too often ignore the fact that students have expectations for what training should offer; instead they prefer to believe that students are sponges, eagerly waiting to soak up all pedagogical information presented in the classroom. Of course, some student expectations will change as students come to understand the complexity of the teaching world. If, however, the preservice experience is to encourage significant progress toward assumption of the professional role, training programs must work to either meet some student expectations or, at the least, to acknowledge that these expectations do exist and must be subject to open discussion and negotiation with students.

STUDENTS' REACTIONS TO THE FORCES OF SOCIALIZATION

In examining how preservice students react to their training environment, it will be argued that recruits are not individuals who willingly submit to all expectations and demands of the teacher education faculty, nor do they unquestioningly succumb to being molded into the type of teacher the training program faculty has determined to be desirable. Instead, recruits play an active role in the socialization process. They have beliefs regarding which faculty expectations are reasonable and unreasonable, ultimately deciding which expectations they will meet and how they will meet them.

Zeichner (1979) indicated that students have conventionally been regarded as passive entities who simply adapt and conform to the forces of socialization. He notes that much research has assumed this functionalist version of socialization in which young teachers are shaped by the social structure of professional culture. He found the functionalist viewpoint, however, inadequate to accommodate the increasing number of research studies indicating that students do not always adapt or conform to school culture. He concluded that, "the dominant view of teacher socialization as a process where the neophyte is a passive entity totally subject to institutional press is rejected. Instead, teacher socialization is portrayed as a dialectical process involving a continual interplay between individuals and the institutions into which they are socialized" (p.1).

This section will document some of what currently is known about students enrolled in professional training programs by describing professional socialization as a dialectical process. Specifically, discussion will focus on how students react to the expectations of their instructors, describing how the power of the student sub-culture may later reinforce desired or undesirable teaching behaviors. Because the literature describing preservice teacher socialization in physical education is sparse, studies in the fields of medicine (Becker et al., 1961; Light, 1979; Merton, Reader, & Kendall, 1957) and nursing (Davis, 1968; Olesen & Whittaker, 1968) will be used to construct a preliminary understanding of what happens in professional training programs. By combining that knowledge with studies in education (Lacey, 1977; Lapin, 1985) and physical education (Graber, 1986, 1988a, 1988b; Steen, 1985, 1986), it is possible to speculate about what may be happening to recruits enrolled in preservice physical education teacher preparation programs.

Studentship

In describing how students react to the forces of socialization, the word studentship will be used to describe a set of behaviors students may employ to progress through a training program with greater ease, more success, and less effort. Described within the framework of the dialectical process, studentship is the means by which students react to the training program environment, enabling them to acquire skills they believe are important while ignoring those which they believe to be irrelevant or dysfunctional. It constitutes a variety of behaviors which empower recruits with the choice, regardless of their reasons for entering teaching or what they expect to receive from training, to decide how they will be molded. As Olesen and Whittaker (1968) discovered in their study of student nurses, studentship emerged when students decided when to study, what to study, how to look interested in the classroom, and how to make other students look more favorable to the faculty. It occurs in any area of training when students manage their image, take short-cuts, cheat, or when they employ other strategies for progressing through the program with greater ease.

When reading this section it is necessary to understand that while some studentship behaviors have clear negative implications for preservice teacher development, many of them must be regarded as benign, or at least as perfectly normal responses given the context in which they occur. In the final analysis, studentship behaviors are coping behaviors. Their appearance may tell us more about aberrations in program than flaws in character. For example, some degree of fronting (faking-it) is part of the daily commerce of all social interaction. Work reduction negotiation often protects students against destructive anomalies in class or program requirements, and behaviors which may appear designed to curry favor with instructors are essential "trying on for size" activities related to internalization of new values. Even cheating, which appears to undermine program goals, must be understood in terms of its etiology rather than simply "blamed" on students or faculty.

When socialization is perceived as a dialectical process in which students push back against the forces that bear in upon them, studentship is not surprising. Students realize they must meet the demands of the training faculty in order to graduate and become certified. They may, of course, elect to comply with faculty demands because they are perceived to be for the best. They may, however, attempt to change the demands or comply with the demands while retaining reservations about doing so. In selecting the latter course, recruits are likely to exhibit studentship behaviors. Based on this dialectical model of socialization, selected studentship strategies will now be discussed in relation to how they have been observed to occur in professional training programs ranging from medicine to physical education.

Psyching-out. One measure of success in any program is the mark of formal evaluation. Students attempt to meet programmatic demands, at least in part, in order to obtain good grades. Students, however, may be uncertain about the precise expectations of the training faculty. Also, programs rarely provide adequate time to study all that may be required (Olesen & Whittaker, 1968). As a result, students may attempt to psych-out the instructor in their efforts to both define and narrow the field of demand and obtain good grades.

Psyching-out a professor is the attempt to discern what might be asked on an exam, what should be included in a paper, or how to act during an internship. It is not the attempt to simply learn more, but an active attempt to determine the exact nature of faculty demands—so that less must be studied or attempted. Some professors may assist students in their quest to discover what they must do. Others will interpret this behavior as laziness or deviousness. These professors find psyching-out behaviors annoying and often respond by saying that they are not willing to "spoon-feed" their students (Becker et al., 1968; Becker et al., 1961; Hughes, Becker, & Geer, 1962; Merton et al., 1957).

Whether or not instructors are willing to assist students by letting them know what is expected, students may respond by only studying what they believe the faculty wants them to know, not what the students believe is important to know. This was particularly true of the University of Kansas medical students (Becker et al., 1961; Hughes et al., 1962). These individuals ceased studying what they perceived was important to know as a doctor and began to study what their professors might want. The medical faculty who didn't give clues to the students were described as being highly unfair and not "playing the game."

Psyching-out, however, is not peculiar to the medical profession. Lacey (1977) studied honors students in one education department whom he grouped into three categories. The first, "cue-deaf," were students who believed working hard was all that was needed. The second, "cue-conscious," attempted to pick up hints regarding what it was faculty favored. The third, "cue-seekers," were individuals who buttonholed staff about exam questions, questioned them over coffee, and attempted to discover what faculty interests were.

During a study of preservice students enrolled in a physical education teacher training program (Graber, 1988a), many students were observed to actively employ psyching-out behavior. As might be expected, students engaged in this behavior most frequently for the purpose of discovering what instructors would ask on the final exam.

Fronting and Image Projection. Fronting and image projection are studentship behaviors exhibited by students who attempt to portray a favorable image of themselves to those who control evaluation. Some students will be better than others at these behaviors because they have proven to be good at controlling the interactions in which they are involved (Strauss, 1959). These individuals often are better at fronting because they possess what Snyder (1980) calls high self-monitoring skills—the ability to mold behaviors to the demands of a social situation, and the capacity to exert sensitive censorship over the way one expresses oneself socially.

Students who are good at exhibiting these studentship behaviors are likely to gain information which is helpful not only to them, but also to those in the sub-culture who are not adept at fronting. For example, Davis (1968) discovered that some student nurses were particularly skilled at fronting. They were able to put on straight faces while asking didactic questions concerning teacher expectations and ways in which performance might fall short of meeting those expectations. Although other students never exhibited conscious awareness of such skilled fronting, they often benefited from what they learned through the adept fronters.

These behaviors occur in many settings and are likely to be displayed any number of ways. In a study examining studentship in two physical education teacher preparation courses (Graber, 1988a), students were discovered to consciously front and project their image in subtle and imaginative ways such as indicating interest in note-taking, volunteering, and paying obvious attention in class. These behaviors also may be present when students display an interest in children and teaching, when they adopt a professional vocabulary, or when they adopt specific teaching behaviors because they are reflective of program values. While these behaviors may seem relatively harmless and unsurprising, as Locke and Dodds (1984) have indicated, something less benign may emerge. If recruits are demonstrating skills and displaying beliefs just to please the faculty or in order to be perceived more favorably, they may as a consequence be distancing themselves from engagement with issues which demand reflection and resolution.

Cheating and Short Cuts. Students who front and manage their image are attempting to be perceived by faculty in a predetermined and positive manner. These same students, however, may engage in behaviors which they don't want faculty to notice. Cheating is one example of a behavior students carefully attempt to hide. If students are caught cheating they are not likely to be perceived favorably by faculty, their previous efforts at image management are seriously undercut, and they are likely to face disciplinary consequences.

Cheating occurs in varying degrees in various settings, and may be perceived differently by different individuals. Although both faculty and student definitions of cheating may be similar if someone is caught blatantly cheating on an exam, there may be other instances where what constitutes cheating is not black or white, and agreement is unlikely. One gray area which emerges can be labeled "taking short cuts."

Becker and his colleagues (1961) observed medical students who did things which the faculty might construe as cheating, but which students considered sensible short cuts. Students were observed copying each other's experiments, though they were to have been done separately. They also were observed attempting to discover what might be asked on an exam. Further, some students who were interviewed actually admitted that they condoned and participated in cheating.

During Steen's (1985) study of professional socialization in a physical education teacher training program, he observed students cheating and devising strategies to improve their scores on a volleyball skills test. Whereas the instructor might have perceived their behaviors as cheating, it was clear that students regarded their actions as rational and necessary short cuts in attempting to achieve their goal—passing the course.

Under conditions in which they feel relatively safe, students may talk readily about engaging in short cutting and cheating. For example, in a study of preservice physical education majors (Graber, 1986), students were interviewed who readily admitted to engaging in various forms of these behaviors. Here students discussed perceived faculty expectations and ways in which they met those expectations. Frequently, students opted to meet perceived demands by employing studentship behaviors which faculty would have determined to be antithetical to the goals of training.

In another study (Graber, 1988b), preservice physical education re-cruits were observed participating in cheating and short cutting to var-ious degrees. While summaries from interviews indicated that the major-ity of students condemned cheating, describing it as an immoral act, incidents of cheating were observed to occur during a final exam. Short cutting strategies also emerged as a primary means of passing through the system with the greatest ease and most success. Here students were ob-served copying work they had previously completed for other classes, relying on other students for ideas, allowing other students to complete their work, and copying the work of students who had previously taken the class. Additionally, the manner in which students took notes was based more on what they would be required to know for the exam and less on what they regarded as was important to remember about teach-ing. Finally, even class attendance was a cog in the machinery of short cutting. When students believed their grade wouldn't be affected if they skipped class, they did so with less trepidation and increasing frequency than when class attendance was a requirement.

Some cheating and taking of short cuts may not pose serious threats to socialization; others will undermine critical intentions of the training program. When these behaviors result in certifying recruits who, as a result of studentship, haven't learned how to teach, the purpose of teacher training will have been seriously thwarted.

Sub-cultures

The word "sub-culture" designates a smaller unit within a larger group, a unit tied together by shared role structures and perspectives. The member individuals share a common interpretation of experience and generate social behaviors based upon a common fund of acquired knowledge (Spradley, 1979). Sub-cultures may develop where common problems are faced and, as was discovered, in the study of medical stu-dents at the University of Kansas (Hughes et al., 1962), they can be very strong. Aspects of a training program sub-culture, such as solutions to problems, may be rediscovered or reinforced as they are passed down from one generation of students to the next (Hughes, 1971). Indeed the most important elements of the sub-culture may prevail even when an individual leaves the common situation of the group (Lacey, 1977).

A sub-culture can be a powerful medium for encouraging student-ship behavior. For example, Lapin (1985) observed teacher training recruits who engaged in "confronting" strategies with the faculty when they attempted to negotiate both exam dates and grades. Physical education recruits also have been observed (Graber, 1988a) using collusion to exert the collective power of the sub-culture to confront instructors about what might be asked on the final exam. Had the sub-culture not been intact, it is unlikely that students could have cooperated in such a delicate and potentially risky exercise of power.

The strength of the sub-culture results in sufficient empowerment of students to allow control of some of the training environment. When a problem arises, such as an assignment which students determine is unreasonable, students can act as a collective bargaining agency in an attempt to negotiate for workload reduction. This action serves to disempower faculty who might be intimidated by a large group of students.

It is not difficult to imagine that a teacher educator might react to the pressure exerted upon them. Teacher educators are, after all, human beings who hope to be liked and respected by their students. In some instances they also will be aware that tenure decisions may be based in some part upon student reactions to the classroom environment. When negotiations occur, and if the basic intentions of the program are not jeopardized, socialization will not be impaired by a degree of give and take. When, however, instructors succumb to the power of the sub-culture at the expense of some learning experiences, particularly those intended to reinforce certain dispositions deemed critical to good teaching, the dialectic of socialization will have produced a net loss.

Playing at the Role

Though it is true that many studentship behaviors may conflict directly with the intentions of the program, producing teachers who have dispositions about teaching unlike those promulgated during training, sometimes studentship behaviors actually may reinforce programmatic goals. Fronting is one example of a studentship behavior that, under the appropriate circumstances, may encourage internalization of the dispositions intended by the faculty.

In a study of student nurses, Davis (1968) discovered a six step process by which individuals came to discard their lay imagery about nursing. After students discovered nursing school was not what they expected, the nursing students began to engage in psyching-out and fronting behaviors. These studentship behaviors, however, eventually led to a step which Davis labeled role simulation. The more successful the students became at playing at the role, the less they felt they were merely simulating it, and the more they gained conviction about being an authentic performer.

Moreover, having lived through the beguiling process of "becoming nurse" through "playing at it," the cognitive groundwork was laid for a less stressful, more wholehearted internalization of the "institutionally approved" version of nursing practice which the school sought to inculcate. (p. 248)

Templin (1984) discusses the importance of role-playing with teaching recruits. He indicates that role-playing brings about mastery of skills and knowledge required of a role, providing growth for the individual and eventually the validation of training. Fronting, therefore, cannot always be regarded as a dysfunctional behavior. If some playing at the role eventually leads to the internalization of training program dispositions, it will have had a positive impact upon the recruit.

THE INFLUENCE OF THE TRAINING PROGRAM

Professional socialization in teacher training programs has been a neglected area of inquiry. Surprisingly, teacher educators have only the most general and impressionistic picture of what happens to students as they progress through training programs. They may be blissfully ignorant of the degree to which students are committed to acquiring and maintaining a professional orientation. Most important, educators often appear to be unaware of the impact of training in areas which recruits deem to be the most relevant, those aspects which they are most likely to bring with them into the field as certified professionals.

From another perspective, the preservice stage of learning to teach has been regarded as a weak treatment, having relatively little long-term influence on recruits. In fact, it has been hypothesized that many aspects of training may be washed-out when students reenter schools as certified teachers. This seems particularly true of liberal perspectives on such issues as pupil control. Zeichner and Tabachnick (1981), however, have argued that other factors may be responsible for what only appears to be wash-out.

Perhaps teacher training is too weak to overcome latent values which persist untouched, or perhaps universities are just as conservative as schools, covertly reinforcing through a tacit hidden curriculum what recruits learned during their long apprenticeship of observation as pupils. Training may be weak because there is a dysfunctional fit between recruits' reasons for entering teaching and the intentions of the training program. The overall power of studentship and the student sub-culture also may be responsible for the weak impact of preservice, particularly if recruits are certified who never buy into the intentions of the training faculty, yet fool teacher educators into believing that they have.

What, then, do students learn? If they actually learn professional skills and dispositions, what will they retain? It is obvious that all students learn something, albeit in various degrees, and that the formal curriculum which exists at the preservice level is the causal agent. Generally, the curriculum can be defined as consisting of all the things that happen to students from which they learn, some of which is intended and some of which is not. An intended curriculum is explicit; it represents a "level of knowing" which is available to both teachers and students, and it is communicated either verbally or in written form. The intended curriculum is present in curriculum guides and lesson plans; it can be overheard in teachers' talks in the faculty room or at departmental meetings. Most importantly, it represents what teachers intend, what they want students to learn. It is probable that students in preservice teacher training will learn how to write lesson plans, how to develop curriculum guides, how to measure the active learning time of their pupils, how to discipline unruly students, and how to utilize various styles of teaching. Whether or not students implement these learnings in their own teaching is generally an individual matter, is largely unknown to the faculty of most programs, and is the ultimate test of preservice socialization.

Students also learn from an unintended curriculum which can have greater impact than the formal curriculum. It is inaccessible to both teachers and students, is unconscious (or at least unattended), and is not readily available for analysis. It controls some undefined portion of what students learn. The hidden curriculum may have a positive function if it reinforces the intended curriculum. If, however, it does not reinforce the intended curriculum, students may receive powerful messages which are dysfunctional to socialization, having the potential for undermining the explicit lessons of the training program. If, for example, teacher educators instruct students on both the construction and merits of lesson planning, yet never utilize lesson plans themselves, students will receive the unintended message that lesson plans are only given lip service in preservice training and are not serious tools used by "real" teachers. As a result, when students are observed in schools it may appear as though training has been "washed-out," when in fact students actually had learned from the hidden curriculum of faculty behavior that lesson planning is a relatively unimportant aspect of teaching.

Wisniewski (1984) emphasized the enormous power of the hidden curriculum by stating, "the hidden curriculum is perhaps a more powerful transmitter of values than the formal curriculum. There is no guarantee that what is taught in courses is what students really learn or believe"

(p. 2). Students may learn more important lessons about teaching from the hidden curriculum than they do from the formal curriculum (Dodds, 1983).

When students in preservice teacher training witness disagreements among faculty members about basic issues in pedagogy, they receive mixed messages (Lawson, 1983a). From this, students may learn that a shared technical culture does not exist for teachers. They may learn to alter their behaviors depending upon which faculty member they are addressing. Eventually they may leave the influence of the training program with beliefs about teaching which are confused or antithetical to good teaching, and it will appear as though wash-out occurred because none of this had been made apparent during training.

Until investigators begin to critically examine how students learn, what they deem to be important, and what they carry with them into training, it will be impossible to assess the impact that training has upon the dispositions which recruits either develop or dismiss in relation to teaching. Though one can always speculate about what factors might be responsible for recruits developing dispositions which are contrary to those espoused during training, it will not be possible to chart the course of preservice socialization.

DIRECTIONS FOR TEACHER EDUCATION

What distinguishes teacher preparation from other areas of professional training are the strong beliefs students carry into the program—the belief that they know what occurs in schools and have little more to learn (Lanier & Little, 1986). Unlike students training for the medical profession, teaching recruits have observed teachers for thousands of hours prior to training, developing very strong images of what teaching is about. The job of teacher educators, therefore, is made much more difficult.

Why should students believe what teacher educators have to say when those mentors have had little recent contact with the public schools, and in some cases, little credibility as models of excellence in teaching? If the program does not offer special knowledge and skills essential to professional practice, why not engage in some form of studentship in order to progress through a training program with greater ease, not having to buy into the trivia which recruits determine to be irrelevant to what they will need as teachers? Under the circumstances which exist in most training institutions, all the student must do is survive the program and then go out and teach in a personally acceptable manner which is already known "to work."

Further, unlike the medical profession, the process of learning to teach is not determined by clear models of correct procedure. Learning the procedures for determining the appropriateness of a teaching style is unlike those for a doctor who is learning how to set a broken leg. Learning to teach, like teaching itself, is enormously complex and fraught with ambiguity.

What directions might teacher educators take to increase the probability that recruits will retain and implement more of what is learned during training? Based upon what we do know or may reasonably suppose about the socialization of tomorrow's physical educators, the following suggestions have logical appeal, if not empirical support.

Examining the Past

It is understood that when recruits enter a program with lingering memories and beliefs from their experiences during pretraining, it will be very difficult for formal training programs to exert enough influence to overcome those beliefs. Unfortunately, beliefs developed during anticipatory socialization may be perpetuated as a result of the failure of the training program faculty to confront, as part of the explicit curriculum, the educational predispositions and beliefs of their students (Freeman & Kalaian, 1985). Because students are neither helped to clarify what they believe nor forced to confront conflicts with alternative belief systems, it seems only natural for students to resist or evade program content which conflicts with existing dispositions.

Instead of ignoring the dispositions developed during pretraining, it would be wise, as Lortie (1975) suggests, to help students examine their past and determine how it has shaped their current beliefs about teaching. His suggestion is certainly reasonable in light of what students are likely to have learned about schools long before entering preservice training. If teacher educators began to design ways to explore and deal with student presocialization as part of preservice training, the potency of the program as a socializing agency might be greatly enhanced.

Developing Commitment

Recruits enter teacher training programs for various reasons, some of which will blend nicely with the intentions of the training program and some of which will prove to be antithetical. In response to the relative ease of entrance into the teaching field, Templin (1984) suggests that training programs might begin to assess whether or not students want to teach, their levels of commitment, as well as implementing strategies for the development of commitment. Recruits who choose teaching because of ancillary rewards such as length of vacations, job security, an opportunity for high autonomy in the classroom, or because teaching either is regarded as an easy major or represents a last career option, are not likely either to be committed or socialized.

Recruits need to be convinced that learning to teach is a career long process which involves much more than a love for children. Helping recruits to realistically assess their reasons for entering teaching can only enhance socialization and the degree to which success might be possible. On the one hand, the recruit who entered teaching because of lengthy vacations might realize that teaching provides many rewards, but the work days are long, tough, and demanding, with many teachers having to supplement their incomes with both summer employment and moonlighting jobs during the school year. They might begin to realize that they are best suited for another field. On the other hand, that same recruit might develop an interest in ideas and learning, showing less concern about vacations.

Examining Student Expectations

Students will enter teacher training programs with expectations for what training should offer. Frequently it is assumed that recruits don't have expectations for training, or if they do, that those expectations are either unimportant or will dissipate once recruits begin to immerse themselves in the everyday aspects of program life. Simply ignoring the existence of expectations shows both naivete about the complexity of socialization and a very significant lack of concern for students. Not unlike other consumers, students pay tuition expecting to receive valuables which will provide them with the necessities for assuming a desired vocation. While consumers usually can return merchandise they determine to be unsatisfactory, recruits have not just made a financial investment, they have exchanged a portion of their lives in preparation for the future. If they exit from training feeling "cheated," it won't be surprising if the imprint of program socialization is barely visible.

Obviously it is not possible, or even desirable, to attempt to discover and meet all the expectations students have for their training, particularly when it is understood that some of those expectations are unrealistic or contrary to the goals of the training program. What is possible, however, is to examine those expectations with the same concern that should be shown when examining the dispositions recruits have developed prior to training. If, for example, the recruit believed practicum training in an urban school was an essential part of preparation, it might be possible to locate such experience. So long as the program has the capacity to provide supervision and reinforcement for professional goals, overall socialization will be enhanced by a small act of respect for individual expectations.

Understanding Studentship

Studentship is a means of reacting to the forces of socialization, empowering students with strategies for progressing through a training program with greater ease and increased chance of success. Frequently students have engaged in this form of behavior because it provides an escape from tasks which they feel lack credibility. If students believe they won't get caught copying the work of a student who had previously received an "A" on an assignment which has no perceived justification or apparent worth, why not copy word-for-word and page-by-page?

Of course, students won't always agree with instructor expectations or understand the relevance of specific assignments. If, however, educators are willing to openly discuss the purpose and value of assignments without becoming threatened, taking great care to insure that short cuts such as copying are made difficult if not impossible, then students will be encouraged to regard learning tasks as legitimate—worthy of effort and significant as a means of obtaining professional skills. Students might, of course, resort to fronting techniques in the process, but a little fronting and role playing is a harmless or even useful trade (Davis, 1968; Templin, 1984).

As reward systems are presently structured, students perceive grades and other forms of teacher approval as a scarce commodity. Accordingly, they will do whatever is necessary to improve the probability of obtaining their share. While a teacher can attempt to eliminate cheating during an exam, that doesn't mean students won't try to psych-out the teacher, attempting to discover what was asked on last year's exam. By shifting the transaction away from zero sum competition, this unhappy consequence might be eliminated. If all students believed they were assured of rewards for demonstrating predetermined levels of competence, they would not feel the extreme pressure to compete for grades and thereby be tempted to employ undesirable forms of studentship.

Examining What Students Learn

Educators must begin to critically examine what students actually learn from preservice training, what aspects of training they deem relevant and irrelevant, and what skills they actually take with them when they exit from training. Until questions such as these are answered, it will be impossible to estimate the relative power of different models for training and impossible to use scientific knowledge as a means of improving preservice education.

Further, educators must begin to examine the curriculum from which students learn. While it will always remain important to examine the intended curriculum in detail, investigators must begin to identify the important messages students receive from the unintended curriculum. Not only does this mean examining individual programs in detail, but it means that individual instructors must begin to examine their own behavior in relation to their impact on students.

Understanding Students' Emotions

There are no simple solutions or easy answers to the complexities of the dialectical process as it plays out in preservice socialization. It is reasonable to believe, however, that if teacher educators became more sensitive to the discontinuities and stresses encountered by students throughout the process of learning to teach, they might have greater control over the socialization process. In a recent study of teacher training, Clift, Nichols, and Marshall (1987) found that undergraduates "were concerned with their survival as students and not as teachers" (p. 13), frequently worrying about specific instructor expectations, what to study prior to a test, and becoming anxious over workload requirements. While the role of teaching may seem somewhat removed from students' lives, the role of being a student is ever-present. Understanding student concerns and how those concerns might influence engagement during preservice seems a priority if teacher educators are to exert a measure of benign control over student responses to training program demands.

Placek's (1985) discovery that a communication gap exists between teacher educators and their students also adds credence to the notion that little attention is paid to students' feelings and dispositions. In her study of preservice physical education majors, she discovered that a communication gap:

> existed not only at a superficial level of disagreement about operational knowledge learned in class, but "what knowledge is most important to learn." The gap has implications not only for teacher educators planning their individual classes, but for departments planning curriculum in teacher education. (p. 13)

If teacher educators can begin to understand students as reacting in perfectly normal ways to the demands and constraints of the teacher training program, they will have acquired powerful new leverage within the training process. To regard students as simply transgressing against the intentions of the training faculty is to misunderstand both undergraduate trainees and the realities of professional socialization.

REFERENCES

Becker, H. S., Geer, B., & Hughes, E. C. (1968). *Making the grade: The academic side of college life.* New York: John Wiley and Sons.
Becker, H. S., Geer, B., Hughes, E. C., & Strauss, A. L. (1961). *Boys in white: Student culture in medical school.* Chicago: University of Chicago Press.
Book, C., Byers, J., & Freeman, D. (1983). Student expectations and teacher education traditions with which we can and cannot live. *Journal of Teacher Education, 34*(1), 9-13.
Chu, D. (1984). Teacher/coach orientation and role socialization: A description and explanation. *Journal of Teaching in Physical Education, 3*(2), 3-8.
Clift, R. T., Nichols, C., & Marshall, F. (1987, April). *Turning opportunities into problems: Anger and resistance in teacher education.* Paper presented at the annual meeting of the American Educational Research Association, Washington, D.C.

Davis, F. (1968). Professional socialization as subjective experience: The process of doctrinal conversion among student nurses. In H. S. Becker, B. Geer, D. Riesman, & R. S. Weiss (Eds.), *Institutions and the person*. (pp. 235-251). Chicago: Aldine Publishing Company.

Dodds, P. (1983). Consciousness raising in curriculum: A teacher's model. In A. Jewett, M. Carnes, & M. Speakman (Eds.), *Proceedings of the third conference on curriculum and theory in physical education*. (pp. 213-234). Athens, GA: University of Georgia Press.

Feiman-Nemser, S. (1983). *Learning to teach* (Occasional Paper No. 64). East Lansing, MI: Institute for Research on Teaching, Michigan State University.

Freeman, D. J., & Kalaian, H. A. (1985, April). *Do traditional teacher education programs alter educational beliefs?* Paper presented at the annual meeting of the American Educational Research Association, Chicago, IL.

Geer, B. (1968). Occupational commitment and the teaching profession. In H. S. Becker, B. Geer, D. Reisman, & R. S. Weiss (Eds.), *Institutions and the person*. (pp. 221-235). Chicago: Aldine Publishing Company.

Graber, K. C. (1986, May). *Teacher socialization during professional preparation: The student response to perceived faculty expectations*. Paper presented at the annual meeting of the New England Educational Research Organization, Rockport, ME.

Graber, K. C. (1988a). *A naturalistic study of studentship in the context of preservice teacher training for physical educators*. Unpublished dissertation: University of Massachusetts at Amherst.

Graber, K. C. (1988b, April). *Making the grade: A qualitative study of teacher preparation classes in physical education*. Paper presented at the annual meeting of the American Educational Research Association, New Orleans, LA.

Hughes, E. C. (1971). *The sociological eye: Selected papers*. Chicago: Aldine-Atherton, Inc.

Hughes, E. C., Becker, H. S., & Geer, B. (1962). Student culture and academic effort. In N. Sanford (Ed.), *The American college*. (pp. 515-530). New York: Wiley.

Lacey, C. (1977). *The socialization of teachers*. London: Methuen.

Lanier, J. E., & Little, J. W. (1986). Research on teacher education. In M. C. Wittrock (Ed.), *Handbook of research on teaching* (3rd ed.). (pp. 527-569). New York: MacMillan Publishing Company.

Lapin, F. M. (1985). Professional socialization: A naturalistic study of students becoming teachers. *Dissertation Abstracts International, 45*(8), 2477A-2478A. (University Microfilms No. 84-26, 174).

Lawson, H. A. (1983a). Toward a model of teacher socialization in physical education: The subjective warrant, recruitment, and teacher education (part 1). *Journal of Teaching in Physical Education, 2*(3), 3-16.

Lawson, H. A. (1983b). Toward a model of teacher socialization in physical education: Entry into schools, teachers' role orientations, and longevity in teaching (part 2). *Journal of Teaching in Physical Education, 3*(1), 3-15.

Light, D., Jr. (1979). Surface data and deep structure: Observing the organization of professional training. *Administrative Science Quarterly, 24*, 551-559.

Locke, L. F. (1984). Research on teaching teachers. Where are we now? *Journal of Teaching in Physical Education, Monograph 2* (summer), 1-86.

Locke, L. F., & Dodds, P. S. (1984). Is physical education teacher education in American colleges worth saving? Evidence, alternatives and judgment. In N. Struna (Ed.), *NAPEHE Annual Conference Proceedings: Vol. 5* (pp. 91-107). Champaign, IL: Human Kinetics Publishers.

Locke, L. F., & Jensen, M. (1970). Heterosexuality of women in physical education. *The Foil*, Fall, 30-34.

Locke, L. F., & Massengale, J. (1978). Role-conflict in teacher-coaches. *Research Quarterly, 71*, 27-40.

Lortie, D. C. (1959). Laymen to lawmen: Law school, careers, and professional socialization. *Harvard Educational Review, 29*(4), 352-369.

Lortie, D. C. (1975). *Schoolteacher: A sociological study*. Chicago: University of Chicago Press.

Merton, R. K., Reader, G. G., & Kendall, P. L. (Eds.). (1957). *The student-physician*. Cambridge, MA: Harvard University press.

Olesen, V., & Whittaker, E. (1968). The art and practice of studentmanship: Backstage. In V. Olesen & E. Whittaker (Eds.), *The silent dialogue*. (pp. 148-199). San Francisco: Jossey-Bass.

Placek, J. H. (1985). *Teacher educators and students: The communication gap*. Paper presented at the Fourth Curriculum Theory Conference, Athens, GA.

Snyder, M. (1980). The many me's of the self-monitor. *Psychology Today, 13*, pp. 33-40, 92.

Spradley, J. P. (1979). *The ethnographic interview*. New York: Holt, Rinehart and Winston.

Steen, T. B. (1985). *Teacher socialization in physical education during early training experiences: A qualitative study*. Paper presented at the National Convention of the American Alliance for Health, Physical Education, Recreation, and Dance: Atlanta, GA.

Steen, T. B. (1986). A case study of teacher socialization in physical education during early training experiences: A qualitative analysis. *Dissertation Abstracts International, 46*(9), 2668A. (University Microfilms No. 85-26,256).

Strauss, A. L. (1959). *Mirrors and masks: The search for identity*. Glencoe, IL: Free Press.

Templin, T. J. (1984). *Developing commitment to teaching: The professional socialization of the preservice physical educator*. Paper presented at the Second National Conference on Preparing the Physical Education Specialist for Children, Orlando, FL.

Templin, T., Woodford, R., & Mulling, C. (1982). On becoming a physical educator: Occupational choice and the anticipatory socialization process. *Quest, 34*(2), 119-133.

Western, J. S., & Anderson, D. S. (1968). Education and professional socialization. *The Australian and New Zealand Journal of Sociology, 4*(2), 91-106.

Williams, J. (1988, April) *Moonlighting among physical education teachers.* Paper presented at the annual meeting of the American Educational Research Association: New Orleans, LA.

Wisniewski, R. (1984). The scholarly ethos in schools of education. *Journal of Teacher Education, 35*(5), 2-8.

Woodford, R. C. (1977). *The socialization of freshman physical education majors into role orientations in physical education.* Unpublished doctoral dissertation, University of New Mexico.

Zeichner, K. M. (1979). *The dialectics of teacher socialization.* Paper presented at the annual meeting of the Association of Teacher Educators, Orlando: FL.

Zeichner, K. M., & Tabachnick, B. R. (1981). Are the effects of university teacher education 'washed out' by school experience? *Journal of Teacher Education, 32*(3), 7-11.

5

Trainees, Field Experiences, and Socialization Into Teaching

PATT DODDS
University of Massachusetts

Almost everyone considers field experiences in teacher-training programs to be critical. In 1963, Conant's critique of teacher education called student teaching the "one indisputably essential element in professional education." Haberman labeled student teaching "the heart and mind of teacher preparation" (1983). Most physical education teacher-education programs now include both early field experiences and student teaching (Placek & Silverman, 1983). Graduates consistently praise field experiences as the most useful part of their undergraduate preparation for teaching, sometimes as the only feature that they believe truly prepared them for their job (Locke, 1984).

Field experiences represent the closest juncture between formal teacher training in universities and on-the-job training in schools. For this alone, researchers and teacher educators should study what happens to trainees in the field.

This chapter explains how socialization processes help trainees learn in field experiences. Introductory definitions are followed by several socialization themes that introduce primary socializing agents and processes affecting trainees during field experiences and present physical education research interpreted in light of teacher socialization theory. The last section states implications for teacher educators who want to increase their influence on trainees during field experiences.

Field experiences (Applegate, 1986, 1987; Dodds, 1985; Zeichner, 1980) are opportunities to interact with typical pupils, usually in regular schools with supervision from a training program professor, a cooperating teacher employed at the school, or sometimes both. Often children come to the university for lessons, sometimes there is no cooperating teacher in schools where trainees go, and sometimes trainees are sent to schools without university supervision. Even so, all these variations constitute preservice practice where trainees work with age groups representing those they will eventually teach, discover how schools function as workplaces, and gather data to make decisions about whether they really want a teaching career.

Field experiences may be "course-imbedded" (integrated with the content or structure of regular pedagogical courses) or stand alone (like student teaching). Early field experiences precede student teaching and are usually shorter. They provide chances to observe children and teachers, assist with small groups, tutor a single child, or find out about a school's daily operations. Student teaching is most frequently the last, longest, and most extensive field experience in which trainees assume (sometimes progressively) full-time teaching responsibilities.

Socialization in field settings includes all processes (some deliberate or conscious, others random or unconscious) through which trainees' present teaching perspectives are changed through encounters with people and situations in schools. Their attitudes toward children, beliefs about education, intentions for what should happen to youngsters in physical education, what they know about sports, and how they think about teaching all are shaped by people and events that help them mold their perspectives.

The changes in trainees' teaching perspectives occurring in field experiences are part of the overall process by which they become members of the teaching profession. Such changes come through a combination of their own agency and that of others, most notably in professional teacher-training programs, their professors and on-site cooperating teachers. In the following discussion, professors' roles include various combinations of teaching and research.

Premises of This Chapter

This chapter proposes an accountability frame for teacher socialization based on particular assumptions. The principal task in professional teacher-training programs is to prepare the best entrants for the teaching work force. To accomplish this, a single, central vision of the ideal teacher must guide each program and professors must adhere to this vision as they teach trainees. This programmatic perspective, supported by training program goals, describes the common teaching attributes graduates ought to share and should be sufficiently flexible and complex to allow both professors and trainees their individualistic variations (personal perspectives), thus avoiding the production of teacher clones. Further, any programmatic perspective advocated by a faculty must broadly conform to the existing cultures of teaching (Feiman-Nemser & Floden, 1986), or the program will prepare teachers unable to enter or remain successfully in the work force.

In maximally effective training programs (Graham, 1987), professors understand how teachers are socialized throughout their lives, who the most significant agents are likely to be, and how socializing influences occur. They consciously use appropriate training strategies to increase their influences consistent with the programmatic perspective. They help trainees understand and use the same professional knowledge base as they develop personal perspectives within that of the program. Professors deliberately set out to bring socialization processes under their control during the training program. Though difficult at best, partially because socialization isn't understood well enough yet, it is even more difficult in field experiences because of the additional contexts and people involved.

Professors who ask the right questions about what happens to trainees in field experiences could learn much about how to orchestrate socializing influences effectively to guide trainees toward the programmatic perspective desired. Such inquiry is made easier by Lawson's applications of social science theory to physical education teacher development (1983a, 1983b, 1985, 1986, 1988). He is curiously silent, however, about those occasions on which trainees are placed in schools as part of their formal training. Extending Lawson's work to field experiences would be an important step in organizing salient questions about field experiences. Unfortunately, current research literature gives few clues about how professors might become more deliberate and effective in using field experiences to intensify their programmatic messages to trainees. Willard Waller's *Sociology of Teaching* (1932) all too accurately describes what little is really known about trainees' field experiences today.

Though many studies demonstrate, for example, that attitudes toward pupils become more custodial during student teaching, or that few early field experiences have specific objectives, and many contradict pedagogical messages from sponsoring university programs, most researchers continue to tackle unrelated research questions on widely scattered topics. Such efforts so far have produced little more than what common sense already illustrates and raise few hopes for being better able to explain, predict, or control how field experiences prepare young teachers.

In addition to Lawson's work, Figure 5-1 shows a particular organization of socialization constructs related to field experiences. This organizational scheme is useful to professors because its categories organize and draw attention to teacher socialization constructs that have (and some that have not) been shown to operate on trainees in the field from the particular vantage point of socializing themes to be explained.

SOCIALIZING THEMES FOR FIELD EXPERIENCES

No matter what the point of departure for considering field experiences as an arena for teacher socialization, several themes cast long shadows across the entire process. By understanding how each theme operates when trainees are in schools, professors can maximize the potential socializing power of field experiences to train the kinds of teachers they want. Though quite divergent positions can be taken with each theme professors can modify the impact of field experiences on trainees when the themes become familiar. Themes offering explanatory theory for teacher-socialization mechanisms include: (a) the need for ecological perspectives about field experiences, (b) the parsimony of the construct "teaching perspective" as an overall frame for considering socialization processes, (c) the pervasiveness of dominant-subordinate power relationships in American society, (d) the clash of cultures experienced by trainees, and (e) the importance of making choices.

The socialization constructs in Figure 5-1 help to explain what constitutes the views trainees hold, how these views are forged, and how they change in field experiences. Recruits develop images of what teachers say, do, believe and value as they mature. These images have several parts (Figure 5-1, Teaching Perspectives) and center on key features of educational settings (Figure 5-1, Conceptual Focuses of Teaching Perspectives). Various people (Figure 5-1, Socializing Agents) use socializing strategies to shape trainees' views (Figure 5-1, External Agents' Socializing Strategies). Trainees themselves also change their teaching perspectives through internal processes that achieve reasonable matches with the images of teaching professionals to which they aspire (Figure 5-1, Trainees' Self-Socializing Strategies).

The Need to Hold Ecological Perspectives About Field Experiences

Zeichner (1987) suggests viewing field experiences from an ecological perspective as a useful strategy for making sense of school contexts. Such an ecological viewpoint—requiring sensitivity to multiple, interwoven influences on trainees from several socializing agents and events at the same time—emphasizes the complexities and bidirectional-

FIGURE 5-1. *Socialization constructs related to trainees' field experiences.*

TEACHING PERSPECTIVES (CONTENT)
   PROFESSIONAL IDEOLOGY
      BELIEFS   VALUES   ATTITUDES
      DISPOSITIONS COMMITMENTS
   KNOWLEDGE
   ACTIONS
CONCEPTUAL FOCUSES OF TEACHING PERSPECTIVES (CONTENT)
   TEACHING/LEARNING
   TEACHERS/STUDENTS
   PE AS SUBJECT MATTER/ SPORT
   EDUCATION/ ATHLETICS
SOCIALIZING AGENTS
   INTERNAL
      SELF
   EXTERNAL
      COOPERATING TEACHER/UNIVERSITY SUPERVISOR
      OTHER TEACHERS AND FACULTY MEMBERS
      PUPILS
      FIELD EXPERIENCE PEERS, OTHER STUDENTS
      FRIENDS, FAMILY, AND OTHER SOCIETY MEMBERS
EXTERNAL AGENTS' SOCIALIZING STRATEGIES (PROCESSES)
   ROLE MODELING
   GOALSETTING, PRACTICE, FEEDBACK, AND ACCOUNTABILITY
   PROMPTING REFLECTION
TRAINEES' SELF-SOCIALIZING STRATEGIES (PROCESSES)
   ROLE PLAYING: ROLE TAKING, ROLE MAKING
      SELECTIVE ROLE MODELING
   INTERNALIZED ADJUSTMENT
   STRATEGIC COMPLIANCE
   STRATEGIC REDEFINITION
      SUCCESSFUL, UNSUCCESSFUL
   STUDENTSHIP (IMPRESSION MANAGEMENT)
   REFLECTION
      MATCHING/COMPARING/CONTRASTING
      RESOLVING DISSONANCE AND CONFLICT
         (COGNITIVE AND AFFECTIVE DIMENSIONS)
   CHOICE MAKING

ity of the social interactions that influence trainees in field experiences. With variations in biography, in already formed personal teaching perspectives, in field sites, and in socializing agents, the potential for trainees to receive competing messages about teaching during field experiences is overwhelming. Other forms of socialization, mediated through such sources as sport and the school bureaucracy, further complicate the situation. It is easy to imagine that trainees sort out with great difficulty what they believe about teaching, what values they hold about education, and how they should act with pupils.

Professors who adopt an ecological view of field experiences are less likely to miss important socializing influences on trainees and are more likely to notice and study interactions among those influences that direct trainees' teaching perspectives toward the ideals held in their training program.

The Construct of Teaching Perspectives

Physical education trainees' teaching perspectives include not only values, beliefs, attitudes, and actions about teaching (Zeichner, 1986) but also a similar set of dispositions about sport. Most physical education trainees are simultaneously socialized through long-term participation in both education and sport as they approach the work of teaching (Burlingame, 1972; Lawson, 1983a, 1983b, 1986; Pooley, 1972).

Professors could use field experiences as ideal opportunities to test how well the various components of trainees' teaching perspectives match; i.e., whether their *beliefs* about physical education and sport are consonant with their personal *values*, whether their *dispositions* to act follow their beliefs and values, or whether their overt *actions* at the field site are consistent with their *attitudes*. For example, a student teacher's *beliefs* that handling student misbehaviors should be done privately may remain intact through fifteen weeks in an inner-city high school, but her public *actions* as she teaches in that setting may change drastically from "soft touch" to "hardnose" because that's the only short-term strategy that will elicit a response from those particular students.

Further, professors need to discover how field experiences test congruence between trainees' teaching perspectives and the perspective advocated in the training program—under conditions that are likely to make serious discrepancies painfully evident. Researchers have documented erosion, entrenchment, and enhancement as prospective teachers' views of teaching adjust to pupils, teachers, and circumstances at field sites (Goodman, 1985a, 1985b, 1986).

Professors need to know whether trainees' teaching perspectives remain malleable during field experiences and how trainees assess their competence and aspirations against the requirements and rewards of teaching they perceive. When trainees enter schools, their teaching perspectives and self-appraisal mechanisms—the subject warrant (Lawson, 1983a; Lortie, 1975)—go along. These clinical opportunities to practice their craft allow keen-eyed observers to see how trainees stack up against their conceptions of the teaching role.

Different dilemmas center on how professors and cooperating

teachers exert influence on the *content* of trainees' teaching perspectives (e.g., one ought to believe that teachers should strive to improve the motor skills of all pupils) and how these socializing agents challenge trainees to *process* their views of teaching—how they match programmatic perspectives, and how both resemble or diverge from views of teaching found in schools. Do trainees' personal perspectives override programmatic perspectives when field sites resemble the schools they attended, or when cooperating teachers' views match theirs? What happens when field sites provide conflicting messages and unresolved dissonance with training programs?

The few physical education studies of teacher socialization during field experiences are valuable as much for what they imply as for what they state. That teaching perspectives of trainees become more custodial, that both cooperating teachers and pupils are important shapers of trainees' perspectives, and that few have wondered about early field experiences shouldn't surprise most readers.

Trainees find out in field experiences that pupil learning is not a high priority for physical educators (Placek, 1983; Placek & Dodds, 1988). They recognize the considerable power groups of pupils have over teachers' actions, and that quick managerial fixes they exert to control their classes soon harden into utilitarian perspectives of "do what works." The dominant view of many physical educators toward pupils is to encourage the highly skilled, ignore the competent bystanders (Tousignant & Siedentop, 1983), and allow pupils to sort themselves by gender groups such as athletes, junior varsity players, "wimps," femmes fatales, and others (Griffin, 1984, 1985).

Student teachers' perspectives are custodial, authoritarian, and utilitarian (Locke, 1984), showing little regard for pupils' learning. Both pupils and cooperating teachers contribute to this (Templin, 1979, 1981). Such teaching perspectives illustrate the "busy, happy, good" syndrome documented by other researchers (Placek, 1983). This may be partially explained by evidence that cooperating teachers' perspectives exhibit conformity, conservatism, and the elitism ethic derived from sport (Sage, 1980). But, it may also be that professors in physical education project a comparable programmatic perspective (Zeichner & Tabachnick, 1981).

Dominant-Subordinate Relationships in American Society

During field experiences, prospective teachers are formally subordinate to cooperating teachers and professors serving as university supervisors. This second theme of the real power differential between trainees and cooperating teachers or professors (who control consequences for trainee performance) reflects the power distribution between all teachers and students in our culture. This power distribution makes it more difficult for trainees to develop personalized teaching perspectives, to make successful role transitions, or to escape the prevailing conservatism that characterizes physical education practitioners.

This functionalist view of teacher socialization during field experiences is mitigated by evidence that trainees respond actively instead of simply adopting the role perspectives of others (Lawson, 1983a, 1983b; Lortie, 1975; Tabachnick, Popkewitz & Zeichner, 1979-80; Zeichner & Tabachnick, 1983). Even so, most characteristics of field experiences maintain trainees as subordinates. Being in schools as guests means classes can never really be theirs. They must accommodate their plans and ways of working with pupils to those of the cooperating teacher, since totally different managerial or academic routines would be problematic for teacher and pupils alike. The cooperating teacher's primary responsibility for the pupils (and only a secondary obligation to the trainees) inherently prevents as much attention being given to trainees as may be needed. When cooperating teachers and professors differ about teaching perspectives they want trainees to learn, they confuse their charges; but, the teachers' influence is strengthened by working group norms that act upon trainees as powerfully as on regular teachers (Haberman, 1978).

The dominant-subordinate power relationship is an important backdrop for the socializing strategies of external agents (other people) and trainees' coping strategies, as these interact to influence their teaching perspectives. Trainees relate to people in many role groups (see Figure 5-1) who are potential socializing agents during field experiences. While cooperating teachers and pupils are most influential, friends, family members, and others cannot be discounted from influencing teaching perspectives. When people tell horror stories of embarrassment in their physical education classes, describe the worst stereotypical "gym teachers" or "coaches," or disparage the physical education major as "underwater basketweaving," the almost universal view of physical education as a marginal school subject is reinforced (Dodds & Locke, 1984). Trainees and professors share this low status appraisal, thus consolidating a subordinate position in the school hierarchy (Goc-Karp, Kim & Skinner, 1985).

Cooperating teachers as socializing agents. Evidence supports the dominant-subordinate theme by showing that cooperating teachers strongly influence student teachers (Zeichner, 1986; Zimpher, 1987). Many student teachers adopt utilitarian perspectives (Iannaconne, 1963; Zeichner & Tabachnick, 1983); mirror many activities of their cooperating teachers (Feiman-Nemser & Buchmann, 1987); and are keenly aware of cooperating teachers' actions they perceive as effective or ineffective (Brunelle, Tousignant & Pieron, 1981).

Several factors intensify cooperating teachers' effects on trainees. The physical isolation of the gymnasium from other classrooms and the necessity for handling equipment or monitoring pupils between classes curtail trainees' interactions with other teachers. After briefly introducing themselves and the school, administrators withdraw quickly into their daily routines—a reminder that schools are to educate children, not those aspiring to teach (Feiman-Nemser & Buchmann, 1987).

Cooperating teachers play significant roles as trainees learn their teaching, organizational and social tasks in school settings (Tinning & Siedentop, 1985). Though deliberate professorial role modeling has been found to change university students' interactions in sport settings (Rolider, 1978), few efforts have been made to transfer this concept to physical education in schools.

The Ohio State supervision research program (Siedentop, 1981) demonstrates that cooperating teacher modeling, combined with other socializing strategies, can change trainees' behaviors with relative efficiency. However, other components of teaching perspectives have not yet come under the control of socializing agents or deliberate strategies. Further research could confirm whether similarity of school subcultures produces consistent messages from cooperating teachers or whether these messages contradict or enhance training program signals.

Pupils as Socializing Agents

Pupils are a major force affecting trainees' views of teaching during field experiences. Every day, trainees face pupils in large groups, confronting the generic problems of management to gain pupil compliance with requested learning tasks (Doyle, 1986). Class management is a primary concern of trainees in field experiences (Placek & Dodds, 1988), and cooperating teachers clearly influence how student teachers regard and address pupil misbehaviors (Balboa, 1988) and social behaviors (Schempp, 1985) in learning to teach. In all field experiences, trainees closely watch pupils' responses to academic and managerial task systems (Allison, 1987; Barrett, Allison & Bell, 1987; Bell, Barrett & Allison, 1985; Belka, 1988; Schempp, 1985; Schempp, 1986; Templin, 1981).

What trainees expect of pupils is connected with physical attractiveness, perceived skill level, perceived social behavior patterns and other characteristics of children, all of which influence trainees' actions as they teach (Martinek, Crowe & Rejeski, 1982). This phenomenon, known as the Pygmalion effect or teacher expectancy theory, may operate more publicly in physical education than other subject matters simply because most pupil responses are readily observable, large movements.

Unlike most trainees, distinctive teachers report few discipline or motivation problems (Earls, 1981) and find great satisfaction in their interactions with pupils. In both cases, socializing influences of pupils may preclude physical educators' sense of accountability for *learning*—for trainees because their most immediate concern is class control, and for experienced teachers because few systemic rewards accrue for producing motor skills in non-elite populations.

Socializing strategies of external agents. Professors and cooperating teachers exert several socializing strategies on trainees, and trainees use several coping strategies to survive and grow in field experiences in a tug of war between dominants and subordinates.

Professors role model by demonstrating specific teaching skills with majors or pupils or discussing their beliefs and attitudes about teaching as ways of transmitting information and values about the professional culture as they see it. This conveys messages about teaching (McKenzie, 1982), but the immediacy of teachers interacting with real pupils at a real school may be even more powerful.

Some professors use a powerful, deliberate socializing strategy supported by research (Siedentop, 1981). Based on behavioral goals for training, professors and cooperating teachers formulate goals for teaching in school settings; provide trainees with progressively sequenced, tightly focused practice leading to goal achievement; saturate them with relevant, specific feedback about their teaching; and apply consequences for success and failure. Likely to effect rapid role transitions from student to teacher (Ratliffe, 1988), this strategy exemplifies efforts to socialize trainees toward particular views of teaching derived from behavioral psychology.

Professors need to test the notion that, in the absence of conscious socializing strategies, trainees may graduate without a programmatic teaching perspective, thus holding only personal ones derived primarily from biography and observations as students. One significant problem in field experiences is that professors and cooperating teachers who neither use common strategies nor hold common goals for professional socialization allow natural contingencies and rewards in schools to override training program messages. This delays student-to-teacher role transition as defined in the program and reduces the major professional socializing agents' relative impact on trainees. The old adage of strength in numbers may be true for maximizing influences on trainees' teaching perspectives during field experiences.

Another socialization strategy in physical education is reflection (after Graham, Holt-Hale & Parker, 1986). Though most professors and cooperating teachers now pay lip service to post-lesson processing of trainees' experiences, sophisticated reflection at much deeper levels could enhance field experiences' impact (Cruickshank, et al., 1981; Ross, 1987). Evidence shows that professors are well-suited to help trainees reflect on teaching (Zimpher, 1987).

Trainees' self-socializing strategies. That the self is a critical socializing agent in learning to be a teacher is widely supported by researchers

(Graber, 1988; Lacey, 1977; Zeichner, 1979; Zeichner & Tabachnick, 1983, 1984). With conscious attention to which beliefs one holds, where these came from, how one's belief system influences actions and vice versa, trainees can actively construct how they feel and act in the teacher role. Thus, they take control over how their teaching perspective changes.

Trainees' social strategies may be required to survive or prosper in field experiences (Lacey, 1977). Most such strategies are rooted in the simple operations of comparing/matching/contrasting, or resolving conflicts or dissonance in field experiences. Trainees assume the protective coloration of compliant behaviors and by using an entire arsenal of adaptive mechanisms such as role playing, internalized adjustment, strategic compliance, positive and negative strategic redefinition (Lacey, 1977; Zeichner & Tabachnick, 1984), selective role modeling (Marrs & Templin, 1983), studentship (Graber, 1988), or impression management (Goffman, 1959), and quite probably other strategies not yet detected by professors.

Teacher trainees have ample opportunity to learn to teach by role playing, a universal human strategy for learning cultural norms. When trainees closely attend to other teachers by imagining themselves teaching the same way, they are role taking (Hewitt, 1984). Eventually, trainees personalize their role play by adjusting the role to themselves rather than vice versa (role making). Field experiences provide organized and supervised role-playing possibilities to enrich trainees' images of themselves as teachers (Templin, 1985) and to enable them to compare personal teaching perspectives with the programmatic perspective through their experience in role playing as teachers. Trainees' role playing takes different forms, as explained later, but all are theme variations of subordinates trying a dominant role.

When trainees adjust internally, they adopt much of the cooperating teacher's teaching perspective, including values, beliefs, and actions (Lacey, 1977). Some trainees selectively choose aspects they wish to emulate, probably those that most closely match their personal teaching perspective (Marrs & Templin, 1983).

In contrast, trainees strategically comply by adopting a teaching perspective different from theirs, while covertly harboring doubts about its long-term usefulness (Lacey, 1977). Strategic compliance closely resembles studentship or impression management (Goffman, 1959; Graber, 1988). When trainees "psych out what the cooperating teacher or professor wants" to be judged successful in field settings, their behavior reveals some understanding that taking actions at variance with their values and beliefs to get through the class means outwardly but temporarily adopting others as a way of gaining entry into the dominant role.

Trainees may strategically redefine some role norms in the school setting by holding separate teaching perspectives from cooperating teachers (Lacey, 1977). When successful (positive variation), trainees get away with doing things differently from the cooperating teacher. But, otherwise (negative variation), they are forced to abandon their notions of "teaching their own way" (Zeichner & Tabachnick, 1984).

Regardless of which coping strategies trainees use in field experiences, they measure all incoming information against the standard of their personal teaching perspective. Trainees form and refine their views of teaching based on congruent, competing, and conflicting data from recruit-stage experiences, teacher-training program influences, and the impact of field experiences.

Neither trainees nor professors are mentioned in studies of physical education field experiences as important socializing agents. No recent study of professors specifically examines their roles in field experiences from a socialization theory viewpoint (Mitchell & Lawson, 1984; Mitchell, 1988; Williamson, 1988). Though professors commonly lament differences between universities and schools, they also affirm field experiences as absolutely essential to their programs (Dodds & Placek, 1988).

Except for student teachers' self-managed behavior change projects and peer supervision (Siedentop, 1981), little evidence indicates how trainees influence their own teaching perspectives—whether all parts are congruent, how discrepancies (e.g., between belief and action) are handled, when they use which coping strategies, or what the long-term effects may be on their teaching. To summarize, though some physical education researchers now use teacher socialization theory to study who and what constitute the most powerful messages about teaching, little attention has been directed in field-experience sites to how trainees, professors, cooperating teachers and pupils interact within the dominant-subordinate power structure of schools.

Professors who understand dominant-subordinate power relationships are better able to analyze socialization agents, socializing strategies used by each, and their relative influences on trainees. Professors who ignore the explanatory utility of dominant-subordinate power relationships are, like their trainees, at the mercy of haphazard natural contingencies of field experience environments and have less chance to affect their charges' teaching perspectives.

The Clash of Cultures for Trainees

A cultural metaphor for schooling (Sarason, 1980) draws attention to a third theme: how teachers, pupils, administrators, and others interact to create socially structured meanings for the conduct of education. Within the culture of each school, participants are aware of meanings that outsiders don't fully understand: norms for behavior, implicit rules for performing educational roles, and tacit expectations for how people treat each other. Much as anthropologists take up residence with an exotic tribe, trainees enter field sites as outsiders who have to discover many norms by trial and error. Trainees experience clashes among the subcultures important in their lives: being a college student while learning a profession, participating in sport while pursuing an education, and living in two decisively different professional worlds.

Personal subcultures clash. Field experiences do not necessarily dominate trainees' daily lives, so the potential impact of other people and events on their teaching perspectives is considerable. Except for student teaching, with its nearly full-time demands, trainees must accommodate three distinct subcultures in their lives: the training program and the field site (both professional), and college student peer group. As the only interface between program and workplace, field experiences bridge the two professional cultures. When the bridge is solid, both cultures support the same vision of a professional teacher (i.e., the programmatic perspective). When the bridge is less well-constructed, trainees must meet two sets of norms and expectations that often are dissonant in irreconcilable ways (Feiman-Nemser & Buchmann, 1985). First, they must demonstrate the teaching role expected by the college training program, at least well enough not to alarm professors. Second, trainees must adapt to the field site, usually adopting teaching perspectives commensurate with how their cooperating teachers play the role.

In addition, trainees are in late adolescence, struggling with peer pressures to party instead of study, working to establish roommate and partner relationships, and handling the first measures of independence from family. In field experiences, they are caught not only between two sometimes contradictory professional cultures, but also by disparities between career preparation and the value system of their daily lives as college students. Time crunches force choices between preparing student teaching lessons and spending time at home, or between meeting friends for a movie and officiating the intramural track meet as a way of cultivating the cooperating teacher. Continual accommodation among various roles leads to social fatigue and consequent failures of adaptation.

Time crunches are small potatoes compared with more serious value conflicts faced almost daily in field experiences. When a professor wants skill teaching and maximum student activity time, while the cooperating teacher wants two days of drills followed by total game play, and the trainee wants to work with the high-skilled pupils because it feels so depressing when a significant part of the class fails to learn, there simply are no alternatives that fully accommodate such divergent values.

Education and Sport Cultures Clash. A second cultural clash for trainees may result from their immersion in education and sport as social institutions. Trainees confront the stuff of sports in their classes—past, present, and future. Many physical educators coach athletics as part of their job. As active sport participants, they have come to believe in the virtues of competition, teamwork, playing hard to win, and a caste system where only a few can be on the first team.

These values of sport contradict those that nominally drive free public education: opportunity for all to participate in sport and movement activities, regardless of skill level, social class, ethnic group, gender, or sexual preference. The notions that cooperation can complement competition or that games can be structured for everyone to win are antithetical to the social and political assumptions that undergird the layperson's vision of sport. Without opportunity to examine those assumptions and experiment with alternatives, trainees will retain that same vision.

While no research has directly tested the relative strength of such sport versus educational value systems in trainees, it seems reasonable that the pervasiveness of sport in American society is mirrored directly in schools and that the values of sport are dominant. It is not yet clear whether a separate educational value system exists or simply reproduces values derived from sport. Nevertheless, which value system permeates trainees' teaching perspectives may be discovered by discerning similarities between sport and educational subcultures.

Teacher/Coach Role Conflict. In 1978, the first report of teacher/coach role conflict was published (Locke & Massengale, 1978), illustrating a different aspect of cultural clash between education and sport. Since then, accumulating evidence leaves little question that the worst of elitist, sexist, racist and homophobic values from sport have invaded the teaching of physical education (Griffin, 1984, 1985). This role conflict rests on the differences between sport and educational values, but some evidence shows that there may be no real differences. Recruits don't seem to recognize teacher/coach role conflict before entering professional training, perhaps because their experiences in sport were simply replicated in physical education (Hutchinson, 1988; Lawson, 1988). Four years later, as student teachers, they don't believe pupil learning is terribly important—indirect evidence that sport's "natural selection" code (not everyone can be an athlete) permeates the gym even during instructional hours. And if cooperating teachers give less attention to physical education classes while preparing in detail for athletic practice, trainees may also believe sport is of greater importance and that coaching takes precedence over teaching.

Some distinctive teachers, while acknowledging sport participation as a strong factor in career choice, believe they have resolved the teacher/coach role conflict (Earls, 1981). Their program orientations are social or affective. But, even though such teachers reject negative values from sport, sport nevertheless remains a significant influence on the multiactivity curricula they teach.

When recruits become trainees, their teaching perspectives may undergo fundamental change or reactionary entrenchment, depending on professors' orientations toward sport and educational value systems. When professors teach only about teaching and almost never about coaching, it is small wonder that trainees luxuriate in their return to schools during field experiences where cooperating teachers speak the forbidden words and model the forbidden practices of coaching.

During field experiences, professors sometimes forget what sport means to trainees, thinking only about instructional programs and pedagogy. For many trainees, this is a time of confusion and growing frustration as they begin to sense deep differences between views of teaching in the school and the university. It also is a time when definitions and expectations about teaching get mixed up with those about coaching. In the absence of direct and persistent confrontation with this issue, the views of cooperating teachers will acquire the aura of "this is the way it really is", which trainees quite naturally heed. When professors are noticeably silent on the same issues, only tacit (and probably negative) messages compete with those sent to trainees in the field. Continued lack of attention to coaching, whatever its valence for professors, will only reinforce the power of school settings to overcome training program influences.

Nevertheless, sport continues to be an important part of trainees' lives, both by time investment and saliency (Dodds, 1988). Trainees in early field experiences worry about balancing time to complete assignments and go on road trips with intercollegiate teams or spend evenings in intramural team play. The opportunity to continue intercollegiate sports participation during student teaching is a concern for trainees, even when it receives active support from professors. For some undergraduates, the opportunity to have a coaching apprenticeship in interscholastic sports is a primary factor in selecting student teaching sites. In sum, sport participation competes for trainees' time during field experiences and constitutes a strong, continuing source of professional ideology that functions in teacher training programs.

What trainees learn in school cultures. Some physical education research (Templin, 1979, 1981) invokes the cultural context of schools to explain how field experiences help trainees learn some of the rules governing teachers. Student teachers learn not only the technical skills and broader role metaphors of teaching through occupational socialization, but also important lessons about how to act at work through bureaucratic socialization (Templin, 1979).

In early field experiences, trainees are sometimes disappointed to learn about constraints on physical educators. In one instance, visiting trainees prepared lessons for junior high pupils only to be delayed two hours by a music concert in the gym and another half-hour by administrators deciding which special schedule was to be followed after the assembly. Finally, they did not get to teach because the class hour was deleted

(Dodds, 1988). It is instructive that they were far more appalled by the obvious powerlessness of the resident cooperating teachers than by the lost opportunity to practice as promised.

Student teachers become experts at doing the right things in the halls, in the teachers' lunchroom, around the principal, and especially in the presence of other regular teachers on the staff. Learning to treat pupils as subordinates is a hard lesson when trainees themselves are subordinate both to cooperating teachers and professors (Templin, 1981). But they must demonstrate both dominant and subordinate behaviors to survive in the school. Student teachers learn the kinds of tasks pupils perform within the subculture of physical education classes (Tousignant & Siedentop, 1983) as well as their own tasks as teachers, including a social task structure for fitting into the school (Tinning & Siedentop, 1985). The enormously powerful effects of school cultures on teachers apparently continue, since distinctive teachers recount progressive changes in their views of physical education since undergraduate training (Earls, 1981).

The Fear That Physical Education Has No Shared Technical Culture. One persistent omission in physical educators' discussions of teacher socialization is the collective failure to consider the *ends* toward which socializing processes lead (Lawson, 1983a, 1983b, 1986, 1988; Schempp, 1985, 1986; Templin, 1979, 1981). While being prescriptive is not appropriate—given the incompleteness of present knowledge about effective teaching—the matter of goals, i.e., the desired outcomes of socialization, must be raised by professors: Toward *what* is socialization supposed to lead?

Professors are obligated to describe explicitly the programmatic teaching perspective held for trainees. This then becomes the standard against which trainees' personal teaching perspectives could be measured. The absence of clearly delineated program goals assures multiplicity of goals. Even in programs where such goals are *described* relatively clearly, there remains the nagging hunch that the real problem is *not using* the goals as the primary index of success in training teachers.

One barrier that prevents defining a programmatic teaching perspective is the absence of a shared technical culture in physical education, i.e., knowledge, skills and dispositions about teaching that require specialized study and exceed the skills of laypersons. Some argue that a modest store of technical knowledge about effective teaching in physical education is available from research and could be used to improve school practice (Locke, 1984; Placek & Locke, 1986; Siedentop, 1983). But, the majority of physical educators clearly have not yet accepted research-derived knowledge as a major basis for their work.

For the most part, the norms and role expectations that *are* shared widely among school practitioners (custodialism, conservatism, and conservation) are not technical. No special, professional training is required since much of the most highly prized wisdom of practice comes from personal participation in sport. Therefore, though physical educators in schools share a subculture within the subject matter, this culture is not technical. Nevertheless, a research-based technical culture of teaching is readily available to professors at universities.

Explanations for this lack of a shared technical culture among physical educators are not simple: It is not school practitioners versus those at the university, for many professors share the custodial orientation of many school physical educators and many in the schools actively pursue the search for research-based technical knowledge for teaching.

Because the very forms of professional knowledge considered important by physical educators in different settings (i.e., schools and universities) are disputed (Lawson, 1985), trainees who interact with professors and cooperating teachers are likely to experience another clash of subcultures. When primary socializing agents neither share nor value a common teaching perspective, and when differences among professors may be even greater than those between one professor and one cooperating teacher, trainees' views of teaching will be shaped by random influences in field experiences rather than coordinated messages reiterating a familiar programmatic teaching perspective.

Professors need to study the relative impact of socializing agents and events, seeking differences and commonalities among subcultures such as elementary and secondary physical educators, professors who arrived via different career paths in their present positions (Helfrich, 1975), genders, and college- and school-based physical educators.

In retrospect, clashing subcultures surround trainees during field experiences. At worst, two professional training settings require divergent behaviors, and neither is totally synchronized with the other or with the late-adolescent subculture of college students. Sport and education compete to influence trainees' value systems, or worse, education merely mirrors and intensifies the miseducative values in sport. Finally, failure to define a truly shared technical subculture as the basis for professional teaching in physical education leaves trainees with conflicting models, mentors, and mindsets about what effective teaching is.

The Importance of Making Choices

As the final socialization theme, the notion that humans make choices is an essential belief required of anyone who takes teacher training seriously. "Human agency", the capacity of participants in teacher education to choose their courses of action, is limited by several factors but almost never entirely erased. Professors, cooperating teachers at field sites, and trainees—all are bound by the nature of their personal biographies, the powerful influences of other players in the game (their socializing agents), and the ongoing press of their teacher-training program.

Where, then, can trainees make choices, and how can they be social-ized to do so? The prerequisite to choice making is recognizing situations in which one's teaching perspectives don't match those of others. For example, professors sometimes realize their interpretation of a stated program goal (e.g., graduates will be able to design physical education programs with strong health-related fitness components) is at variance with that of other professors; cooperating teachers notice discrepancies with professors in how teaching is defined; and trainees may be aware that their cooperating teachers value coaching while professors simply fail to discuss it. In such circumstances, although awareness leads to choosing, choices may range from ignoring the dissonance noted to ad-dressing it verbally and behaviorally.

Failure of trainees to believe in choice making reduces their oppor-tunity to influence their socialization into teaching. On the other hand, belief in choice-making potential, however limited by programmatic constraints, makes it possible for trainees to shape their views of teach-ing, to align these views with others' views when it makes sense to do so or to be deliberately at variance, and to continue changing their personal perspectives as ways of being students of teaching.

Specific implications of this choice-making theme for teacher train-ing reside in the virtual impossibility of predicting accurately how strongly any socializing agent will influence someone's views of teaching, from whom or how the most potent messages about teaching will come, or how long the effects of those messages will last. For instance, when trainees retrospectively analyze which childhood teachers affected them most, or discount what teacher educators say to them during discussions about the purposes of public education in the United States, they may be making conscious choices, not simply reacting to quantity or quality of incoming information.

Professors have good reason to applaud their window of influence on trainees' teaching perspectives if they can encourage their charges to choose components of their personal perspectives deliberately rather than "go with the flow" of unexamined messages. Professors who wish to maximize their influence on trainees' views of teaching should help them become informed consumers of every incoming educational message, regardless of source.

IMPLICATIONS FOR PROFESSORS

Socializing trainees during field experiences to adopt particular teaching perspectives that will both display the programmatic vision of an ideal teacher and help the trainee enter the workplace and cultures of teaching easily is an extremely difficult task because so little is known about teacher socialization in these settings. There is little understanding of the ecology of single field experiences, let alone how several may accumulate or mesh with others or with other components of the training program. Something is known about skills and behaviors within trainees' teaching perspectives but little about how their attitudes are formed or changed, what happens to particular dispositions over the course of their time at field sites, or whether all parts of the perspective ever become consistent.

The dominant-subordinate theme has never been directly explored in light of teacher socialization but seems a reasonable lead to pursue when studying trainees in field experiences. Knowing specific mechanisms by which various agents and strategies of socialization operate on trainees is now beyond our grasp in terms of bringing these under control to serve training program goals. And the first steps in research are still being taken to address the ways membership in different subcultures affects trainees while they're in schools. The following points are offered for professors to consider as they continue their work of socializing trainees via field experiences.

1. *All people associated with field experiences don't necessarily share the same teaching perspectives.* They frequently disagree about
   a. what teaching professionals are (what ought physical education teachers to be like?);
   b. how to train teaching professionals (how ought we best to prepare young teachers?);
   c. the subject matter of physical education (what ought school physical education programs to be like?).

   When these conditions are true, no training program will strongly affect its trainees' views of teaching until the perspectives of all participants become broadly similar. Where such views differ in even modest ways, trainees will cling to whatever seems most familiar, workable, and helpful. Certainly trainees are unlikely to risk even tentative assumption of perspectives that they know one or more of the profession's gatekeepers will disapprove. Professors and cooperating teachers who struggle toward a single, mutually acceptable programmatic teaching perspective encourage trainees to step into the teacher role more quickly and comfortably.

2. *Professors must design deliberately progressive, sequential, and well-timed field experiences that clearly support the programmatic teaching perspective.* Each field experience should coincide with relevant theoretical pedagogy activities, be long enough to serve its specific purpose without wasteful repetition, and be accompanied by adequate opportunities for processing and returning to previous material for reexamination. In short, each

field experience should involve serious reflective activities that require trainees to match, compare, and contrast what happens in that natural setting with their views of teaching and with those found in their field site and university program.

Trainees integrate earlier life experiences with current professional training (including field experiences) by absorbing components compatible with what they already know, believe, or try. Professors should continually support trainees in questioning such automatic responses and in trying new approaches to see how those fit their teaching perspectives.

Since first-hand teaching experience doesn't by itself professionally socialize trainees to exhibit programmatic teaching perspectives, professors must intervene by getting trainees to match, compare, and contrast what's going on in the field setting with their views of teaching. Because early biography and school experiences remain dominant influences in shaping teaching perspectives, professors must examine field experiences to determine how these reinforce earlier conceptions of teaching or introduce alternative possibilities. Analysis is not enough: Programmatic perspectives must be clear, explicit, actively advocated and modeled by faculty, and reiterated by cooperating teachers if trainees' personal teaching perspectives are to be shaped toward those identified for the training program.

3. *Professors intentionally must explore implications of sport within field experiences.* Even when field experiences and cooperating teachers match training program courses and professors with regard to teaching perspectives, physical education trainees face frequently conflicting messages from sport about teaching, learning, and kids—messages all too often elitist, racist, sexist, and homophobic—in short, not the messages most training programs include in their program goals. By encouraging open discussion about the effects of sport on trainees engaged in field experiences, the collusion of silence is broken. Opposite viewpoints are then more likely to be expressed, compared, and changed. Since sport may affect trainees' teaching perspectives positively and negatively, raising it to seriously reflective levels can do much to enhance the possibility that all participants will understand better their views of teaching.

4. *The processes of reflection and choice making must become interwoven themes that are apparent in all field experiences.* Clear signals about programmatic perspectives, the role modeling that professors and cooperating teachers do, the design of coursework and field experiences, and the accountability system for trainees to demonstrate their teaching perspectives—all aspects

of the program should consistently reinforce the two processes of reflection and choosing that are characteristic of teaching professionals. These should be part of the programmatic teaching perspective. Because trainees sometimes choose personal variations or alternatives, regardless of overall program strength or consistency, professors should be satisfied if most trainees are making significant progress toward stated program goals and are aware of when and why they choose to deviate from the programmatic teaching perspective.

These four implications merely represent many that could be drawn from socialization research as organized within the themes presented earlier in this chapter. Beginning with the premise that all participants in field experiences don't necessarily share a single teaching perspective allows professors to explore what perspectives are represented among the players and how those perspectives influence the trainee's experiences at that site. Professors with the same premise can try strategies directly focused on describing and discussing various teaching perspectives as ways of influencing others.

A haphazard series of field experiences makes little sense if teacher educators advocate a shared programmatic teaching perspective for graduates. Professors are the only socializing agents in position to lead efforts toward linked, progressive field experiences. We must constantly try to take vantage points outside the immediate situation to discover how school-based and university-based physical educators—together—can produce the best, mutually acceptable, and workable field experiences in which trainees will adopt the programmatic teaching perspective as the integral core of their personal perspective.

Reflection and choice-making themes for field experiences provide natural opportunities for analyzing the impact of both education and sport and their implications for teacher trainees. Of course, professors must learn to be reflective themselves before they can help trainees learn such skills. Continuous practice in making conscious choices about teaching and in reflecting about the consequences of such choices enriches the impact of field experiences and gives trainees enhanced opportunities to become students of their own teaching—the ultimate goal of effective teacher-training programs. Researchers have a particularly rich field of inquiry in observing such activities in teacher-training programs.

REFERENCES

Allison, P. (1987). What and how preservice physical education teachers observe during an early field experience. *Research Quarterly for Exercise & Sport* 58:242-249.
Applegate, J. (1987). Early field experiences: Three viewpoints. In M. Haberman & J. Backus (eds.), *Advances in Teacher Education* 3:75-93. Norwood, NJ: Ablex.

Applegate, J. (1986). Undergraduate students' perceptions of field experiences: Toward a framework for study. In J. Raths & L. Katz (eds.), *Advances in Teacher Education* 2:21-38. Norwood, NJ: Ablex.

Balboa, J-M. (1988). Student teachers' views of their responses to pupil misbehavior in physical education classes. Doctoral dissertation. University of Massachusetts, Amherst.

Barrett, K., Allison, P. & Bell, R. (1987). What preservice physical education teachers see in an unguided field experience: A followup study. *Journal of Teaching in Physical Education* 7:12-21.

Bell, R., Barrett, K. & Allison, P. (1985). What preservice physical education teachers see in an unguided early field experience. *Journal of Teaching in Physical Education* 4:81-90.

Belka, D. (1988). What preservice physical educators observe about lessons in progressive early field experiences. *Journal of Teaching in Physical Education* 7:311-326.

Brunelle, J., Tousignant, M. & Pieron, M. (1981). Student teachers' perceptions of cooperating teachers' effectiveness. *Journal of Teaching in Physical Education Introductory Issue*:80-87.

Burlingame, M. (1972). Socialization constructs and the teaching of teachers. *Quest* 18(Spring):40-56.

Conant, J. (1963). *The education of American teachers*. New York: McGraw-Hill.

Cruickshank, D., Holton, J., Fay, D., Williams, J., Kennedy, J., Myers, B. Hough, J. (1981). *Reflective teaching*. Bloomington, IN: Phi Delta Kappa.

Dodds, P. (1985). Delusions of "worth-it-ness": Field experiences in elementary physical education teacher education programs. In H. Hoffman & J. Rink (eds.), *Physical Education Professional Preparation: Insights and Foresights* 90-109. Reston, VA: AAHPERD Publications.

Dodds, P. (1988). Who socializes trainees in early field experiences? Messages, media, and mentors. Manuscript submitted for publication.

Dodds, P. & Locke, L. (1984). Is physical education in American schools worth saving? Evidence, alternatives, judgment. In N. Struna (ed.). NAPEHE Proceedings, 5:76-90.

Dodds, P. & Placek, J. (1988, April). Teacher educators' views on success/nonsuccess in teaching. Paper presented at AERA, New Orleans.

Doyle, W. (1986). Classroom organization and management. In M. Wittrock (ed.), *Handbook of Research on Teaching* (3d ed.). 392-431. New York: Macmillan.

Earls, N. (1981). Distinctive teachers' personal qualities, perceptions of teacher education and the realities of teaching. *Journal of Teaching in Physical Education* 1:59-70.

Feiman-Nemser, S. & Buchmann, M. (1985). Pitfalls of experience in teacher preparation. In J. Raths & L. Katz (eds.), *Advances in Teacher Education* 2:61-74. Norwood, NJ: Ablex.

Feiman-Nemser, S. & Buchmann, M. (1987). When is student teaching teacher education? *Teaching and Teacher Education* 4:255-274.

Feimann-Nemser, S. & Floden, R. (1986). The cultures of teaching. In M. Wittrock (ed.), *The Third Handbook of Research on Teaching* 505-526. New York: Macmillan.

Goc-Karp, G., Kim, D. & Skinner, P. (1989). Professor and student perceptions and beliefs about physical education. *The Physical Educator* 43:115-120.

Goffman, E. (1959). *The presentation of self in everyday life*. Garden City, NY: Doubleday Anchor Books.

Goodman, J. (1985a). Field-based experience: A study of social control and student teachers' response to institutional constraints. *Journal of Education for Teaching* 11:26-49.

Goodman, J. (1985b). What students learn from early field experiences: A case study and critical analysis. *Journal of Teacher Education* 36(6):42-48.

Goodman, J. (1986). Making early field experiences meaningful: A critical approach. *Journal of Education for Teaching* 12:109-125.

Graber, K. (1988). A naturalistic study of studentship in the context of preservice teacher training for physical educators. Unpublished doctoral dissertation. University of Massachusetts, Amherst.

Graham, G. (1987, June). The developing physical education teacher and coach: Empirical and research insights. Paper presented at the AIESEP Conference, Trois-Rivieres, Quebec, Canada.

Graham, G., Holt-Hale, S. & Parker, M. (1986). *Children moving: A teacher's guide to developing a successful physical education program*. (2d ed.) Palo Alto: Mayfield.

Griffin, P. (1984). Girls' participation patterns in a middle-school team sports unit. *Journal of Teaching in Physical Education* 4:30-38.

Griffin, P. (1985). Boys' participation styles in a middle school physical education team sports unit. *Journal of Teaching in Physical Education* 4(2):100-110.

Haberman, M. (1978). Toward more realistic teacher education. *Action in Teacher Education* 1:1-8.

Haberman, M. (1983). Research on preservice laboratory and clinical experiences: Implications for teacher education. In K.

Helfrich, M. (1975). Paths into professional school. *Sociology of Work and Occupations* 2:169-181.

Hewitt, J. (1984). *Self and society: A symbolic interactionist social psychology* (3d ed.). Boston: Allyn and Bacon.

Hutchinson, G. (1988). Sports instructor, recreation director, or fitness specialist? The perspectives high school students interested in becoming physical educators have about the physical education teacher role in schools. Dissertation in progress, University of Massachusetts, Amherst.

Iannaccone, L. (1963). Student teaching: A transitional stage in the making of a teacher. *Theory into Practice* 2:73-81.

Lacey, C. (1977). *The socialization of teachers.* London: Methuen.

Lawson, H. (1983a). Toward a model of teacher socialization in physical education: The subjective warrant, recruitment, and teacher education. *Journal of Teaching in Physical Education* 2:3-16.

Lawson, H. (1983b). Toward a model of teacher socialization in physical education: Entry into schools, teachers' role orientations and longevity in teaching. *Journal of Teaching in Physical Education* 3:3-15.

Lawson, H. (1985). Knowledge for work in the physical education profession. *Sociology of Sport Journal* 2:9-24.

Lawson, H. (1986). Occupational socialization and the design of teacher education programs. *Journal of Teaching in Physical Education* 5:107-116.

Lawson, H. (1988). Occupational socialization, cultural studies, and the physical education curriculum. *Journal of Teaching in Physical Education* 7:265-288.

Locke, L. (1984). Research on teaching teachers: Where are we now? *Journal of Teaching in Physical Education.* Monograph 2.

Locke, L. & Massengale, J. (1978). Role conflict in teacher/coaches. *Research Quarterly* 49:162-174.

Lortie, D. (1975). *Schoolteacher: A sociological study.* Chicago: University of Chicago Press.

Marrs, L. & Templin, T. (1983). Student teacher as social strategist. In T. Templin & J. Olson (Eds.), *Teaching in Physical Education* 118-128. Champaign, IL: Human Kinetics.

Martinek, T., Crowe, P. & Rejeski, W. (1982). *Pygmalion in the gym: Causes and effects of expectations in teaching and coaching.* West Point, NY: Leisure Press.

McKenzie, T. (1982). Research on modeling: Implications for teacher educators. *Journal of Teaching in Physical Education* 1:23-30.

Mitchell, M. (1988). Perceptions and preferences of physical education methods teacher educators in Ohio. Dissertation in progress, Ohio State University, Columbus, Ohio.

Mitchell, M. & Lawson, H. (1984, July). Career patterns and role orientations of professors of teacher education in physical education. Paper presented at the Olympic Scientific Congress, Eugene, OR.

Placek, J. (1983). Conceptions of success in teaching: Busy, happy, and good? In T. Templin & J. Olson (eds.), *Teaching in Physical Education* Champaign, IL: Human Kinetics.

Placek, J. & Dodds, P. (1988). A critical incident study of preservice teachers' beliefs about teaching success/nonsuccess. *Research Quarterly for Exercise & Sport.* 46-56.

Placek, J. & Locke, L. (1986). Research on teaching physical education: New knowledge and cautious optimism. *Journal of Teacher Education* 37:24-28.

Placek, J. & Silverman, S. (1983). Early field teaching requirements in undergraduate physical education programs. *Journal of Teaching in Physical Education* 2:48-54.

Pooley, J. (1972). Professional socialization: A model of the pretraining phase applicable to physical education students. *Quest* 18(Spring):57-66.

Ratliffe, T. (1988), Preparing physical education teachers: Gaining, losing, and standing still. Manuscript submitted for publication.

Rolider, A. (1978, May). Effect of modeling, instruction, and grade incentive on supportive verbalization among peers in a college physical education class. Paper presented at Midwestern Association of Behavior Analysis, Chicago.

Ross, D. (April, 1987). Teaching teacher effectiveness research to students: First steps in developing a reflective approach to teaching. Paper presented at AERA annual meeting, Washington, D. C.

Sage, G. (1980). Sociology of physical educator/coaches: Personal attributes. *Research Quarterly for Exercise & Sport* 51:110-121.

Sarason, S. (1980). *The culture of the school and the problem of change.* (2d ed.) Boston: Allyn & Bacon.

Schempp, P. (1985). Becoming a better teacher: An analysis of the student teaching experience. *Journal of Teaching in Physical Education* 4:158-166.

Schempp, P. (1986). Physical education student teachers' beliefs in their control over student learning. *Journal of Teaching in Physical Education* 5:198-203.

Siedentop, D. (1981). The Ohio State University supervision research program summary report. *Journal of Teaching in Physical Education* Introductory Issue:30-38.

Siedentop, D. (1983). *Developing Teaching Skills in Physical Education.* Palo Alto: Mayfield.

Tabachnick, R. & Zeichner, K. (1983). *The impact of student teaching experience on the development of teacher perspectives.* Madison, WI: Wisconsin Center for Education Research.

Tabachnick, R., Popkewitz, T. & Zeichner, K. (1979-80). Teacher education and professional perspectives of student teachers. *Interchange on Educational Policy* 10:12-29.

Templin, T. (1979). Occupational socialization and the physical education student teacher. *Research Quarterly* 50:482-493.

Templin, T. (1981). Student as socializing agent. *Journal of Teaching in Physical Education* Introductory Issue:71-79.

Templin, T. (1985) Developing commitment to teaching: The professional socialization of the preservice physical educator. In H. Hoffman & J. Rink (eds.), *Physical Education Professional Preparation: Insights and Foresights.* 119-131. Reston, VA: AAHPERD Publications.

Tinning, R. & Siedentop, D. (1985). The characteristics of tasks and accountability in student teaching. *Journal of Teaching in Physical Education* 4:286-299.

Tousignant, M. & Siedentop, D. (1983). A qualitative analysis of task structures in required secondary physical education classes. *Journal of Teaching in Physical Education* 3:47-57.

Waller, W. (1932). *The sociology of teaching.* New York: John Wiley & Sons.

Williamson, K. (1988). A phenomenological description of the professional lives and experiences of physical education teacher educators. Doctoral dissertation. University of Massachusetts, Amherst.

Zeichner, K. (1979). The dialectics of teacher socialization. Paper presented at the annual meeting of the Association of Teacher Educators, Orlando, FL.

Zeichner, K. (1980). Myths and realities: Field-based experiences in preservice teacher education. *Journal of Teacher Education* 31:45-55.

Zeichner, K. (1986). Individual and institutional influences on the development of teacher perspectives. In J. Raths & L. Katz (eds.), *Advances in Teacher Education* 2:135-164. Norwood, NJ: Ablex.

Zeichner, K. (1987). The ecology of field experience: Toward an understanding of the role of field experiences in teacher development. In M. Haberman & J. Backus (eds.), *Advances in Teacher Education* 3:94-117. Norwood, NJ: Ablex.

Zeichner, K. & Tabachnick, B. (1981). Are the effects of university teacher education "washed out"? *Journal of Teacher Education* 32:7-11.

Zeichner, K. & Tabachnick, B. (1983, April). Teacher perspectives in the face of institutional press. Paper presented at AERA, Montreal, Quebec, Canada.

Zeichner, K. & Tabachnick, B. (1984, April). Social strategies and institutional control in the socialization of beginning teachers. Paper presented at AERA, New Orleans.

Zimpher, N. (1987). Current trends in research on university supervision of student teaching. In M. Haberman & J. Backus (eds.). *Advances in Teacher Education* 3:118-150. Norwood, NJ: Ablex.

6

Socialization and Inservice Teacher Education

SARAH DOOLITTLE
*University of Massachusetts
at Amherst*

SUSAN SCHWAGER
Montclair State College

Ms. Smith requests a professional day to attend a workshop at the local college on using computers for fitness testing. Her request is approved, and she spends the day learning how to use software that will enable her to compile and report her students' fitness scores. She is excited about the prospect of using the computer printout to communicate with parents and to accumulate some statistics which might be used to support her physical education program. After the workshop day she returns to the district and enthusiastically explains the computer innovation to her director and colleagues.

The director promises to order the materials necessary. He does so only after repeated reminders from Ms. Smith and the materials finally arrive four months after the workshop. Meanwhile her attempts to interest her colleagues in using the software are not very successful. They either seem to prefer "the way we've always done it," or agree they could use the program, but are not able to schedule sufficient time to meet with her to learn how to run the program. Ms. Smith decides to use the computer for the scores from her own classes. She signs up for access to the school's computer lab, and finally finishes collecting the scores, but has trouble setting up and running the program. She eventually abandons the computer in favor of the old way of tallying scores.

This vignette is fictitious, but it is an example of an actual inservice program. The teacher's experiences reflect some of the problems associated with typical inservice programs. Inservice programs are intended to promote improvements in existing school practices, but often fall short of their goals. Ideas brought back from inservice workshops often do not succeed in the school setting unless the school's natural resistance to change is taken into account.

In this chapter, we suggest that inservice teacher education is intended to counteract the negative effects of teacher socialization in the schools. It is meant to continue teachers' formal education, and challenge the status quo of teachers' practices and school programs. We present a description of the most common forms of inservice offered to physical educators, and suggest some characteristics which have been featured in recent successful inservice efforts. We then offer two examples of physical education inservice programs which currently have some impact on local teachers and programs, primarily because they attempt to work with the realities of teachers' work in schools.

SOCIALIZATION AND TEACHER EDUCATION

We know that teachers learn to teach not only through formal teacher preparation, but also through what has been called the socialization process: through observation of and experience with schools as students and as teachers. Socialization is unstructured and unsystematic, yet is a powerful determinant of teaching practice. By adopting many of the prevailing practices of their new workplace, the stability of the school is maintained. This allows novice teachers to become part of the system with minimum disruption.

While socialization can be essential to the smooth transition of teachers from teacher education to full teaching responsibility, socialization also can serve to perpetuate ineffective teaching practices and lackluster programs. Beginning teachers assume full responsibility from their first day, and usually work alone. What they learn through experience may be, for the most part, unexamined and unguided (Lanier & Little, 1986). Even assuming initial teaching competence, continuing the development of teaching skills, and incorporating program innovations is often problematic within complex school settings. Inservice education can provide the opportunity for teachers to continue learning about their profession in a more structured way. It is designed to encourage certified, experienced teachers to consider new ideas, and to implement changes in their existing programs.

We have chosen to define inservice teacher education so that it contrasts with pre-service teacher education. According to Locke (1984), *inservice teacher education* "includes all of the operations used to continue the education of teachers after they are certified for teaching and employed in a professional position" (p. 13). In its broadest sense, inservice teacher education also includes the supervision of teachers, staff development, and program development. *Supervision* consists of functions initiated by the administrator for the purpose of improving an individual teacher's instructional practices (Stillman, 1987). *Staff development* refers to organized education or learning opportunities for natural groups of teachers and others (administrators and other support staff) responsible for implementing school programs. The aim of staff development is to alter the group's professional practices. *Program development* is designed to improve or change what is taught, to alter the formal curriculum, teaching approaches, and/or the organization for instruction. The difference between program and staff development is one of emphasis. Staff development focuses on altering the professional practices of school personnel; program development is directed at what teachers are to provide. Inservice teacher education may consist of any or all of these development intentions, but the central issue for all inservice teacher education is to continue the professional education of school personnel, and to encourage positive change in existing instructional practices.

COMMON FORMS OF INSERVICE EDUCATION

This section details the various forms of physical education inservice education. Inservice programs found in the physical education literature have been grouped into two categories (originally suggested by Locke (1984), but which have been enlarged here to encompass program development): on-site staff and program development, including inservice teacher supervision and program development; and off-site staff and program development. Though the inservice literature appears to contain much more prescription than empirically based description, a preference has been given to reports of actual development efforts with real school programs, and with experienced physical education teachers.

On-Site Inservice Programs

On-site programs are most frequently characterized by "top-down" initiation, selection of goals and process, and recruitment of participants.

The most common forms of these are formal and informal teacher supervision, and "superintendent's day" workshops.

Supervision is perhaps the oldest form of inservice teacher and program development, and is conducted through formal and informal means. Most teacher contracts have specifically defined supervision and evaluation procedures, and maintaining and improving instruction is the explicit intention. But, most formal systems are performed in a perfunctory way, unless the teacher is new or the administrator is faced with collecting evidence for promoting or dismissing a teacher. Instructional improvement and professional development is rarely pursued in a conscious and deliberate manner through formal supervision (Stillman, 1987). It appears that the formal procedures are too tightly connected to union policies and personnel evaluation to have a strong influence on changing teacher practice, unless the teacher is a novice, or is seriously deficient.

Stillman's 1987 study of the staff development practices of physical education administrators found that it is informal supervision which appears to contribute to the teachers' development. Stillman reports that administrators routinely "walk-through" the gym to see for themselves "what's going on," and base much of their assessment of teachers and programs on frequent, brief, and informal supervisory visits. Administrators in the Stillman study reported that they only recorded these observations in writing when they asked the teachers' permission, and usually did so to formally recognize good work which might not otherwise become part of formal evaluation observations (Stillman, 1987).

The importance of informal supervision is further implied in the numerous studies which suggest that the influence of the immediate administrator is crucial for creating and maintaining exemplary school programs (Beerman, 1987; Faucette, 1984). Effective supervision for teacher and program development appears to consist of an authentic, supportive personal relationship, and the "clout," or administrative influence, necessary to provide resources. For teachers to voluntarily accept a challenge to change their professional practices, the supervisor must be able to cultivate a positive personal relationship with teachers, to devote a fair amount of time toward the instructional program (which is often difficult when the physical education administrator is also responsible for the most visible athletics programs), to set an overall tone for high quality teaching, and to be able to listen, question, give feedback, and help teachers set and achieve goals for their instructional programs.

A second common form of on-site inservice education is the district- or school-based workshop day. Again, this is usually a administration's requirement for teachers. Participants meet as school groups, though in some cases entire district staffs or small departmental and interdepartmental groups are arranged. Because teachers meet in natural groups for discussion, applying ideas to the unique context of the school is facilitated. Workshop days are usually initiated by district level administrators or school principals. Program format is usually lecture-discussion, lasting one-half to one day, and is conducted by an invited consultant or expert. The content of the inservice day ranges widely, but is usually based on a theory or model which promises school improvement if it can be learned and applied in the school setting. When follow-up activities are planned (such as focused assessment and planning, meetings, and class observations) this application, or implementation is more likely to occur.

Off-Site Inservice Education

Off-site staff development generally takes the form of graduate course work, non-credit short courses, conference days, or day-long workshops, which may or may not include follow-up, and which occur outside of the teacher's school district. Participation is usually initiated by an individual teacher (a "bottom-up" rather than "top-down" approach) who may or may not request compensation from school districts. Programs are offered by local colleges, professional associations, or state education agencies. Topics focus on specific program areas, or on supplementary teaching skills of interest to the participant (i.e., coaching clinics, computer applications, mainstreaming, or sex equity).

Off-site teacher education groups are composed of teachers from a number of school districts, and may represent several different school levels, from a wide range of public and private schools. These development activities last for a defined period of time, from one day to one academic term. Beyond the individual teacher's attempts to apply the ideas, off-site programs include little or no support or follow-up in the school setting. (Regarding activities offered by professional organizations and state and federal agencies concerned with physical education, off-site programs will be mentioned only briefly here. They will be discussed more fully in Chapters 7 and 14.)

Summary

The most important criticism of these common forms of inservice teacher development is that they are likely to have little or no impact on what teachers do in their classes. Although the literature is full of prescriptive ideas which should be incorporated by teachers in school settings, there are fewer descriptions of inservice efforts which have documented actual changes in existing practices. Howey and Vaughan (1983) identify a number of general problems which contribute to the limited impact of on-site and off-site staff and program development opportunities: 1) a lack of respect for the school and class context of the participants; 2) little continuity among inservice offerings, and virtually no follow-up to support changes teachers try out in their classrooms; 3) a perception among teachers that the program offered is to correct a deficiency rather than contribute to the normal development of a professional; and 4) a perception that the teacher is the sole person responsible for improving instruction in schools.

In physical education, Zakrajsek and Woods' (1983) survey found that teachers are disenchanted with available inservice opportunities. They are more likely to avoid "opportunities" for continuing their education than they are to seek out and get involved in developing their professionalism. Teachers who do attend often criticize inservice presentations as "too theoretical" or impractical for use in their classes.

On the whole, inservice teacher and program development appears to have limited success in breaking down the resistance to change and development which is fostered by the socialization forces existing in schools. Still, despite limited impact, school district administrations, education agencies and professional organizations continue to offer inservice education. By analyzing the successes and failures of past efforts, staff and program developers are beginning to find solutions to some of the problems of inservice education. Descriptions of programs which have reported successful results in schools contain a number of similar features. These features have become a foundation of a theory for designing and analyzing what works in inservice teacher education.

SUCCESSFUL INSERVICE TEACHER EDUCATION

Reports of successful staff and program development consistently cite the importance of the school or district's provision of time, space, equipment, materials, expertise, and funding needed to support realistic growth and change. Changing established practices requires long-term, substantial commitment from those who control school resources. But, change is fundamentally an individual endeavor. Administrators and teachers do not necessarily view staff and/or program development as a part of normal teaching duties (Schwager & Doolittle, 1988; Stillman, 1987). Some teachers feel professional commitment includes continually seeking to innovate; others do not. There is evidence to support the idea that teachers can change what they do in response to organized inservice activities, although this professional development may or may not occur.

Opportunity and motivation are two important issues to address if teachers are going to participate in an inservice or staff development program (Lanier & Little, 1986), and incorporate the suggested changes. Opportunities for teachers to develop and change must be made available by school districts through either off-site or on-site inservice programs. Motivation can be personal and intrinsic, or can be in response to incentives offered by the teacher's school or district (inservice credit, salary increments, released time).

Common Features of Successful Inservice Education

Successful inservice efforts appear to take into account the characteristics of experienced teachers in schools, and to design the inservice teacher education to work in light of these characteristics. Common features of the inservice opportunities which are repeated in available literature are the following:

- recognition of teachers as adult learners
- ownership
- collegiality
- practicality
- support from administration and school board
- change over time

Recognition of teachers as adult learners. When inservice teacher education is regarded as an opportunity for the development of professional skill or judgment, rather than a obligation to correct deficiencies, teachers tend to respond in a more positive way (Bolin, 1987, Howey, 1985; Lieberman & Miller, 1984a). Teacher development research has led the field in assisting inservice developers to recognize various developmental stages for teachers (e.g. Glickman, 1981; Zumwalt, 1986), and to undertand there are likely to be different professional needs for different teachers (Bents & Howey, 1981; McGreal, 1983).

Feiman-Nemser and Floden (1986) identified three major approaches to teacher development which have spawned inservice teacher education programs. It is suggested that if developers use procedures matched to the targeted teachers' levels of cognitive development or professional concerns, the intervention is more likely to have an effect on teachers, and presumably on teachers' programs.

Teacher development from the cognitive development approach recommends that developers provide programs that challenge teachers' cognitive capacities through an appropriate learning environment. The goal is to help teachers progress to higher stages of conceptual, ego, or moral development. The rationale is that teachers at higher stages have demonstrated more proficient teaching practices: responsiveness, flexibility, empathy, and humane and democratic decision-making (Sprinthall & Thies-Sprinthall, 1983). Recommendations for teacher development programs based on this approach include placing teachers in carefully selected, experienced-based role-taking activities, guiding careful and continuous reflection, balancing discussion, reflection and teaching with these activities, continuing programs with year-long follow-up activities, providing personal support and challenge for growth, and assessing the impact of such programs for each individual (Sprinthall & Thies-Sprinthall, 1983, pp. 28-31.). Programs incorporating various systems of reflection (e.g., keeping personal teaching journals) can be associated with a cognitive development approach to teacher development.

Teacher development programs also can be designed on the stages of concern teachers pass through as they experience imposed changes (Fieman-Nemser & Floden, 1986). Fuller (1969) first defined three stages of concern: survival, where teachers question their personal adequacy as compared to their responsibilities; mastery, where teachers focus on managing the tasks; and impact, where teachers' effects on students become the most central concern (Feiman-Nemser, 1986). Hall translated this framework into stages of teachers' concerns about school change, and designed assessments which determine the individual teacher's progress toward a goal of efficiently using the innovation as defined. In addition, appropriate interventions were suggested to help teachers move through the stages (Hord, Rutherford, Huling-Austin & Hall, 1987). This approach is most often used in staff development programs which have specifically defined goals for specific groups of teachers.

A third approach may be termed the advisory approach, and is characterized by individualized support for teachers' self-identified needs and interests (Fieman-Nemser & Floden, 1986). Consultants or developers from teacher centers and other agencies work over a period of time as assistants and resources, at the request of the teacher, and concentrate on both guiding professional growth and creating more effective educational programs for students (Apelman, 1986). The advisor's educational beliefs are made explicit at the outset, but agendas are not imposed, and formal teacher evaluations are not conducted. The advisor may perform a variety of functions (such as observing in the classroom, providing information and materials, and modeling teaching practices with students) depending on what the teacher hopes to change. Teacher centers and peer supervision/collaboration/mentoring are examples of teacher development programs which are based on the advisory approach.

Available research on teacher supervision demonstrates the extensive impact teacher development has had on that type of inservice teacher education (at least theoretically), but other types of inservice education appear to be less responsive. In the physical education literature on inservice teacher education, the teacher development approach most often applied is the concerns-based model. Faucette (1987), Knowles & Hord (1981), McBride (1986), and Schwager (1983) have conducted research that compared teachers' stages of concerns with their implementation of program changes. Recommendations from these studies include recognizing and attempting to accommodate individual differences in inservice offerings, providing activities for teachers matched to the various stages, and planning to conduct development over a sustained period of time, with frequent structured follow-up activities.

Studies based on teachers' reported needs point out the importance of planning inservice programs that match the concerns of teachers (Knowles & Hord, 1981; Schwager, 1986). McBride, et al (1986) examined experienced teachers' concerns and found that even after several years of teaching, teachers remained at the lower levels of a concerns continuum. Their concerns centered around issues of discipline and class control. The researchers also report that physical education teachers continued to need positive feedback from colleagues and supervisors, and were often unsure as to their professional status.

Researchers in physical education program development suggest that developers begin by investigating the needs of physical education programs. Helping teachers to assess their program priorities, and then addressing the needs selected for attention leads to more effective program improvement (Anderson, 1987).

To plan inservice teacher education programs that accommodate a range of cognitive levels and personal concerns requires the kind of re-thinking on the part of developers and supervisors that teachers have had to make when they individualize instruction for mixed ability classes. Inservice developers cannot assume teachers are homogeneous, nor that they will respond positively to issues important only to experts outside of the school teaching context.

Ownership. Teachers need to be involved in making decisions about the planning and implementation of inservice development programs in which they participate. Most researchers have recommended that teachers' participation should be voluntary and that teachers should have a role in deciding the aims and the process of the development effort (Anderson, 1987; Bird, 1984; Dillon-Peterson, 1981; Lieberman & Miller, 1984a; Sarason, 1982; Schwager, 1983). Locke (1984) says that the opportunity for sharing in the overall program goal is directly related to the success of that program:

if teachers do not have a major part in deciding what inservice to have (what skills to develop or problems to solve) the probability of long-term success is small. (p.51)

Collegiality. Teachers working alone can make some changes in their own classes; however, a program or school wide change requires cooperation from the people who make up that environment. But developing collegiality can be difficult. The isolation of teachers within schools is well-documented and is one of the distinctive qualities that sets teaching apart from work in other professions. Most teachers' schedules are so restrictive that finding time for planning with other teachers during the school day is extremely difficult. When this isolation is broken down through team teaching, sharing office space, frequent meetings with colleagues, or visitations to other classrooms, teachers begin to share concerns and ideas for instructional improvement. There is evidence to support the idea that collegial support and follow-up for instituting new ideas have influenced teachers to implement improvements discussed at off-site courses and workshops (Faucette, 1984; Lieberman & Miller, 1984a; Schwager & Doolittle, 1988; Wade, 1984).

Lanier & Little (1986) note that:

by teachers' reports, collegial work adds to the pool of available ideas and materials, the quality of solutions to curricula problems and teachers' own confidence in their collective and individual ability to refine their work. (p. 562)

Change is difficult for most people. The barriers against change are diminished when a group of colleagues supports the trying out of a new idea.

Practicality. If teachers are to make changes in what and how they teach, the suggestions for change made in the context of inservice development must be practical and relevant to their day-to-day work (Anderson, 1987; Goodlad, 1983; Lieberman & Miller, 1984a; Locke, 1984; Schwager, 1986). Teachers are more likely to participate on projects that can directly affect what they are able to do with their classes than activities to increase their base of abstract knowledge. Concrete, workable ideas that can be adapted to suit their unique class contexts are welcomed by experienced teachers (Locke, 1984). More abstract principles can also be of interest as long as they are grounded in practical examples (Lanier & Little, 1986; Howey, 1985).

Inservice development ideas need not be narrow and idiosyncratic, but with little time for reflection and less time for fully discussing ideas with colleagues, it is not surprising that teachers are most interested in teaching tips that can be easily adapted to their own situations and which make their day-to-day work seem easier and more satisfying.

Knowles and Hord (1981), McBride, Bogess and Griffey (1986), Oliver (1987), Schwager and Doolittle (1988) and others have investigated the specific interests physical education teachers have for inservice development work. These studies are nearly all in agreement that teachers would like inservice workshops to address the following practical issues: discipline and class management techniques, motivational ideas, strategies for co-ed and mixed ability classes, new teaching strategies and activities, and program planning.

What makes ideas practical is a respect for the daily realities of working teachers. Making sure teachers' concerns are considered is a first step. When inservice starts where the teachers are, rather than where the developers are (Lieberman & Miller, 1984b), teachers seem to find the ideas more worthwhile.

Administrative support. The allocation of school system resources such as teacher time and responsibilities, facility scheduling, equipment, materials, and funding, are crucial to making teacher and program development feasible. If teachers are to consider continued learning and instructional innovation as part of their jobs, teachers need not only the financial support of release time in an otherwise overcrowded teaching year, but the expectation of quality teaching and innovation from their administrators. Superintendents' workshop days are only one way to demonstrate the school district support of continuing professional development. Because long term projects seem to have a greater impact on programs than one day workshops, arranging working time outside of the classroom can represent an administration's commitment to teacher development and program improvement. Without this long-term time support, reflection and discussion with colleagues, consultation with specialists, and experimentation with new ideas and materials are not realistic (Lieberman & Miller, 1984b).

In particular, the principal or direct supervisor seems to be the most important gatekeeper for meaningful program and teacher development (Goodlad, 1983; Lieberman & Miller, 1984a; Sarason, 1982). Several follow-up studies of inservice programs have indicated the principal as a primary factor for the success of the implementation of an innovation (Faucette & Graham, 1986; Ratliffe, 1985). In physical education, the department head, director of physical education, or the athletics director appears to be the administrator with the greatest influence over the success or failure of staff and program development (Anderson, 1982; Beerman, 1987; Schwager, 1983; Stillman, 1987). Ironically, the principal and athletic director also are responsible for many immediate and demanding details in conducting the daily affairs of a school or large athletic program. Teacher and program development often stay on the back burner.

Teacher and program development tend to be low priority issues unless the administrator makes deliberate efforts to allot time and energy to those ends. Faucette's (1984) in-depth study of the impact of inservice programs on two elementary teachers vividly illustrates the teachers' attribution that their principal is required for the implementation of inservice education. Beerman's (1987) study of outstanding high school physical education programs repeatedly cites the physical education department head and the high school administration as enabling factors for outstanding physical education programs.

Change over time. Implementing changes in teaching and programs requires adequate periods of time. One-day workshops provide ideas, but adapting those ideas requires reflection, planning, and experimentation. When teachers are expected to spend most of their day in classes with students, they also cannot be expected to plan for and incorporate new and unfamiliar procedures.

Administrators demonstrate their commitment to development when they arrange released time or extra pay for this professional work. While the research suggests that monetary rewards are not associated with successful inservice development (Locke, 1984; Wade, 1984), compensated, professional time for thinking, planning, monitoring and discussing is essential.

In successful inservice efforts, the timing of project tasks is arranged with insight into how much extra work teachers can assume in addition to their normal duties. The natural rhythms of the school day, terms, and year are taken into account. Almond (1985) suggests that there are two fruitful periods in the school year when physical education teachers can devote some time to thinking and trying out instructional ideas in their classes: the first falls just after the start of the school year; the second is in late winter, before the rush at the end of the school year.

The rhythm of the coaching seasons also can be considered when planning inservice activities for physical education teachers (Earls, 1981). If teachers are coaching after-school activities, planning changes for the instructional program often take on a lower priority. Because physical education teachers are more likely to be influenced by shared facilities and extracurricular activities than their classroom colleagues, inservice developers need to become cognizant of the seasonal constraints which have an impact on the teaching environment. Planning the development process with teachers and administrators facilitates the timing of a project within the limitations of normal school work.

Summary

These features of successful inservice teacher education are difficult to implement on a continuing basis. Simply allotting the time necessary for teachers to meet and plan changes is not practical for most school districts. Teachers are expected to spend their time teaching children, not improving their skills or school programs.

Since schools have not often managed to provide successful inservice, local colleges and universities have engaged themselves in inservice teacher and program development. Because the universities have recognized the problems with more traditional inservice forms, and because they stand to gain indirect benefits from working with teachers, university-school collaboration is an increasingly recurring form of inservice teacher education, which appears to make a difference to teachers and their programs.

In addition to the traditional roles universities play in teacher education, providing pre-service teacher education, graduate course work for teachers, and private consultation with individual schools or districts, some universities have initiated partnerships with local schools. These partnerships may be an alternative approach to teacher and program development that take into account the realities of teachers' work in schools. They illustrate one way to incorporate the features of successful inservice teacher education previously detailed.

TWO MODEL INSERVICE PROGRAMS: UNIVERSITY-SCHOOL COLLABORATION

There are advantages of school-university collaboration for teachers and for the university. School teachers have the sense that long-term relationships can develop, allowing for follow-up to conferences and continued support for changes. The university can become a hub for interested teachers in various districts, creating an "invisible college" of practitioners interested in innovation in their teaching. The university connection is also valued since it is more likely to separate program and staff development from administrative evaluation of teachers and other political issues within the school district.

The university can locate teachers and programs with various strengths; and, since universities need to place students in quality programs and graduate students need to conduct research with teachers or in schools, field-based access is facilitated. Over a sustained period of time, the university can understand the politics of individual school districts, and recognize feasible goals and processes which may be implemented. Personal relationships between teachers and professors can become the basis for trying out ideas. Providing financial support for local teachers and school administrators who are interested in staff and program development can be viewed by the university as important and relevant community and professional service.

Disadvantages from the school's point of view are that the local college may be too familiar a neighbor, and ideas and programs initiated by the university may be seen as intrusive. Schools also recognize that for any service the university provides to local schools, reciprocal service can be expected for university programs. Schools may be expected to accommodate field-based studies and pre-service student teachers. Disadvantages from the university's viewpoint include the responsibility for maintaining contact and familiarity with local school issues as well as sound educational ideas. Furthermore, it is the university's responsibility to establish constructive working relationships with school administrators and teachers. They must be able to translate theory into practical programs suitable for the school contexts. Finally, universities do not normally recognize school service as important to tenure and promotion of professors. Substituting school service for research may not be regarded by the university as worthwhile professional activity.

Nevertheless, school-university collaboration should be considered a more effective approach toward the improvement of instruction in schools. Two examples of such partnerships in physical education demonstrate how the features of successful teacher and program development have been implemented to increase the impact of inservice teacher and program development in schools. What makes these inservice approaches different is their sensitivity to the constraints of the school settings, and to the practical expertise of teachers.

Second Wind

This is a four-year-old university-based staff development/inservice program that services physical educators in Massachusetts schools. The major source of financial support is the state university: one full time faculty member and several graduate assistants are assigned to run the inservice programs. Revenues also are accumulated from federal and state staff development grants, and staff development honoraria from school districts.

Second Wind has articulated five goals which guide its work:

1. to institutionalize work with physical educators in the schools as an integral part of departmental responsibilities at the University of Massachusetts;
2. to facilitate communication and professional development among physical educators at all levels (K-college);
3. to assist the continuing evaluation and development of school physical education programs;
4. to provide the means for teachers to improve and expand their instructional skills;
5. to create an opportunity for college physical education teacher educators to ground their work with pre- and inservice teachers in the realities of life in schools. (Griffin & Hutchinson, 1988).

The staff members of Second Wind work with individual teachers, a physical education staff in a single school, or an entire district's physical education teachers on projects of interest to the teachers. They also facilitate networking among teachers across school districts by organizing programs designed for physical education teachers at specific levels (elementary, junior high school, high school), and encourage teachers to visit each other's schools. Second Wind maintains communication with school administrators by notifying them of planned development activities and of their teachers' participation.

Griffin & Hutchinson (1988) describe the varied programs conducted by Second Wind that have focused on teacher-identified needs. For example, they have assisted in teachers' implementation of entire new curriculums, health related fitness units, adventure activities, and educational gymnastics units. They comment that Second Wind has had a positive impact not only on the schools with which they have worked, but the university programs as well. "Our public school colleagues, with their insistence on practicality, keep us in touch with the realities of schools" (p. 189).

Second Wind illustrates one way to implement programs which respect teachers as adults capable of developing new professional practices. The Second Wind staff conducts projects based on several theories of teacher development, but each project includes teacher ownership, collegiality, practical ideas, productive relationships with school administrators, and a respect for the time it takes to create changes in school settings.

The Physical Education Program Development Center

Since 1979, physical education teachers and directors from six school districts in New York state have collaborated with Teachers College, Columbia University on school-based program development. Housed in one of the districts, the Center's purpose is to promote on-going program and staff development in the participating districts. The university provides released time for a faculty member, and funding for graduate assistants to conduct workshops and other activities. The school districts contribute annual dues and provide release time for teachers to attend workshops.

The Center staff facilitates school district efforts to improve teaching and existing programs in a variety of ways:

1. encouraging each district to assess current programs, and establish priorities for change;
2. conducting periodic workshops that focus on topics identified by teachers and physical education directors; and
3. visiting teachers in their schools to monitor progress and to offer suggestions for program changes. (Anderson, 1987)

Anderson (1988) lists several projects recently conducted which were designed to meet the specific needs of the participating teachers. For example, projects have focused on fitness programming, elective programming and management, curriculum writing and revision, competency based program segments, adaptive programs, and alternative elementary activities and management techniques.

Anderson notes that this school-centered partnership has been effective to some extent in promoting on-going program and staff development in the schools. In addition, the graduate students who serve as facilitators for projects are able to conduct descriptive studies about program and staff development.

Again, this staff and program development effort utilizes teacher development approaches to creating change in member school programs. The Center is based on the features of long-term relationships with teachers, administrators, and university specialists working collegially on teacher-owned, practical problems and interests. The success of this collaboration may be directly attributed to a respect for the nature of teaching in schools, and the difficulty of promoting change within schools.

SUMMARY

Socialization can have both positive and negative effects on producing and maintaining quality programs and teaching in physical education. Teacher educators are not recognizing the impact of socialization on how teachers work in schools, and why innovations often fail. Inservice teacher education programs are now being re-designed to work constructively within the constraints of school realities. We have offered two examples of how teacher educators can work with teachers and administrators to provide opportunities to revitalize their programs and refine their teaching skills. Although these partnerships are difficult to initiate, collaboration between physical educators in schools and universities can be mutually beneficial.

REFERENCES

Almond, L. (1985). Principles of a 12-month inservice course. Unpublished conference paper. AIESEP. Garden City, New York.

Anderson, W. G. (1982). Working with inservice teachers: Suggestions for teacher educators. *Journal of Teaching Physical Education, 1*(3), 15-21.

Anderson, W. G. (1987). Five years of program development: A retrospective. G. Barrett, R. Feingold & C. Rees (Eds.) *Myths, Models and Methods in Sports Pedagogy.* Champaign, IL: Human Kinetics.

Anderson, W. G. (1988). A school-centered collaborative model for program development. *Journal of Teaching Physical Education, 7*(3), 176-183.

Apelman, M. (1986). Working with teachers: The advisory approach. In K.K. Zumwalt (Ed.) *Improving Teaching.* Alexandria, VA: ASCD.

Beerman, M. (1987). Outstanding characteristics of high physical education. Unpublished doctoral dissertation. Teachers College, Columbia University.

Bents, R. H. & Howey, K. R. (1981). Staff development: Change in the individual. In B. Dillon-Peterson (Ed.) *Staff Development/Organization Development.* Alexandria, VA: ASCD.

Bird, T. (1984). Mutual adaptation and mutual accomplishment: Images of change in a field experiment. *Teachers College Record, 86*(1).

Bolin, F. S. (1987). Reassessment & Renewal in Teaching. In F. S. Bolin & J. M. Falk (eds.) *Teacher Renewal: Professional Issues, Personal Choices.* New York. Teachers College Press.

Dillon-Peterson, B. (1981). Staff development/organization development: Perspective 1981. In B. Dillon-Peterson (Ed.) *Staff Development/Organization Development.* Alexandria, VA: ASCD.

Earls, N. F. (1981). Distinctive teachers' personal qualities, perceptions of teacher education, and the realities of teaching. *Journal of Teaching Physical Education 1*(1), 59-71.

Faucette, N. (1984). Implementing innovations: A qualitative analysis of the impact of an inservice program on the curricula and teaching of two elementary physical education teachers. Unpublished doctoral dissertation. University of Georgia.

Faucette, N. (1987). Teachers Concerns and Participation Styles During Inservice Education. *Journal of Teaching in Physical Education 6*, 425-440.

Faucette, N. & Graham, G. (1986). The impact of principals on teachers during inservice education: A qualitative analysis. *Journal of Teaching Physical Education 5*, 79-90.

Feiman-Nemser, S. & Floden, R. E. (1986). The cultures of teaching. In M. C. Wittrock (Ed.) *Handbook of Research On Teaching.* New York: Macmillan.

Fuller, F. F. (1969). Concerns of teachers: A developmental characterization. *American Educational Research Journal, 6*, 207-226.

Glickman, C. D. (1981). *Developmental Supervision.* Alexandria, VA: ASCD.

Goodlad, J. I. (1983). *A Place Called School.* New York: McGraw Hill.

Griffin, P. & Hutchinson, G. (1988). Second Wind: A physical education program development network. *Journal of Teaching Physical Education 7*(3), 184-189.

Hord, S. M., Rutherford, W. L., Huling-Austin, L. & Hall, G. E. (1987). *Taking Charge of Change*. Alexandria, VA: ASCD.

Howey, K. R. (1985). Six major functions of staff development: an expanded imperative. *Journal of Teacher Education*, Jan-Feb.

Howey, K. R. & Vaughan, J. C. (1983). Current patterns of staff development. In G. A. Griffin (Ed.) *Staff Development*. Chicago: NSSE.

Knowles, C. J. & Hord, S. M. (1981). The concerns based adoption model: tools for planning, personalizing and evaluating a staff development program. *Journal of Teaching Physical Education 1*(1) 24-37.

Lanier, J. E. & Little, J. W. (1986). Research on teacher education. In M. Wittrock (Ed.) *Handbook of Research on Teaching*. New York: MacMillan.

Lieberman A. & Miller, L. (1984a). School improvement: Themes and variations. *Teachers College Record. 86*, 4-19.

Lieberman, A. & Miller, L. (1984b). *Teachers, Their World and Their Work: Implications for School Improvement*. Washington, D. C.: ASCD.

Locke, L. F. (1984). Research on teaching teachers: Where are we now? *Journal of Teaching Physical Education*, Monograph 2.

McBride, R. E., Bogess, T. E. & Griffey, D. C. (1986). The concerns of inservice physical education teachers as compared with Fuller's concerns model. *Journal of Teaching Physical Education 5*, 149-156.

McGreal, T. L. (1983). *Successful Teacher Evaluation*. Alexandria, VA: ASCD.

Oliver, B. (1987). Teacher and school characteristics: Their relationship to the inservice needs of teachers. *Journal of Teaching Physical Education 7*, 38-45.

Ratliffe, T. (1985). The influence of school principals on management time and student activity time for two elementary physical education teachers. *Journal of Teaching Physical Education 5*, 117-125.

Sarason, S. B. (1982). *The Culture of the School and the Problem of Change*. Boston: Allyn & Bacon.

Schwager, S. M. (1983). The planning, implementation and analysis of a program development project in elementary physical education. Unpublished doctoral dissertation. Teachers College, Columbia University.

Schwager, S. M. (1986). On-going program development: Teachers as collaborators. *Journal of Teaching Physical Education 5*, 272-279.

Schwager, S. M. & Doolittle, S. A. (1988). Teachers' reactions to activities in ongoing program development. *Journal of Teaching Physical Education 7*, 240-247.

Sergiovanni, T. J. (1982). Toward a theory of supervisory practice: Integrating scientific, clinical and artistic views. T. J. Sergiovanni (Ed.) *Supervision of Teaching*. Alexandria, Va: ASCD.

Stillman, A. (1987). Staff development practices of district wide physical education administrators. Unpublished doctoral dissertation. Teachers College, Columbia University.

Sprinthall, N. A. & Thies-Sprinthall, L. (1983). The teacher as an adult learner. In G. A. Griffin (Ed.) *Staff Development*. Chicago: University of Chicago Press.

Wade, R. K. (1984). What makes a difference in inservice teacher education: A meta-analysis of the research. Unpublished doctoral dissertation. University of Masschusetts.

Zakrajsek, D. & Woods, J. L. (1983). A survey of professional practices: Elementary and secondary physical educators. *Journal of Physical Education, Recreation and Dance*, 54(9): 65-67.

Zumwalt, K. K. (1986). Working together to improve teaching. In K. K. Zumwalt (Ed.). *Improving Teaching*. Alexandria, VA: ASCD.

7

The Influence of Professional Organizations on Teacher Development

MARIAN E. KNEER
University of Illinois at Chicago

A learned profession is a body, or collection of persons, engaged in an occupation requiring extensive education in a branch of science or liberal education. Members of a learned profession are called professionals. Teachers are professionals. Members of a learned profession often form organizations to promote their collective interests, such as welfare issues relating to salaries and benefits, teaching policies and practices, and social and ideological issues. Members use political action, collective bargaining and various communication modes to share knowledge and skills to promote their goals. Organizations more concerned about collective bargaining usually are called unions; those more concerned with promoting and improving service are called professional organizations.

The primary goal of a professional organization is to promote and improve its service and the conditions surrounding the conduct of that professional practice. Normally, professional organizations are called associations, and the largest usually are organized on a national, regional, and/or statewide basis. Members pay dues to support their association and elect members as officers to develop the policies and procedures to conduct their business. Leonard (1980) states:

> The word association is a synonym for formal organization. We use the former term instead of the latter to minimize confusion with the sociological concept of "social organization." This latter term is much broader than what we wish to convey. . . . An association is a special purpose group which is deliberately constructed to seek specific objectives, goals and values . . . (p. 42)

Teachers' interests are served by two major types of professional organizations: process oriented and content oriented. Process oriented teacher organizations are primarily interested in purposes and goals relating to the conditions of teaching. The American Federation of Teachers (AFT) and the National Education Association (NEA) are process oriented professional teacher organizations open to membership to all teachers regardless of subject and/or level specialization. Content oriented organizations are primarily interested in purposes and goals which relate to teachers of a specific subject. The American Alliance for Physical Education, Health, Recreation and Dance (AAHPERD) is an example of a content oriented organization.

There are many professional associations that serve physical education. These associations range from very small to very large, and serve single interests, such as the North American Society for Sport History, to those of many interests such as the AAHPERD. The AAHPERD has over 34,000 members and is the largest professional organization in the United States serving the interests of physical education teachers. It serves many interests through an alliance of five Associations concerned with dance, health, leisure, sport for girls and women, sport and physical education, and research and administration in all areas. The Alliance is organized on a national and district basis. Each state has its own independent association which has close symbiotic ties with the Alliance. For example, the Canadian Association for Health, Physical Education and Recreation (CAHPER) serves the professional members in Canada.

In addition, there are professional organizations for physical education professionals in higher education; sub-disciplinary research associations for exercise physiology, sport psychology, sport sociology, biomechanics, sport history, sport philosophy and motor learning and control; and physical education fraternity related associations. Sub-disciplinary associations are mainly interested in the sharing of research through meetings and the publications of their own journal. Also, there are sport associations designed to improve the coaching of sports. Many of these also are organized on a national, regional, and/or statewide basis. Indeed, Morford (1972) stated:

Any professional organization not capable of developing its own knowledge, effectively monitoring and evaluating social change in light of its knowledge is doomed to failure since it will be unable to provide for society's demands. (p. 92)

One of the major problems of teacher organizations in the United States is that policies and practices are locally determined and essentially state controlled. Therefore, there is a need for state professional organizations to focus on these provincial-type problems. National organizations serve an important role in setting a professional consensus to guide the direction of local practice and to help in the solution of state problems which may affect teaching conditions. However, membership in a national organization does not always require membership in the state association. Consequently, communication and a focused effort is often difficult to achieve.

Currently, the AAHPERD and the physical education state associations are separate organizations. Approximately half the AAHPERD membership also belong to the state physical education association. Most state physical education associations are concerned about sharing of information and skills through conventions and publications. Several of the larger states are very active in the political arena to gain state support for mandating sufficient instructional time for physical education in the state's schools and for gaining physical education supervisory staff in their state office of publication instruction. Illinois, for example, is one of the largest state physical education associations in the United States. It has been successful in gaining and maintaining the only daily physical education mandate to local school districts.

Professional organizations serve as an important socializing agency for both pre-service and in-service physical educators. This socializing capacity is gained through the dynamic interaction of the organization's membership within its structure and function (Leonard, 1980). The strength of the socialization process is related to the quality and quantity of the membership, the success of its projects and the seriousness of the problems besetting the profession.

Members utilize their professional organizations in three different ways. One type of member is very active in the sense that he or she attends conventions, reads the organization's publications, and may even serve the organization on committees and in positions of leadership. A second type of member belongs to the professional organizations but rarely serves the organization, seldom attends conventions, and does not generally read the publications. Metzler and Freedman (1985) reported that only about a third of the physical education teacher educators were active in the AAHPERD, and about half were active in their state associations. Table 7-1 identifies the involvement of physical education teacher educators in professional organizations. Kneer (1986) reported that less than one fifth of the secondary teachers in Illinois belonged to the state association and/or read its professional literature. She reported that the reasons given for not attending workshops and/or conventions were failure to receive support from their employer, conflicts in duties, and other personal problems. A third type of member is usually very inconsistent in their use of professional services. Seiter (1984) states that one-third of the AAHPERD members drop out annually and are replaced by members who are new or who are renewing their membership. A review of records shows a relationship of new memberships to the geographic area in which a convention is held. Since membership in the sponsoring organization of a convention is required, new members are attracted because of their propinquity to the meetings. These members often drop their membership the next year. Another factor is the failure of some members to renew their membership. Apparently, theirs is not a strong commitment to the professional organization.

Special effort is made by most professional physical education associations to attract and serve the interests of the pre-service teacher. These attraction efforts include giving representation to student members on governing bodies, special student programs at conventions, and student columns in publications. Reduced membership and conference fees are given to student members in order to encourage early interest and entry into professional organizational life. In 1984, 8 percent of the AAHPERD members were students (Seiter, 1984).

The services of professional organizations given to teachers is both direct and indirect. Direct service is accorded to those who are members

TABLE 7-1. *Involvement in Professional Organizations* (Percent of Sample)*

	Very Active	Somewhat Active	Little Active	Not Active	% PETE Members
AAHPERD	9.4	25.1	45.0	11.5	91.2
State/Local AAHPERD	32.7	25.1	19.3	5.8	83.0
Other P.E. & Sport	4.7	9.4	23.4	6.4	43.9
Coaching Associations	8.8	4.7	11.1	1.7	26.3
District AAHPER	5.3	5.8	5.8	2.3	19.3

*Metzler, M. & Freedman, M. (1985). Here's looking at you PETE: a profile of physical education teacher education faculty. *Journal of Teaching Physical Education*, 4 (2), 128.

to the professional organization. These services are manifested to members through: (1) social facilitation encouraged by members serving as a form of reference groups, who share ideas and research and provide a form of group identification; (2) pressure to gain uniformity and standards fostered through communication; (3) power which is dependent upon the quality and quantity of members; (4) leadership by elected and employed representatives; and (5) motivational trusts which are based upon group aspirations and the extent to which members cooperate or compete. Indirect service is accorded to those who are not members but whose professional lives are influenced by professional organizations in terms of the power and pressure exerted through standards, legislative activity, and communication.

This chapter will explore these socialization services, their relative impact on the pre-service and the in-service physical educator, the problems that affect the effectiveness of the organization to influence professional behavior, and a projection for the future role of professional association influence on professional development.

DIRECT SERVICES

Social Facilitation

Most associations provide, as a minimum, an annual conference or convention and one or more journal. These activities are designed to socially facilitate the professional members' ability to expertly perform their teaching tasks. They are carried out by members who share ideas, strategies, and research which have improved, or hold promise for improving, the learning and practice of physical education. Clearly, the intent is to gain conformity to acceptable practice, to reinforce conforming behavior, or to replace nonconforming behavior with universal and normative behaviors and values. In addition, special conferences and workshops are offered on a regional basis to bring information closer to the aspiring or practicing professional. Other services frequently provided are commercial exhibitions of the latest textbooks, uniforms, equipment, and educational agencies. The internalization of the information given through the spoken and written word is dependent upon the degree to which the members can perceive value and/or the feasibility to use this information in their present or future practice. Studies by Kneer (1986), Kelley and Lindsay (1980), Placek (1987), and Safrit and Wood (1986) show that this internalization effect is not very widespread. Their work shows that on the average, less than 25% of the profession know about or use innovative ideas. These findings no doubt support the notion that teachers are mainly interested in solutions to their perceived unique problems. However, these studies included both members and non-members of a professional physical education association. Since the vast majority of the profession are not members, the results may be misleading as to the influence of the organization.

Periodicals and books often are published by professional organizations. The AAHPERD publishes the *Journal for Physical Education, Recreation and Dance, Strategies,* and the *Research Quarterly for Exercise and Sport.* The first two publications feature articles practical in nature, which can be readily applied to practice. The latter reports research that has been conducted in the sub-disciplinary areas. It is through reading the newsletters and journals that physical educators and coaches can stay abreast of improved ideas for practice. The AAHPERD publishes a wide variety of books on specialized topics ranging from youth sports to physical activity and human well being. Metzler and Freedman (1985) studied the extend to which physical education teacher educators (PETE) subscribed to Journals that were pertinent to their area of study. They found that 85% received the *Journal for Physical Education, Recreation and Dance* and that 47% received the *Research Quarterly for Exercise and Sport.* Table 7-2 identifies the subscription data relative to journals most often taken by PETE faculty.

TABLE 7-2. *Journals Most Often Taken by PETE Faculty*

	Percent
Journal of Physical Education, Recreation and Dance	85.0
Research Quarterly for Exercise and Sport	47.4
Journal of Teaching Physical Education	18.1
State AAHPERD	18.1
Kappan	15.8
Physical Educator	15.2
Health Education	15.2
Quest	14.0
Physician and Sportsmedicine	9.3
Athletic Journal	4.0

*Metzler, M. & Freedman, M. (1985). Here's looking at you PETE: a profile of physical education teacher education faculty. *Journal of Teaching Physical Education,* 4 (2), 128.

Social Pressure

Social pressure is an attempt by an individual or group to gain acceptance of a value, belief, and/or practice by implicitly or explicitly threatening the non-conformist with the notion that they are out of step or practicing unacceptable behavior. Since social theory has confirmed that most human beings wish to be in conformity with societal values and practices, the setting of standards and guidelines for practice become powerful tools. Therefore, one of the functions of a professional organization is to set standards, guidelines, and/or to write position papers to give direction as well as to evaluate quality practice. This function is expected to exert pressure on members, nonmembers, the employer, and the public to conform to acceptable procedures in the conduct of physical education and sports. Standards, guidelines, and/or position papers have been written, for example, on professional preparation of physical educators and coaches; elementary, middle and secondary school physical education; grades and eligibility for athletics; and drug education.

Pressure to conform is exerted not merely by developing and publishing these documents, but by widely disseminating them to schools, colleges, governmental agencies, and other educational groups. One project of the AAHPERD, Physical Education Public Information (PEPI), has survived for almost two decades carrying out its mission to bring to public attention the standards and values relative to physical education. The National Association for Sport and Physical Education (NASPE), a member of the AAHPERD, developed guidelines for elementary, middle and secondary school physical education and has cooperated with the National Creditation Association for Teacher Educators (NCATE) to develop evaluative criteria and plans to administer the evaluation of physical education professional preparation program. NASPE has representation on the National Study of School Evaluation team to develop criteria for secondary school physical education and athletic programs. Through these efforts, NASPE is exerting pressure to control the quality of the professional preparation program for pre-service physical educators and the programs conducted by the in-service physical educator. No study has been conducted which can give evidence to the effectiveness of these efforts. However, it is a commonly held belief that physical education programs in the United States do not generally conform to the expected quality standards.

Power

Power is the influence a professional organization's members can exert by joining together. The strength of that influence depends partly upon the attractiveness of the group, partly upon its communication ability, and partly upon the acceptance of the purpose. Power is crucial to increase pressure to conform to the standards set by the organization and to embrace the value of the practice. Often the larger the organization, the more powerful it is or is perceived to be. However, the prestige of the members of a professional organization often can overcome the power exerted by the size of the group. For example, membership in the American Academy for Physical Education is limited and exclusively formed. Although this group seldom ventures into the political arena, their support on an issue would carry considerable power within the profession. For example, during the struggle to determine the appropriate content for physical fitness test batteries, they passed a resolution which strongly supported health-related physical fitness testing. This resolution was widely disseminated and was used as compelling evidence to persuade the AAHPERD to promote a new thrust in fitness testing called *Physical Best* which promotes health-related fitness testing. Nevertheless, the Academy and AAHPERD have small memberships in comparison to the number of teachers who are not members of either group. Consequently, it is no surprise that Safrit and Wood (1986) found that there is limited knowledge and use of health-related physical fitness tests. Obviously, a more inclusive representation of teachers as members may serve to improve communication. On the other hand, organizational power is diminished because the association is evidently not sufficiently attractive to most physical educators to become members of it.

The direction of the power function of a professional organization is often toward significant others. These significant others in education are the public, related educational organizations, school officials, and legislators. One type of power function is to develop and distribute information which identifies the benefits of physical education and the quality controls needed to significant other groups. This information is delivered through articles prepared by members for publication in media accessed by these significant others, speeches at their meetings, and by direct and indirect contact with them. An excellent example of a project designed to influence policy is the AAHPERD "Fit to Achieve" program. The purpose of this program was to gain quality daily physical education programs in the United States. A public relations agency was employed to draw up the plans which included massive media involvement, a celebrity as a national chairperson, printed and videotaped information, a local involvement plan, and a legislative program. The budget for the "Fit to Achieve" program was estimated to be over two million dollars. The program would take several years to accomplish.

The rise of state and national "Legislator Fitness Days" is another attempt to gain power. These events are designed to increase awareness of the need for physical education and ultimately to gain support by legislators. The AAHPERD has a director of public/legislative affairs with sufficient staff support. This office works at the national legislative level and with the state physical education organizations Public/Legislative Affairs Committees. The AAHPERD was successful in 1987 in obtaining a Congressional Resolution endorsing physical education as part of the educational process in U.S. schools. Many state organizations employ lobbyists to work politically for appropriate support for physical education in their schools. The Illinois Association for Health, Physical Education, Recreation and Dance (IAHPERD) publishes a bi-monthly public relations newsletter entitled, *Governmental Action News*. They will use, no doubt, the Congressional Resolution to influence legislative support for governmental matters which affect physical education.

Another manifestation of power is the opportunity that professional organizations are given to be represented on relevant committees of other agencies and/or organizations. NASPE has representation on several Olympic and other international competitive sport organizations. The AAHERD has a working relationship with the President's Council for Physical Fitness and Sport (PCPFS) and most state associations have similar relationships with the Governors' Council on Sport and Physical Fitness and/or their state education agency. The AAHPERD tried unsuccessfully to influence the PCPFS to support the exclusive use of health-related fitness tests as a basis for their award program. Much of this failure may be attributed to the lack of support and knowledge about health-related fitness testing as reported by Safrit and Wood (1986). NASPE and the National Association for Girls' and Women's Sports (NAGWS) have representation on various rules committees for selected sports. These power functions vary in their effectiveness in changing and/or influencing professional development.

Summary: Power is necessary to effect support for organizational goals. Professional physical education organizations in the United States have developed mechanisms to exert power to provide for and to improve physical education in the nation's schools. The success of these efforts has been minimal because of the organization's failure to attract the majority of physical educators as members in order to gain support for their goals and to communicate with them.

Leadership

Leadership influences the professional lives of the members of the organization, as well as the leaders. The quality of the leadership given to the professional organization is critical to the attainment of its goals. All professional organizations depend upon the volunteer help of its members to perform policymaking decisions and often to carry out programs. The larger organizations will employ staff to carry out many of the approved functions and programs. The AAHPERD maintains a large headquarters in Reston, Virginia and is staffed by over 50 employees. The employees are assigned clerical, fundraising, membership, publication, public relations, legislative, and archival duties.

Staff financial support for the operation of a professional organization is gained through membership dues, publication and advertising sales, grants, and fundraising events such as the "Jump Rope for Heart" project. Most state associations employee an executive director and/or business manager. Fundraising projects often are conducted in cooperation with related organizations who share many of the same goals. For example, the "Jump Rope for Heart" project is a fundraising event sponsored by the American Heart Association. School children agree to jump rope for a specified period of time in return for financial donations. This project nets funds for both organizations and encourages an aerobic activity for children.

There are two major kinds of professional leaders. One is the professional member who volunteers time to serve as an elected officer or committee member to help develop policy and/or to carry out the organization's work. These leaders are either elected or appointed. The second type member may or may not serve in a capacity to develop the organization's policies or to carry out its projects but whose scholarly papers, either written or spoken, serve to give direction to professional practice.

The leadership given by professional members either through service or through scholarly activity influences not only the profession, but also the leader's professional life because of the personal prestige gained from assuming the leadership role. This prestige results from the visibility and/or quality of the leadership. It places the leader on a higher social/professional level in a form of influence stratification. Professional upward mobility is frequently an outcome. This is especially true for physical educators who are employed in colleges and universities where such activity is highly valued. Leadership activity gives visibility to the employing educational institution and serves to verify professional dedication and often professional competence. Teachers who work under merit pay conditions frequently will receive salary increases based upon the quality and quantity of their work as well as support for professional rank promotion.

The quality of the leadership will directly influence the organization's goals and the attainment of them. In the mid-1960s, the leadership of Sara Jernigan, Katherine Ley, and Phoebe Scott, all presidents of the AAHPER's Division of Girls' and Women's Sports (DGWS), were primarily responsible for helping girls and women to attain increased competitive sport opportunities. I, as a past president of NASPE, was able to develop policies which focused the organization on efforts to gain support for quality daily physical education programs in the United States. Projects developed were support for a Curriculum and Instruction Resource Center with the University of Georgia, plans to identify legitimate outcomes in elementary and secondary schools, and programs aimed at gaining public support. The extent that these projects will be successfully completed will depend upon continued leadership support until the goal is attained.

Motivation

The ability of the professional organization to motivate its members to strive for quality practice depends upon the member's perception of the value of the innovation or his or her belief that the recommended procedures are possible, given their educational setting. Unfortunately, I believe, that since less than one fourth of all physical educators belong to a professional physical education organization, the commitment to improve professional performance is not high (Kneer, 1986). Non-members frequently want to know "what do I get for my dues." There is some evidence that teachers become more interested in the work of a professional organization when it is working on their personal survival goals such as mandating programs because it insures jobs, salary, and working conditions (Lortie, 1973). Several years ago, Illinois doubled membership dues to obtain money to employ a lobbyist to help maintain the current grade 1-12 daily physical education mandate. This was accomplished with no loss in membership. However, most physical educators' salary and working conditions problems are addressed by the local teachers' association which is affiliated either with the NEA or the AFT.

Professional organizations try to motivate their members to conform to quality controlling guidelines by offering recognition programs, publications, and convention programs. NASPE has programs designed to recognize the outstanding physical education major in each college and university, elementary and secondary teacher of the year, coach of the year, and athletic director of the year. Scholarship is recognized through "Scholar of the Year" programs. These programs are carried out on state and regional bases. Although there is no evidence these recognition awards motivate teachers to improve their teaching and coaching, members appreciate the awards. The AAHPERD publishes books and journals conveying ideas and current research which have the possibility of motivating improved practice. Conventions, workshops, and special topic conferences are held annually on a national, regional, and state basis to motivate effective practice. NASPE supports three substructures for physical educators: Council on Physical Education for Children, Middle and Secondary School Physical Education Council, and the College and University Physical Education Council. These structures serve to gather and distribute information that will improve professional practice. All too often, as stated by Cross (1987, p.499) what teachers want to know is "what works in my setting and with my kids."

Leaders are rewarded by the visibility of their work and office. In addition, most professional organizations have honor and/or service award programs for recognizing service and other professional contributions. Leadership is further rewarded through the hierarchial organization of the various association. For example, a successful leader in a state association often is selected to serve in regional and national organizations with similar goals.

Summary: Professional organizations strive to motivate both members and non-members to support and utilize practices which have potential for improving the quality of physical education programs by rewarding quality programs and physical educators and by sharing information.

INDIRECT SERVICES

Indirect service is accorded to those who are not members but whose professional lives are influenced directly by professional organizations in terms of the power and pressure exerted through standards, legislative activity, and communication. The amount of influence these services exert will vary depending upon the perceived needs of the non-members, their knowledge of the association's work, or the amount of external pressure exerted. Seiter (1984) reports that only 8% of the pre-service teachers belong to the AAHPERD. They most often are influenced in terms of the readings assigned to them in the professional literature, the quality of the professional program, available jobs, expectations, and standards for pre-service performance. Their non-membership is curious since Metzler and Freedman (1985) found that 91% of the physical education teacher educators were members of the AAHPERD. The in-service teacher will be directly affected when a professional organization effects legislation which will influence programs and practice. For example, the Illinois State Board of Education (ISBE) adopted goals and objectives for physical education which were developed by the IAHPERD with ISBE support. These goals and objectives will affect all physical educators in Illinois regardless of their membership status. The "Fit to Achieve" program explained earlier is designed to encourage parents and school officials to exert pressure to adopt policies that will give rise to quality daily physical education.

Another indirect service is the availability of the publications of professional organizations through libraries and by direct purchase of books, pamphlets, and guidelines from the AAHPERD or similar organizations. Workshops, conferences, and conventions are open to non-members. In some instances, they must join the sponsoring organization, or pay an additional fee, to attend. This practice is one method employed by professional associations to encourage membership. Professional organizations constantly attempt to recruit new members. Consequently, few professional physical educators are unaware of the services and benefits of membership.

EFFECTIVENESS OF PROFESSIONAL ORGANIZATIONS

The effectiveness of the various professional organizations on professional development is related to the quality and quantity of membership, success of projects, and the magnitude of the problems which beset them.

Membership

The socialization of pre-service teachers begins with anticipating the world of a physical educator. Burlingame (1972) points out that this process is influenced by reference groups and by the training period. Dewar and Lawson (1984) report that these reference groups influence physical education recruits differentially. Males are more influenced by their high school coaches and their father; whereas women are more influenced by their physical education teacher, mother and older brother(s). Role modeling is an important socializer. The relative influence of teacher educators concerning the professional membership of pre-service teachers is questioned since so few pre-service teachers belong. Perhaps this is because, as Metzler and Freedman (1985) report, that even though teacher educators generally belong to the AAHPERD, less than half are actively involved.

Pooley (1971) and Lortie (1969) stress that the most powerful factor in shaping the professional behavior of a teacher is the in-service work environment. However, Seiter (1984) reports that of the total membership in AAHPERD, 45% are teachers and 22% are teacher/coaches. The remaining members are in non-physical education occupations. Kneer (1985) studied the professional membership of secondary school physical educators from randomly selected Illinois high schools. She found that less than half of physical education teachers belonged to a professional physical education association, but 83% belonged to a coaching association. Indeed, as pointed out by Massengale (1981), Templin, Woodford and Mulling (1982), and Chu (1980), physical educators have a preference for coaching over teaching and are beset with conflict problems between teaching and coaching. It appears that faculty participation in professional organizations may not be as powerful as survival as a coach. It is not surprising that when AAHPERD members were asked to identify their priority interest, sport and athletics were identified as a low priority (Seiter, 1984). The AAHPERD does not attract coaches as members.

The Seiter (1984) AAHPERD study reveals that approximately half of the membership elementary and secondary teachers, and about one third of the members are in higher education. The potential membership of physical educators in NASPE, an association of the AAHPERD, has been estimated to be over 200,000. It currently has approximately 24,000 members. Therefore, the NASPE attracts about 15% of the professional physical educators in the United States. Consequently, the socialization influence of NASPE is essentially non-existent except for members.

Seiter (1984) probed the members' feelings about their support for Alliance activities. Table 7-3 below provides her data. The present activities of the AAHPERD are supported by the members. The setting of standards is an important function, as evidenced by the desire for even more activity in this area. Another valued activity is cooperating and assisting with other associations. It appears that the current level of providing teaching materials is satisfactory.

The Seiter AAHPERD study indicates that members rank periodicals, newsletters, and the publication of books as their top three preferred services. This result supports the finding by Kneer (1986) that in-service secondary teachers most often reported reading of professional literature to be their major source of in-service education.

TABLE 7-3. Means for Alliance Activities*

Activity	Mean
Produce position statements	1.2
Respond to national issues	1.6
Liaisons with other national organizations	1.7
Assistance to state associations	1.7
Promote visibility	1.8
Provide curriculum requirements	1.8
Provide teacher standards	1.8
Provide curriculum materials	1.8
Provide media library	2.1

Note: 1 = More, 2 = Same, 3 = Less

*Seiter, M. (1984). American Alliance Membership Survey. Unpublished Paper. American Alliance for Health, Physical Education, Recreation and Dance. Reston, VA. p. 23.

Projects

Burlingame (1972) noted that teachers are initially more concerned about surviving in the classroom than in improving the quality of their practice. The survival concern may explain the result obtained by Seiter (1984) that members' top problem and priority for action by the AAHPERD was public support for physical education and the "selling" of programs. Seiter (1984) concludes her report by saying, "it is safe to say the services the membership wants the most are 'hands on' services which touch their lives in some real and concrete way" (p. 35)

The various professional organizational activities have been successful in serving the membership for providing services that it can control such as periodicals, position statements, publications, criteria, and guidelines. When projects require public support, they are less successful. However, one of the more successful projects occurred in the mid 1960s when the AAHPERD through the Division of Girls and Women's Sports, was highly successful in contributing the current support for girls and women's athletic programs in schools, colleges, and the Olympics. Davenport (1984) reported that AAHPERD membership on the United States Olympic Committee Women's Advisory Committee and subsequent DGWS sponsored National Institutes on Girls Sports were the springboard for ultimately influencing the professional lives of both men and women physical educators/coaches because it permitted girls and women to participate more fully in competitive activities. Although this influence may have contributed to the conflict in roles played by teacher/coaches, it did increase interest in sports participation by girls and women.

In spite of a plethora of projects geared toward giving recognition and support for physical education programs, minimal success has been realized. In the early 1970s, the AAHPERD launched the Physical Education Public Information (PEPI) program. Although that program is still functioning, physical education programs have been reduced because of the national movement to improve education in areas other than physical education. The "Fit to Achieve" program, cited earlier, is still another attempt. This project differs from PEPI because it plans to use professional public relations agencies to plan and carry out the program.

At the beginning of the 1980s, NASPE decided to encourage physical educators to use conceptual knowledge as part of the objectives of their programs. As a result, the *Basic Stuff Series* was published (Kneer, 1981). The Series became a best seller of the AAHPERD, with over 20,000 books sold. A second edition is now available. But did it change teacher behavior? Placek (1987) conducted a study to determine the influence of such a project on change. She surveyed the 966 members AAHPERD had recorded as purchasing the Series between 1982 to May 1986. This total represents less than 1% of the physical educators in the United States. Of that total of 966 purchasers, only half reported they were actually using the books. The AAHPERD publication office reports that the major purchasers have been college and university bookstores. In fact, over 150 colleges and universities have adopted the *Basic Stuff Series* as part of their programs. Perhaps the impact is greater on pre-service teachers. It may be too early to judge the impact of promoting conceptual knowledge in physical education. It appears that many of the educational reforms promulgated by state education agencies are including objectives based upon knowing how and why the body moves.

Another project conceived to give teachers "hands on" help was the "Justification Project," which published a book and an interpretation booklet which contains all known research supporting the need for physical activity. However, it also identified that most physical education programs were presently ineffectual (Seefeldt, 1986). These publications should assist teachers and administrators in justifying the need for physical education.

Summary: Teachers are more interested in projects which contribute to their survival in the gymnasium. However, these projects usually require public support and are more difficult to achieve success. It may not be possible to achieve the "survival goal" without achieving a change in the quality of physical education programs.

PROBLEMS

There are four major problems related to the potential impact of professional organizations upon the professional development of physical educators: (1) poor quality physical education programs, (2) poor image of the physical educator, (3) inability of the physical educator to control his or her professional life, and (4) influence of college and "survivor" members on professional organizations.

Quality of physical education programs. Although one may beget the other, the inability of physical education to achieve creditability in the schools and minds of the public results in unacceptable teaching conditions in terms of time, equipment, and class size. Koceja et al. (1987) reported that these conditions were cited as the most serious problem besetting secondary teachers. This condition creates a despairing attitude among physical educators. Burlingame (1972) states that the physical educator operates alone, is rewarded alone, and is given little or no support. As a result, there is little apparent reason for shifting radially or for listening to others. Professional organizations are not, therefore, viewed as important. On the other hand, Templin (1987) stated one of the impediments to the future of the public school teacher is professional isolation. He laments that the isolation of physical educators is characterized by infrequent contact with colleagues and what does occur is seldom related to improving instruction and the curriculum. The value of professional organizations may not be understood, but in reality the organizations do have the capability of lessening isolation.

Some problems are of our own making. The lack of a clear mission for physical education makes it difficult to articulate what should be expected, though a clear body of knowledge exists relative to recommended practices. Kneer (1986) found at least a 50% gap between theory and practice. Subjects in her study stated the recommended practices were not necessary or needed. Kelly and Lindsay (1980) assessed the knowledge obsolence in physical education and found that both inservice and pre-service teachers were below acceptable standards.

Image of the physical educator. Squires (1981) stated that the average reading level of teacher trainees was such that reading the professional journal may not be possible. Templin, Woodford and Mulling (1982) report that physical education attracts and admits students who are the lowest in academic achievement and who prefer coaching to teaching. These factors contribute to poor programs and ultimately to a poor image of a physical educator. The notion of becoming a member of a professional physical education association may not be viewed as important by the teacher or the administrator.

Lack of control over professional life. Teachers do not have control over their professional lives, as do physicians and lawyers. The United States educational system is controlled by externally developed policies democratically determined through legislation. The application of these policies are subject to the idiosyncratic preferences of local school officials in deference to local and state intentions. Teachers are expected to account for their competence by carrying out these policies (Darling-Hammond, 1987). The cost for membership in professional associations and the costs for attending professional conferences and conventions are mostly the responsibility of the teacher. Yet, reward for competence is rarely given. As a matter of fact, one of the most often stated reasons for not attending professional meetings is the failure of the school to release the teacher to attend. Lortie (1973) reported that only 22% of the schools rewarded professional attendance.

Lack of control over professional organization. Although elementary and secondary physical educators outnumber college physical educators two to one in the AAHPERD, a review of membership involved in leadership and substructure service positions shows that the reverse is true. This situation is not an overt act by the professional association, but is most likely related to the two previous problems cited (lack of control over professional lives, and the ability and interest of the non-college teacher). Dreeben (1973) reported that "most research is carried out by academics and is published in scholarly teacher journals and teachers tend not to be consumers of it" (p. 469). As a result, non-college physical educators do not believe their professional associations know about their problems and/or care about viable solutions. Furthermore, many researchers may feel no responsibility to share their knowledge with the field professional. Some have abandoned the AAHPERD for participation in their subdisciplinary association. Interpretations of research are most often reported at conventions and in journals by professional preparation professors. A good example of this process occurred over the appropriate tests to evaluate physical fitness. Disparities exist relative to knowledge between field professionals, college teachers, and college researchers.

Summary: Professional associations are more attractive to college teachers and may impact on less than 20% of the available physical education community. Members of the AAHPERD are satisfied with the services provided and activities that relate to controlling the quality of physical education practice (Seiter, 1984). However, they see public support for physical education to be a top problem and identify it as a priority project of the AAHPERD. Professional projects which extend beyond the membership have had limited impact on practice because of the difficulty of a minority of teachers, and reaching a majority of non-members. Furthermore, projects which are designed to influence the public have been relatively unsuccessful because of insufficient power to influence public policy. Finally, the overall impact on the socialization of physical educators is essentially negligible because of problems relating to quality programs, teacher image, control over professional lives, and control within the professional organization.

IMPLICATIONS

The professional development of physical educators is a lifelong process, beginning with the pre-schooling, intensifying with formal college professional preparation, and continuing after graduation. The quality of that development is highly dependent upon the effectiveness of professional organization. Consequently, the relatively low impact of physical education associations on teacher development has serious implications. These implications are related to: (1) improving the role of professional associations, (2) solving the teacher/coach problem, (3) increasing the power of the professional organization, and (4) conducting research in this area.

Improving the role of professional organizations

Templin, Woodford, and Mulling (1982) identify the academic background of the in-service teacher as a major problem in effective teacher development. They stress the need for professional preparation programs to raise entrance standards as a primary remedy and rightfully point out the financial implications for colleges to install their recommendation. Certainly NCATE standards can somewhat control the quality of the program which may help to remediate the entry academic level of recruits. However, these standards have been in place for years, yet the image problem of physical educators persist. Therefore, a national association such as NASPE must begin to investigate ways to control the quality of the professional development programs in much the same way as the medical and legal professions. Current reforms in education have touched on this approach, but from a political rather than a professional base.

The effectiveness of social pressure applied through position papers, standards, and criteria is dependent upon knowledge about them. NASPE, or another similiar organization, must improve dissemination strategies. All too often, these documents are distributed only to the members, which is but a small proportion of the profession, and are seldom distributed to those who control the educational environment. Efforts must increase to foster interaction with educational policy makers at all controlling levels. This effort should include papers delivered through educational administrators' professional organizations, articles published in their journals, and discussions with legislators relative to physical education professional concerns and goals.

Physical education professional organizations need to increase their promotion programs to encourage physical education teacher educators to facilitate the attendance of their pre-service teachers at association workshops, conferences and conventions and to work with other educational professionals associations to demand that schools facilitate their faculty members to attend. Professional organizations should become partners with other educational professional organizations to help change the administrative/teacher relationships within the school setting, and to obtain for teachers a greater control over their professional lives. Sage (1975) points out that if professional organizations are impotent in their role of influencing appropriate professional development of teachers, other socializers will take over in a less controlled manner. Currently, several agencies are offering certification programs for youth sport coaches, fitness specialists, and wellness leaders.

Finally, the physical education profession must decide what are the legitimate outcomes of physical education programs. Failure to identify to the public the nature of a "physically educated person" will continue to confuse our professionals as well as our students. NASPE has formed a committee to determine the legitimate outcomes in physical education.

Teacher/Coach Problem

Segrave (1980) reported that 62% of the prospective physical education teachers preferred coaching to teaching. Further, Chu (1980) found that male teachers/coaches spend 36.6 hours per week in preparing for coaching and 2.7 hours for teaching preparation, even when not coaching. Another problem is time. Chu reported that the teacher/coach spends 68 hours per week in both duties. If the teacher/coach is conscientiously pursuing both occupations, he or she is overworked. Kneer (1987) identified four solutions: (1) make coaching part of the teaching load, (2) separate the two occupations and hire full time coaches in the school, (3) take athletics outside the school, and (4) reduce practice time and game schedules. It is time that physical education through the collective effort of its national organization develop and promote solutions to this problem which shapes the teacher's image and the quality of physical education programs.

Organizational power

The political structure of the AAHPERD requires collective agreement by other associations for any thrust of major proportions. This agreement is difficult to gain without diluting the thrust. A national professional organization, such as NASPE, may not have sufficient power under the umbrella of the AAHPERD. Perhaps a new configuration of affiliation is needed to provide the power to influence public policy for physical education and to build the cooperative political structures within and between related organizations. This configuration may be a confederation of associations which would allow more autonomy without losing the necessary interrelationships. Only in this manner can the expressed needs of physical educators to gain public support for physical education be gained. Griffin and Ward (1986) stated "the reform movement in teacher education will probably be judged largely on the basis of the degree to which coalitions of educational organizations can orchestrate the various pieces toward mutually responsible leaderships" (p. 12).

The important research discoveries need to be shared with the public and the profession. All professional organizations, regardless of size or purpose, need to disseminate their important work through news releases and journals that reach a more diverse professional population.

Finally, all too often untrained volunteer members are expected to carry out promotional plans. Association members are physical educators carrying out full time jobs. They are not qualified to be public relations experts, solicitors, and lobbyists; nor do they have the time. Professional physical education associations simply must financially support their organization sufficiently to employ the expertise needed to gain power.

Research

There is a shocking lack of research available to identify the kind and nature of professional association interaction with members and nonmembers, the acceptance and compliance with standards, the effect of special projects to achieve specified goals, and the overall effectiveness of physical education programs. Research is needed to identify why membership in the AAHPERD turns over one third annually. Why do members leave? Why do they return? Why don't they join? There is little or no research available that can identify the number of physical education programs that comply with recommended standards and criteria. Information is needed to determine the extent to which members and nonmembers are aware of professional leadership to promote quality programs and instruction.

FUTURE

Professional organizations should be major socializing agents for the professional development of both the pre-service and in-service teacher. Their role in collectively bringing to bear direct and indirect influence upon professional physical educator lives through sharing of knowledge and the leadership to gain power to effect needed change is of utmost importance to the dynamic and viable survival of the profession. Morford (1972) eloquently stated our future as follows:

> Obviously a profession is an organization dedicated to doing things for people, thus its survival is dependent upon its usefulness and value to society. A professional field becomes known by the things it does and how well it does them. Of great concern to those within the profession should be the manner in which knowledge is acquired so as to arrive at the position of knowing that what it does is good, sound, and appropriate to the needs of its clients. (p. 92)

Therefore, it is imperative that physical education professional associations become the powerful influence that they can be on the professional development of in-service and pre-service teachers. This influence shall extend to controlling the quality of the professional inducted as well as their pre-service and in-service continuing education. Public interest in quality education and the physical well being of youth should begin to exert pressure to improve the practice of physical education. This pressure ultimately will force a solution to the teacher/coach problem, and the need for a more cooperative interaction between field professionals and physical education researchers so that a mutual sharing of problems and solutions can occur to enrich their professional development.

REFERENCES

Burlingame, M. (1972). Socialization constructs in the teaching of teachers, *Quest. 18*, 54.
Chu, D. (1980). Functional myths of educational organization: college as career training and the relationship of formal title to actual duties in upper secondary school employment. *Proceedings of the Annual Conference of the National Association for Physical Education in Higher Education, 2*, 30-46.
Cross, K. P. (1987). The adventures of education in wonderland: Implementing educational reform. *Phi Delta Kappan*, March, 499.
Darling-Hammond, L. (1987). Teacher professionalization versus democratic control. *Basic Education, 31*, 2-5.
Davenport, J. (1984). The American Alliance/U.S. Olympic Committee Relationship. *Journal of Physical Education, Recreation and Dance, 55* (3), 18-19.
Dewar, A. & Lawson, H. (1984). Subjective warrant and recruitment into physical education. *Quest, 36* (1), 24.
Dreeben, R. (1973). School as a workplace. In R. Travers (Ed.), *Second handbook on research on teaching*. Chicago: Rand McNally.

Griffin, G. & Ward, B. (1986). Policy and decision making contexts of reform in clinical teacher education. In Hoffman, J. V. & Edwards, S. A. (Eds), *Reality and Reform in Clinical Teacher Education.* New York: Random House.

Kelly, E. J. & Lindsay, C. A. (1980). A comparison of knowledge obsolescence of graduating senior and practitioners in the field of physical education. *Research Quarterly for Exercise and Sport, 51* (4), 636-644.

Kneer, M. (Ed.) (1981). *Basic Stuff Series I & II.* Reston, VA: American Alliance for Health, Physical Education, Recreation and Dance.

Kneer, M. (1985). Will the parade pass us by? claims, causes and cures. *Illinois Journal of Health, Physical Education and Recreation, 3,* 18.

Kneer, M. (1986). Description of physical education instruction theory/practice gap in selected secondary schools. *Journal of Teaching Physical Education.* (5), 91-106.

Kneer, M. (1987). Solutions to the teacher/coach problems in secondary schools. *Journal of Physical Education, Recreation and Dance.* 59 (2), 28-29.

Koceja, D. M., Sodona, C. J., Updyke, W. F., & Willett, M. S. (1987). Attitudes of secondary physical education teachers in the United States: regional differences. Unpublished manuscript, Indiana University, Department of Physical Education, Bloomington, Indiana.

Leonard, W. M. (1980). *A Sociological Perspective of Sport.* Minneapolis: Burgess Press.

Lortie, D. C. (1969). The balance of control and autonomy in elementary school teaching. In A. Etizioni (Ed.). *The Semi-Professions and Their Organization: Teachers, Nurses, Social Workers.* New York: Free Press.

Lortie, D. (1973). Observation on teaching as work. In R. Travers (Ed) *Second handbook on research and teaching.* Chicago: Rand McNally.

Massengale, J. D. (1981). Role conflict and the teacher/coach: some occupational causes and consideration for the sport sociologist. In S. Greensdorfer and A. Yiannakis (Eds.) *Sociology of Sport: Perspectives.* West Point, New York: Leisure Press.

Metzler, M. & Freedman, M. (1985). Here's looking at you PETE: a profile of physical education teacher faculty. *Journal of Teaching Physical Education, 4* (2), 128.

Morford, W. R. (1972). Toward a profession, not a craft. *Quest, 18* (Spring), 92.

Placek, J. (1987, March). Paper presented at the Curriculum Theory Conference, Athens, GA.

Pooley, J. C. (1972). Professional socialization: a model of the pre-training phase applicable to physical education students. *Quest, 18* (Spring) 57-66.

Safrit, M. J. & Wood, T. M. (1986). The health-related physical fitness test: a tri-state survey of users and non-users. *Research Quarterly for Exercise and Sport, 57* (1), 27-31.

Sage, G. H. (1975). Socialization of coaches: antecedents to coaches beliefs and behaviors. *Proceedings of the Annual Conference of the National Association for Men,* 124-130.

Seefeldt, V. (Ed.) (1986). *Physical Activity & Well Being.* Reston, VA: American Alliance for Health, Physical Education, Recreation and Dance.

Segrave, J. (1980). Role preferences among prospective physical educator teacher/coaches. *Proceedings of the Annual Conference of the National Association for Physical Education In Higher Education,* 543-62.

Seiter, M. M. (1984). American Alliance Membership Survey. Unpublished Paper. American Alliance for Health, Physical Education, Recreation and Dance, Reston, Va.

Squires, M. M. (1981). A comparative analysis of the relationship between the reading achievement of prospective teachers and the readability level of professional literature. *Dissertation Abstracts International,* 41-3539-A (University Microfilms, No 81-02, 785).

Templin, T. (1987). Some considerations for teaching physical education in the future. In D. Massengale, (Ed.) *Trends toward the future of physical education.* Champaign, Illinois: Human Kinetics Press.

Templin, T., Woodford, R., & Mulling, C. (1982). On becoming a physical educator: Occupational choice and the anticipatory socialization process. *Quest, 34* (2), 119-133.

8

From Rookie to Veteran: Workplace Conditions in Physical Education and Induction Into the Profession

HAL A. LAWSON
Miami University

SCHOOLS AS WORK ORGANIZATIONS

Most analyses of schools and specific curricula such as physical education focus exclusively on the content and process of students' learning. Such a focus on children and youth is warranted because schools exist, first and foremost, to provide structured opportunities for the development of children and youth. Schools are, however, more than *learning* places for children and youth. Schools and school systems also are in-

Tom Templin, Alison Dewar, Dave Belka, and Dick Moore provided assistance in the development of this chapter.

creasingly complex bureaucracies, which vary somewhat according to their urban, suburban, and rural locations. In short, schools double as *work*places, which process *teachers* as well as students. It is timely to explore the ways in which the work of, and work conditions for, physical education teachers affects their careers, personal lives, and their students' experiences in physical education. We will begin with the kind of induction into the physical education profession that teachers are able to experience.

TWO STAGES OF PROFESSIONAL INDUCTION

Induction into the physical education profession should occur in two stages (Lawson, 1983a; 1983b). The first stage is teacher or professional education.

Ideally, during their higher education experiences and coursework, prospective physical education teachers are provided knowledge, values, sensitivities, and skills, which together comprise the model physical education teacher. Teacher education programs have achieved one of their central purposes when recruits welcome and internalize such knowledge. Prospective teachers begin to think and act like other physical education professionals. Moreover, the emergence in individual teaching recruits of a common denominator of perceptions, thoughts, and skills indicates that personal identities are being transformed into professional identities. A "master identity" has been formed when it becomes impossible to distinguish professional values from personal values, or personal perceptions and aspirations from professional perceptions and aspirations. Knowing Jane or John as a person automatically implies knowing Jane or John as a physical educator. This is the first stage of induction, and it should occur during teacher education (Lawson, 1983a; 1983b).[1]

Ideally, the transition from teacher education to full-time employment is relatively easy. Student teaching experiences and select coursework are intended to facilitate this transition. Such transition-easing experiences are aimed at connecting teacher education, the first stage of induction, with the second stage, actual entry into the first, full-time teaching position. Although some adjustments and minor frustrations are expected in all new teaching positions, the ideal situation is one in which the new teacher finds familiar and appropriate work expectations and responsibilities in the school. The new teachers find a high degree of correspondence and compatibility between the aims and content of teacher education and actual teaching practice. Furthermore, with each passing month, and each passing year, each teacher gains increasing

---

[1] The conception of induction here is drawn from the dominant and conservative view of professions, a view that presently is being criticized by cultural studies specialists.

amounts of comfort, confidence, and competence. On-the-job performance thus brings more identity-bestowing and identity-reinforcing experiences, the likes of which began in teacher education programs. As a result, commitments to physical education are finalized (Steen, 1988; Templin, 1985) and the master identity of the teacher becomes firmly established. Ideally, then, induction into the physical education profession is complete and successful for the majority of teachers.

Unfortunately, such ideal inductions may constitute the exception more than the rule in physical education. We will summarize briefly reasons for the induction problem in teacher education and then give more extensive attention to problems of actual teaching practice, the second stage of induction.

The Variable Impact of Teacher Education

We know that teacher education does not in all cases provide the first stage of a professional induction. We do not know the extent of this problem because it is a new area of research in physical education. There is research on classroom teachers (Lortie, 1975). Also, important, new research and scholarly work on physical education's teacher education recently has been initiated (Dewar, 1987; Lawson, 1986, 1988; Steen, 1985). Moreover, Locke (1984) has completed an important monograph, which is devoted to a review of the literature on teacher education in physical education, and Bain's book chapter (forthcoming) is an invaluable contribution to the literature. All of this literature can be blended with literature on the occupational socialization of physical education teachers to produce three, related explanations for an induction problem in teacher education.

1. Some prospective teachers engage in short term compliance and impression management in order to complete individual courses, receive their bachelor's degree, and gain provisional teacher certification. They do not, however, take seriously the aims and content of teacher education. Some prospective teachers actively contest and even reject the aims and content of teacher education. Others view teaching physical education as a career contingency, a job for which they must prepare if they want to achieve their aspirations (e.g., become a coach). For these teaching recruits, biography, not teacher education, influences their work-related values, knowledge, sensitivities, and skills.
2. Teacher education programs are not structured and conducted in ways that are conducive to a professional induction. This is a multifaceted problem: for example, the content of teacher education courses is not sequenced and staged appropriately; teacher education professors fail to agree among themselves about program

goals and educational processes; and courses and experiences related to the development of occupational commitment are rare.
3. The variability among school physical education curricula makes it impossible for teacher education programs to correspond to all curricula. The lack of a perceived fit between teacher education and school curricula weakens the effects of teacher education.

To reiterate, these three kinds of reasons are related. They interact to reduce the overall effectiveness of teacher education programs. In both teacher education and school curricula, there are differences within, as well as across, institutions regarding the standards that comprise effective physical education and teacher preparation. Little wonder, then, that there is "an induction problem" associated with teacher education.

It follows that problems with the first stage of induction will affect the second stage. A scenario, which has on the surface some explanatory appeal, can be sketched that introduces such induction problems.

Induction Problems in the Schools

Not all of the graduates of teacher education programs leave higher education possessing somewhat uniform expectations and aspirations as well as valuing the same knowledge, sensitivities, and skills. The schools they enter as beginning teachers differ as do physical education programs within and across these schools. Such differences reduce the likelihood that the aims and content of teacher education will correspond to school practice. Rather than marking a smooth or relatively easy transition from teacher education, then, the first teaching position often brings "reality shock." Caught in the contradictions and differences between teacher education and school practice, new teachers experience psychological stress. They quickly learn that they must make a choice between the perspectives of teacher education and those of school practice. The decision is not difficult to make because classes have to be met and occupational survival may be at stake. Many new teachers start taking their cues from experienced teachers in the same or similar schools and contemplate even greater conformity with school traditions. Thus begins the so-called "wash-out effect," wherein school practices progressively erode the effects of teacher education.

Such is the scenario on the surface. Now we need to look beneath the surface in order to learn more about schools as work organizations. Schools differ, and so do beginning teachers. Hence, there are differences in the ways schools socialize new teachers and in the ways new teachers respond to those kinds of socialization. Once these differences are understood, the scenario will lose some of its surface appeal.

ORGANIZATIONAL SOCIALIZATION AND CULTURE

Schools are work organizations. Like all work organizations, a school attempts to socialize its new members. New teachers are targets for *organizational socialization*. This process of organizational socialization is intended to allow new teachers to learn their school's *organizational culture*. The following discussions explore these two concepts and their import for workplace conditions for physical education teachers.

Organizational Socialization

Organizational socialization proceeds on the basis of interaction and learning. It should allow new teachers to "learn the ropes" and become accepted in their schools. Socialization differences among schools, even schools in the same district, eventually become known to teachers, and the occupational mobility of selected teachers can be explained in part by the attempts these teachers make to find a better workplace (Becker, 1952).

While acknowledging differences among schools' organizational socialization, it also is imperative to look for ways in which schools may be similar in their approaches to this process. The search for similarities in the process of organizational socialization may proceed on the basis of the six tactical dimensions of organizational socialization, which have been identified by Van Maanen and Schein (1979). These dimensions were summarized in a previous work as follows:

The organizational socialization of teachers may be *collective* or *individual*; with others, they experience the "we're in the same boat" feeling, which makes socialization more powerful than if the individual faces it alone. Second, socialization may be *formal* or *informal*. Third, it may be *sequential* or *random*; that is, it may proceed in a planned, step-wise progression or characterized by an absence of such an order. Fourth, socialization may be *fixed* or *variable*; it may proceed according to a well-developed timetable or there may not be a fixed time frame. Fifth, socialization may be *serial* or *disjunctive*; teachers may be taken "under the wing" of an experienced mentor who doubles as a role model or confronted with a "sink or swim by onself" situation. Finally, socialization may include *investiture* or *divestiture*; new sensitivies, knowledge and skills gained in teacher education may be welcomed and accommodated, or ridiculed and rejected. These are six tactical dimensions of organizational socialization. (Lawson, 1983b, p. 7)

There are four features of this view of organizational socialization that merit emphasis.

First of all, school officials may or may not have selected the tactics for their organizational socialization. Organizational socialization is not always a rational process because the socialization tactics that are employed may not have been paired deliberately with predetermined socialization outcomes. Custom and tradition may be as much responsible for the socialization of new teachers as a rational plan. When this occurs, conflicting or contradictory processes and messages are likely, and this reduces the effectiveness of such organizational socialization, resulting in variability among new and experienced teachers.

Secondly, such variability within and across schools in their organizational socialization is a basis for conflict within teacher education programs. When there is a "wash-out effect," organizational socialization is in part responsible for it.

Thirdly, the work orientations and actions that teachers exhibit are attributable in part to how they learned them: *how* teachers are socialized influences *what* (or whether) they learn. Van Maanen and Schein (1979) emphasize, for example, that different socialization tactics are linked to three different work orientations. New teachers may develop a *custodial orientation*, an orientation aimed at the protection and preservation of existing policies and practices in the school and physical education. Some new teachers may develop either of two kinds of innovative orientations. They may be *content innovative*, meaning that they change selected ways in which teaching is done, or they may become *role innovative*, meaning that they revolutionize physical education and the role of the physical education teacher in their school. Selected socialization tactics are associated with these work orientations (Van Maanen and Schein, 1979).

1. Schools with socialization tactics that are collective, sequential, variable, serial, and involve divestiture will breed custodial orientations in new teachers.
2. Schools with socialization tactics that are individual, informal, random, disjunctive, and involve investiture, will nurture innovative orientations in new teachers. (Lawson, 1983b, p. 7)

The fourth feature of organizational socialization is that it is especially potent at so-called "boundary passages." Organizational boundaries are invisible to outsiders, known only to insiders. For example, it shall become apparent that a new teacher is not accepted and trusted automatically by other teachers and school administrators. There is a trial or testing period during which the new teacher is perceived by others as an outsider, and the new teacher is acutely aware of this status. Gradually, the new teacher gains trust and acceptance. In short, this person has crossed an organizational boundary, called an inclusionary boundary.

Once this boundary has been crossed, the new teacher is included as a genuine participant in selected teacher discussions and activities.

Two other organizational boundaries are a functional boundary, which separates those who can actually do the work of teaching from those who cannot, and a hierarchical boundary, which separates persons who have formal authority and power (department heads, principals) from those who do not (new teachers, teacher aides). Clearly, new teachers often must cross boundaries simultaneously. They must cross both the inclusionary and the functional boundaries; their abilities to cross one may influence their abilities to cross the other. For example, it is difficult for a new teacher to gain acceptance among veteran teachers (cross the inclusionary boundary) if this person cannot gain control of classes and actually teach (cross the functional boundary). Organizational socialization is especially powerful during these times and stages when such boundaries need to be crossed (Van Maanen and Schein, 1979).

Schools are similar to the extent that they employ the same kinds of organizational socialization tactics and seek the same kinds of teacher work orientations—either custodial, content innovative or role innovative. Another potential source of similarity is among school's organizational cultures.

Organizational Culture

Organizational socialization refers to how new teachers interact and learn. Organizational culture refers to what it is the new teachers learn. Organizational culture may be defined as follows:

Any organizational culture consists broadly of long-standing rules of thumb, a somewhat special language, an ideology that helps edit a member's everyday experience, shared standards of relevance as to the critical aspects of the work that is being accomplished, matter-of-fact prejudices, models for social etiquette and demeanor, certain customs and rituals suggestive of how members are to relate to colleagues, subordinates, superiors and outsiders, and a sort of residual category of some rather plain "horse sense" regarding what is appropriate and "smart" behavior within the organizational and what is not. All of these cultural modes of thinking, feeling and doing are, of course, fragmented to some degree, giving rise within large organizations to various "subcultures" or "organizational segments."

Such cultural forms are so rooted in the recurrent problems and common experiences of the membership in an organizational segment that once learned they become viewed by insiders as perfectly "natural" responses to the world of work they inhabit. This is merely to say that organizational cultures arise and are maintained as a way of coping with and making sense of a given problematic environment. (Van Maanen & Schein, 1979, p. 210).

A school's organizational culture is largely unwritten. It consists primarily of deeply embedded assumptions, which are accepted and professed by veteran and powerful school personnel, about the school and its functions. This organizational culture has two functions. It helps the school and its members meet external environmental demands, and it facilitates the internal integration of diverse school workers (Schein, 1986, pp. 8-9).[2] Organizational culture should be learned and internalized by all new teachers. It shall become apparent that while all teachers may learn this culture, some will not accept it or its parts, nor will they internalize it. Such acts of rejection are common in all work organizations, including schools. Amended or entirely new versions of organizational culture then appear among groups of teachers. Here is the basis for organizational sub-cultures, which are to varying degrees at odds with the dominant organizational culture that is espoused by the school's administration. An example of an organizational culture follows.

Jane was a secondary school teacher.[3] Her reflections on her school's organizational culture illustrate selected aspects of a school's organizational culture.

There were certain explicit attitudes, behaviors and administrative duties that were expected of all of the teaching members of the staff. The behavioral requirements of this role were clearly outlined and defined in the staff policy booklet. This booklet contained the policy and rules for general staff conduct and guidelines for behavior in a variety of different situations. These included guidelines for general school discipline, staff discipline, administrative duties, communication within and without the school and staff and pupil dress and conduct.

Every new member of the staff was issued this booklet, and we were told to read it, learn it and apply it to our behavior in the school. . . . This process ensured that we all developed the same awareness of and first exposure to the culture of the school. The experience was one of divestiture in the sense that we were presented with these guidelines for the purposes of mastery and application. Here were the rules, all we had to do was adhere to them and apply them.

The immediate consequence of this socialization tactic was that

---

[2] Some oversimplification of organizational culture is unavoidable here. See Schein (1986) for depth and breadth.
[3] This and other quotes are derived from autobiographical case studies completed by experienced teachers, 1982-88.

I adopted a custodial orientation to my role. I read the booklet, learned the rules, and applied them to my work. This total acceptance of the culture and adherence to the status quo was, for me, a very practical solution to an immediate problem. I was faced with a totally new situation, with children who all knew the rules of conduct acceptable within the school, and, for whom, putting the teacher to the test was a good way of establishing how well I knew and was prepared to apply these rules. Following the booklet to the letter provided a way of coping with an unknown situation and surviving with my credibility in tact.

I discovered as I began to interact and discuss certain aspects of my role with established members of the staff that they did not in fact apply the policy guidelines and rules and did not always act in a manner consistent with the behaviors I had been led to believe were sacrosanct. These individuals had developed their own standards and codes for behavior and used these to maintain the desired ends of order and discipline.

This realization obtained through informal social interaction resulted in a change in my orientation towards my role. I started to model my behavior on that of successful experienced teachers and I adapted and selectively applied certain aspects of the "code of conduct" to my behavior. In essence, I was redefining some of the *means* towards achieving the ends which I had internalized and accepted during the first stage of my organizational socialization. This change from a custodial to a more content innovation orientation was only possible after I had become an insider in the organization and as such had displayed enough of the suitable forms of behavior to be allowed to move inwards on the inclusionary dimension of the organization.

Symbolic and actual struggles among teachers and school administrators occur over their competing cultures. Consequently, work groups, called occupational communities, are formed around such sub-cultures. These and other salient points will become more understandable as we examine workplace conditions for physical education teachers.

WORKPLACE CONDITIONS FOR THE PHYSICAL EDUCATION TEACHER

Another way in which schools and school physical education teachers may be analyzed for their differences and similarities is the workplace conditions that new and veteran physical education teachers create and experience. Organizational cultures and sub-cultures are part of these conditions, but the need exists for a more elaborate analysis of these conditions.

An overview of the factors influencing workplace conditions for the physical education teacher is presented in Figure 8-1. The categories for these influences range from personal-social to political and economic. It is important to emphasize three features of this conceptualization of workplace conditions. These categories and influences interact with each other, both within and across the categories. Furthermore, the specific influences and their parent categories may be used to analyze specific aspects of both organizational socialization and organizational culture. The third feature is extremely important: just as these influences may shape and change the orientation and actions of physical education teachers, so too can teachers act upon and shape these influences. Changing and shaping these influences constitutes a major challenge confronting new and experienced physical education teachers. This observation shall become apparent as each of the categories is analyzed.

Political and Economic Factors

The United States Constitution delegates the responsibility for education to each of the 50 states. The states, in turn, delegate selected policy decisions and functions to local school boards. This is the political and economic context for physical education.

States vary in their requirements for physical education (Mitchell & Earls, 1987). There are differences in the number of grades in which physical education is a required subject, and in the number of days, hours, and minutes allocated for physical education instruction. Variations also exist in the specificity of the content of physical education, in the credentials and backgrounds of the persons who may be assigned to teach physical education classes, and in the resources that states allocate specifically to physical education.

The same can be said of local communities as they interpret and implement state standards for physical education. Communities exert their own influences, and these may be apart from state standards and requirements. An example, which is offered tongue-in-cheek, illustrates this point. In some communities in the state of Indiana, there is no question that basketball instruction will be included in physical education. The only question is whether there will be sports activities other than basketball!

There are political and economic influences that have a direct bearing upon the work of the physical education teacher. Ultimately, the status of physical education in the schools has as its origins such state and local political and economic influences. Changing the status of physical education in the schools requires political activitism by physical education teachers and others concerned with physical education programs.

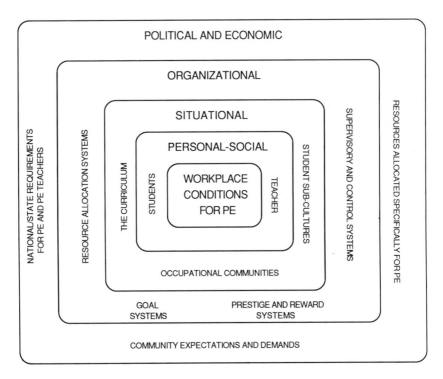

FIGURE 8-1. *Interactive Factors Influencing Workplace Conditions for the Physical Education Teacher*

Organizational Factors

Each school is a work bureaucracy, and its bureaucratic norms often are at odds with professional norms offered in teacher education (Lawson, 1983b; Templin, 1979). Each school has at least four kinds of systems. One such system is the goal system, which orients the school toward singular or multiple purposes. For example, a school may be college preparatory, vocational- technical, or comprehensive, and its goal system reflects and fuels this organizational orientation. A second system is designed and employed for the allocation of resources such as equipment, facilities, and funds for professional development and staffing assistance. Another is for the control, supervision, and evaluation of teachers' work performances. Yet another is more invisible than the other two: This is the prestige and reward system that is an integral part of the dominant organizational culture. These four systems are related, and they influence workplace conditions in physical education.

For example, listen to John, an experienced teacher of elementary physical education as well as English, to gain some understanding of organizational prestige systems and their impact on a teacher's work.

Another realization I had was that physical education was not very high on the prestige ladder in the structure of my school. This was something that I learned in my student teaching assignments, but supressed prior to graduation. This lack of prestige manifested itself in many ways. The first way was in regard to the principal. When I was in the gym, the principal rarely came to observe me teach. It seemed that the only time he came to the gymnasium was if a student was injured. In contrast, when I taught English I was regularly observed.

A second area where I perceived a lack of prestige was in regard to the rest of the faculty. Some of these faculty members would bring their classes to the gym early, and pick them up late. Also, when we were talking about students, the other faculty members would ask questions about their behavior, attitude and success in English, but not in the gym. The other faculty members also used physical education as a reward and punishment tool. If a student was misbehaving, he ran the risk of losing his physical education classes for a period of time. It was as if physical education was a privilege, not a class. This was a practice which I tried very hard to stop, but the principal didn't wish to confront the rest of the faculty on this matter.

One final instance which confirmed the lack of prestige which I held in the school came late in my first year. After a couple of students had been hurt while outside during recess, I was asked by the principal to supervise the students while they were outside. I later mentioned this to a group of teachers during lunch. One of them replied, "I don't see any problem with that, gym class is just supervised play." The further my socialization process progressed, the more my lack of prestige within the school was reinforced.

With my rank within the school clearly in mind, I began to look for ways to keep up my motivation as a physical education teacher. I began to look very hard for ways to internally replace motivation which I lost with the loss of prestige. However, as time passed, I found myself losing motivation. I began to see signs in myself which reminded me of the teachers I worked under when I student taught.

I believe the lack of prestige causes many physical education teachers to become separated from the rest of the faculty. I feel it may also lead to more serious effects such as loss of enjoyment for the job, and even cause teachers to eventually leave the field.

Resource allocation systems are equally important, and they interact with the prestige and goal systems. Joan was a secondary school teacher. Her assessment of her teaching conditions is revealing.

The transition from student and student teacher to teacher was quite dramatic for me. I found that I was not totally prepared for some of the events that happened during teaching. As a result, I did a lot of "scrambling" to survive. There were so many new responsibilities all at once that it took quite a while for me to adjust.

. . . I was tormented by many dilemmas and doubts. The way the program content was planned and the scheduling of gym time were the major sources of mental anguish. Having the use of the gym on alternate eight-day cycles (of which I met each class five times) was certainly not enough time to pretest, teach a skill and then evaluate it. As a result, I fell into teaching something to a class for five days, then we didn't have the use of the gym so we went elsewhere and did something different. There could be no continuity developed within such a system. This system merely allowed exposure to a certain activity and because there wasn't enough exposure and continuity, there was little sense in evaluating the final outcome. To complicate matters further, a grade was not given for PE, only a participation mark of one to five. When I tried to evaluate for the knowledge of rules in a sport, for example, I found that the students were not motivated to learn the rules or study for the test because they knew that their PE participation mark would not affect their grade point average. . . . I felt I was helpless in the situation and largely developed a custodial approach to my work. . . . In addition, because of the above mentioned situation, I felt doubt. . . . In this case, the school system, its budget, lack of facilities and poor time tabling took precedence over the needs of the students.

Joan perceived the relationship between the school's prestige and allocation systems:

. . . the PE curriculum didn't seem to be as important as other subjects in the school. You didn't see the math teacher losing the use of his classroom for an eight-day cycle with each class. . . . I felt, is my job really necessary and is my work really valued?

In short, organizational factors have a major bearing on teachers' work and their longevity in teaching.

Situational Factors

Interacting with broader organizational factors are situational influences. Among these are student sub-cultures, occupational communities, and the nature of the physical education curriculum.

Although more research needs to be completed, there is a growing amount of evidence that student sub-cultures exist in each school, and that these sub-cultures impact the effectiveness of physical education programs and affect the work of physical education teachers (Griffin, 1983; Tindall, 1975; Wang, 1977). Sport and exercise, together with socioeconomic status, may be among the most important factors in the formation of these student sub-cultures. Two things are relatively clear. These sub-cultures influence the work of teachers, sometimes making it easier and at other times making it difficult or almost impossible. For example, groups of students frequently contest and reject traditional sports and games instruction (Corrigan, 1982; Hendry, 1978; Willis, 1977). Furthermore, these sub-cultures impact the functional curriculum for physical education, i.e., what is actually taught to and learned by students.

In the same vein, the curriculum for physical education influences the work of teachers. A curriculum is defined here as a prescribed course of learning and performance for students, together with the experiences and activities, which are intended to facilitate such learning and performance. State curriculum guides not withstanding (Mitchell & Earls, 1987), there is reason to believe that not every school has an agreed-upon formal curriculum and that not every teacher views learning as a necessary and important outcome of physical education. Clearly, this influences the work of physical education teachers. Work completed in Scotland (Hendry, 1978) illustrates this point and helps to explain why some physical education teachers may emphasize their work as coaches more than their work as teachers.

> It would seem that the physical education teacher, although a specialist in his own right and enjoying the same basic salary as other certified teachers in the country, is distinctly aware of this "marginality." Since physical education is a "nonexaminable" subject it cannot be evaluated in the same manner as classroom subjects, thus there is every possibility that subjective criteria may be used by the rest of the pedagogy in assessing standards which give the subject its status within the school. Indeed classroom colleagues see any status that does exist coming via games successes, thus the fortunes of school teams may be paralleled with school examination results. (Hendry, 1978, p. 35)

In short, if the curriculum does not emphasize learning and performance, and if teachers do not evaluate this performance and share results with colleagues, then physical education teachers will suffice with low status in the school, or seek status through their coaching responsibilities.

Teachers also join together to form work groups called occupational communities. Occupational communities have four related characteristics: (1) each member of the group believes he performs the same kind of work; (2) each member identifies more or less positively with his work; (3) each member believes that group members share the same kinds of values, perspectives, and problems; (4) the activities of group members blend the realms of work and leisure (Van Maanen & Barley, 1984).

Sometimes the circumstances of the physical education teacher's work influences their interaction and their community membership. Again, Jane's situation illustrates this point.

The physical education department in the school was isolated as a separate sub-unit and was located in two areas within the school. The physical location of the department working areas determined that during intervals and between teaching periods we often had to use the time to travel from one area to another. This had quite a significant influence on my socialization in the school as I did not have time to go to the main staff room and interact with other members of the staff, and the only other individuals I came into contact with were members of the physical education department.

Occupational communities also are instrumental in organizational socialization and organizational culture. Consider Doug's case:

When I first arrived at my school I was not truly accepted by any of the major functional groups. I was a teacher in transition, who was seeking to become a respected, central and working member of staff. My professional involvement began when I was at a relatively young age, and I looked it. Entering this school I did not have any previous teaching experience. The staff and administrators had to decide if I was an effective teacher. My youthful age and inexperience did not make the acceptance automatic. Since teachers operate in their own rooms, behind closed doors, the evaluation is not of the visible kind. Most of the communication and assumptions are based on here-say from students and/or mostly by the conversations about students and the school, that occurs as you sit around with fellow workers at meetings and at lunch hour. This informal testing of my abilities, motives and values decided how much personal and professional respect I was to receive.

Gaining respect was a slow process for me. I was a first year teacher who was overwhelmed with course planning and marking work. I did not have a great deal of time for informal conversations or volunteering for meetings with fellow workers. Gradually though, my abilities were tested and towards the end of the first year I felt that I had become an "insider" to the organization. Fellow workers gradually began sharing their opinions and philosophy on all aspects of the school organization. In my first year I had thus moved from the edge of the organization, where I was only interested in performance, to a more central role of sharing information within the organization.

Passage through the outsider-insider boundaries changed me considerably. Most of my first year I was very tense and anxious about my profession and performance in it. Suggestions given by staff and administration were often readily accepted in order to reduce my apprehensions. Use of tests, labs and exercises given by others, was prevalent. I tried to conform to values and beliefs I gradually began to perceive as important in the organization. Organizational socialization was changing me.

. . . My experiences in both teaching and coaching were very similar to what was expected. Most teachers on staff were young, enthusiastic, and out-going. Staff games at noon hour, afterschool softball games and week-end and summer hiking trips were all a part of my first two years experience.

In brief, Doug's membership in an occupational community facilitated his acceptance in the school and helped his work. This impact is further substantiated in the next testimonial:

A large turnover in staff and a new principal were two major changes that occurred during the next two years of my teaching. During this period of time, due to the above changes, discontinuity began. Coaching became more difficult as the staff was less inclined to help me. Generally, there was an attitude change by the staff in the school. The worth of the extracurricular and physical education programs was being questioned. In talking to fellow workers in other schools, such negative attitudes were present in many of these schools.

Thus, occupational communities are important influences on teacher's work. They may facilitate or constrain this work, and, in both cases, there are attendant effects upon a teacher's enthusiasm, morale, and commitment.

PERSONAL-SOCIAL FACTORS

Political-economic, organizational, and situational factors all influence the interactions between individual teachers and students. Such influence not withstanding, teachers daily confront the realities associated with close interaction with students in isolated work situations. Teaching can be lonely work (Lortie, 1975).

Students, individually and collectively, influence the workplace conditions for physical education teachers as well as work orientations and actions. Students are socializing agents for teachers (Lawson, 1988; Templin, 1981), and the functional acts of teaching proceed in large part in accordance with what students will permit. Acceptance and enthusiasm by students are the desired norms. Unfortunately, student apathy and even rejection of physical education content are well documented. Different kinds of behavioral norms among students foster in teachers attendant work orientations and behaviors. For example, if students do not like and value physical education, they likely will pose behavior problems for teachers. Teachers, rather than devoting all of their time and effort to instruction, will be forced to concentrate on discipline. Therefore, there can be different versions of physical education and different workplace conditions in the same school.

Teachers also influence students. Just how much influence an individual teacher may exert with apathetic or hostile students remains an important question. Answers to this question are highly contextual, involving political-economic, organizational, situational, and personal-social factors.

Two related teacher orientations appear to be especially salient for workplace conditions in physical education. One is the teacher's orientation toward student learning. It makes a difference if teachers view student learning as an intended outcome of physical education and then act appropriately. On the other hand, there is evidence suggesting that not all teachers view learning as a necessary outcome of physical education (Placek, 1983), and their attendant acts help to create and maintain a different set of workplace conditions for physical education.

A second orientation relates to coaching responsibilities. Some analysts have suggested that teaching and coaching responsibilities are incompatible (Locke & Massengale, 1978; Templin, 1980). These analysts have described this incompatibility as "role conflict," in essence locating responsibility for the problem in the school's organizational structure.

There is, however, another side to the story, a side that emphasizes the teacher's responsibility for an imbalance between teaching and coaching. For some teachers, instructional physical education may have been from the time they entered teacher education programs a career contingency. In other words, these teachers have gained preparation for teaching and have consented to teach because this was the best or only way for them to coach. Such persons will bring divergent orientations and behave differently than teachers for whom teaching is a firm career choice. In both cases, workplace conditions are affected, and, in both cases, individual actions and orientations, not just organizational structure, are responsible for these conditions.

To recapitulate, new teachers inherit workplace conditions that result from a variety of factors (review Figure 8-1). These factors interact. They may facilitate, constrain, or prevent effective work practices. Yet, it also is true that teachers, with their students, can influence and even author their workplace conditions.

WORKPLACE CONDITIONS AND INDUCTION INTO THE PHYSICAL EDUCATION PROFESSION

New or rookie physical education teachers become veterans as they are able to prove themselves to their colleagues, students, and work supervisors. Veteran status is gained when rookie teachers have crossed functional and inclusionary organizational boundaries. New teachers are able to cross the functional boundary when they have demonstrated to the satisfaction of their peers and work supervisors the work-related knowledge, values, sensitivities, and skills that are valued by school administrators and other teachers. New teachers cross the inclusionary boundary when they gain acceptance in an occupational community, a group of like teachers who share the same kinds of work, work perspectives, and whose relationships meld the realms of work and leisure. It is difficult to pinpoint the timing and dynamics for every transition from rookie to veteran. Like workplace conditions for physical education teachers, the timing and dynamics of such boundary passages appear to be highly variable among individuals and among (if not within) schools.

All schools are not alike, and certainly workplace conditions for physical education teachers vary. Neither are new teachers alike because there are differences in the intent, content, and impact of their teacher education programs. Thus, the work of teaching physical education does not lend itself to the kind of professional induction that some analysts have envisioned and advocated. This concept of an induction is directed toward a singular model for a physical education teacher. Such an induction is predicated upon uniformity, conformity, and work autonomy. By contrast, in physical education the transition from rookie to veteran teacher is marked by diversity, some deviance from professional norms and values, and heteronomy more than autonomy. The case of physical education may be more aptly described as a "culture of variability" rather than a "culture of professionalism."

Furthermore, the concept of an induction into a profession implies that the new teacher develops a national or universal perspective on his or her identity as a physical education teacher. "The profession" in this perspective remains in the forefront of each teacher's mind, and each person's orientation is more cosmopolitan than local. Granted, in physical education's culture of variability some teachers will develop, maintain, and display such an identity and orientation. On the other hand, this same culture of variability, is responsible for work identities, orientations, and actions that deviate significantly from the norms of professionalism. If new teachers are not uniform in their orientations and identities when they complete teacher education programs, then each school's organizational socialization and organizational cultures only add to this variability, emphasizing the here-and-now as well as located work identities, orientations, and responsibilities.

For many new teachers, it is membership and acceptance in the local occupational community, not the national profession, that is prized and pursued, at least in the initial years of teaching. And it is the occupational community's norms, more than professional or dominant organizational norms, that gain salience in the mind of the new teacher. Hence, future research should attend to the formation, orientations, and actions of such occupational communities, together with their organizational sub-cultures or "idiocultures" (Fine, 1987). An enhanced understanding of occupational communities promises new and important insights into the transition from rookie to veteran physical education teacher.

Physical education's culture of variability is produced and repro-duced in the daily acts of teacher education and actual teaching practices in elementary and secondary schools. Such variability will not vanish until there is greater consensus among the persons and organizations respon-sible for the design, conduct, and evaluation of teacher education and school programs. Until a consensus is reached, both among persons in physical education and with others who also control the fate of physical education programs, there is little reason for optimism regarding im-provements in the workplace conditions for physical education teachers. It follows that if there are few or no improvements in workplace condi-tions for teachers, there is little reason to believe that children and youth will be treated to improvements in their school physical education expe-riences, or that there will be significant changes in the job satisfaction and work identities of physical education teachers. Many such teachers will continue to leave physical education teaching for other careers. And when they do, new employment opportunities for the next generation of new teachers will present themselves, starting anew the transition from rookie to veteran physical education teacher in workplace conditions that are highly variable.

REFERENCES

Bain, L. L. (in press). Physical education teacher education. In W. Houston, M. Haberman, & J. Sikula (Eds.). *Handbook of research on teacher education.* New York: MacMillan and the Association of Teacher Educators.
Becker, H. S. (1952). The career of the Chicago public schoolteacher. *American Journal of Sociology, LVII,* 47-477.
Corrigan, P. (1982). *Schooling the smash street kids.* London: Macmillan.
Dewar, A. (1987). The social construction of gender in physical education. *Women's Studies Interna-tional Forum, 10*(4), 453-466.
Fine, G. (1987). *With the boys: Little league baseball and preadolescent culture.* Chicago: University of Chicago Press.
Griffin, P. S. (1983). "Gymnastics is a girl's thing": Student participation and interaction patterns in a middle school gymnastics unit. In T. Templin & J. Olson (Eds.), *Teaching in physical education.* Champaign, IL: Human Kinetics.
Hendry, L. B. (1978). *School, sport, and leisure.* London: Lepus Books.
Lawson, H. (1983a). Toward a model of teacher socialization in physical education: The subjective war-rant, recruitment and teacher education. *Journal of Teaching in Physical Education, 2*(3), 3-16.
Lawson, H. (1983b). Toward a model of teacher socialization in physical education: Entry into schools, teachers' role orientations and longevity in teaching. *Journal of Teaching in Physical Education, 3*(1), 3-15.

Lawson, H. (1986). Occupational socialization and the design of teacher education programs. *Journal of Teaching in Physical Education, 5*, 107-116.

Lawson, H. (1988). Occupational socialization, cultural studies and the physical education curriculum. *Journal of Teaching in Physical Education, 7*(4), 265-288.

Locke, L. (1984, Summer). Research on teaching teachers: Where are we now? *Journal of Teaching in Physical Education,* Monograph 2, 3-86.

Locke, L., & Massengale, J. (1978). Role-conflict in teacher-coaches. *Research Quarterly, 71*, 27-40.

Lortie, D. (1975). *School teacher: A sociological study.* Chicago: University of Chicago Press.

Mitchell, M. & Earls, R. (1987). A profile of state requirements for physical education K-12. *The Physical Educator, 44*(3), 337-343.

Placek, J. (1983). Conceptions of success in teaching: Busy, happy, and good? In T. Templin & J. Olson (Eds.), *Teaching in physical education.* Champaign, IL: Human Kinetics.

Schein, E. H. (1986). *Organizational culture and leadership.* San Francisco: Jossey-Bass.

Steen, T. B. (1985). A case study of teacher socialization in physical education during early training experiences: A qualitative analysis. *Dissertation Abstracts International, 46*, 2668A. (University Microfilms No. 85-26, 256)

Steen, T. (1988). Looking for commitment to teaching: Suggestions for teaching education. *Quest, 40*(1), 74-83.

Templin, T. (1979). Occupational socialization and the physical education teacher. *Research Quarterly, 50*(3), 482-493.

Templin, T. (1980). Teacher/coach role conflict and the high school principal. In V. Crafts (Ed.) *Proceedings, National Association for Physical Education in Higher Education, Volume II.* Champaign, IL: Human Kinetics Publishers.

Templin, T. (1981). Student as socializing agent. *Journal of Teaching Physical Education, 1*(1), 71-79.

Templin, T. J. (1985). Developing commitment to teaching: The professional socialization of the preservice physical educator. In H. Hoffman & J. Rink (Eds.), *Physical education professional preparation: Insights and foresights.* Reston, VA: AAHPERD.

Tindall, B. A. (1975). Ethnography and the hidden curriculum in sport. *Behavioral and Social Science Teacher, 2*(2), 5-28.

Van Maanen, J. & Barley, S. (1984). Occupational communities: Culture and control in organizations. In B. Staw & L. Cummings (Eds.). *Research in organizational behavior, Vol. 6* (pp. 287-365). Greenwich, Conn: JAI Press.

Van Maanen, J. & Schein, E. (1979). Toward a theory of organizational socialization. In B. Staw (Ed.). *Research in organizational behavior* (pp. 209-261). Greenwich, CT: JAI Press.

Wang, B. M. (1977). An ethnography of a physical education class: An experiment in integrated living. Doctoral dissertation, University of North Carolina at Greensboro, *DAI,* 1977, 38, 1980A-1981A. (No. 77-21750).

Willis, P. (1977). *Learning to labor: How working class kids get working class jobs.* New York: Columbia University Press.

9

Running On Ice: A Case Study of The Influence of Workplace Conditions on a Secondary School Physical Educator

THOMAS J. TEMPLIN
Purdue University

> The administration creates as difficult a time as they can for us in this discipline. They hold us accountable for what we do, but don't give any help and make it more difficult for us to do it.

This statement represents the analysis of a mid-career, female secondary school Physical Education teacher who feels the emotional drain and frustration of her work. As the reader will learn, it reflects the erosion of the conditions under which she toils, her dissatisfaction as a teacher, and the marginality of her subject area within the school curriculum. This teacher's experiences in many respects mirror those of other struggling PE teachers (Locke, Griffin, & Templin, 1986) and reflect the literature which suggests that PE is a troubled subject area in our public schools (Dodds & Locke, 1984; Siedentop, 1986; Taylor, 1986; Templin, 1987).

Of course, it would be in error to suggest that all programs and all PE teachers reflect such a "gloom and doom" scenario. Many programs exist in which the conditions necessary for teacher effectiveness and satisfaction prevail. Unfortunately, documentation of such programs is rare (Graham, 1982; Siedentop, Mand, & Taggart, 1986; Templin, 1983).

It is the purpose of this chapter to discuss and describe various workplace conditions which influence teachers' work. In order to accomplish this, a case study will be presented in which the effects of school conditions on the teacher (hereafter Sarah), previously quoted, will be illustrated.[1] It should be clear from this biographical account that positive workplace conditions are prerequisite to promoting school, program, and teacher effectiveness. This has been documented within this text by Lawson, Evans, and Sage as well as by others (Cuban, 1987; Frymier, 1987; Goodlad, 1983a, 1983b; Little, 1987; Lortie, 1975; Schwartz & Olson, 1987; Shulman, 1983). As Goodlad (1983b) suggests:

For all schools, the priority item always to be on the agenda is the quality of life in the workplace—its assessment and improvement. Creating a satisfying place of work for the individuals who inhabit schools is good in its own right, but it appears also to be necessary to maintain a productive educational environment. (p. 59)

Goodlad is joined by Frymier (1987) who emphatically commented on his concern for the importance of creating a desirable workplace for the teacher:

. . . there are many people in policy and administrative positions who mouth pat phrases about the importance of teachers and teaching then proceed to undercut teachers by creating conditions of work that blunt their enthusiasm and stifle their creativity. I see such actions as a kind of "neutering" of teachers. (p. 9)

"Neutering" may be a strong term to some, but it represents the product of organizational socialization in which teacher effectiveness and satisfaction may be effected. It relates to Frymier's (1987) concern for understanding that curricula, policies, personnel, programs, and precedents are powerful forces that effect a teacher's work.

---

[1]This chapter is an extension of research previously reported (Templin, 1988). This research was theoretically grounded in the developmental work by Levinson and his associates (1978) and utilized an ethnographic approach. Primary sources of data came from taped interviews and school and departmental documents.

As Lawson points out in Chapter 8, one must take into account these factors because they reflect the interplay of personal, institutional, cultural, and environmental forces. Further, one must recognize that the conditions of the workplace can work in two directions—any condition or set of conditions has the potential to facilitate, or constrain the teacher's ability to perform and be satisfied in the teaching role. Teaching is problematic and teachers may react and be socialized in different ways as various factors impact everyday work. This is the dialectical nature of teacher socialization (Lacey, 1977, 1987).

Hence, as one examines the context in which Sarah works, various questions may be forwarded:

- What are the goals of the school and PE program department in relation to a student's physical education?
- What are Sarah's goals?
- How are school, department, or Sarah's individual goals facilitated or constrained?
- What contextual factors contribute toward the success or failure of these goals (i.e., curriculum, teacher roles and workload, administrative expectations and leadership, students, teacher rewards, teacher collegiality, teacher decision-making, facilities and equipment, and professional development)?

Schematically, Figure 9-1 depicts the variety of contextual factors which have impacted on Sarah's teaching career and which will be analyzed in relation to her life as a teacher. It is important to note that these factors are, in most instances, interconnected or interdependent. For example, the school principal's role, attitude toward, and association with those in physical education may well influence the PE curriculum, facilities and equipment, teacher decision-making, teacher rewards, and professional development opportunities.

From this analysis it should be clear that schools are more than learning places for children and youth. Schools and school systems also are increasingly complex bureaucracies which double as work places—work places which process teachers as well as students. Again, this chapter's intent is to explore the selected ways in which contextual factors in one school have affected the work—in essence, the life and career—of one secondary school teacher.

Before preceding, I wish to point out some cautions related to how this chapter is presented. First, it is skewed in a negative direction—it is limited to a rather dismal picture instead of a profile which might provide a more positive image of the workplace. Secondly, it is based on one teacher's perceptions of her workplace. It does not include interview data from her colleagues, students, administrators, or others in her role set. It is a mid-career teacher's view of her world and our (her's and mine)

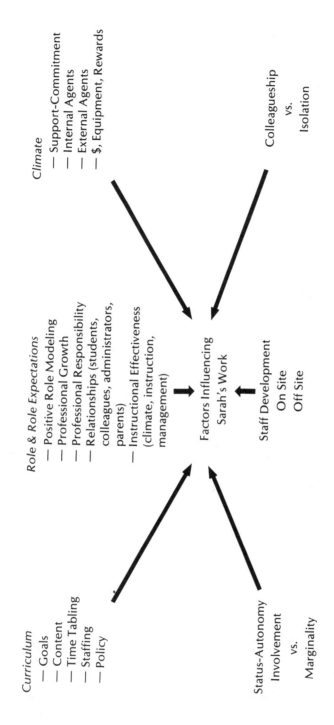

FIGURE 9-1. *Factors influencing Sarah's work*

interpretation of it. Finally, the chapter is written for the most part, in the present tense because the conditions under which our subject must live persist. They endure in the present, are a part of her past, and in all likelihood will remain with her in the future.

SARAH AND INDUCTION

Sarah is a 41-year-old secondary school physical education teacher who has taught for 14 years in the large Midwestern City in which she was raised. She teaches in the same high school (hereafter, Smith High School) that she attended as a adolescent and within the same school system that she completed her student teaching. Sarah has a bachelor's and master's degree in physical education and health and is licensed to teach both subjects. Finally, she has coached various sports throughout her tenure in the high school of 1,500 students.

Induction

Sarah was in a unique position for her employment at Smith High School having been a former student of the school and having done her student teaching at a local junior high. Sarah perceived compatibility between herself and the school based on her previous experience as a student and in relation to her preparation at the university.

They had seen me in action because I did my student teaching at one of the junior high's and at that time I was also involved in athletic training and I was the first female graduate from the university with an athletic training certificate. I was the first female to be involved in athletic training at Smith. So I have a lot of firsts. They knew my capabilities, they knew my philosophy, and I was a native. I had an interest in the community and they are going to be more accepting with an individual they feel comfortable with than with an outsider they know very little about. All those things combined probably made me a good candidate in their eyes.

When I started I was fairly well prepared. I knew from my schooling how to build a progression, a sequence. What you had to do, the drills that went into developing this specific skill. All I had to do was sort out the basic skills that were specific to that age group and what was needed in the sequencing of their skill levels . . . I didn't have a whole lot of preparation to do because it was so ingrained in my undergraduate training that it was a natural for me. It was easy for me to see where we had to move and what had to be done and the manner in which I was going to do it. So the preparation in the early years was basically an evaluation type and hand out information to the students. So I didn't have a lot of hours on end for preparation, setting up lesson plans and doing all that. It was more the process of conveying information to students, the handouts and stuff that I used and then the written evaluative tool which was the test. That wasn't very difficult for me either because I had my objectives. I knew what was supposed to be incorporated in it.

However ideal the situation appeared initially for Sarah, she was not naive in realizing that the fit was not altogether perfect. Sarah also recognized that the "honeymoon" during induction was short lived, particularly in terms of student attitudes toward learning.

When ever you come out of a university program, you have high expectations of idealistic objectives and the realism hits you the first day of school because nothing ever works the way it's supposed to or rarely does it work the way it's supposed to. The expectation was that you have kids that are coming to you to learn and the realization is that that's not always the case. As the years have gone on our society has become so complex and so different with its needs that I perceive education as being real irrelevant to a lot of kids. We use to have a dynamite school, the curriculum was the best in the state, the respect for teachers in the community and the respect for teachers from kids was great. I was proud when I first started to say, "Hey, I'm a teacher at Smith." It didn't bother me when people asked me what I do. I said, I teach. But now it's a whole different story.

What once was a smooth pathway into teaching has become a very rocky road. We need to look beneath the surface in order to understand Sarah's plight, to understand the conditions which has made the travel over her 14 years very rough at times.

THE WORKPLACE

The Curriculum

Most secondary school PE curricula have multiple objectives: fitness development, skill acquisition, personal-social development, cognitive development, and affective development. These traditional objectives are promoted through a variety of physical activities during a student's PE experience. Most states require at least two semesters of PE and many programs offer PE beyond the basic requirement (Mitchell & Earls, 1987).

It is reasonable to assume that the degree to which curricula prioritize and, in fact, operationalize these objectives or combinations of them, will determine the overall impact of the curriculum on student learning. Equally, influence also may extend to the teacher; that is, how objectives and activities impact upon the teacher's work. Thus, a curriculum, whether it is overt, hidden, or both, may set the tone not only for student learning but for teacher effectiveness, satisfaction, the division of labor within a staff, and the image PE projects to students, administrators, teachers, parents, and the community.

As Lawson (1983c) stated, "although created by humans, curricula may act back upon their creators by socializing them" (p. 363). For example, Dewar (1985) and Templin, Savage and Hagge (1986) provide examples of the way in which curricula, intended to improve professional practice, may in fact deskill or deprofessionalize teachers' work. Through imposed, routinized, or even the implementation of pre-packaged curricula, teaching becomes controlled. Teachers experience the proletaranization of their work and become deskilled (Apple, 1983; Gitlin, 1983). This, as Dewar (1985) suggests, represents a "decrease in the autonomy and control that teachers have over the conception and execution of their work" (p. 164).

One should recognize, however, that even curricula that are self designed and controlled may lead to deprofessionalization. The major characterization and criticism of most PE programs center on PE as play, "recess," or supervised recreation wherein little curricular or instructional prowess, creativity, or novelty is witnessed. Reproduction and maintenance of a sports and games curriculum (Lawson, 1988) is prevalent. Regardless of objectives or content, teachers play little role in affecting student learning. Goodlad (1983b) found PE may be high in liking, but low in relevance to students. A parallel conclusion may be applied to teachers—they may like or prefer the role of supervisor of a sports and games curriculum, but they recognize it may be irrelevant to students and toward maintaining their skills as teachers.

In many respects, Sarah has been deskilled through the curriculum at Smith. She has had little autonomy or control in determining the curriculum, staffing decisions, or scheduling of activities or space. She is only "reskilled" (Dewar, 1985) to the extent to which Sarah attempts to remain a pedagogically competent and committed practitioner. Unfortunately, in Sarah's mind, her commitment toward effective teaching is waning.

Sarah fully recognizes and is angered by the fact that the PE program at Smith is classified as "non-academic." Sarah believes the curriculum is far from promoting the objectives of the school (Smith Faculty Handbook, 1987-8):

> In theory and in practice we believe we must strive to offer a variety of attractive curricular and extracurricular programs; to give students the opportunity to develop further intellectual, *physical*, social, and artistic skills; to provide opportunities for social relationships; and to stimulate constructive use of leisure time. (p. 2)

Sarah believes such a philosophy is "universal with most schools" and that the PE curriculum specifically is aimed at "developing motor skills, fitness, coordinator balance, agility, social skills, and understanding rules and the nature of games."

Unfortunately, Sarah sees little correspondence between philosophy and objectives and the effect of those activities offered. Students, and consequently teachers, are constrained initially by time and policy constraints. Sarah explains:

Being able to touch upon goals or whether we satisfy them is the real question. We touch upon them, but we don't know to what degree we fulfill them. Learning is an ongoing process and there's never enough time. It seems you can only do so much with the time that's allotted. Our state allots us only a minute amount of time for secondary PE. We're not governed to require more than a credit—that's a semester their freshmen year and one their sophomore year. That's five hours a week for 18 weeks—that's a total of 36 weeks or a total of 180 hours of PE minus interrupted classes for pep sessions, etc. Once they have accomplished that, they are not required to take anymore class through graduation. With our country's so-called "fitness craze," the policy provides for a very marginal experience. So in terms of the time we have to fulfill our objectives, it is very, very limited.

Equally, the way in which activities are structured presents difficulties as well. It appears that teachers are hardpressed to facilitate learning when activities are blocked into short, three-week units. Students often rotate from one three-week unit of activity and teacher to another and the rotation revolves around a six-week unit of swimming. One consequence of this system is that each PE teacher rarely has the same group of students for more than three weeks during a semester. For example, only once has Sarah worked with one group for an entire semester (this group engaged in six different activities over 18 weeks). The next longest time frame in which Sarah taught any one group was six weeks. An examination of her schedule (Figure 9-2) reflects the lack of continuity and the heavy preparation time (10 different activities) that confronts Sarah and her colleagues.

The structure is contrary to a philosophy which suggests learning is a priority. Rather, it appears to correspond more directly to a "recreational" or "introductory" and "cost effective" rationale frequently seen in many secondary schools. This rationale suggests that by giving students a brief introductory experience to a variety of activities, they will use the introduction to pursue self-directed activity once graduated from high school. Whether this is true remains unresearched.

Sarah is frustrated by her schedule, the structure of the curriculum, and its introductor emphasis, but feels powerless in changing it:

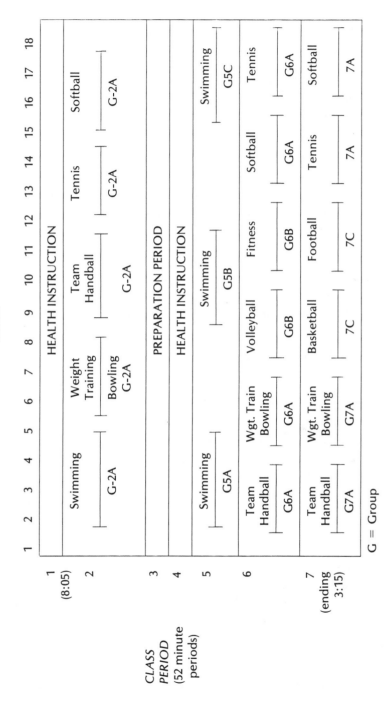

FIGURE 9-2. Sarah's teaching schedule

G = Group

This does bother me, but what control do I have over it? That's part of my frustration. We don't have the flexibility from the school corporation by them saying—"Hey, you people know what you need to do, you have control over what you want to do as a department." Our philosophy has always been, and I'm not always in agreement with it, to do lots of different activities. They are always aware and conscious of the use of the facility. Are we using good use of our space? It's a cost effectiveness situation here. So we don't have enough control over our own program to say we're going to offer nine weeks of fitness, six weeks of swimming, and maybe another activity. With the philosophy the way it is, it's not really academic in nature where kids can get a real grasp of something and really use it. It's like trying to run on ice in street shoes. You can't get anywhere.

A necessary condition for Sarah for her effectiveness and satisfaction as a teacher is linked to a focused and well scheduled curriculum which may be truly linked to the stated objectives of the program. Equally, she desires to be empowered to control what is offered and the way in which activities are offered in terms of length and staffing. Unfortunately, the reverse is true as Sarah teaches a variety of activities to constantly changing and large groups of students. The size of her classes has not gone unnoticed by Sarah.

In a PE class, there's no way you can teach 39 kids and really do a good job of teaching. You can do a good job of managing, but that's it. We have the largest class size in the school.

In summary, Sarah finds herself in a traditional sports and games curriculum. Learning appears to be a secondary focus as the structure of the curriculum is primarily introductory and recreational in nature. Sarah works with ever-changing, large groups and is focuced to recognize that curricular maintenance and management have become a key to surviving in her role. She senses becoming deskilled as a result of this curricular structure and yet she feels rather helpless in changing the curriculum or the attitudes of others who are quite content with it.

There is little question that the Smith curriculum is one contextual factor that has made teaching rather difficult work for Sarah.

Teaching Workload and Role

Closely linked to the PE curriculum is the teacher's role in executing the curriculum and school policy. This may be explained by examining the role expectations of the school administration as well as those of an individual teacher. Institutional and personal expectations may reflect either congruence or conflict; that is, the teacher may experience satisfaction or conflict depending on the tasks expected of the teacher. This should be apparent already in relation to Sarah's view of the Smith curriculum.

Based upon the objectives of most schools' PE departments, one would assume that a PE teacher's role would be defined in terms of such role expectations as: lesson and unit planning; effective teaching (establishing sound climate, instructional, and management practices); evaluation of instruction and curriculum; service through curricular and extracurricular roles; maintaining positive relations with students, administrators, teaching colleagues, and parents; and engaging in professional development activities.

Again, a teacher may experience role congruity or conflict depending on the extent and nature of role demands. Both intra role and inter role conflicts may abound and determine one's effectiveness and satisfaction in a role or roles. Certainly, PE teachers who often assume the dual role of coach (not to mention other roles held concurrently with teaching and coaching) are highly susceptible to the problem of role conflict as pointed out by Sage (Chapter 11) in this text.

The bottom line is what does the workplace demand or expect of the teacher and how does it effect the teacher's work?

Expectations. Within the faculty handbook of Smith High School, specific administrative expectations for teachers are outlined. Figure 9-3 delineates these expectations, which will be discussed through the remainder of this chapter.

Although these expectations are never explicitly reviewed with teachers, Sarah suggested that the administration assumes that teachers know what they are and that they should be fulfilled. Although Sarah believes she attempts to meet the expectations in each area, she admits that many are increasingly difficult to demonstrate. Sarah has tried to maintain high expectations for her students, maintain enthusiasm for them, and meet instructional expectations of the administration, yet she struggles to do so. She fights the frustration of the "play" mentality in the curriculum and she battles students' attitudes that suggest education is largely irrelevant. Sarah reflects on her frustration:

> It seems like I'm the freak in the system. That I feel my responsibility is to teach, not to manage and sometimes I feel I'm the only one that feels teaching is important. Everybody else says, just get through, just manage it. There's a fear too that I'm going to have to adjust to the management situation and I don't like that at all. So there's an inner conflict battle within myself knowing that I'm a teacher and what I've been hired to do and it disgusts me to see that kind of thing happening in other people and disgusts me to think even more that I may

Personal Characteristics
— Shows a positive attitude toward students, subject manner, general school environment.
— Provides a model for students (self control, punctuality, courtesy, respect, friendliness, integrity).

Professional Growth
— Remains professional current.
— Participates in required in-service.
— Participates in faculty and departmental meetings.
— Participates in planning opportunities.
— Sets professional goals.

Professional Responsibility
— Assumes personal share of responsibility for the general operation of the school (hall monitor, pep sessions, volunteers for extra curricular events, enforces school rules).
— Completes assignments on time.
— Maintains complete and accurate records.

Relationships with Students
— Displays fair and consistent attitudes, encourages high expectations, explains regulations.
— Shows an interest in students, is friendly, enthusiastic, gives positive reinforcement and maintains a sense of humor.

Relationship with Staff
— Works and communicates effectively with staff.

Relationships with Parents and Community
— Informs parents of student's academic progress and degree of cooperation with school rules.

Classroom Management
— Provides an atmosphere conducive to learning.
— Encourages students to set and maintain high standards of classroom behavior.
— Uses clear and appropriate objectives.
— Plans effectively via written daily and unit lesson plans.
— Provides effective instruction in relation to reviewing and presently new material, evaluation, and the use of a variety of teaching materials and techniques.
— Assures safety.

FIGURE 9-3. *Administrative expectations for teachers at Smith High School*

become one of those people. So there's a real inner conflict going on with me . . . I think that's what has made me so unhappy because I can't give in to the "roll out the ball" syndrome, play syndrome. Play is good, but I think in an educational setting at the level we're at, some interaction, feedback, information, transfer has to take place.

This is why Sarah finds it difficult and even hypocritical to be expected to meet certain expectations related to instructional effectiveness when instruction (versus supervision) has such a low priority in the PE curriculum. This difficulty may be further linked to the relationship between administrative expectations toward fair and accurate evaluation of students and the PE curriculum. Sarah comments on the determination of student grades in relation to the curriculum pattern at Smith:

You get a sheet with total points. You don't know how it's broken down. It gets complicated because a grade could reflect six weeks of swimming and a three-week unit, 3 three-week units, or 2 three-week units of three weeks of swimming. It's a headache—a hassle. I don't know how you keep track of students. That's why I went to the administration. I can't be accountable to my students under this system. If we're going to be recreation, fine, let's be pass/fail. But no—you are to teach. That's the complication, but we aren't assisted. It gets more and more difficult to teach. That's the conflict. The longer you are in it, the harder it is.

Workload. Beyond the expectations for Sarah's role as a teacher, one must acknowledge the time demands of teaching. This is particularly true of physical education teachers who are often called upon to coach. It is not unusual for the PE teacher/coach to put in 10 to 12 hours a day for the majority of a school year.

The pace and routine of Sarah's workload was very demanding. As described earlier, she teaches six periods a day and has one preparation period. This schedule included four PE classes (10 activities per semester) and two health classes. In addition, she coaches one spring sport which ran from February through May. She starts the school day at 7:30 and is usually home between 5:00 and 9:00 at night, depending on her coaching responsibilities. Sarah perceives her workload as being demanding:

My workload is very stressful. When I talked to the superintendent, I told him I am working harder now than when I started teaching. But nothing is being done to alleviate that stress. There could be some small changes—significant changes—that would alleviate the stressful situation. From the time I hit the door there's no time to relax, unwind, interact with your associates. The bells ring and the students come. The bells ring and the students leave and another group comes in and it's so regimented all day long and by the time you get done with seven periods you're whipped . . . During the prep period you found yourself running a lot to get stuff organized, visual aids, printed material, computer stuff and I just found myself just spinning my wheels not getting too much done. Just totally being worn out because of the pace you have to go at. Also, I found myself getting more and more frustrated because there's no time to interact, to sit down and work on things.

Equally, Sarah's combined roles of teaching and coaching have brought added stress to her work. She feels the demands of her roles make exemplary role performance in each impossible:

It gets in the way because it's another demand placed on you and your fatigue level increases. It's (coaching) an added responsibility without adequate time to prepare for it. So, something has to give. In my situation, they both give. I don't neglect one over the other, but I'm not at full capacity in either.

Various strategies to resolve teacher/coach conflict have been recommended (Kneer, 1987; Templin, 1981). Sarah suggested one basic adjustment to her schedule:

Ideally, if you have responsibility for coaching, you should have a half load, half coaching and half teaching . . . There's only so many things you can do in a day's time and there's also personal needs you have to weigh with teaching and coaching. It's like you're a machine and you live just to teach and coach. There are more demands in each role, in life, and the time allotted has not changed.

Thus, with the specific responsibilities and expectations of each role, Sarah finds her roles very demanding relative to her perception that: 1) PE is of little meaning to students, colleagues and administrators, which is reflective of a "introductory" curriculum and which, at times, deters Sarah from exemplary role performance; and 2) the combined demands of teaching and coaching make her job even more stressful. Yet, Sarah remains in the coaching role because she gains satisfaction from interacting with students/athletes, and it gives her some additional discretionary income.

RELATIONSHIPS

It seems reasonable to suggest that one of the primary criteria for a satisfactory workplace is one in which the teacher is able to cooperate not only with students, but with fellow teachers, administrators, and parents as well. Such a proposition is well supported in available literature (Duckworth & Carnine, 1987; Feiman-Nemser & Floden, 1986; Goodlad,

1983b; Little, 1987; Martinek, 1981; Tangri & Moles, 1987; Templin, 1987). It appears to be an evident truth that when a teacher is able to interact positively with students as well as collaborate with and is supported by those with whom one works, teacher effectiveness and satisfaction are enhanced. Students, colleagues, and school administrators can serve as "significant others" in setting favorable work conditions for the teacher. They may serve as socializing agents in facilitating successful (versus troubled) role performance.

Students

As described in Figure 9-3, Sarah is expected to display fair and consistent attitudes with students while maintaining high expectations. She is expected to be friendly and enthusiastic, and to reinforce students positively.

Sarah has attempted to meet these expectations throughout her career. Although Sarah perceives education as "being irrelevant to a lot of kids," her motivation to stay in teaching is linked to her desire to interact with adolescents and help them grow and become physically educated. Such a stance, however, has become increasingly difficult for Sarah to maintain. For example, those students enrolled in advanced physical education classes presented new difficulties to Sarah:

> I'd rather not teach these classes. The clientele in those classes are kids who flunked Basic PE [required one semester of freshman and sophomores] two or three times. They come in with the attitude "it's an easy credit," that they don't have to do anything but play, that it's not a structured learning environment. I had 30 kids signed up for team sports. On the very first day when kids found out what the course outline was and what they were going to be expected to do, I had 10 kids drop the class. There was going to be work involved and they didn't want that, they just wanted to play. If there isn't learning going on, why do we have an educational establishment?

Secondly, in relation to the students enrolled in Basic PE, Sarah is able to distinguish those students who make her job enjoyable from those who transform her role into that of a supervisor.

> I have two different groups in the day. The freshmen have been very receptive, have been very willing to do note taking, do drills, take feedback, and try to improve. You have kids willing to learn. I have two classes [sophomores] where the students make it horrendous to get anything done. These kids are immature, disrespectful, hateful, and destructive. They make it bad for me and those kids who want to learn. So you have everything. This depends on the administration and what they allow the students' attitude to develop toward.

Sarah is concerned about those students who needed special attention and assistance, and is stressed by the additional responsibility they present:

There's so many kids that need help . . . I wasn't prepared to deal with all this kind of stuff—divorce, court, father's got him six months here and the mother's got him six months there, and he's bouncing back and forth, and the mother has a boyfriend that's living with her, and then the kid comes to school and he's wired anyway. My health assignment is irrelevant to the kid who's worried about his life and surviving. We are here to educate these kids, not to deal with their home problems—their psychological or personal needs versus academic needs. We cannot deal with these kinds of things. I spend most of my time in my toughest classes with behavioral problems. This shouldn't be my responsibility. I'm not a psychologist. I'm a physical educator—I'm a teacher. I have subject matter I need to deal with and I feel the administration needs to support that kind of attitude in that we are here to educate.

Sarah's remark relates to her aversion to her never-ending roles as a parent surrogate, counselor, and disciplinarian. Although Smith High School defines strategies and guidelines for its teaching staff for the resolution of disruptive behavior, they are not automatic deterents to these problems. Certainly, such behavior is a constant companion or condition of teaching. Smith's guidelines (Smith Faculty Handbook, 1987-8) stem from a philosophy which suggests:

1. The teacher must be empathetic in the solution of student problems
2. The words *firm, fair,* and *friendly* are the teachers' keys to better discipline. (p. 33)

As a consequence, teachers are expected to regard each student with the rights and respect due any individual. Sarah is expected to uphold 25 Do's and Don'ts (Figure 9-4) and to promote a positive approach to discipline. In line with the philosophy of the school which, again, suggests teachers are (Smith Faculty Handbook, 1987-8):

encouraged to develop a better understanding of student problems by consulting with counselors, teachers, and parents. Also, once a student has been disciplined, the teacher should follow up and make a special effort to aid the student in conforming with school expectations. In general once a student is down, don't keep him there, but give him a helping hand. (p. 36)

Teachers are expected to resolve their students misbehavior on their own and to seek the help of an assistant principal only for the most se-

DO'S

1. One should be fair at all times. . . . Consistency is mandatory.
2. One should be enthusiastic, courteous, and above, maintain a sense of humor.
3. One should let students know he cares.
4. One should establish a minimum number of rules.
5. One should make sure the punishment fits the misdeed.

DON'TS

1. One should never get into a "do it or else" situation.
2. One should never punish the entire class for the actions of a few.
3. One should avoid arguing with students.
4. One should not overburden students with demands beyond their ability.
5. One should not harp on small imperfections and minor infractions.

FIGURE 9-4. *Dos and Don'ts of discipline at Smith High School*

rious cases. Teachers are expected to have written discipline plans and to enforce disciplinary procedures outlined in both faculty and student handbooks. The Smith PE program's written plan expects students to adhere to the following: 1) learn to his/her potential, 2) participate in a constructive manner, 3) to not hinder any student from learning, 4) to not hinder any teacher from teaching, 5) follow the basic rules and safety procedures of the class, and 6) uphold all rules of the school and community. Any disruption of the above may result in five disciplinary steps which range from a verbal reprimand to the removal from the class for a semester. The word "may" is emphasized because in reality according to Sarah, the Smith system does not adhere to that exact rule. Sarah explained:

> I feel the administration gives them too many times to mess up. They get three times to mess up in my class, three times in every class. That's 21 times before they're out. I think if a kid is in trouble one time in class, get it taken care of there, but don't give him 20 other times in other classes. I think it should be three strikes, period, and you're out.

Thus, Sarah's relationship with PE students reflect both satisfaction and dissatisfaction. Unfortunately, the latter seems more common and Sarah's major reason for entering teaching—working with kids—"has become less of a reason to stay in teaching" for Sarah.

Teaching Colleagues

When addressing the issue of teacher isolation, Templin (1988) suggests that "teachers rarely engage in activities whereby personal and professional support for one another is given or whereby pedagogical problems may be solved (p. 197)." It has been documented that collegiality is an important development, as an important source for intrinsic reward for teachers, and as a way to gain a sense of pedagogical unity with others (Little, 1987). Hence, one's colleagues have the potential to be a very important support network. On the other hand, if one works in physical or philosophical isolation from co-workers, one's work experience may become conflict ridden. Again, a necessary condition for the workplace would be one in which co-workers could work together, create together, enjoy the satisfactions of teaching together, and solve problems together.

Sarah likes the people with whom she works. She has a cordial relationship with her fellow PE teachers and finds it easy to interact with them. At the same time, however, she is frustrated by the fact that the majority of her PE colleagues don't share her high commitment to teaching.

There's a definite conflict in our philosophies and that makes the relationship and the working condition a little uneasy, but I'm not the only one who has that. I would feel bad about feeling that way if I were the only one who felt it, but there are teachers who are outside the discipline that feel the same way. We have our differences and we get them out on the table and we talk about them. . . . We plan and we all say yes, this is what we're going to do, but when it comes down to running it in the class, I'm not sure what transpires . . . There may be times in there when they do teach, but it's not on a day-to-day basis.

Thus, Sarah perceives divisiveness of philosophy in relation to that identified earlier, namely, the learning versus play mentality.

You have basically two kinds of physical educators who represent two philosophies. You have the one philosophy where its a discipline, its academic, and its applied science. Then you have the other side which says PE is play. It's merely to experience. Two, maybe three (out of six teachers) hold it's more than play. So we're split. We have trouble supporting one another and I know that's where a lot of the problem is. I said to the department head, if we can't unite and do what we say we should do, then we don't have a leg to stand on. Yet, he continues to divide the department . . . He's not concerned for PE and that's the philosophy of the school corporation. I don't think our students need that agenda.

This division presents a problem for Sarah when students come to her with lessons from other PE teachers' classes. It is difficult for students to understand that Sarah prioritizes teaching and learning over just playing.

Different philosophies from another individual [teacher] and you have to change the kids' philosophy . . . When the kids rotate to me from a "play" teacher, the kids have a harder time adjusting.

This point was illustrated earlier when nearly one-third of her advanced students dropped her class after learning of Sarah's expectations.

Equally, Sarah perceives the reaction from her colleagues is rather demeaning.

People may think, hey, that Sarah goes around acting like she's department head and doing this and stirring up trouble. Why doesn't she leave it alone? Nobody has ever told me that directly, but that's the feeling I get from their actions. I have the students' concern at heart. It's a question of professional ethics and responsibility.

Even with her concern for professional integrity, Sarah does, at times, question her fit within the program.

Well I wonder, I've got all these people around me who don't agree with me or don't seem to hold the same ideal. I get to thinking, boy, I'm in the wrong place because I'm like a weird puzzle part that doesn't fit.

Fortunately another colleague who is in the initial stage of her career serves as a source of support for Sarah. She commented on this relationship.

She's very, very well disciplined and goal oriented with objectives in mind with her teaching and so that's been a reinforcement to me to know I'm not the lone duck in the puddle. She and I have many of the same philosophies and move in the same sort of direction. We do explanation, demonstration, practice, and then lead up games to play situations. We give the kids feedback. We're always interacting.

Thus, with the exception of this one teaching colleague, Sarah is frustrated by the lack of a shared commitment to the teaching/learning process among the other PE teachers. The department head provides little leadership and appears to do little in modeling teacher effectiveness. In this context, Sarah wonders periodically, if her commitment is worth the struggle.

Administrators

One earmark of school effectiveness is that school administrators are respected leaders who lead and collaborate effectively in the school (Duckworth and Carnine, 1987). Effective leaders must be caring, involved, supportive, knowledgeable of school programs, and willing to decentralize authority and decision making. As Goodlad (1983b) found in the Study of Schools, the principal and the principal-teacher relationship are key factors in teacher satisfaction. As Goodlad (1983) states:

> It appears that mutual trust between principal and teachers, considerable autonomy in the classroom for teachers, support for teachers by the principal, and respect for each other as professionals are important elements in the healthy school workplace. (p.52).

Such a thesis is supported by Ratliffe (1986) in his research involving the school principal and physical educators. For example, Ratliffe suggests that in order for physical educators to gain curricular and instructional control, teachers must become "proactive" rather than reactive in attempting to influence programmatic events. This requires, as Ratliffe (1986) states:

> Opening up channels of communication with people (the principal and faculty colleagues) who make decisions; decisions which will be based upon what they know and do not know about physical education in your school; decisions which control the quality of your professional life. (p.86)

The physical educator must become a socializing agent in attempting to influence one's own professional and personal future within a school.

Sarah's perception of the school's administration is similar to her perception of the majority of teaching colleagues. She feels frustrated by a lack of collegiality and support in her periodic attempts to improve the PE program. However, it is important to recognize that Sarah has opened the line of communication; she is trying to improve the situation and become proactive.

Her most recent attempt involved meetings with both the principal of Smith and the superintendent of the school corporation.

> I've talked to the principal and the superintendent and it's a back and forth type of situation. They're not committing that one's in charge or the other's in charge. It's the proverbial passing the buck routine. So you're in limbo and you don't know what's going on. They won't make a decision. They won't say.
>
> I talked to the principal first and he recommended I go to the superintendent. I asked him what is the philosophy of the school corporation toward PE? I said I need to know whether we are trying to teach these kids something or if we are just trying to give them a vent for stress. Is it going to be recreation in nature or is it supposed to be an educationally structured setting? The other question was how committed are you in a program in PE? The third question was what about stress situations in the teaching environment. We need

more faculty. We need more staff members in PE because we have the highest class size in the building. If, in fact, we are part of the process then we need to address the fact that we are not flexible or innovative in our curriculum, we do not have adequate staff members, our class size is so high that we cannot do the job.

On all three of these questions I got skirted. It was like that everyone has the tendency to think that their discipline is the most important in the school. I said if you don't think it's important, and I get the feeling it's low on the priority list, I want to know that so I can make some adjustments to my expectations. I don't have to have high expectations when it doesn't match your expectations.

One example of a mismatch is Sarah's concern for the addition of a PE classroom needed for lectures, testing, and the presentation of audiovisual material. Sarah received little support for such an idea.

We have asked for classrooms, yet the kids have to take tests on the gym floor. What does that do for your professional image? You can't give a lecture in here [the gym] because the noise level is so high you can't get your students to hear you. If you want to use a video or another audio-visual, you can't do it. I asked the superintendent why we don't have classrooms and he said we don't need them.

Another mismatch of expectations exists between Sarah and the department chair in relation to the equipment needed for proper instruction.

When we started tennis, I sorted out six out of 24 rackets that had loose grips, broken strings, or cracked head frames. We had flat balls that you can sink your fingers from one side to another . . . There's a big cement manhole in the middle of our playing field. I have asked and asked to have that taken care of . . . There's a budget, but I don't have any idea what it is. He [the department chair] doesn't show us. He asks us what we want, but we never get it. He asked about videotapes, too. I gave him my order but he lost the list. I'm still waiting.

Thus, the issue of professional integrity has become an issue of practicality for Sarah. Even though she "battles" once in awhile with school leaders about philosophy, curriculum, staffing, and the facility and its equipment, she senses she is forced to live with the present structure and without administrative support. Although change should not always rest in the principal's office or with a department chair (Lieberman and Miller, 1984), in Sarah's case, a little bit of assistance would make Sarah's work easier.

It hasn't always been easy to deal with liking someone or working with someone you like when they are so far off of what you believe in . . . I've changed . . . at times I've had to overlook some of the things that are not right just to get through.

Sarah perceives she is learning to live with a situation that her colleagues, teachers and administrators, apparently are quite content with.

Parental and Community Involvement

When discussing the future of physical education, Templin (1987) suggested:

> the constituency for whom public school physical education teachers work will be increasingly important, and if we are to improve the status of the teaching ranks with this constituency, we will need increased interaction, mutual respect, and increased coordination of goals and design of physical education. Partnerships must be formed. (p.64)

This notion relates to research which suggests that the positive and enthusiastic involvement of parents and other citizens of the school community is yet another trademark of good schools (Goodlad, 1983a, 1983b; Tangri & Moles, 1987). It is reasonable to suggest that these individuals could be significant socializing agents in how a school or teacher may operate. Whether parents and others are supportive or create conflict for teachers and programs may well determine individual and curricular effectiveness in a school. Examples of the positive effect of community involvement may be found in the federally sponsored Urban/Rural School Development Program (Joyce, Hersh & McKibben, 1983) and, more specific to PE, a curriculum development project recently conducted in the Lincoln, Nebraska public schools (Austin and Willeke, 1986). In both cases, teacher and curriculum development was positively effected through exchanges of ideas, assessment of school and community needs, and discussion of and implementation of programs. Feelings of anomie were decreased and a sense of efficacy increased as teachers and community members were brought closer together. Teachers look for and need positive involvement from agents outside the school. These agents can make teaching an easier task.

The Smith Faculty Handbook (1987-8) states as one of its objectives "that we should strive to make every effort to involve the community on an effective and meaningful partner in the educational process" (p. 3). Equally, in relation to administrative expectations, teachers are expected to "inform parents of students' academic progress and degree of cooperation in the school rules" (Smith Faculty Handbook, 1987-8), p. 12).

In terms of community involvement in relation to PE, Sarah believes her school falls well short of meeting the objective presented above. In her 14 years at Smith, parents and other community members rarely have played an active role in influencing staff or curriculum development. Sarah's statement reflects the marginal status of PE in the school.

There are some who care, but they are very small in number. If you don't have an administration that supports you, how can you get support from the community? So, parents are rarely involved. There is an advisory council, but I don't believe they have even concerned themselves with PE. After all, [Sarah stated facetiously] it's just PE.

Ideally, Sarah hopes for the formation of a committee that would focus on the curricular and staff development.

I'd probably work on a joint effort. Somehow pulling interested people from the community, from the university, from business, and within the school into some sort of common goal and commitment for grades K-12. But, this isn't going to happen.

Thus, agents outside the school have little impact on Sarah or PE at Smith.

TEACHER REWARDS

Given the tone of the preceding discussion, one probably wonders what keeps Sarah teaching. What rewards does she gain from teaching? Certainly, analyzing the rewards of teaching is yet another area which enables one to understand the work of teachers and yet another condition of the work place.

The rewards of teaching are typically categorized in terms of extrinsic, intrinsic, and ancillary rewards (Lortie, 1975). Extrinsic rewards are defined in terms of money, status, and power. Intrinsic rewards, also known as psychic rewards, are usually attached to the teachers' perception of the value of serving, and helping students, collegial support, enjoyment of teaching activities, and personal and professional growth through teaching. Ancillary rewards are associated with the stability of income, tenure, short working hours, and frequent holidays.

"Teachers vary in the importance they attach to both extrinsic and intrinsic rewards" (Feiman-Nemser and Floden, 1986, p.510). Equally, while teachers have depended primarily on intrinsic rewards (Lortie, 1975), these rewards are waning. As a consequence, the reward and career system of teaching "continues to favor recruitment rather than retention and low rather than high involvement" (Lortie, 1975, p.99).

Extrinsic rewards

Wealth, status and power are rarely the standard for classroom teachers. Although average salaries have increased since 1983, many teachers continue to struggle financially and must moonlight in order to supplement their income (Williams, 1988). The salaries of beginning teachers are lower than any other field requiring a bachelor's degree. Equally, salaries peak sooner and at a lower level than other college degree level positions (Shulman, 1987).

Although merit pay and career ladder structures have surfaced to promote financial and career mobility incentives, such structures have problems. For example, Rosenholtz and Smylie (1984) found various problems connected to merit pay in relation to measurement and colleagueship in a school. Such problems may be linked to career ladder systems as well. Teachers themselves operate off an egalitarian ethic which opposes individual differentiation beyond any financial gain or upward mobility through one's seniority and/or educational training.

Teaching, physical education in particular, is still considered a low status occupation. Teaching is scorned work and such a tarnished image prevents many from considering teaching as a career choice. Teachers are sensitive to and suffer from the "lack of respect syndrome" (Schwartz & Olson, 1987) which, in essence, is an occupational hazard. PE teachers and PE in general suffer greatly from this syndrome (Bain, 1983; Hendry, 1975).

Intrinsic Rewards

Assuming the relative absence of extrinsic rewards and the cultural and structural nature of most schools, the primacy of intrinsic rewards appears to be greater than extrinsic rewards. However, again, these rewards may fluctuate and seem to be waning. They may be more powerful to recruitment to the career than to the satisfaction and retention of teachers in their work. Power is lost due to the changing nature of teaching; teachers once found satisfaction in teacher-student relationships, collegial stimulation and support, and a strong service orientation. This is less true today (Feiman-Nemser & Floden, 1986).

PE teachers enter teaching because of their desire to serve society, their love of children, and the enjoyment they receive from their association with sport and physical activity (Templin, Woodford, and Mulling, 1982), yet the glow of these rewards may become dim as evidenced by various case studies (Locke, Griffin & Templin, 1986) which reveal oppressive work conditions for PE teachers.

Ancillary Rewards

These rewards—economic security, tenure, short and flexible work hours, frequent holidays—are best summarized by Lortie (1975):

Ancillary rewards affect entry to a given line of work more than the effort of those in it . . . Ancillary rewards are present. Whether one makes high or limited effort on the job . . . they may restrain a person from leaving the occupation, but they are unlikely to affect the effort he exerts on a day-to-day basis. (p. 103)

Thus, beyond the pressures related to tenure, these rewards are perhaps the most constant rewards gained by the teachers. With few exceptions, the tenured teacher can count on a monthly salary and set vacation periods. The teacher can count on a work schedule which is relatively small in hours in comparison to the time required of other workers. The schedule is more flexible and allows the teacher to devote more of himself to other outside interests and even outside employment.

The attractiveness of lesser time demands on the PE teacher/coach is, of course, diminished. PE teaching or teaching in other subject may be a career contingency for those who elect to coach and as such, they are committed to the extra time demands involved in coaching. Of course, along with coaching comes the hard earned reward of additional income.

Sarah has experienced the waning of her intrinsic work rewards. She enjoys and is rewarded by those students who make her work satisfying, yet she experiences less and less of this feeling. In fact, she experiences little student respect, little collegial stimulation, and little administrative support. She provides a retrospective of her perceptions:

They [rewards] are getting less and less and less. The rewards, all the things I went into it for—we had a dynamite school, the curriculum was the best in the state, the respect for teachers in the community, the respect for teacher from kids. I was proud when I first started to say, boy, I'm a teacher at Smith. It didn't bother me when people asked me what do I do, I said, I teach. But now, it's a whole different story. The kids' attitudes have changed. I get less respect. It's not the money and it's getting to a point where it's not the kids anymore.

In terms of rewards generally and in relation to the limited praise she has received from school administrators, Sarah feels little satisfaction. She wants praise to translate into meaningful administrative commitment and support:

There are really no rewards. Support in the form of verbal praise isn't enough. I want them to substantiate it—by them to back it up through action, and commitment. It's a falsehood for them to say you're doing a good job, but we can't help you in reducing class size, getting equipment, or restructuring the teaching schedule or curriculum.

Sarah feels strongly about the fact her school system has done little to enhance career mobility for its teachers. She is in favor of a career ladder structure and suggests that determining individuals for certain positions would not be difficult.

There's nothing in the teaching field. Here you can become a principal or counselor, that's about it. I think it would be simple to do [creation of a career ladder system]. You look at professionalism. You look at expectations. You look at success. You look at one's rapport with others. The people who are successful at working with people, meeting objectives, and being professional are the ones who go up.

Status is an absent reward as well. Sarah is not unlike many PE teachers who believe that PE is of marginal importance within the school curriculum. She based her claim on changing values in society, curricular priorities, and the attitude of physical educators themselves.

I think that physical education is perceived as not as important as reading, writing, and arithmetic per se because it doesn't have anything to do with making money. It has to do with taking care of oneself to live a happier life. To a lot of people the only thing that's valued in life is the money. So it's a value system and it's whatever your priorities are. Some people prioritize money as being the number one thing and health is clear down here.

Sarah suggested that the PE facility itself was subject to takeover at anytime for the purpose of other school activities.

Everybody uses the facilities so there's no specialness about what we do . . . We have the music people come in and use the gym and our classes aren't there and so on and so forth. Then it also projects the idea that this is not important. This PE class is not important because other things take priority.

It is ironic that the marginal status that PE held in the school was reinforced by PE teachers themselves. In Sarah's view incompetent teaching had contributed to such an image.

I think if we as physical educators had said, "hey we're going to do this right and this is what it's all about," then it would be different, but we've gone through so much of roll out the ball . . . that it is going to be difficult to change.

Sarah does find one reward of teaching in her summer vacation. It seems paradoxical to find one reward of teaching to be connected to disassociation from teaching. Her time off is a welcome respite from the strain of work. Sarah used an interesting metaphor in this context:

The time off you get after the nine months you are in the foxholes is nice—you need to regroup, reexamine the year, curriculum, to relax; and attend to personal concern.

Thus, beyond the security of a steady income and school vacations, the rewards of teaching are almost non-existent for Sarah. She finds herself wondering if it is worth the effort.

It seems the longer you stay in the fight the more dissatisfied you get and you can see the handwriting on the wall . . . the hassles you go through and the lack of respect, you lose your self-respect. You see yourself losing ground.

PROFESSIONAL DEVELOPMENT

The final condition to be addressed in this chapter is a condition necessary for the professional growth of the teacher—specifically, the provision of systematic outlets whereby a teacher may develop pedagogically. Although the process is directed at teacher development, the intent of the process is targeted toward school and departmental change. Ultimately, it is aimed at improving student opportunities to learn.

Traditionally, most schools address professional development through one day, on site inservice workshops in which special topics related to teaching are discussed by "outside" experts. Although teachers may learn or gain new insights, these events are typically viewed as parochial and insignificant because they rarely, if ever, replace those pedagogical or curricular elements so firmly embedded in the culture of the school (Goodlad, 1983a). In essence, these elements represent the embeddedness of many of the conditions previously discussed in this chapter, constrain the implementation of new ideas and strategies. Locke (1984, p.52) once stated, "teachers can be taught what they will not use," but perhaps it may be more appropriate to state: teachers can be taught, but they may be constrained to use that which they have learned. Regardless of the wording, this represents yet another paradox of teachers' work and of professional development. This thesis may be applied to one's involvement in other development activities such as university coursework and professional conferences, and through professional literature.

The failure of on-site programs also may be applied to off-site development activities (Locke, 1984). The reason for failure goes beyond the cutural embeddedness of school and instructional norms, but also relates to failing to meet the necessary criteria for successful staff development efforts (Schwager and Doolittle, 1988):

a. There must be personal and institutional commitment by school personnel (time and money).

b. Target improvement should be "owned" by the participants expected to implement the change (teachers need decision making and responsibility).
c. Changes should be practical, having a direct influence on real, day-to-day school problems.
d. Groups of teachers and other specialists, including administrators, need to collaborate over a period of time and with respect for each others' expertise. (p. 240)

The characteristics have been implemented in various projects through the Physical Education Program Development Center (Anderson, 1988) from 1980 to the present and are reflected in inservice and other mentoring models employed in various school districts throughout the country (Gray, & Gray, 1985; Martinek & Schempp, 1988; Showers, 1985; Templin & Savage, 1982). These development centers have led to teacher, program, and school effectiveness. They have promoted colleagueship through ownership and shared decision-making as well as peer mentoring. Quite simple, they have assisted teachers by establishing a system which suggests program and adult development is important.

As noted earlier in this chapter, one major expectation of the Smith administration for its teachers relates to their professional growth. Teachers are expected to remain professionally current, participate in required in-service, participate in faculty and departmental meetings, participate in planning opportunities, and set professional goals.

Sarah suggested that she meets all of these expectations, but it is the degree to which she is involved in such activities that determines the significance of these expectations. For example, she rarely has the time or energy to stay abreast with professional literature; her preparation time is used for planning versus collegial interaction and reading professional journals. Equally, she is usually too tired to engage in such activity after school. She does participate in required in-service and faculty or departmental meetings, but rarely finds these activities of great value for her own instruction. Not surprisingly, departmental meetings are usually devoid of substantive curricular or instructional issues. While inservice meetings have added new insights to Sarah's generic knowledge base, they have never addressed physical educational issues specifically. Furthermore, topics and/or speakers have never been solicited from Sarah and her colleagues.

Although Sarah sees the potential benefits of peer observation and interaction, these activities are non-existent in Sarah's work experience. Time seems to be the major constraint preventing this activity even though some administrative support was evident.

I think it would be very good to do that [peer interaction] and our principal has suggested that we observe other teachers during our prep period, but we don't have the time and they don't create more open time for us. I've had the opportunity to do that with one individual (Sarah's younger PE colleague) which is really helpful, but as far as a unified departmental and school effort to interact with one another, there's no time to do it.

Equally, Sarah suggested attending professional meetings. Although permitted within her school system, professional meeting attendance doesn't appear to be greatly encouraged. In fact, Sarah suggests that the process of applying for a leave is so cumbersome that she is discouraged even to consider such activity.

Often when you ask to go to a conference they say, well if we can find a sub for you or you've already been to one. So they don't really like teachers to be out for any reason. If you have been to one conference then that's pretty much your limit for the year. I quit asking because it was such a hassle to leave. They may fund the registration fee, but that is it. If you go, then they ask for implications for the school or program and nothing ever happens. Either scheduling can't be arranged or no funding. It's a hassle.

It appears that Sarah is in a situation where professional development has little meaning. Although development is an expectation of the administration for teachers at Smith, Sarah's perception is that such an expectation is unreal. Time for collegial interaction is not formally structured and inservice activities hold little practical value. As a consequence, Sarah is on her own to promote self growth which, under her circumstances, is difficult to achieve. Unfortunately for Sarah, her colleagues, her administration, her program, and its students, most people seem quite content with things as they are in PE.

SUMMARY

Shulman (1983, p. 492) states, "a teacher with adequate competence who is confronted with compatible mandates may remain unable to respond because of the working conditions of the schools." This appears to represent, for the most part, Sarah's experience as a secondary PE teacher. It seems clear in Sarah's case, that her effectiveness and satisfaction is not so much a function of her pedagogical competence, but a function of the conditions under which she must struggle. In review, her workplace may be summarized as follows:

1. It lacks a focused, well coordinated curriculum in which to teach
2. It demands many roles and long hours with insufficient facilities and equipment

3. It lacks insufficient planning time and significant staff development time
4. It centers on practical pedagogy, play and recreation, versus appropriate academic foci
5. It centers on managing disruptive behavior versus teaching and learning
6. It is isolated; little collegial stimulation exists
7. It provides few intrinsic rewards and little or no opportunity for career mobility
8. It is routine work—it does not vary significantly from day to day
9. It is powerless and lacks status within the school

Such a characterization would seem to be devastating for most teachers for it is in direct opposition to those necessary conditions needed to promote school and teacher effectiveness (Cohen, 1987; Frymier et al., 1984).

One is inclined to wonder why Sarah remains at Smith. This is a bit of a mystery, but it probably lies in her desire to teach 20 years (six years remain) and then return for a Ph.D. in teacher education. Equally, it is grounded in her persistence to try to redefine the structure, attitudes, and behavior related to physical education at Smith. This appears to be a monumental challenge because in all likelihood, Sarah will remain in a Catch-22 situation. If she conforms to existing norms for teacher behavior (which she admits to doing periodically), she will endorse that which is contrary to her own beliefs about teaching. In contrast, if she continues to employ standards and expectations in her own classes, she will remain frustrated by the fact that such behavior is not normative in the department, nor encouraged by administrators, or well received by some students. She will remain pedagogically isolated and retarded. She can "battle" for what she knows is best for her and her students, but such a battle will be met by counter-resistance.

Neither strategic compliance or strategic redefinition (Lacey, 1977) may be certain strategies for improving Sarah's satisfaction in her role. She may not become more satisfied through impression management nor through challenges to others. These are commonplace strategies; but in Sarah's case, their potential effectiveness seems limited. It seems unlikely that without power, Sarah will be able to "achieve change by causing or enabling those with formal power to change their interpretation of what is happening in the situation" (Lacey, 1977, p. 73). In all probability, the program and conditions at Smith will remain unaltered unless Sarah and her colleagues are empowered. The empowerment of teachers is, of course, another necessary prerequisite to improving the conditions of the workplace (Maeroff, 1988; Mertens & Yarger, 1988).

Sarah's situation is one in which the interplay between individual volition and institutional constraints demonstrates the problematic nature of the socialization process. It raises the need for more study, and in particular, the need for biographical, case study, and life history research which may be the best methods for studying teacher socialization. This raises the need for detailed studies of schools, PE programs, and teachers relative to identifying those work place characteristics needed to promote effectiveness. It is important to remember, however, that the identification of such characteristics are not useful "unless they are accompanied by details of the structure, function, content and processes used to achieve an identifiable level of effectiveness" (Schwartz & Olson, 1987, p. 597).

I have attempted to provide this detail by illustrating that contextual factors of the workplace are powerful forces that influence a teacher's knowledge, attitudes, and behavior. This influence seems more significant than one's training or past experience. Hence, it appears to be a logical point in time where reform movements link teacher effectiveness with improvements of the conditions under which teachers must work. I believe that what all teachers like Sarah want in the workplace is a chance to be in control of, enthusiastic about, and supported and appreciated in their work. That seems to be a reasonable expectation for any employee in any organization.

REFERENCES

Anderson, W. (1988). A school-centered collaborative model for program development. *Journal of Teaching in Physical Education, 7,* 176-183.
Apple, M. (1983). Curricular form and the logical of technical control. In M. W. Apple & L. Weiss (Eds.). *Ideology and practice in schooling.* Philadelphia: Temple Press.
Austin, D. & Willeke, M. (1986). A curriculum development study: School/community collaboration. *Journal of Physical Education, Recreation, and Dance, 57,* 50-53.
Bain, L. (1983). Reaction to work, gender, and teaching. In A. Jewett (Ed.), *Proceedings of the Third Conference on Curriculum Theory in Physical Education.* Athens, Georgia.
Cohen, M. (1987). Improving school effectiveness: Lessons from research. In V. Richardson-Koehler (Ed.), *Educators' Handbook: A research perspective.* New York: Longman.
Cuban, L. (1987). Cultures of teaching: a puzzle. *Educational Administration Quarterly, 23,* 25-35.
Dewar, A. (1985). Curriculum development and teachers' work: The case of the basic stuff series in physical education. In M. Carnes (Ed.), *Proceedings of the Fourth Conference on Curriculum Development in Physical Education.* Athens, GA.
Dodds, P. & Locke, L. (1984). Is physical education in American schools worth saving? Evidence, alternatives, judgement. In N. Struna (Ed.), *Proceedings of the National Association of Physical Education in Higher Education.* Champaign, IL: Human Kinetics.
Duckworth, K. & Carnine, D. (1987). The quality of teacher-principal relationships. In V. Richardson-Koehler (Eds.), *Educators' handbook: A research perspective.* New York: Longman.
Feiman-Nemser, S. & Floden, R. (1986). The cultures of teaching. In M. Wittrock (Ed.), *Handbook of research on teaching.* New York: Macmillan Publishing Co.
Frymier, J. (1987). Bureaucracy and the neutering of teachers. *Phi Delta Kappan, 69,* 9-16.
Frymier, J.; Cornbleth, C.; Donmoyer, R.; Gansneder, B.; Jeter J.; Klein, M.; Schwab, M.; and Alexander, W. (1984). *One hundred good schools.* West Lafayette, IN: Kappa Delta Pi.
Gitlin, A. (1983). School structure and teachers' work. In M. Apple & L. Weis (Eds.), *Ideology and practice in schooling.* Philadelphia: Temple Press.
Goodlad, J. (1983a). The school as workplace. In G. Griffin (Ed.), *Staff development: Eighty-second yearbook of the national society for the study of education.* Chicago: The University of Chicago Press.
Goodlad, J. (1983b). *A place called school.* New York: McGraw-Hill.

Graham, G. (Ed.). (1982). Profiles in excellence: Processes and teachers in children's physical education. *Journal of Physical Education, Recreation, and Dance, 53*, 37-54.

Gray, W. & Gray, W. (1985). Synthesis of research on mentoring teachers. *Educational Leadership, 43*(3), 37-43.

Hendry, L. (1975). Survival in a marginal role: The professional identity of the physical education teacher. *British Journal of Sociology, 26*, 465-476.

Joyce, B., Hersh, R., and McKibbin, M. (1983). *The structure of school improvement.* New York: Longman.

Kneer, J. (1987). Solutions to the teacher/coach problem in secondary schools. *Journal of Teaching in Physical Education, Recreation, and Dance. 59*(2): 28-29.

Lacey, C. (1977). *The socialization of teachers.* London: Methuen.

Lacey, C. (1987). Professional socialization of teachers. In Dunkin, M. (Ed.), *The international encyclopedia of teaching and teacher education.* Oxford: Pergamon Press.

Lawson, H. (1983a). Toward a model of teacher socialization in physical education: The subjective warrant, recruitment and teacher education. *Journal of Teaching in Physical Education, 2*, 3-16.

Lawson, H. (1983b). Toward a model of teacher socialization in physical education: Entry into schools, teachers' role orientations, and longevity in teaching. *Journal of Teaching in Physical Education, 3*(1), 3-15.

Lawson, H. (1983c). A theoretical foundation for curriculum studies in physical education. In A. Jewett, M. Carnes, & M. Speakman (Eds.), *Proceedings of the Third Conference on Curriculum Theory in Physical Education.* Athens, GA.

Lawson, H. (1988). Occupational Socialization, Cultural studies, and the physical education curriculum *Journal of Teaching in Physical Education 7*(4), 265-288.

Levinson, D. J.; Darrow, C.; Klein, E.; Levinson, M.; and McKee, B. (1978). *The seasons of a man's life.* New York: Knopf.

Lieberman, A. & Miller, L. (1984). *Teachers, their work, and their world: Implications for school improvement.* Alexandria, VA: Association for Supervision and Curriculum Development.

Little, J. (1987). Teachers as colleagues. In V. Richardson-Koebler (Ed.), *Educators' Handbook: A reserach perspective.* New York: Longman.

Locke, L. (1984). Research on teaching teachers: Where are we now? [Special issue] *Journal of Teaching in Physical Education.*

Locke, L., Griffin, P. and Templin, T. (Eds.) (1986). Profiles in struggles. *Journal of Physical Education, Recreation and Dance, 57*(4), 32-63.

Locke, L. (1986). What can we do? *Journal of Physical Education, Recreation and Dance, 57*(4), 60-63.

Lortie, D. (1975) *Schoolteacher: A sociological study.* Chicago: The University of Chicago Press.

Maeroff, G. (1988). Blueprint for empowering teachers. *Phi Delta Kappan, 69*, 472-477.

Martinek, T. (1981). Pygmalion in the gym: A model for the communication of teacher expectations in physical education. *Research Quarterly for Exercise and Sport, 52*, 58-67.

Martinek, T. & Schempp, P. (Eds.). (1988). Collaboration for instructional improvement: Models for school-university partnerships. [Special Issue] *Journal of Teaching in Physical Education, 7*(3).

Mertens, S. & Yarger, S. (1988). Teaching as a profession: Leadership, empowerment, and involvement. *Journal of Teacher Education, 39*, 32-37.

Mitchell, M. & Earls, R. (1987). A profile of state requirements for physical education K-12. *Physical Educator, 44*, 337-343.

Ratliffe, T. (1986). Influencing the principal: What the physical educator can do. *Journal of Physical Education, Recreation, and Dance. 57*, 86-87.

Rosenholtz, S. & Smylie, M. (1984). Teacher compensation and career ladders. *The Elementary School Journal, 85*, 149-166.

Schwager, S. & Doolittle, S. (1988). Teachers' reactions to activities in ongoing program development. *Journal of Teaching Physical Education, 7*, 240-249.

Schwartz, H. & Olson, G. (1987). Stress and burnout. In V. Richardson-Koehler (Ed.), *Educators' handbook: A research perspective.* New York: Longman.

Showers, B. (1985). Teachers coaching teachers. *Educational Leadership, 42*, 43-48.

Shulman, L. (1983). Autonomy and obligation: The remote control of teaching. In L. Shulman and G. Sykes (Eds.), *Handbook of teaching and policy.* New York: Longman.

Shulman, L. (1987). Professional issues. In V. Richardson-Koehler (Ed.), *Educators' Handbook: A research perspective.* New York: Longman.

Siedentop, D. (1986). High school physical education: Still an endangered species. *Journal of Physical Education, Recreation, and Dance, 58*, 24-25.

Siedentop, D., Mand, C. & Taggart, A. (1986). *Physical education: Teaching and curriculum strategies for grades 5-12.* Palo Alto, CA: Mayfield.

Tangri, S. & Moles, O. (1987). Parents and the community. In V. Richardson-Koehler (Ed.), *Educators' handbook: A research perspective.* New York: Longman.

Taylor, J. (1986). Surviving the challenge. *Journal of Physical Education, Recreation, and Dance, 57*(1), 69-72.

Templin, T. (1981). Teach/coach role conflict and the high school principal. In V. Crafts (Ed.), *Proceedings of the National Association of Physical Education in High Education*. Champaign, IL: Human Kinetics.

Templin, T. (Ed.). (1983). Profiles of excellence: Fourteen outstanding secondary school physical educators. *Journal of Physical Education, Recreation, and Dance, 54*, 15-36.

Templin, T. (1985). Developing commitment to teaching: The professional socialization of the preservice physical educator. In H. Hoffman & J. Rink (Eds.), *Physical Education professional preparation: Insights and foresights*. Reston, VA: AAHPERD.

Templin, T. (1987). Some consideration for teaching physical education in the future. In J. Massengale (Ed.), *Trends toward the future in physical education*. Champaign, IL: Human Kinetics.

Templin, T. (1988). Teacher isolation: A concern for the collegial development of physical educators. *Journal of Teaching in Physical Education, 7*, 197-207.

Templin T. (1988). Settling down: An examination of two women physical education teachers. In J. Evans (Ed.), *Teachers, Teaching and Control in Physical Education*. pp. 57-81. Lewes: The Falmer Press.

Templin, T. & Savage, M. (1982). The basic stuff as a magic feather: Managing the interface between the university and the public schools. *Journal of Physical Education, Recreation, and Dance, 53*, 23-26, 29.

Templin, T., Savage, M. & Hagge, M. (1986). Deprofessionalization and the physical education. In *Trends and Developments in Physical Education: Proceedings of the VIII Commonwealth and International Conference on Sport, Physical Education, Dance, Recreation, and Health*. London: E. & F. N. Spon. Ltd.

Templin, T., Woodford, R., & Mulling, C. (1982). On becoming a physical educator: Occupational choice and the anticipatory socialization process. *Quest, 34*, 119-133.

Williams, J. (1988, April). *The moonlighting experiences of physical education teachers in New York State*. Paper presented at the annual meeting of the American Educational Research Association, New Orlean, LA.

10

The Psycho-Social Dynamics of the Pygmalion Phenomenon in Physical Education and Sport

THOMAS J. MARTINEK
*University of North Carolina
at Greensboro*

My interest in the Pygmalion phenomenon was reinforced by an experience that took place several years ago when I was a new faculty member at The University of North Carolina, at Greensboro. At that time the physical education department was in the process of hiring a new assistant professor. As with most departments, this process involved reviewing the papers of several candidates and then selecting those who would visit the campus for an interview. It was expected that consensus would be reached on the candidate best suited for the position.

For candidates who were *clearly* unqualified or real "hot shots," there was strong consensus. Unfortunately, there was an incredible disparity of opinion for those who fell somewhere in the middle. Everyone had his own criteria for the ideal candidate.

It became obvious that there were many subtle factors influencing faculty evaluation of the candidates. Such factors as doctoral programs, advisors, ages of the candidates and their philosophical leanings toward professional training all became salient pieces of information as to their success within our department.

As a result of these expectations, the candidates were treated differently. For instance, one candidate who was regarded less favorably was asked more probing questions about his research which required considerable analysis and defense during the interview. It is also interesting that this candidate came to his interview wearing an earring. For some of the more conservative faculty such apparel was totally inappropriate for a university professor; the candidate didn't have a chance, no matter how strong his vita. For others, the jewelry represented someone who might offer a "breath of fresh air" to an otherwise traditional faculty.

However, those who were viewed more favorably were given the benefit of the doubt, and less detailed explanations of their research was required. Many of the interactions focused on general issues related to professional preparation. This enabled these candidates to be more relaxed than the others and, therefore, more interactive and less defensive, reinforcing the positive expectations of the faculty.

I began to realize more fully the power of expectations in influencing social interactions and human behavior. At the same time, I became interested in the seminal work of social psychologist Robert Merton (1948) who provided the theoretical foundation for explaining expectancy effects in different social settings. He believed that certain social phenomena were, to a large extent, influenced by the expectations of the individual members of a society. It was not until 20 years later that Merton's concept of the self-fulfilling prophecy came to the attention of educational researchers (Clark, 1963; Goldberg, 1963). The Rosenthal and Jacobson (1968) study at the Oak elementary school created the most interest and controversy about the self-fulfilling prophecy. In their study they manipulated teacher expectations to see if they would become self-prophetic. The findings indicated that in the early grades, teachers' expectations were associated with student performance. Since the Oak school experiment, researchers have conducted well over 100 studies relating to teacher expectations; other writers have provided scholarly critiques that have both supported and debated the degree to which teacher expectations affect student performance.

Historically, physical education researchers have not conducted investigation in this potentially important area. Not until recently have physical education researchers and sport psychologists begun to build a significant body of knowledge to support the notion that the self-fulfilling prophecy prevails in the gymnasium and athletic field as well as the classroom (Brown, 1979; Crowe, 1977; Martinek, 1983; Horn, 1984).

In an effort to develop a theoretical framework for physical education instruction, I initiated a series of descriptive and experimental studies that examined the dynamic processes of the self-fulfilling prophecy. This line of research has been conducted for more than a decade and continues to provide an enriching and yet complex explanation of how teacher expectancy effects operates in physical education and sport.

In the following sections of this chapter a model that has emerged from this research will be presented from which teacher expectancy effects can be partially explained. Specifically, the model will describe how expectations are formed and communicated, and to what extent they influence student behavior and performance.

THE TEACHER EXPECTANCY MODEL FOR PHYSICAL EDUCATION AND SPORT

The Teacher Expectancy Model for Physical Education and Sport was adapted from earlier ones proposed by Good and Brophy (1978) and Merton (1948), which used the concept of the self-fulfilling prophecy to explain the social events occurring in the classroom. The model suggests that: a) teachers form expectations of their students from perceptions gained through a number of impression cues related to student characteristics; b) from these perceptions certain expectations for the future performance of the student are formed; c) expectations can affect the quantity and quality of the interactions between the teacher and student; and d) the student perceives and interprets the interactions and may or may not perform in a way that is consistent with the original expectations. The concept of the expectancy loop also was proposed to demonstrate that self-prophetic student behavior can perpetuate the initial expectations held by the teacher (Martinek, 1981a; Martinek et al, 1982).

Subsequent to the development of the above model, several studies have attempted to validate the various steps of it. A major goal of these studies has been to confirm the existence of the expectancy phenomenon operating in physical education and sport (Crowe, 1977; Horn, 1984; Markland & Martinek, in press; Martinek, 1980; Martinek, 1983; Martinek & Karper, 1982; Martinek & Johnson, 1979; Rejeski et al., 1979). Many of these studies indicate an association between teacher expectations and certain types of teacher behaviors and, in some instances, performance behaviors and affective states.

Although the expectancy-performance relationship appears to be straightforward, there are important exceptions to consider. For example, research has shown that poor performance does not always come from low expectations. Similarly, high expectations have not always been found to guarantee good performance (Brophy & Good, 1974; Good, 1987; Martinek, in press; Martinek et al, 1982; West & Anderson, 1976). Therefore, there are significant differences in opinion about the degree to which teachers' expectations are likely to function as self-fulfilling prophecies.

In order to clarify the Pygmalion phenomenon, the following sections will provide various studies representative of this model.

Impression Cues and Perceptions of Students

The formation of teacher expectations is based upon the teacher's perception of certain student characteristics. These characteristics, called impression cues, can come from actual observation of the student or past information from outside sources (i.e., academic records, other teachers). Though the existence of expectations is difficult to dispute, it is apparent that even to the most naive observer identical information gained about a student may not lead to the same impression for two or more teachers. Expectations are highly subjective and mediated by outside factors.

Taguiri (1969) has suggested three major factors that affect teachers' perceptions of students: a) characteristics of the teacher, b) attributes of the student about whom some judgment is being made, and c) the social situation of which the impression cues are viewed.

For example, look at the case of a teacher who is drawn to a student because the student symbolizes a conflict or problem experienced by the teacher in his/her childhood. Under such circumstances, strong biases might operate. Consequently, the child may be given extra support and attention during instruction. The teacher needs to perceive the student as capable. Failure by the child would serve as a reminder of the teacher's own vulnerability.

Characteristics of the teacher. Specific examples of teacher characteristics include such things as intelligence, self-concept, reactive versus nonreactive personality, and rigid versus flexible character (Brophy, 1983). Although few studies have looked at this dimension, some have shown interesting findings regarding "high bias" and "no bias" teachers. Babad et al. (1982) reported conflicting results when comparing "high bias" and "no bias" teachers on data collected using quantitative and qualitative measures. The objective measures showed no significant differences between "high bias" teachers and "no bias" teachers in terms of educational ideology, dogmatism, political views, defensiveness, locus of control, extroversion, and impulsiveness. However, qualitative analysis showed that "high bias" teachers were regarded as more autocratic, rigid, distant, impulsive, and preferential in their teaching behavior. It appears, therefore, that "high bias" teachers produce most of the self-fulfilling prophecy effects and that most of these are described as positive rather than negative effects.

Other combinations of characteristics also can produce considerable variety among teachers in the way they interact with their highs and lows. For example, while some teachers may think that low-expectancy students require more structured learning experiences than high-expectancy students, they may in fact be unable to provide the necessary structure because of their own personal style of teaching (Hamachek, 1972). This is especially true when a teacher is impulsive by nature and mediates a large degree of student decision-making during the teaching process. This becomes an apparent problem when the personality style is so inflexible that it gets in the way of the teacher's ability to plan and organize appropriate teaching strategies for low-expectancy students. Brophy (1983) believes that we are a long way from being able to predict with any accuracy why teachers differ in the way they are affected by their own expectations. He has found that some teachers feel less responsible to do something about their low achievers. Others will make extraordinary efforts to monitor and interact with them (Rejeski et al., 1979). In either case, it appears that future research must take into account individual teacher characteristics when developing clearer interpretations of effective and ineffective teaching strategies.

Characteristics of students. Researchers also have determined the role that specific student characteristics play during impression formation. These cues are typically viewed as either static (i.e., sex, race) or dynamic (behavioral disposition, performance). The nature of cues are important in that the possibility of changing a teacher's expectations may be reliant on whether the student's characteristics are changeable or not. In either case, these cues form the basis from which a teacher's expectations emerge.

Static cues that are thought to be especially salient in physical education are handicapped versus non-handicapped, sex, and physical attractiveness (Crowe, 1977; Karper & Martinek, 1982; Martinek & Johnson, 1979). For example, research with mainstreamed classes (Martinek & Karper, 1981) has shown that elementary physical educators have significantly lower expectations for their handicapped students' social relations with classmates. However, nonsignificant differences were found between the two groups for expectations for physical performance, cooperative behavior, and ability to reason. Given that the intended outcomes of mainstreaming are to develop and improve integration of handicapped and nonhandicapped children, these findings have implications regarding those problems encountered by handicapped children who are mainstreamed into programs with social goals.

Student gender is another static cue that affects expectancy formation. Our society has always been influenced by stereotypic beliefs concerning sex-appropriate behaviors. In addition, it is common for people to perceive that certain competencies are directly limited by specific sex-related characteristics. For example, there is substantial evidence that teachers overrate the intelligence and the academic potential of young girls (Palardy, 1969; Doyle et al, 1972). Furthermore, after an extensive review of the literature, Brophy and Good (1974) concluded that teachers, irrespective of sex, are more negative in their attitudes concerning young males, particularly regarding their potential as behavior problems. These perceptions probably arise from an awareness that males are characteristically more independent and assertive than females, qualities which often conflict with traditional, more conservative, teaching styles.

There is every reason to believe, then, that teachers and coaches employ sex stereotypes when evaluating children in physical activity settings. This position is supported by research and philosophical writings (Crowe, 1977; Herkowitz, 1977; Methany, 1970; Sutton-Smith & Rosenberg, 1961) suggesting that activities requiring strength, speed, or endurance are perceived as inappropriate for females. Interestingly, a recent investigation utilizing an elementary school population (Corbin & Nix, 1979) found further support for such stereotypes. The girls in this study expressed lower self-confidence than did boys when they anticipated competing at a traditionally "masculine" task. These results are consistent with research by Brawley and his colleagues (Brawley et al., 1979) in which college-aged females expressed lower performance expectations toward an endurance task than a comparable group of males. An interesting point in this latter investigation was that a pretesting of the task had failed to reveal that the males would outperform the females. This finding offers rather convincing evidence for the perceived ineptitude of women toward tasks demanding physical prowess.

A rather intriguing aspect of the Corbin and Nix (1979) study was that after the girls had experienced success in cross-sex competition, their self-confidence improved significantly. The implication inherent in this research is that physical skills have a potentially powerful role to play in changing traditional views of women in society. Unfortunately, if teachers and coaches do not exhibit confidence in women, there is a good possibility that the self-fulfilling prophecy will maintain the status quo.

An interesting proposition is that a child's physical attractiveness biases the quantity and quality of student-teacher interaction and thus becomes an important mediator of the self-fulfilling prophecy. To test the hypothesis that physically attractive children are perceived more favorably, Dion (1972) presented coeds with photos of children who varied in attractiveness. A story was then presented in which the child depicted in the photo had committed either a mild or severe antisocial act. Results showed that severe transgressions were seen as more typical of unattractive than attractive children. When asked which children would be more likely to repeat the antisocial behavior, consensus favored the unattractive children. Also of interest was the finding that, among children committing antisocial acts, attractive children were perceived to be more honest and pleasant. In a later study, Dion (1974) demonstrated that women (but not men) were more lenient in punishing attractive rather than unattractive children.

Some evidence has begun to surface in physical education supporting the link between student attractiveness and teacher expectations. In one of my studies (Martinek, 1981b), I found that highly attractive students were expected to perform better in physical activities and to be more socially adept with their peers than less attractive students. They also appeared to affect the teacher-student interactions.

In a follow-up study (Martinek & Karper, 1984a), it was discovered that the attractiveness cue was especially influencial in expectancy formation for older age groups than young groups. These data suggested that as children get older, attractiveness becomes increasingly related to performance expectations.

The findings that physical attractiveness can influence perceived ability, character, and performance evaluation make this an extremely important variable to consideration in research dealing with Pygmalion effects and motor performance. It has particular relevance to grading in physical education, because contact with individual students often is minimal in public education. Under such circumstances, when precise information regarding children's characteristics is vague, one would predict the effects of social stereotypes to be strong.

Thus far, we have examined various types of static cues that influence teachers' perceptions of children. There is little doubt, however, that numerous examples of dynamic cues also interact with expectancy formation. It is important to note again that dynamic cues differ from static ones in that they are behaviorally oriented and may change according to the learning task.

One type of dynamic cue that has been investigated is the student's expression of effort as perceived by the teacher. Recent studies (Martinek & Karper, 1982; 1984a) have demonstrated that both effort and attractiveness in upper elementary grades were directly related to overall teacher expectations, especially for social prowess and thinking ability. This finding becomes more relevant when we look at the numerous ways teachers reward and punish in order to elicit higher levels of motivation and participation rather than better performance.

Furthermore, Ansorge and his associates (Ansorge et al. 1978) have demonstrated that when judges' ratings of gymnasts are normally ranked from poorest to best, there is a tendency for judges to rate later performances higher, irrespective of the actual merit. Subsequent study (Scheer & Ansorge, 1979) has shown that certain judges are more inclined to be affected by such biases. Specifically, it has been shown that judges who are external in their locus of control are influenced by order effects, while judgments made by internals are not affected by such bias.

In summary, it is important to note that the examples included are in no way exhaustive; additional cues might relate to family history, personality patterns, and emotional handicaps. It is the task of future researchers to identify and integrate cues used in the process of teacher expectations so teachers might gain some control over their negative effects.

Social climate/context. We can see how specific social climates or learning environments can impact on personal perceptions. Contrast the expectations a teacher might have for a relatively weak student in an independent problem-solving learning environment with that characterized by traditional teacher-directed methodology. In general, the belief is that weak students will make greater gains in structured settings, a prominent characteristic of the latter environment.

In physical education, motor ability may be salient in forming teachers' expectations. However, it is not clear how these expectations may be affected by the goal structure and social climates in various environments where motor skills are taught. In physical education, for instance, three different contexts typically are created by activities which are either competitive, individual (noncompetitive), or cooperative in nature (Dauer & Pangrazi, 1984; Johnson & Johnson, 1979; Martinek & Karper 1984b; Orlick, 1982). Within competitive, individualized, and cooperative activity instructions, the motor ability of a child may differ, and, therefore, variably influence the teacher's expectations for them. As a result, the interaction patterns between the teacher and his/her high and low expectancy students may significantly vary from context to context.

This hypothesis was partially tested in a recent study of 126 elementary age children and three physical education teachers (Martinek & Karper, 1986). The purpose of the study was to determine the differential effects of competitive, individualized and cooperative instructional settings on expectation formation and dyadic interactions.

High and low ability groups were determined by giving a standardized motor skills test. Teacher expectations were determined by asking the teachers to assign an expectation rating to each of their students prior to each instructional phase. It was found that teachers had higher expectations for the highly skilled group when the students were engaged in activities that were individualized or competitive. The low skilled students were expected to do better in cooperative types of activities. Inspection of the interaction data also showed that teachers gave more technical feedback to high ability students during the individualized phase, and were more empathetic to low skilled students during competitive activities.

Similar studies have looked at context effects in the sport setting (Horn, 1984; Rejeski, et al. 1979). For example, Horn (1984) investigated two athletic settings, game versus practice, in terms of the interaction patterns between high and low expectancy softball players and their coaches. The results indicated that coaches did exhibit differential patterns of behaviors toward the two groups of athletes. However, the differences were evident in game situations only; comparable effects were not found during the practice sessions. Unlike other studies that have supported the theory of the self-fulfilling prophecy, the differences found in Horn's study indicated that low expectancy athletes received more technical feedback. In addition, low expectancy groups received more reinforcement after successful performance than did high expectancy groups. Horn's findings seem to indicate that coaches are compelled to give more information to those individuals who are perceived as having the lowest amount of skill. This was especially true in game situations where mistake contingencies were prevalent.

Expectations and Dyadic Interactions

Another aspect of the teacher expectancy model includes the differential interaction patterns resulting from teacher expectations. Researchers have documented the ways teachers communicate with their high and low expectancy students. (In fact, the majority of teacher expectancy research has focused on this area of the model.) Rosenthal (1974) described a four factor model that emerged from a meta-analysis of over 30 studies. The model suggests that specific types of teaching behaviors maximize student achievement if they:

1. Create a warm socioemotional climate with their students (Climate);
2. Give them more feedback about their performance (Feedback);
3. Teach more material as well as more difficult material (Input); and
4. Give a greater number of response opportunities (Output).

Though Rosenthal's four factors provided a rather substantial beginning in the development of social psychological theory, today's teachers of physical education might benefit if additional specific behaviors were identified and implemented for education and inservice purposes. In addition, since teachers appear to be affected more by low expectations than high expectations, there is a special need to find how these low expectations are being communicated. In reviewing the expectancy research, several specific teaching behaviors related to low teacher expectations in the physical education setting have been identified.

1. Teachers gave less praise (verbal and nonverbal) to low expectancy students (Crowe, 1977; Markland & Martinek, In press; Martinek & Johnson, 1979; Martinek & Karper, 1984a, 1984b, 1986; Martinek, In press; Rejeski et al., 1979).
2. Teachers asked less analytic questions and provided fewer response opportunities to low expectancy students (Crowe, (1977); Martinek & Johnson, 1979; Martinek & Karper, 1984b, 1986).
3. Teachers gave low expectancy students less evaluative comments to their responses (Crowe, 1977; Markland & Martinek, In press).
4. Unanswered questions were rephrased or repeated less for low expectancy students (Crowe, 1977).
5. Fewer dyadic contacts were directed to low expectancy students (Brown, 1979; Martinek & Johnson, 1979).
6. Less information on content-related behaviors was directed toward low expectancy students (Brown, 1979; Rejeski et al., 1979; Martinek & Karper, 1984a; 1984b; 1986).
7. More criticism (verbal and nonverbal) was directed toward low expectancy students (Templin, 1981; Martinek, 1984a; 1984b).
8. Acceptance and use of student ideas and actions were less for the low expectancy students (Martinek & Johnson, 1979; Martinek & Karper, 1981; 1986).
9. Low expectancy students initiated few interactions with their teachers (Crowe, 1977; Horn, 1984; Martinek & Karper, 1984b).
10. More direction was given to low expectancy students. That is, teachers appeared to be more directive in getting those students to do various tasks (Martinek & Karper, 1984a; 1986).
11. Low expectancy students are given more technical feedback (Horn, 1984; Rejeski et al. 1979).

The reader is strongly cautioned when trying to apply the above findings to actual instructional practice. Though research on student-interaction appears to be vigorous, the summary of the findings just presented do *not* necessarily represent a characterization of effective instruction. Instead, they should serve as guidelines for supervisors and teachers to use in their planning.

There are other factors when considering instructional differences between high and low groups. For example, Brophy (1983) suggested that differential interaction patterns may be a function of the student's own behavior, as opposed to teacher bias. High expectancy students may attain higher frequencies of praise because they exhibit more successful performance behavior; they give the instructor more reasons to respond positively. This concept was partially tested in a study by Templin (1981), who looked at the socializing role that student behavior has in the formation of student teachers' concept of behavior control over their students.

By using both quantitative and qualitative methodologies, Templin examined the degree to which high and low achieving students' behavior affected the student teachers' ideas about dealing with their own behavior. Results of the study revealed that the teachers shifted from a humanistic approach to pupil control and, further, to one that was more custodial in nature. Concerning high and low achievers, the results also indicated that the student teachers did, in fact, formulate positive and negative attitudes in accordance with certain student attributes. That is, the teachers appeared to have a more positive bias toward students who were conforming, cooperative, orderly, and high-achieving. This in turn affected the teachers by causing them to use more controlling behaviors with low-achieving students.

An important implication of this study was that the low achieving students' off-task behavior preoccupied most of the teachers' attention, causing them to become more custodial during the student teaching term. Similar results were reported by Martinek and Karper (1984a), who found that low teacher expectations for the social behavior of early elementary students caused teachers to distribute more convergent direction-giving behaviors to these students. It also was found that these expectations were positively related to the amount of off-task behavior that low expectancy students displayed during physical activity instruction.

Student Perceptions of Individual Teacher Treatment

While teacher expectancy studies seem to indicate that some teachers treat high and low achieving students differently, it also appears that not all students are affected the same way by the teacher's interaction with them (Brophy, 1983). One reason for this is the considerable variability in the way that children actually perceive and interpret instructional events. Unfortunately, there has been a paucity of research in physical education that has looked at the role student interpretations of teacher treatment plays in the current theorizing of the effects of teacher expectations. Although several students in the same classroom setting may perceive similar teacher actions directed toward them, there may be considerable variability in the way students interpret and place value on them. Knowing how they interpret behaviors would help to explain why some expectancy effects vary so greatly from student to student. It is important that researchers begin to explore the specific causes that high and low expectancy students attribute to the teachers' actions.

One way of doing this is by using an attributional model to help explain the interpretative processes used by high and low expectancy students when they perceive certain teacher behaviors being directed toward them. According to attribution theory, students often attribute the causes of performance to either personal reasons (i.e., ability) or to factors outside the control of the individual (i.e., task difficulty) (Weiner, 1979). Darley and Fazio (1980) have extended this theory to describe how teaching behaviors may be interpreted by a student as being attributed to both internal and external factors. They contend that perceived teaching behaviors can be described by the student as being attributed to one of four causes.

The first is characterized by self-attributions. When using self-attributions, a student may attribute the teacher's actions as being caused by personal factors. For instance, the student may interpret the teacher's criticism as justified because he or she thinks: "I should have been paying attention."

A second type of attribution may be directed toward the teacher. Rather than personally assuming responsibility for the teacher's actions, students may attribute the actions to dispositional characteristics of the teacher; i.e., "the teacher doesn't like girls anyway." By doing this, the student justifies the teacher's actions to external factors rather than personal ones.

The third type of attributions are those related to the situation rather than to teacher or personal factors. For example, a student who receives disapproval from the teacher following an unsuccessful attempt at a task might attribute the behavior to the difficulty of the task or other elements in the learning environment (i.e., other students, equipment, space allocation) which were interferring with his or her attempt to execute the task.

Finally, students may use more complex attributions to explain the teacher's actions toward him or her. These types of attributions are characterized by a combination of factors related to the other three attributional categories. For example, a student's interpretation of teacher praise could be due to both the personal skill attributes and the teacher's perceptibility in acknowledging a correct response. Therefore, the student perceives the teacher behavior as a result of an interaction between personal and teacher attributes.

Validity of the Attributional Model

Recently, I attempted to test the validity of Darley and Fazio's attributional model (1980) with elementary physical education classes (Martinek, in press). The intent of this study was to determine how high and low expectancy students attribute causes to the perceived teaching behaviors. During an interview process, elementary age students were asked to describe the causes for the teacher actions that were perceived as being directed toward them. Each cause was classified into one of the four attributional categories presented by Darley and Fazio.

Attributional data revealed that low expectancy students tended to attribute teacher reprimand to personal causes much more so than high expectancy students. This was especially true for teacher responses related to behavior management. This finding implies that low expectancy students may believe their misbehavior is a stable trait, one that is difficult to change. According to Ames (1984), such self ascriptions can lead to low self-concept and a continuance of poor social behavior and low motivation. The study's findings also indicated that high expectancy students thought that any punitive action directed toward them was a function of certain teacher characteristics. Therefore, high expectancy students appeared to have a greater tendency to attribute teacher reprimand to external causes.

Again, it is important to underscore the influential role that student interpretation of teacher behaviors plays during the expectancy cycle. Darley and Fazio (1980) contend that if environmental or teacher attributes are seen as causal elements for the teacher's behavior, the responses of students may be much different than if the student attributed them to personal factors. Specifically, they believe that behaviors are likely to be more in line with the teacher's expectations if teacher and environment are considered causal elements, thus confirming the teacher's expectations. It is important to note, however, that not all students behave in a way that is consistent with the teacher's expectations. For some students, self-perceptions may be so strong that any counter-expectations may have little or no affect on the students.

According to Brophy and Good (1974), this is contingent on the degree to which the student believes or accepts the teacher's statement concerning the expectations for the student. For example, in a study by Biddle and Moore (1973), elementary students are conditioned to believe or not to believe the expectancy statements of students concerning the probable success on a given task. It was found that students conditioned to believe the teacher's predictions demonstrated low performance following low expectation statements from the teachers. Conversely, it also was found that students conditioned not to believe these statements showed no impairment of performance under negative expectation conditions. It was concluded that if direct communications of expectancies are to function as self-fulfilling prophecies, they must be credible to the students. In turn, this credibility is established with accuracy and success in predicting the student's achievement.

The Influence of Attributional Patterns on Student Performance

Along with the identification of specific attributional patterns, consideration needs to be given to the ways these patterns actually influence motivation and performance. One subtle influence is seen in the way teachers communicate ability estimates of their students.

Although most research seems to imply that giving praise and encouragement to a student will result in increased levels of motivation, remember that not all students interpret praise as a direct indication they are perceived as being skillful. Likewise, criticism does not always communicate to the students they lack sufficient skill proficiency (Brophy, 1983). Studies by Lanzetta and Hannah (1969) and Weiner and Kukla (1970) have indicated that specific teaching behaviors such as praise, help-giving, and empathy appear to provide some students with information that the teacher estimate of their ability is low. They also found that blame, reprimand, and indifference tended to convey information that the student's ability was high.

Meyer (1982) offers an explanation to this paradox. He suggests that the nature of the learning tasks may significantly interact with the way students interpret certain teacher behaviors. He contends that the perceived difficulty of the learning tasks for which the student is praised or criticized may be highly influential in forming the student's self-perception of ability. For example, the teacher may give praise to a student for performing an easy task or exhibit empathy for struggling with difficult tasks. The teacher also may help this student more than other students, even though the student didn't ask for it. The student might conclude, therefore, that the teacher does not think he/she is very capable; thus, the self-perception of ability is lowered.

If Meyer's theory is correct, then low expectancy students may be placed in a "no win" situation where low expectations become internalized. Ultimately, the likelihood of success at other tasks is significantly decreased. As a consequence, the student acquires a state of learned helplessness (Seligman, 1975); low expectancy students believe that failure is eminent in most everything they attempt. Dweck, et al. (1980), and Martinek & Karper (1983) believe that if students learn that their responses have little to do with the outcome from their efforts, they will simply give up. The teacher's expectations may be so strong and inflexible that no matter how hard the student tries (or doesn't try), the interpretation of the outcomes by the teacher will always be the same. As a result, the student acquires a "what's the use" complex (Martinek et al., 1982). We, then, might expect students with low expectations to remain inhibited to responding to various motor tasks presented by their teacher or to persevere with primitive or inappropriate response strategies in an effort to camouflage their feelings of inadequacy.

OTHER ISSUES CONCERNING THE PYGMALION PHENOMENON

In physical education and sport, continued research into the mediating effects of the Pygmalion phenomenon is tantamount. Clearer interpretation and understanding of expectancy effects can be learned only when researchers begin to apply more refined methodological approaches to their research questions. Several important issues have been addressed in this chapter; many others exist. In this section I would like to address two critical issues. The first focuses on the need to study teacher expectations from a multidimensional perspective.

Much of the past research concerning expectancy effects has focused almost exclusively on performance expectations. Few studies, if any, have addressed teacher expectations as a multi-dimensional construct. That is, teachers may have other expectations for their students, such as for their students' social relations with their peers, their cooperative behavior in class, and their ability to synthesize directions and concepts given during instruction. For example, a teacher may have high expectations for a student who participates in competitive games because the teacher believes the student possesses the skills needed to succeed in those types of games. However, the teacher may have different expectations when the same student is engaged in activities which are less competitive and require more problem-solving skills. Consequently, it is quite possible that these expectations may operate differentially during the instructional process and that student-teacher interaction patterns may vary in relation to these expectations.

A recent study (Martinek & Karper, 1986) looked at the differential effects of specific types of teacher expectations on motor ability and dyadic interactions during individual, competitive, and cooperative units of instruction. The results showed that the instructor's expectation for the student's ability to understand the tasks was the strongest predictor of motor ability. This relationship was especially evident when students were engaged in either individualized or cooperative units of instruction. Specifically, it was found that expectations for understanding tasks were significantly higher for high ability students than for low ability students during individualized instruction. In the cooperative unit, however, opposite findings were found. High ability students were expected to understand the tasks given to them more than low ability students. The results of this study support the notion that certain units of instruction cause specific expectations to be more salient than others. Given the array of teaching conditions that exist in the physical education setting, the need to identify potential effects of specific expectations relative to these conditions is vital for gaining insight into instructional practice.

A second area of study should focus on student behavior and the extent to which it strengthens or changes original expectations. In addition, there is some uncertainty about the conditions in which students behavior may activate a change in teacher-student interactions despite the lack of substantial change in teacher expectations.

It is not uncommon for us to misjudge another person. For example, you are told by a friend that John, a new acquaintance, is extremely disorganized. Immediately, you mentally associate related traits: he is sloppy, careless, and habitually tardy. Although on the surface John appears to be disorganized, it is readily apparent that he is quite structured in his approach to almost any endeavor undertaken. This premature misjudging is found in the schools, too.

Interestingly, little research has dealt with the issue of change in perceptions other than correlational research which appears to suggest that teacher expectations remain relatively stable across time. We might ask, however, why expectations remain stable and under what conditions.

One of the reasons for stable expectations may be due to the concept of perceptual salience (Martinek et al., 1982). This idea is based on the premise that when we expect certain behaviors from others, we pay special attention to evidence which might support our beliefs and ignore others which run counter to our expectations. It also has been suggested, by way of the Pygmalion model, that teachers will cause certain behaviors to occur in children that are consistent with their perceptions. For example, if a child is thought to be lazy and the teacher treats him/her appropriately, the child will be discouraged from being more enthusiastic toward learning tasks. Therefore, the teacher's perception of that child's laziness remains unchanged, or even strengthened.

However, Good and Brophy (1978) believe certain circumstances may cause some expectations to change. They suggest that the credibility of the source of information plays a major role in modifying expectations. Information about a child that comes from individuals who have close contact with the child (i.e., parents, other teachers) as opposed to those who have less contact (school clinician, principal) represent more credible sources of information. In general, our interactions are less biased if we are uncertain about how judgments were made. Further research on this issue is warranted.

Another condition affecting change in teacher expectations relates to the disposition of the student. Students with strong self-concepts and high achievement motivation are more self-sufficient and less apt to believe a teacher's expectation than those with low self-concepts and low achievement motives. The implications are that across time the former students persist despite the possibility of negative overtures from the teacher (Martinek et al., 1982). Eventually, the continual display of achievement behavior will cause the teacher to change his/her original expectations. To date, there are no data to support this relationship.

SUMMARY

The Pygmalion phenomenon in today's gymnasiums continues to play a major role in establishing positive and productive instructional practices. Because today's teachers are forced to emphasize performance and absolutes, it is little wonder that expectancy effects have such a profound influence on the student. At the same time, we continue to proselytize humanism in our physical education curricula, there is a fundamental need to reexamine our philosophy and direction in education. We need to alter our goals of teaching; that is, instead of "teaching to learn" we should be embracing the philosophy of "learning to learn."

By adopting this philosophy, we would be focusing our teaching on developmental competence. This is not to be confused with the concept of competency-based instruction. The former seeks to develop performance potential in students; the latter represents a "measuring stick" by which self worth is determined. It is ironical that the use of a performance based system often breeds anxiety over the quality we wish to produce. At the same time, providing students with skills to learn will result in high levels of motivation and, thereby, better performance behaviors.

Therefore, it was my intention to communicate the scientific merit of the Pygmalion phenomenon in physical education and sport and to raise the level of awareness about its dynamic role in fostering positive teacher-student relationships.

REFERENCES

Ames, C. (1984). Achievement attributions and self-instructions under competitive and individualistic goal structures. *Journal of Educational Psychology, 76,* 478-487.
Ansorge, C., Scheer, J., Laub, J., & Howard, H. (1978). Bias in judging women's gymnastics induced by expectations of within-team order. *Research Quarterly, 49,* 399-405.
Babad, E., Inbar, J., & Rosenthal, R. (1982). Pygmalion, Galatea, and the Golem: Investigations of biased and unbiased teachers. *Journal of Educational Psychology, 74,* 459-474.
Biddle, S. & Moore, J. (1973, February). The effects of prior conditioning to expectancy statements on persistence and non-presistence of attention. Paper presented at the annual meeting of the American Educational Research Meeting, New Orleans.
Brawley, L., Landers, D., Miller, L. & Kearns, K. (1979). Sex bias in evaluating motor performance. *Journal of Sport Psychology, 1,* 15-24.
Brophy, J. (1983). Research on the self-fulfilling prophecy and teacher expectations. *Journal of Educational Psychology, 75,* 631-661.
Brophy, J. & Good, T. (1974). *Teacher-student relationships.* New York: Holt, Rinehart & Winston.
Brown, J. (1979). Description of dyadic student-teacher interaction in physical education activity class. Unpublished doctoral dissertation, University of North Carolina at Greensboro.
Clark, K. B. (1963). Educational stimulation of racially disadvantaged children. In A. H. Passow (Ed.), *Education in depressed areas.* New York: Columbia Press.
Corbin, C. & Nix, C. (1979). Sex-typing of physical activities and success predictions of children before and after cross-sex competition. *Journal of Sport Psychology, 1,* 43-52.
Crowe, P. B. (1977, April). *Research on teacher expectations.* Paper presented at the annual convention of the American Alliance for Health, Physical Education, Recreation and Dance, New Orleans, LA.
Darley, J. M., & Fazio, R. H. (1980). Expectancy confirmation processes arising in the social interaction sequence. *American Psychologist, 35,* 867-881.
Dauer, V., & Pangrazi, R. (1984). *Dynamic physical education for elementary school children* (6th ed.). Minneapolis: Burgess.
Dion, K. (1972). Physical attractiveness and evaluations of children's transgressions. *Journal of Personality and Social Psychology, 24,* 207-213.
Dion, K. (1974). Children's physical attractiveness and sex as determinants of adult punitiveness. *Developmental Psychology, 10,* 772-778.
Doyle, W., Hancock, G., & Kifer, E. (1972). Teachers' perceptions: Do they make a difference? *Journal of the Association of the Study of Perception, 7,* 21-30.
Dweck, C., Goetz, R., Strauss, N. (1980). *Sex differences in learned helplessness: An experimental and*

naturalistic study of failure, generalizations, and its mediators. *Journal of Personality and Social Psychology, 36*, 441-452.

Goldberg, M. (1963). Factors affecting educational attainment in depressed urban areas. In A. H. Passow (Ed.), *Education in depressed areas.* New York: Columbia Press.

Good, T. (1987). Two decades of research on teacher expectations: Findings and future directions. *Journal of Teacher Education,* July-August, 32-47.

Good, T., & Brophy, J. (1978). *Looking in classrooms* (2nd ed.) New York: Harper & Row.

Hamachek, D. (1972). Personality styles and teacher behavior. *Education Forum, 36*, 313-322.

Herkowitz, J. (1977). Sex role expectations and motor behavior of young children. In M. V. Ridenour (Ed.), *Motor Development: Issues and Applications.* Princeton, NJ: Princeton Book Co.

Horn, T. (1984). Expectancy effects in the interscholastic athletic setting: Methodological considerations. *Journal of Sport Psychology, 6*, 60-76.

Johnson, D., & Johnson, J. (1979). Cooperation, competition, and individualization. In H. Walberg (Ed.) *Educational Environments and Effects.* Berkley, CA.: McCutchan.

Karper, W., & Martinek, T. (1982). Differential influence on various instructional factors on self-concepts of handicapped and nonhandicapped children in mainstreamed physical education classes. *Perceptual and Motor Skills, 54*, 831-835.

Lanzetta, K.T. & Hannah, J.E. (1969). Reinforcing behavior of "naive" trainers. *Journal of Personality and Social Psychology, 11*, 245-252.

Merton, R. K. (1948). The self-fulfilling prophecy. *Antioch Review, 8*, 193-210.

Markland, R. D. & Martinek, T. (in press). Descriptive analysis of coach augmented feedback given to high school varsity female volleyball players. *Journal of Teaching in Physical Education.*

Martinek, T. (in press). Confirmation of a teacher expectancy model: Student perceptions and casual attributions of teaching behaviors. *Research Quarterly for Exercise and Sport.*

Martinek, T. (1980). Student expectations as related to a teacher's expectations and self-concept in elementary age children. *Perceptual and Motor Skills, 50*, 555-561.

Martinek, T. (1981a). Pygmalion in the gym: A model for the communication of teacher expectations in physical education. *Research Quarterly for Exercise and Sport, 52*, 58-67.

Martinek, T. (1981b). Physical attractiveness: Effects on teacher expectations and dyadic interactions in elementary age children. *Journal of Sport Psychology, 3*, 196-205.

Martinek, T. (1983). Creating "Golem" and Galatea" effects in physical education instruction: A social psychological perspective. In T. Templin & J. Olson (Eds.), *Teaching physical education.* Champaign, IL: Human Kinetics.

Martinek, T., Crowe, P., Rejeski, W. (1982). *Pygmalion in the gym.* West Point, NY: Leisure Press.

Martinek, T., & Johnson, S. (1979). Teacher expectations: Effects on dyadic interaction and self-concept in elementary age children. *Research Quarterly, 50*, 60-70.

Martinek, T. & Karper, W. (1981). A teacher's expectations on handicapped and nonhandicapped children in mainstreamed physical education classes. *Perceptual and Motor Skills, 52*, 327-330.

Martinek, T. & Karper, W. (1982). Canonical relationships among motor ability, expression of effort, teacher expectations and dyadic interactions in elementary age children. *Journal of Teaching in Physical Education, 1*, 26-39.

Martinek, T. & Karper, W. (1983, summer monograph). The influence of teacher expectations on ALT in physical education instruction. In P. Dodds & F. Rife (Eds.), Time to learn in physical education. Blacksburg, VA: *Journal of Teaching in Physical Education* (monograph 1).

Martinek, T. & Karper, W. (1984a). Multivariate relationships of specific impression cues with teacher expectations and dyadic interactions in elementary education classes. *Research Quarterly for Exercise and Sport, 55*, 32-40.

Martinek, T. & Karper, W. (1984b). The effects of competitive and noncompetitive instructional climates on teacher expectancy effects in elementary physical education classes. *Journal of Sports Psychology, 6*, 408-421.

Martinek, T. & Karper, W. (1986). Motor ability and instructional contexts: Effects on teacher expectation and dyadic interactions in elementary physical education classes. *Journal of Classroom Interaction, 21*, 16-25.

Methany, E. (1970). Symbolic forms of movement: The female image in sports. In G. H. Sage (Ed.) *Sport and American Society.* Reading, MA: Addison-Wesley.

Meyer, W. (1982). Indirect communications about perceived ability estimates. *Journal of Educational Psychology, 74*, 888-897.

Orlick, T. (1982). *The second cooperative sports and games book.* New York: Pantheon Books.

Palardy, J. (1969). What teachers believe—what children achieve. *Elementary School Journal, 69*, 370-374.

Rejeski, W. Darracott, C., Hutslar, S. (1979). Pygmalion in youth sport: A field study. *Journal of Sport Psychology, 1*, 311-319.

Rosenthal, R. (1974). *On the social psychology of the self-fulfilling prophecy: Further evidence for Pygmalion effects and their mediating mechanisms.* New York: MSS Modular Publications.

Rosenthal, R. & Jacobson, L. (1968). *Pygmalion in the classroom: Teacher expectation and pupils' intellectual development.* New York: Holt, Rinehart & Winston.

Scheer, T. & Ansorge, C. (1979). Influence due to expectations of judges: A function of internal-external locus of control. *Journal of Sport Psychology, 1*, 54-58.

Seligman, M. (1975). *Helplessness: On depression, development, and death.* San Francisco: Freeman.

Sutton-Smith, B., & Rosenberg, G. (1961). Sixty years of historical changes in the game preferences of American children. *Journal of American Folklore, 74*, 17-46.

Taguiri, R. (1969). Person perception. In G. Lindsay & E. Aronson (Eds.) Handbook of social psychology. Cambridge, MA: Addison-Wesley.

Templin, T. (1981). Student as socializing agent. *Journal of Teaching in Physical Education.* (Introductory issue), 71-19.

Weiner, B. (1979). A theory of motivation for some classroom experience. Journal of Educational Psychology, *71*, 3-25.

Weiner, B. & Kukla. (1970). An attributional analysis of achievement motivation. *Journal of Personality and Social Psychology, 15*, 1-20.

West, C. & Anderson, T. (1976). The question of preponderant causation in teacher expectancy research. *Review of Educational Research, 46*, 613-630.

11

Gender As A Socializing Agent In Physical Education

PAT GRIFFIN
University of Massachusetts at Amherst

The purpose of Title IX, the 1972 federal law prohibiting gender dis-crimination in education, was to serve as a legal lever to force changes in schools that would provide more equitable opportunities for girls and boys in academics, athletics, and physical education. In response to Title IX, the tradition of gender-segregated classes in physical education was to end, as gender could no longer be used as a criterion for assigning students to classes. The vision was that all physical education classes would be coed.

Gender restrictions placed on participation would be removed and, as a result, girls and boys would learn to participate together. Girls, with their increased opportunities in athletics and physical education, would improve their skills and assert their right to share in the joys of sport participation. Boys would learn that girls can be skilled performers, that losing to girls isn't humiliating, and that dance and gymnastics can be fun and enriching activities. In the mid-1970s we anticipated the future when we would be able to step back with satisfaction to survey our coed classes, as all students shared in the new freedom from traditional gender role restrictions.

If this vision seems out of focus, it is because things have not worked out the way we planned. Our efforts to implement coed classes and to change participation patterns among girls and boys in physical education have failed. Both casual observation and recent research on boys' and girls' participation show that gender remains a salient factor in physical education classes.

When students exhibit differences in performance and interest, both teachers and students often attribute these differences to gender. Gender is frequently used by both teachers and students as a criterion for dividing students into instructional or social groups within a class. In some schools, even relationships among physical education staff are clearly divided along gender lines: the men and women teachers don't speak to one another. Even caricatured teaching styles often are attributed to gender differences: men throw out the ball and lean against the gym wall, while women spend too much time lecturing about the rules or doing drills.

Some teachers would argue that coed classes are even more destructive to girls' sport participation than gender-segregated classes. The intimidation, hassling, and ridicule girls endure from male classmates in some coed classes do little to enhance their sport skills or their enthusiasm for sport participation. Other teachers believe that coed classes have destroyed physical education as an instructional activity. Because of the wide discrepancies in skill and interest they see in a coed class, these teachers have thrown their hands up, the ball out, and resigned themselves to providing little more than a recreation period.

As we move toward the 1990s, rather than working with the rosy coed vision once anticipated, more and more teachers are closing the gym divider (if it still works) and quietly resegregating classes by gender. This trend is encouraged by the weakened enforcement of Title IX over the last eight years as teachers who only grudgingly taught coed classes under the threat of legal action, realize that no action is taken when they resegregate classes. Perceptions of gender and its role in mediating participation and performance in physical education proved to be far too deeply rooted for the mere mixing of boys and girls in the same classes to change.

Our failure to make significant changes in the ways girls and boys participate in physical education is due largely to two factors. One, we have not examined carefully enough how gender is conceptualized by both teachers and students and how deeply rooted that conceptualization is in the larger societal context. Two, we have been naive in our attempts to address gender inequity in physical education. By framing the problem as one of simply providing equal access, we have failed to question the structure of sport and physical education and the sacred meaning they have in a male-dominated society.

My purpose in this chapter is to critically analyze, from a feminist perspective, gender socialization in physical education and sport. Integral to such an analysis are the following characteristics: (a) grounding the discussion in a socio-historical context; (b) recognizing differential power relationships among different social groups by gender, race, and class; (c) promoting social change and the empowerment of subordinate cultural groups by race, class, and gender; and (d) placing an imperative on elaborating the perspectives and experiences of women in a male-dominated society. Analysis of physical education and sport from a critical feminist perspective has been largely lacking, with the exception of some feminist sport sociologists (Birrell & Richter, 1987; Boutilier & SanGiovanni, 1983; Hall, 1987; Sabo & Runfola, 1980) and some physical education teacher educators (Bain, 1985; Dewar, 1987).

GENDER CONCEPTUALIZATION IN PHYSICAL EDUCATION AND SPORT

How we think about gender has tremendous implications for how we analyze gender socialization in physical education. Dewar (1987) identified four ways that physical educators treated gender issues in a college physical education program. These are (a) gender as a performance variable, (b) gender as an issue of sex difference, (c) gender as an issue of inequality, and (d) gender as a socially constructed set of power relationships. These four ways of thinking about gender form the framework for this discussion of gender socialization in physical education.

In most of the literature in physical education and in discussions among physical educators, gender is framed as a performance variable or an issue of sex difference. Perusal of the *Research Quarterly for Exercise and Sport* supports this observation. Gender is implicitly or explicitly defined as a personal biological trait. One's biological gender is used as the basis for explaining gender differences. Moreover, these differences often are thought of as dichotomous and static. That is, men and women belong to two discrete nonoverlapping categories and their differences are unchangeable. From this frame of reference, the biological definition of gender forms the basis for social and psychological gender expectations for men and women. Thinking of gender only as a biological trait results in the belief that gender differences are natural. Therefore, attempts to change significantly the sport participation and performance of girls and boys in physical education are futile.

There are, of course, real physical differences between females and males. When these differences are exaggerated or generalized in ways that ignore the tremendous overlap in male and female sport performance and interest, however, they form the core of the rationale to restrict women's sport participation. Arguments against the inclusion of women in sport altogether, explanations for the poor sport performance of so many girls, justification of the restriction of women to certain sports, and reservations about the wisdom of coed physical education are usually rooted in this biological definition of gender: girls are more prone to injury; men will always be bigger, stronger, and faster than women; girls' elbow, shoulder, or hip structures make them throw and run the way they do; girls aren't naturally aggressive or competitive.

In contrast to this biological perspective on gender, the literature encouraging coed physical education and demanding more resources for women's athletics treats gender as a socially constructed issue of inequity. Most feminists in physical education have taken this perspective. Many studies of gender issues in physical education available in the *Journal of Teaching in Physical Education* take this perspective (see Reference section for examples). Gender differences are framed as a societal discrimination problem to be solved by the expansion of opportunity for girls and women in sport.

From this perspective, most sport performance and interest differences between boys and girls are not biologically based but are the result of inequitable distribution of resources, opportunities, and rewards in sport. Consequently, performance gaps will narrow and gender differences will lose their significance as girls take advantage of increased sport opportunities. The focus, then, is on making teachers and coaches aware of gender bias and stereotyping in physical education so they will change their expectations of students and provide more equitable treatment to girls and boys. This perspective is based on the naive assumption that once teachers are aware of the errors of their ways and change, the problem will be solved. It's only a matter of providing the appropriate instructional resources to help teachers make the transition from gender discrimination and bias to gender fairness.

A conflict occurs when teacher educators, sex equity consultants, and teachers who think of gender as an issue of inequity lock horns with colleagues and students who think of gender as a biological trait. They all may see performance and interest differences between girls and boys in physical education, but they attribute those differences to disparate causes: biology, and social inequity. As a result, they have different perceptions of the possibility, or even the desirability of change.

Both perspectives, defining gender as a biological trait and dealing with gender as an issue of social inequity, ignore the importance of questioning the deeper structure of sport and physical education and their relationship to how gender is conceptualized. From the biological perspective, efforts to change gender socialization are futile because gender differences are biological. Consequently, there is no need to question the current structure of sport and physical education. From the inequity perspective, efforts to change gender socialization in physical education involve helping girls get more of what boys have had all along. The focus is on getting girls into sport and getting fair treatment once they're there. No concerted effort is made to change the structure of sport. At best, gender equity proponents hope that by including more girls and women in sport and implementing coed classes, concomitant changes will occur in the structure of sport and physical education, moving toward a more humane and inclusive, rather than masculine and exclusive, norm.

A third way of thinking about gender in physical education and sport is to conceptualize gender as a socially constructed set of power relationships. From this perspective, the function of gender as it is socially constructed is to perpetuate a male-dominated society. This perspective is a radical departure from thinking of gender as a biological trait or as an issue of inequity, the more typical perspectives taken by physical educators.

Our lack of success in changing the basic gender dynamics in physical education and sport is a result of our failure to understand the importance to the maintenance of a male-dominated society of accepting gender as a biological trait. Framing gender as an issue of inequity is too simplistic and ignores the necessity of thinking of gender as a biological trait in justifying the power imbalance between men and women. In addition, we have failed to understand the importance of sport and physical education as contemporary social institutions in maintaining that imbalance.

Taking the perspective that gender is a set of socially constructed expectations and power relationships allows us to examine gender socialization in physical education in a new way. This perspective forces us to move beyond the question, *how* are girls and boys socialized into "gender-appropriate" behaviors in physical education, to the question, *why* are students socialized into these particular behaviors rather than some other set.

This perspective rejects the assumption that girls and boys act the way they do in physical education because gender is biologically based. Boys don't emerge from the womb with a passion for football or an innately perfect overhand throwing pattern. It isn't natural or inevitable for girls to prefer sitting to running or to be movement-impaired (Bennett et al. 1987). These are learned behaviors, and serve a function in our culture for gender socialization to be constructed in this particular way.

Two questions emerge from this discussion: (a) What is the function of gender as it is socially constructed? and (b) What role do physical education and sport play in maintaining the current social construction of gender?

WHAT IS THE FUNCTION OF GENDER AS IT IS SOCIALLY CONSTRUCTED?

Little research is needed to support the claim that we live in a white, male-dominated society. Many major institutions in our society are controlled by white men. All three branches of our government (executive, judicial, and legislative) are predominantly white and male. Leadership in all of our other major social institutions (religion, law, business, education, and medicine, for example) is overwhelmingly white and male. Sport and physical education are no exception: white men hold most positions of power.

When gender is perceived as a set of socially constructed power relationships, its function in supporting and justifying a male-dominated society can be understood. Biologically based conceptions of gender justify the inequitable distribution of power between men and women. Separate, nonoverlapping, and static conceptions of gender serve the purpose of differentiating males and females. Further, attributes associated with the masculine gender role are more highly valued in all social institutions outside the home and family. Achievement in the public world of work calls for toughness, leadership, decisiveness, aggressiveness, competitiveness, autonomy, independence, and strength. Not so coincidentally, all of these qualities are associated with the male gender role. Attributes associated with the feminine gender role—gentleness, cooperativeness, passivity, dependence, and nurturance—are defined as incompatible with success in the work world. Moreover, men learn to despise anything they perceive to be feminine in themselves or in other men.

Men and women who defy gender roles by exhibiting behavior associated with the other gender are subject to ridicule and suspicion unless they compensate for their nonconformity by proving their fidelity to the appropriate gender in some other way: the outstanding female athlete who is also a cheerleader, or the male ballet dancer who is notorious for his numerous sexual liaisons with women. Men and women are socialized into and internalize these socially constructed gender roles as natural and inevitable. This acceptance is necessary if the male-dominated structure of our society is to be maintained. When we begin to question the naturalness and inevitability of gender roles, we begin to question the biological basis for the power imbalances between women and men in our society.

WHAT ROLE DO PHYSICAL EDUCATION AND SPORT PLAY IN THE MAINTENANCE OF THE CURRENT SOCIAL CONSTRUCTION OF GENDER?

The usual perspective taken in the physical education literature is to examine the role of gender socialization in sport and physical activity participation. From a critical feminist perspective, this is the wrong question because neither the concept of gender nor the structure of sport is examined. When gender is perceived as socially constructed rather than biologically based, the more appropriate question is, what role do physical education and sport (as they are currently structured) play in gender socialization?

Despite Title IX and 15 years of struggle, physical education and sport remain male domains. Though statistics reflect increased sport participation among girls and women, these percentages do not come close to the participation percentages for men and boys (Boutilier & SanGiovanni, 1983). Men and boys still receive more encouragement to be athletic (some would say boys are required to be athletic), receive more financial and other rewards for their participation, and in general invest far more time doing, talking about, and watching sport than girls or women do (Lewko & Ewing, 1980). Additionally, both print and broadcast media provide steady and overwhelmingly male sports coverage (Boutilier & SanGiovanni, 1983).

Observation studies of coed physical education classes have shown that boys dominate participation in team sport games (Bischoff, 1982; Griffin, 1981, 1984, 1985a; Solomons, 1980). Moreover, Greendorfer and Lewko (1978) found that the school played a minor role in socializing girls into sport. This finding highlights the importance of focusing more attention on the underlying structures of physical education and gender and their roles in our culture if we are to effectively change gender participation patterns in sport.

From a biologically based perception of gender, sport and physical education as male domains are natural and reflect inherent gender differences in ability and interest. From a socially constructed perception of gender, sport as a male domain serves a specific function in gender socialization. Boutilier and SanGiovanni (1983) identify three functions that sport serves for men and boys: (a) socialization into the male gender role, (b) denigration of women and femininity, and (c) provision of an appropriate outlet for male expressiveness and intimacy. Sport is a training ground where boys and men learn to be competitive, aggressive, tough, and to fight for their place in the male dominance hierarchy (Fine, 1987; Sabo, 1986). The ubiquitous practice of picking teams in physical education serves as a metaphor for this sorting out function in sport. Those doing the picking and those picked first gain public affirmation for their high place in the masculine pecking order. Those picked last or are not picked at all suffer the public humiliation of having their status as losers in the masculinity game confirmed.

In sport, boys learn that softness, weakness, vulnerability, timidity, and physical incompetence are feminine traits to be avoided at all costs. Indeed, for a boy to be called a girl, be compared to a girl, or lose to a girl in sport are the ultimate insults to masculine pride.

Sport also provides one of the only places where men can acceptably express unrestrained emotion without fear of being called gay or woman-like. Tears shed over lost games and leaps of joy following wins are acceptable public emotional displays in the sport context. Expressions of male intimacy, strictly forbidden in other interactions, are acceptable in sport. Hugs, fanny pats, and close physical contact in the contest are all accepted male-to-male interactions in the sport context. The comradery and deep affection male sport buddies often have for each other is evidence of the important role sport plays in male relationships with other men. In sport, men and boys bond together and test themselves against each other in masculinity rites seemingly as sacred as any religious ritual.

If the function of sport is to teach boys how to play their gender roles and to differentiate themselves from girls and feminine gender role behavior, then what place do girls and women have in sport? In this social construction of gender, the presence of girls and women in sport devalues the function sport serves for men and boys. If girls and women can play sport with the same degree of intensity and commitment that boys and men can, then sport loses its special status as a masculinity rite. In short, women in sport in a male-dominated society are an intrusion, marginal participants in an alien environment. As long as sport and physical education are perceived as vehicles to teach boys how to be men, women will never be more than peripheral participants, whether varsity competitors or members of the third period gym class.

To preserve sport and physical education as male turf, women are intimidated and discouraged from participation. Threats and innuendos about the sexual orientation and gender identity of women in sport are powerful inhibitors of female athleticism. Athletic women are continually on the defensive about their "femininity." Women and girls internalize the message that they are biologically inferior to men and that an intense involvement in sport betrays an inappropriately masculine nature.

Bryson (1987) suggests two other processes by which sport is maintained as masculine activity: ignoring and trivializing. Boutilier & SanGiovanni (1983) review several studies that document the sparse media coverage of women's sport as compared to men's sport. Even when the same event includes male and female performers, as in triathlons, marathons, or tennis matches, the bulk of media coverage is typically devoted to the men. In many schools, it would not be unusual to have a men's football team slogging through a losing season receive far more attention than a women's field hockey or soccer team vying for the national championship. This ignoring and trivializing of women's sport reinforces the perception that women do not participate in sport, and when they do their accomplishments are unimportant.

From this perspective, that sport and physical education serve an essential function in maintaining a male-dominated culture, it comes as no surprise that coed physical education has had little impact on gender-related participation. Simply mixing students by gender in physical education cannot begin to change the deeply rooted function sport plays in teaching boys to be men in a male-dominated society.

To preserve this function, girls must learn that they do not belong in sport, or to accept their peripheral role as participants in a masculine domain. Even our best intentions to provide equal opportunities for girls and boys in physical education classes are sabotaged by the competitive sport-oriented nature of the curriculum. As long as physical education curriculum is primarily comprised of competitive team sport activities and teachers and students accept a biologically based definition of gender, the masculine training function of sport in a male-dominated society will overwhelm any counteragenda of gender equity.

Most of the research on gender-related participation and sex equity in physical education as well as casual class observation support the claim that coed classes have not solved the problems of gender inequity in the gym. Girls and boys participate and interact with each other in stereotypical ways (Griffin, 1984, 1985a; Solomons, 1980, Wang, 1978). Boys engage in more than their expected share of active participation in team games (Bischoff, 1982; Griffin, 1981; Solomons, 1980). Boys ignore and hassle girls in classes (Griffin, 1983). Teachers continue to have gender-biased perceptions of and explanations for student behavior (Griffin, 1985b; Martinek et al., 1982) and teachers have more interaction with boys than with girls (Dunbar & O'Sullivan, 1986).

The curriculum remains largely a collection of competitive team sport activities that, traditionally, have appealed more to boys than to girls. A masculine elitist competitive norm of participation pervades classes (Kollen, 1983), so that less competitive and less skilled participants, girls and boys, are shunted to the side as more aggressive students are allowed to dominate class games. Though there are exceptions to these patterns, both casual conversations with teachers and observation of classes attest to their pervasiveness in most sport and physical education settings.

By understanding the role sport and physical education play in gender construction and socialization, it is possible to look at behavior in the gym from a different perspective. Teachers and students are imbedded in their experience of socially constructed gender roles. Having grown up in a society that teaches us that gender roles are natural, appropriate, and inevitable, it is difficult to step out of this construction of reality to envision another. Many teachers and students do not even perceive gender roles to be a problem. Conceptualizing gender as a personal biological trait affecting performance makes gender an extremely salient factor in the gym. Students are separated by gender, performance expectations are gender-related, and teacher perceptions of student interest in physical education are affected by gender. Our embeddedness in gender roles as they are socially constructed constricts our perception of what is possible, not only for others, but for ourselves as well. Gender may be the single most powerful socializing agent in the gym perpetuating the status quo in our male-dominated society.

What does this analysis tell us about gender socialization in physical education? Our efforts to expand participation options for girls and boys have ignored the underlying functions of traditional gender roles in a male-dominated society. We have underestimated how deeply rooted our conceptions of gender are in understanding ourselves and making sense of the world. We have failed to appreciate the difficulty of stepping out of traditional gender roles as well as the pressure to conform to them. Moreover, we have ignored our discomfort with people who step out of bounds or ask us to.

Instead we have relied on simplistic appeals to fair play and equity. We have promoted mechanical and methodological strategies that encourage the inclusion of girls in sport, but do not directly address the sexist structure and function of sport and physical education. Though grouping by abilities, using a variety of teaching styles, avoiding sexist language, and restructuring game play all are excellent teaching strategies, they also are superficial changes without an accompanying shift in how teachers conceptualize gender and the role of physical education and sport in gender construction.

PROSPECTS FOR CHANGE IN GENDER SOCIALIZATION AND IN PHYSICAL EDUCATION

Gender socialization is complex and deeply rooted in our culture. Additionally, this construct is related to sport and physical education in complicated and confusing ways. We must recognize that changing gender socialization in physical education in the 1970s and 80s is only part of an ongoing socio-historical evolution. Because this change challenges the foundations of our male-dominated society, it will meet with fierce resistance. Because we all are embedded in that society, resistance comes from within ourselves as well as from others. For these reasons, change will be slow and progress uneven.

We must begin to question the structure and function of sport and physical education. We can no longer focus on interactions and teaching methods within the structure without thinking critically about the structure itself and its relationship to the larger society. This shift in focus requires that we think about the issue of gender socialization in physical education in much broader terms.

We must reflect on our own conceptualizations of gender. Dewar (1987) has given us a useful conceptual framework from which to start the process of identifying how we think about gender and what effect our conceptualization has on our work and personal lives. We must identify our own fear and resistance to changing our conceptualization of gender. We need to recognize that changing conceptions of gender is an evolution of consciousness, not merely a change in attitude. This conceptual change requires a major shift in our view of ourselves and other people.

Changing conceptions of gender must be a personal process as well as an abstract one. As a result, this change has great potential for being personally threatening, as we give up what is comfortable and familiar to explore new ways of thinking about gender. How we think about gender affects not only how we teach or coach, but also how we live and our relationships with friends, lovers, colleagues, family, and children. If we are to change how gender is constructed, we cannot limit our commitment to gender equity to our work lives. Change will come from the inside out as we unlearn the rules for a masculinity and femininity game we have known for a long time.

For all of these reasons, our prospects for changing gender socialization in physical education depend on our willingness to engage in a lifelong process of thinking critically about gender, not only in the gym, but everywhere. Clearly, the task is more complicated than we thought when Title IX was passed in 1972.

IMPLICATIONS FOR TEACHER EDUCATION AND RESEARCH IN PHYSICAL EDUCATION

This discussion of gender socialization in physical education has focused on classes where students are engaged in motor activities. All research on gender issues in physical education, with the exception of Dewar (1987), has focused on the K-12 curriculum. However, before teacher educators can effectively address gender issues with beginning or experienced physical activity teachers, we must begin to address these issues among ourselves. We must examine the culture of teacher education and question the role gender plays in our professional relationships. Sears (1985) describes the importance, and difficulty, of integrating a "woman's perspective" into teacher education.

We in physical education teacher education need to analyze critically the effects of gender on our profession's development. Why is it that in many teacher education programs women are the teachers and men are the researchers? Why are those perceived to be "giants in our field" primarily men? Why is it that when sex equity is addressed in teacher education programs it is usually women who must do the confronting and the teaching? In answering these tough questions, teacher educators must avoid easy, simplistic, or defensive explanations. If we are not willing to explore the effects of gender socialization on college professorship and membership in the community of physical education scholars, then we cannot effectively address the same issues with students in our undergraduate classes or with our colleagues in the schools.

To seriously and effectively address gender socialization in physical education, teacher educators must interact with each other, undergraduate physical education majors, and physical educators in the schools in the following ways:

(a) Challenge the conception of gender as simply biologically based.

(b) Examine the structure and function of physical education and sport in a male-dominated society.

(c) Challenge our perceptions and stereotypes of inherent and socially constructed gender differences.

(d) Frame the discussion in such a way that men and women share the responsibility for addressing gender issues in physical education. To the extent that gender issues are "ghettoized" as women's issues only of concern to women in a male-dominated profession, no real change is likely. Women in physical education can no longer afford to accept gratefully the private verbal support of those male colleagues who claim to deplore gender inequity. It is important that supportive male colleagues speak and act out their convictions as well.

(e) Identify how both men and women can benefit from the process of questioning and working together to change a male-dominated society in general education, and physical education in particular. Allowing the discussion to polarize into a win-lose debate between men and women serves no purpose except to awaken the feminist consciousness of some women who did not previously understand the deeply rooted fear and anger some men feel about addressing gender inequities.

(f) Recognize that this process will be difficult and ongoing. Taking a course, attending a workshop, or reading a book on gender stereotyping in physical education is only a start. Effectively addressing gender issues in physical education means unlearning a lifetime of expectations and beliefs about being male or female. We cannot trivialize the scope of gender issues by assuming that if we took a course on sexism last semester, then further discussion of the issue in subsequent semesters is redundant.

(g) Accept this as a personal change process, not only an academic or abstract discussion. This requires that men and women consider stepping out of bounds and breaking rules in the game of gender as we have known it. Even the simple equity strategy of asking a man to teach aerobics to music can be perceived as personally threatening if this activity falls outside his boundary of acceptable behavior for men. Yet, we must all be willing to challenge ourselves in similar ways if we are to make a difference.

Reframing gender as a social construction also has implications for research in physical education. To date, most research on teaching physical education focuses on intraclass events: interactions among teachers and students, the effects of different teaching strategies on student learning, and determining student activity time are several of the research themes that comprise the bulk of the body of knowledge in teaching physical education. Though some of these studies focus on describing gender differences in participation and performance, few studies critically examine the concept of gender or the structure of physical education in a male-dominated society. We need to develop a tradition of research that broadens our focus beyond intraclass events to make connections between what is happening in physical education and the broader socio-historical context. Bain and Jewett (1987) call for the development of such a critical theoretical perspective in physical education teaching and curriculum research.

We need to inform our data analyses with an explicit awareness of social diversity issues that influence both our perspectives as researchers and the actions and beliefs of the teachers and students we study. Specifically, we need to integrate an awareness of how we and our research participants think about gender, race, ethnicity, class, or other social group memberships. By acknowledging power imbalances among different social groups and giving a voice to those less frequently heard in our research (women, disabled people), we can move beyond a context-free description of what is happening in the gym to engage in a rich and grounded discussion of socialization in physical education. The inclusion of a diversity of voices in the ongoing research dialogue will bring all of us to a deeper understanding of physical education and its relationship with the rest of our lives as members of a diverse and dynamic culture.

I began this chapter with a discussion of our profession's attempt to implement gender equity laws. I believe that the changes we have made are superficial, not structural, and that the time period from 1970-1990 is a mere hiccup in the evolutionary process of social change in how we conceptualize gender. There is, however, an inevitability to the change process. The history of women's participation in sport and in the larger society tracks a slow and uneven, but consistent journey toward liberation from the restrictions of rigid gender roles. Each of us as physical education professionals must decide what role we will play in this evolution: to either facilitate or resist change. There are no other choices. To decide to do nothing supports the status quo in a male-dominated society. Each of us will be either part of the problem or part of the solution.

I hope what I have presented will be provocative. If it angers some physical educators and energizes others, I will feel successful because I believe we must shake ourselves up before we can begin to see things a new way. We need to identify contradictions and inconsistencies in how we understand gender. We must begin to see the absurdity, destructiveness, and loss of resources that result when we insist that gender constitutes two separate, hierarchical, and non-overlapping categories into which we assign people on the basis of their genitals.

Most importantly, we must challenge the necessity, desirability, and, ultimately, the viability of a male-dominated social structure and the role we play as physical educators in maintaining this social structure. The alternative is living with what we have: another generation of boys who assume entitlement in sport and eagerly struggle to mold themselves into the restrictive model of masculinity a male-dominated society demands . . . another generation of girls who assume disablement in sport and settle for the lowered expectations and aspirations that femininity in a male-dominated society requires.

REFERENCES

Bain, L. (1985). A naturalistic study of students' responses to an exercise class. *Journal of Teaching in Physical Education*, 5 (1), 2-12.
Bain, L. & Jewett, A. (1987). Future research and theory building. *Journal of Teaching in Physical Education*. (Monograph). 6 (3), 346-362.
Bennett, R., Whittaker, G., Woolley Smith, N., & Sablove, A. (1987). Changing the rules of the game: Reflections toward a feminist analysis of sport. *Women's Studies International Forum*, 10 (4), 369-380.
Birrell, S. & Richter, D. (1987). Is a diamond forever? Feminist transformations in sport. *Women's Studies International Forum*, 10 (4), 395-410.
Bischoff, J. (1982). Equal opportunity, satisfaction, and success: An exploratory study on coeducational volleyball. *Journal of Teaching in Physical Education*, 2 (1), 3-12.
Boutilier, M. & SanGiovanni, L. (1983). *The Sporting Woman*. Champaign, IL: Human Kinetics.
Bryson, L. (1987). Sport and the maintenance of masculine hegemony. *Women's Studies International Forum*, 10 (4), 349-360.
Dewar, A. (1987). The social construction of gender in physical education. *Women's Studies International Forum*, 10 (4), 453-466.
Dunbar, R. & O'Sullivan, M. (1986). Effects of intervention on differential treatment of boys and girls in elementary physical education lessons. *Journal of Teaching in Physical Education*, 5 (3), 166-175.

Fine, G. (1987). *With The Boys: Little League Baseball and Preadolescent Culture.* Chicago: University of Chicago Press.

Greendorfer, S. & Lewko, J. (1978). The role of family members in sport socialization of children. *Research Quarterly, 49,* 146-152.

Griffin, P. (1981). One small step for personkind: Observations and suggestions for sex equity in coeducational physical education classes. *Journal of Teaching in Physical Education,* Introductory Issue, 12-17.

Griffin, P. (1983). Gymnastics is a girl's thing: Student participation and interaction patterns in a middle school physical education unit. In T. Templin & J. Olson (Eds.), *Teaching in Physical Education.* Champaign, IL: Human Kinetics.

Griffin, P. (1984). Girls' participation patterns in a middle school team sports unit. *Journal of Teaching in Physical Education, 4* (1), 30-38.

Griffin, P. (1985a). Boys' participation styles in a middle school physical education team sports unit. *Journal of Teaching in Physical Education, 4* (2), 100-110.

Griffin, P. (1985b). Teachers' perceptions of and reactions to sex equity problems in a middle school physical education program. *Research Quarterly for Exercise and Sport, 56* (2), 103-110.

Hall, A. (Ed.) (1987). The gendering of sport, leisure, and physical education (special issue). *Women's Studies International Forum. 10* (4).

Kollen, P. (1983). Fragmentation and integration in human movement. In T. Templin & J. Olson (Eds.), *Teaching in Physical Education.* Champaign, IL: Human Kinetics.

Lewko, J. & Ewing, M. (1980). Sex differences and parental influences in sport involvement of children. *Journal of Sport Psychology, 2,* 62-68.

Martinek, T., Crowe, P., & Rejeski, W. (1982). *Pygmalian in the gym: Causes and effects of expectations in teaching and coaching.* West Point, NY: Leisure Press.

Sabo, D. (1986, November). Sports, patriarchy, and male identity: Wrestling with the legacy of the plow. Keynote address presented at the First Multidisciplinary Conference in Sport Sciences for the Nordic Countries, Lillchamer, Norway.

Sabo, D. & Runfola, R. (Eds.). (1980). *Jock: Sports and male identity.* Englewood Cliffs, NJ: Prentice-Hall.

Sears, J. (1985, July). The hollowness of credibility: Gender and the culture of teacher education. Paper presented at the National Coalition of Sex Equity in Education Conference, Williams Bay, WI.

Solomons, H. (1980). Sex role mediation of achievement behaviors and interpersonal interactions in sex integrated team games. In E. Pepitone (Ed.), *Children in cooperation and competition.* Lexington, MA: D.C. Heath.

Wang, B. (1978). An ethnography of a physical education class: An experiment in integrated living. (Doctoral dissertation, University of North Carolina, 1977.) *Dissertation Abstracts International, 38,* 1980-A.

12

Moving Up and Getting Out: The Classed and Gendered Career Opportunities of Physical Education Teachers

JOHN EVANS AND TREFOR WILLIAMS
University of Southampton

DEFINING THE CONDITIONS OF WORK

It would not be much of an exaggeration to state that currently in Britain, as in the United States (Greene, 1985; Apple, 1986), a teacher's lot is not a happy one. One would need to look long and hard over the contemporary educational scene to find a time when teachers had been subjected to so many pressures emanating from so many varied sources, while the expectations placed upon them had been so high and when they were expected to administer so many changes in the content and method of their educational practice. Like other critical analysts of the contemporary educational scene (Apple, 1986; Ozga, 1988), we, too, claim that teaching in Britain is going through a period of crisis, "from which it is likely to emerge in very different form to that of the '60s and '70s. The nature and conditions of a teacher's work in schools are being fundamentally altered by a number of policy initiatives (for example, the implementation of a national curriculum, new forms of assessment), the cummulative effect of which is to greatly increase central government control over the teaching force" (Ozga, 1988 p. xiv).

The origins of these changes cannot be detailed here[1], but briefly we might note that since the mid-1960s, schools in Britain have come repeatedly under attack from the conservative voices of the political left and recently from those more powerful and organized on the radical right (see Ball, in press; Davies, 1986). Throughout this period, schools and teachers within them have been variously blamed for damaging educational standards, promoting ill discipline among children, and failing to supply industry with an adequate supply of talent and skilled manpower. They have been repeatedly but incorrectly (Bates et al., 1984) identified as at the root of Britain's poor economic performance and the high levels of unemployment in the country, especially among its youth, and for what is reputed to be the nation's moral decline. Physical educationalists have not escaped this critique (Evans, 1988). They, too, have wrongly been accused of adopting radical left-wing policies and crude egalitarian ideas and blamed for supporting innovations (involving, for example, health related fitness and cooperative game forms) which not only, it is claimed, damage the production of Britain's sporting talent, but also the promotion of competitive and individualistic attitudes that are vital both to an individual's performance in the paid work place and Britain's future economic success.

Unsurprisingly, these criticisms of the teaching force have badly lowered the morale of the profession and dramatically altered the way in which outside publics (parents, industrialists) think about teachers. They also have "paved the way for a level of political intervention in the nature and content of state education provision which makes the comprehensive school experiment of earlier years by contrast pale into a deep and

---

[1] As Ozga (1987), we would stress that this crisis has its origins in the wider, extra-school economic context. As she points out, "the crisis in teaching is not new but forms an episode in a relationship between teachers and the state which is characterized by different degrees of tension, depending on the extent of the need to exert control over the teaching force. In times of economic crisis, foreign competition and political dissensions, the central state tends towards strong, directive management which imposes controls on teacher recruitment, training, salaries and status, and curriculum and examination context" (p. x). With Ozga, however, we would also emphasize that this control over teachers is never complete or easily secured.

irrelevant insignificance" (Evans & Davies, 1988). A variety of policy initiatives have been implemented that include, among others, alterations to both the pattern of in-service and initial teacher training and the content of training that is intended now to emphasize technical competence rather than intellectual development. And after a long and often bitter dispute between the teacher and the government over pay and conditions of work, a dispute that has had profound effects upon PE, teachers have had to accept changes in the contractual relationships between themselves and their employers (effectively the government), which involves the abolition of their negotiating rights (Ozga, 1988). They have also had to come to terms with the arrival of a national curriculum and new forms of examinations, with the loss of autonomy and control over the content and evaluation of schooling that these may entail.

All of this, with an underfunding of educational practice and the negative effects of a declining secondary school population (falling rolls), has ensured that the expansion and optimism of the 1960s has sadly and dramatically given way to a period of contraction and a widespread and deep sense of pessimism and insecurity as teachers see themselves being under-valued, poorly rewarded, and losing control over the nature of their work. However, though all teachers are subject to these patterns and changes, we suggest that individuals do not subjectively experience them in a uniform way, nor do they individually or as members of a subject group possess the same degree of power or resource to confront, challenge, or resist their individual conditions of work (Evans & Davies, 1988), or improve or advance their educational opportunities and career possibilities. Teachers' careers are structured (limited or facilitated), by ideologies in the school work place that influence and differently define the position and status both of men and women and the academic and "non-academic" (practical) curriculum; and that these ideologies have their bases in wider society.

Within the current career and occupational structures of the educational work place, competition between individuals and between subject groups is a fundamental feature of life in school and an inescapable aspect of individual advancement through teaching. Although individual teachers may in theory have equal access and opportunities for career advancement both within the subject and to areas outside PE, they do not have equal status, social, or professional resources to bring to the competitive stakes. Teachers' opportunities to change the conditions of their work or advance their careers may be structured by their sex, or the occupational status of their subject. As others have pointed out (Ball, 1987), there are very clear patterns of advantage and disadvantage in the career opportunities of teachers; physical educationalists do not feature too well within them. These patterns are deeply ingrained in the educational system and extend across schools to provide structural advantages for certain groups and disadvantages for others. The most significant, in Ball's view, is the organization of and different status imputed to subject departments. This pattern benefits and privileges some teachers and dis-benefits others. Ball quotes "If a Headship is the target, then for *teachers of equal experience* the best chances of achieving this goal lie with (the subjects of) history, physics, French and maths" (cited in Hilsum & Start, 1974, p. 83). In short, some subjects and the teachers that staff them lack credibility and influence in the eyes of significant others (head teachers, local education authority policy makers), the gatekeepers to career op-portunities. This status is reflected both in the type of subject of teachers who achieve positions in the senior hierarchy of schools, and in the dis-tribution of salary scale points and senior positions within and between subjects (Evans & Davies, 1988; Williams, 1988).

PE teachers are far less likely to rise above the mid-levels of the salary scale within their subject department than are other subject teachers (Department of Education and Science, 1982). But, subject status alone does not account for the difficulties that some teachers experience when seeking promotion or looking for a job. As will be pointed out (Apple, 1986; Ball, 1987; Deem, 1978) women are often profoundly disadvan-taged in terms of career rewards by male dominance in administration positions across various sectors of schooling and within and between specific subject areas. Even in the primary or elementary sector teaching force in Britain (as in the United States) in which women outnumber men, the latter are disproportionately represented in senior positions. This is because the language and structure of schooling and the subject departments inside them are often deeply shaped by patriarchy. The gatekeepers to jobs are predominantly men and they (Burgess, 1986) do not always believe women are either capable or suitable, because of their competing family and work roles, for advancement to senior positions. In Britain, PE departments in the co-educational secondary sector have long existed as separate entities with clearly different and distinct curriculum for boys and girls. There is often a teacher in charge of girls' PE, and there is usually a head of PE overseeing both boys and girls. This person (Bur-gess, 1986; Scraton, 1985) is almost invariably male. We will suggest that these patterns have been exacerbated in recent years as economic cuts have depleted resources (human and physical). This, as Scraton (1985) points out, has sometimes meant that PE staff members have not been replaced or have been replaced with part-time appointments. These have tended to be women who have left their jobs, not from any lack of commitment, but because of lack of opportunity and the power of some men to enact their gender-stereotypical imagery upon the careers of men and women.

The Research

Our data are drawn from a study of British physical education teachers in Hampshire Secondary Schools, which was undertaken in 1987 (Williams, 1988). In total, 72 mostly 12-16 co-educational comprehensive schools (serving ages 12-16) were included in the study. A questionnaire was issued to each teacher in charge of boys' PE and each teacher in charge of girls' PE. Responses were received from 50 male and 50 female teachers representing just over 80% of the schools. The questionnaire survey generated a wealth of qualitative and quantitative data. In this discussion, we want to concentrate mainly on the data relating to the teachers' position, and status in PE and the broader school context, and their perspectives on their careers in a period of educational contraction and change.

Teachers: Position, Responsibilities, and Status

Most of the teachers in the study had entered PE teaching for a number of reasons, but chief among them were their love of sport (Whitehead & Hendry, 1976), and the positive influence that PE teachers had had upon them in their own school careers. For the majority of these individuals, PE had been their first career choice; most had progressed through specialist PE colleges, which they felt had well-equipped them to teach PE but not a second curriculum subject. The majority had left college with a Certificate in Education[2].

The average age of the males in the study is 37.2, and of the females, 34.1. The males had an average of 14.5 years of teaching experience, the females, 11.2 years. However, although we find an average age and experience difference between males and females of just more than three years, when we examine the distribution of responsibilities, reward, and status between men and women a rather striking pattern emerges. Although most of the teachers in the study operated in schools with a male and a female in charge of boys' and girls' PE, in 84% of these schools it is a male teacher who holds responsibility as overall head of the PE department. Clearly this also has implications for the way in which rewards, in the form of salary scale posts, are distributed between men and women (see Table 12-1).

You will note, 88% of the men, by contrast with 38% of the women, had achieved scale 3 or 4 positions (the top salary scale, before moving on

---

[2] In the late 1970s, teaching in the primary and secondary sectors of education in Britain became an "all graduate entry" profession. Teachers qualify by taking either a three-year Bachelor of Education (B.Ed), a four-year B.Ed honors course, or a three-year specialist (subject based) degree course plus a one-year Post Graduate Certificate in Education course. Prior to this, most teachers entered the profession after three years' training with a Certificate in Education though some could stay on an additional year to achieve a bachelor's degree.

TABLE 12-1. Distribution of Salary Scale Points Between men and women PE teachers.

Men	Salary Scale Posts	Women
2%	1	12%
10%	2	50%
66%	3	32%
22%	4	6%

to senior management positions). How might we explain this distribution of responsibility, reward, and head of department status? It could be suggested that this picture reveals little more than the allocation of reward for age and years of teaching experience. There is some evidence for this; there are more younger women than men in the sample. However, a close examination of the data reveals that even when men and women have comparable teaching experience, it is the men who tend to be positioned on the higher salary scales (Williams, 1988). It might also be suggested that this positional difference is an expression of the abilities of the teachers concerned; however, there is no evidence for this in our study[3].

Common-sense notions (like some psychological and economic theories) sometimes conceive of ability as a property of the individual (like hair or eye color) and suggests that it is this ability that largely determines an individual's competence and position in life[4]. In Britain, as in the United States, a meritocratic ideology permeates society as well as the school systems that helps reproduce and support it[5]. In this ideology, everyone has the same chance to advance to the top to experience success and satisfaction; individual attainment is seen largely as a function of how hard individuals work and their inherent ability or talent. But this is a view that takes little cognizance of the way in which individual abilities,

---

[3] If ability is adjudged simply in terms of academic qualifications, the women in our study had more of it than the men.

[4] Indeed, this is a view in much of the literature on teachers and professionalism, which, as Lawn and Grace (1987) point out, constructs a view of organized teachers

"as making steady historical progress toward a clear set of professional goals. Their analyses has been located within liberal versions of social mobility theory, premised upon an essentially benevolent (or nationalist) view of the state and a sense that expertise, aspiration and responsible behaviour will ultimately be rewarded. In effect, this liberal, evolutionary, social mobility view of organised teachers has failed to illuminate the actual class and gender relations of teaching" (p. ix).

[5] I am grateful to Tom Templin for pointing out to me that the ideology of meritocracy may be finding further and more obvious expression in the United States as "career ladders" increasingly find their way into schools to create a situation wherein teachers are "selected" and financially rewarded (given "merit pay") for different responsibilities, and that many teachers are opposed to this development because of its negative effects on themselves and their colleagues. One can find in Wexler (1988) an excellent discussion of these trends in the United States, which have their parallels on the British scene.

identities, and opportunities are structured and constrained by institutional arrangements and ideologies that pervade the educational work place as in other areas of social life and that together ensure that often beneath the rhetoric of meritocracy, openness, and contest, a system of sponsorship successfully but implicitly prevails.

Ball (1987) has made the point that women teachers may validly be regarded as a distinct interest group within the school if only because the overall pattern of their career development is so different from that of men. There is a growing body of evidence to suggest that women are severely disadvantaged by male dominance in schools. Many women have to manage two careers, one in the paid educational work place, the other in the unpaid context of family life; still they have to bear the main responsibility for child rearing and servicing other family members' needs. This dual role often has important implications for how women are perceived in schools and concomitantly for their occupational careers. More than 40% of the women in our study had taken a break from teaching to meet "family responsibilities". Only 8% of the men had had a break from teaching and none of them for this reason. Even though the break, in most cases, seems to have been short, many of the women felt it had severely disadvantaged them in the career stakes because, in their view, senior management regarded them with suspicion and now doubted their commitment to a career in teaching. As one teacher said:

> Once you start a family you are regarded almost as a part-time teacher as far as career prospects are concerned."

Others mentioned the hostility they had faced on returning to school, particularly from older colleagues, who made it plain that they felt women should be at home with the children rather than teaching. One female teacher summed up this particular problem.

> Many of my older male colleagues don't disguise the fact that they think it almost immoral of me to return to school so soon after the baby. Mind you many of these still believe that women teach for "pin" money. Equal opportunity? Sexual equality? That really is a myth!

In the view of these teachers the ideology of *familism* (Arnot, 1984) that "exaggerated identification with the myth that the family is the only place where a woman may experience self-fulfillment," was firmly established in the thinking of significant others in the work place. It was this, in their view, that operated as a substantial constraint on their career opportunities.

What is found then, is a situation in which within the organizational culture of the school, commitment is defined not only as a particular form of behavior (a continuous or unbroken involvement in teaching) with a set of attributes (knowledge, expertise, experience) associated with it, but also as an attitude toward the position and place of paid employment in the life style of the individual. The upshot of this is that within the career stakes, commitment (and all its constitutive elements) can be seen as either synoyomous with or as an indissoluble component of teaching or teacher ability. Clearly, it is men, not women whose lives are structured by the dual responsibilities of family and paid work, who are more likely to have the capacity and the opportunity to display such talents.[6]

THE CAREER AMBITIONS OF PE TEACHERS

It is hardly surprising that we find this differential distribution of rewards, responsibilities, and status giving rise to different career ambitions among men and women. While most of the men in the study having reached the top in PE, have their sights set firmly on getting up and out of PE (mainly into the pastoral system[7]), women still see the next step as making it up to the position of head within the PE department or simply continuing as a teacher of physical education.

In the study, many of the men (62%) are looking toward a move into a senior position in the pastoral system. It will be revealed, however, that many also feel they have come to a halt in their careers and that they are stuck in a job that they no longer want but from which they cannot easily depart. By contrast, some 14% of the women see their next step as moving up in the PE department to a position of head and 52% feel that they will 'remain as a PE teacher' (see Table 9-2). We can only speculate on the reasons for this apparent commitment to and contentment with teaching PE. For many, perhaps, teaching without the responsibilities of head of department is the only means of coping with the dual demands of the family and school; others may find a harsh realization that in the competi-

---

[6] As others (Evett, 1988) we stress the conventional concept of "career," as a continuous progression through a series of hierarchically arranged positions, is quite inadequate when considering the working lives of women. It is a concept that may have frustrated the career opportunities of women and the analyses of their working lives and experiences. For an excellent discussion of the concept of commitment and its bearing on teachers' careers, see Sparkes (1988).

[7] In many state secondary schools in Britain, "pastoral care" is viewed as an important aspect of educational provision. The term tends to refer to the non-instructional aspects of the roles of teachers and others in schools, those concerned with the social, emotional, and psychological well-being and development of children. This work is facilitated by "pastoral structures" (which sit alongside academic structures), which may take the form of intra-school divisions (e.g. houses or year groups), with such roles as head of pastoral care, head of house, or school counselor, year master and form (class) tutor built into them. "These structures are support-giving, reassuring convivial institutions whose functioning makes possible the fullest and happiest development of the individual pupil's school career(s)" (Best, Jarvis and Ribbins, 1980). The pastoral structure has its own hierarchy, from class tutor to head of pastoral care, a position usually taken by the (or one of the) deputy heads of the school. Some have argued that these "structures" are often more concerned with the control of children than with caring for them (Corbishley and Evans, 1980). PE teachers have long been thought suitable for such caring or controlling pastoral roles.

TABLE 12-2. The Career Ambitions of PE Teachers

Anticipated next position	MALE (N = 50) %	FEMALE (N = 50) %
Head of Department	4	14
Management	12	6
Pastoral	62	30
Adviser	2	4
Lecturer	0	4
Remain as PE Teacher	12	52
PE and Classroom Teacher	4	12
Out of Teaching	12	0

tion for senior positions in the department or school they would invariably fair badly against their privileged male colleagues. As one female teacher stated:

There is virtually no chance of a woman becoming head of department in this school. The head would never contemplate a female head of department, and my only chance of promotion is in pastoral care or a move to an all girls' school.

What we find, however, is a situation in which womens' opportunities to climb the career ladder in PE are structured not only by the ideology of patriarchy as it pervades the school system, but also by mens' opportunities to get out of the subject. These also are limited, by the hegemony of the academic curriculum that places physical education and its teachers in a position of marginality and low status in the school curriculum.

As noted, some subject teachers seem to be implicitly sponsored to achieve senior management posts within the school hierarchy, (Ball, 1987; Hilsum & Start, 1974). PE teachers, like others in "practical subjects," do not tend to fair well in the selective thinking of appointment panels. There is little doubt that many of the male teachers in our study felt their career opportunities were extremely limited by the way in which significant others in the school hierarchy thought about PE and imputed low status to the subject. Many considered that their best hope lay in their promotion into the pastoral system—a common route for PE teachers (Bell, 1986; Sikes, 1988)—though some felt even this was a "structured opportunity" in that they were being channeled in this direction by senior management who saw only the social and affective domain of schooling as suitable for the "non-academic" PE teacher. However, although 40% of the men had attended courses in pastoral care, there was among many a growing sense of doubt that even these efforts to meet the expectations of management would ultimately bring them career advance. As one male teacher illustrates:

> What is the point in course attendance, when we have little or no chance of promotion beyond head of department level? At best you meet an adviser who may help you within PE. But, as I am already a head of department, I see little point in course attendance.

It is also evident that the contemporary conditions of schooling, particularly the long period of industrial action and the contraction in the education system, had further exacerbated these teachers' problems of achieving promotion. Many of the male teachers felt that getting out of the subject depended upon their capacity either to achieve for themselves and their subject a high public profile in and outside the school (through the production of successful sports teams), or display their academic credentials by teaching a second (non-PE) academic subject. Throughout the period of industrial action (1984 to 1986), however, teachers were required by their unions to fulfill only their contractual duties. This meant that many PE teachers and other subject teachers could not or would not continue to make available opportunities or support (in the form of coaching, for example) for extra school sport.

In effect, the industrial action severely constrained one of the most important means traditionally available to PE teachers in Britain to display their credentials, their commitment to teaching and coaching, the quality of their department, and their competences as teachers. In short, they were constrained in their endeavors to produce and publicly display their abilities at producing successful sports teams. The decision to support the union action had thus put enormous strain on teachers as they weighed the consequences of their decisions for their careers. As one male teacher stressed:

> Since we stopped school matches I know the head is far from happy with the PE department. I'm sure he feels we should have continued against our union's advice. My chances of a further promotion with this head have disappeared.

They also were subjected to pressure from senior management who, in a period of conflict between employer and employee and often between teachers in schools, were eager to maintain at least a public front of order, continuing commitment, and productivity.

PE staff members have long acted as a point of contact between school and parents during the provision of extracurricular sporting activities, and when these stopped, members of senior management were often unhappy with PE departments. One male PE teacher said:

> We realized many parents would be unhappy (about the cessation of

school matches, etc.), and the head and deputy I'm sure resented the PE staff because of the conflict this causes with parents. At least it made them analyze the amount of hours PE staff put in, which is very often taken for granted by parents and heads.

Furthermore, many men felt that their opportunities to achieve a higher visibility as academic teachers by teaching a second non-PE subject became limited. Despite the cessation of teacher action, many teachers from other subject areas who had previously given help to the teaching of PE had not "returned" to give this commitment. They, too, may have been severely demoralized by the period of teacher action and the limited support for teachers and the educational system shown by the government. The contraction in the educational system that has resulted from a combination of falling rolls and government under-resourcing has also meant that PE teachers are either not being appointed or taken on only as part-time or second-subject teachers. This diminishing supply of trained and "helper" PE teachers has limited PE teachers' opportunities to develop their teaching in a second academic subject. In our study, 67% of the teachers taught only PE and many felt that they were now increasingly being "locked in" to teaching more and more P.E.

CHANGING THE GAME

It is hardly surprising that facing these conditions of work, with few career opportunities, and feeling that as a profession they could expect to receive little support from seniors inside the institution or publics, parents, or politicians outside it, many of the teachers in our study felt deeply frustrated, even alienated, from teaching. As one female teacher remarked, perhaps capturing the attitude of many others.

> Why should we continue to work all hours when we are constantly criticized by all sections of society, especially by our own secretary of state?

More than 80% of the men and 40% of the women in the study are now looking for a career outside PE and 85% of the teachers could name PE teachers who had already left the profession. Said a male teacher:

> Yes, of course, I know PE teachers who have left teaching—who doesn't? I have lost three from my department in the last eight years, and part of the fault is my inability to move on to create a promotion for them. I only wish I had the courage to leave and try something new, but at my age it is too big a risk.

Finding satisfaction in work was now increasingly difficult, and some clearly had begun to search for this in activities outside school[8]. One of the female teachers in the study said:

> I've now developed other interests outside school. I work in a pub, part time, and as far as I'm concerned I'm happy to work a normal school day like everyone else.

Similarly, a male teacher said:

> I've always been a keen gardener and I have started selling shrubs, cuttings, etc. in the extra spare time since school sporting activities ceased. I can earn more money, am more relaxed—why should I change back?

Statements such as these suggest that many teachers now are only going through the motions of the job of teaching PE. In a context where they feel there is minimal support for them, their subject, or for teachers in general, they are not prepared to invest energies or time over and above that which is required to fulfill their contractual obligations.

SUMMARY

The data provided lend support to the claim that in Britain today the PE teachers' lot is not a happy one. We hope, too, that they give something of a feel for the demoralization and frustration felt by PE teachers over their current conditions of work and the limited opportunities for advancement which these provide. PE teachers face problems and difficulties that "high status" subject teachers do not, and this makes the task of finding satisfaction in work, and of realizing ambitions and hopes, a special problem for them. As we have seen, female teachers can be doubly disadvantaged by the attitudes of men and the ideology of patriarchy, and by the hegemony[9] of the academic curriculum that puts teachers and the subject of PE in a position of marginality and low status. Whitehead and Hendry (1976, section 2, part B) made this point strongly, claiming that PE teachers, although specialists in their own right, find that their

---

[8] "Moonlighting," it seems, is a common feature of life for many teachers in the United States (and I thank Tom Templin for bringing this to my attention). Many studies have estimated that up to 50% of PE teachers in the United States engage in such activity. However, whether this is because of disatisfaction with teaching or the poor pay and conditions of work, I am unable to say; though clearly teachers in the United States have been subjected to the same sort of criticism and vilification by the radical right as their British counterparts (Wexler, 1982).

[9] There is little space here to provide detail of the various ways in which the term "hegemony" is used in critical social theory. For our purposes, we find the definition provided by Kirk, McKay, and George (1986) most helpful. For them, "hegemonic struggle" is a "dualistic process whereby groups competing for power attempt to attain cultural dominance first, by having their specific and historically contingent values and practices accepted as 'obvious' and 'given'; and second, by incorporating and/or marginalising oppositional or alternative values and practices." When a group's set of values and practices become hegemonic, then, the "agenda is set" with respect to what is culturally "reasonable", "realistic", or "normal".

prestige is markedly different than that of other subject teachers; they are marginalized because they are not considered central to the instrumental function of the school. But, we need to ask, why are the subject of PE and its teachers so positioned? Why is it assumed the PE curriculum does not have cognitive or academic components? Why is the practical accorded less status than the academic or the instrumental? It may well be the case that these statuses reach out to a broader social and economic context and a general value system in capitalist societies, which encourages theoretical knowledge and undervalues a practical, physical or "playful" orientation (Kirk, McKay, & George, 1986). Teachers in schools, like society at large, tend to celebrate and reward general knowledge rather than technical knowledge, the work of the mind rather than the work of the hand and the body. As critical theorists have long pointed out, one of the main rules of the school is to recognize and reward mental labor and denigrate manual labor (Giroux, 1983).

In so doing, teachers help to reproduce conventional social class and cultural hierarchies and categories. In this respect, women in PE are profoundly disadvantaged by a co-mingling of both class and gender ideologies. Together these ideologies interact to reproduce particular conceptions of teacher ability in schools, which ensure that men and women PE teachers are disadvantaged by their status, and women by their sex, in the contest for advancement or in their endeavor to improve the conditions of their work. A meritocratic ideology in this context begins to look like a facade that hides an often less than subtle system of sponsored mobility in which women in particular are badly disadvantaged and disbenefitted.

It is equally evident that these difficulties experienced by teachers have been exacerbated in a period of economic and educational contraction, a context in which there are fewer pastoral or academic posts to apply for (Bell, 1986) and fewer opportunities for the teachers to display their competencies to important gatekeepers of their professional careers. The consequence may well be an aging population of PE teachers working in jobs they no longer enjoy and from which they cannot easily escape, and knowing that the longer they remain in their posts the less likely they are to achieve their career ambitions. Others have made the point that in a "meritocratic system" of contest mobility, age can be an important credential in the competition for advancement. Among individuals in comparable position, those who are older may well be assumed to have taken longer to reach that attainment and so it may be inferred that they must have lost some competition along the way and possess less ability than their peers. This type of inference might be used to stigmatize individuals who are old for their jobs (Rosenbaum, 1986).

Finally, we would acknowledge and stress that we have hardly begun to touch the surface of the processes in which the identities of men and women teachers are constructed and constrained in the process of PE, in which their identities and opportunities are structured by the conditions of their work and the ideologies that prevail within them. Indeed, our data are not sufficiently qualitative or detailed to allow us to fully explore how, in particular circumstances, individual teachers experience or attempt to challenge, improve, or change their conditions of work (Templin, 1988; Sykes, 1988). In the quest to understand these processes and the issues that they generate, much work lies ahead.

REFERENCES

Apple, M. (1986). *Teachers and Texts.* New York and London: Routledge and Kegan Paul.
Arnot, M. (1984). A Feminist Perspective on the Relationship Between Family Life and School Life. *Journal of Education, Vol. 166* issue 1, 5-24.
Ball, S. (1987). *The Micro-Politics of the School.* London and New York: Methuen.
Ball, S. (in press). Comprehensive Schooling, Effectiveness and Control: an analysis of educational discourse. In R. Slee, (ed.), *Education, Disruptive Pupils and Effective Schooling.* London: Macmillan.
Bates, I., Clark, J., Cohen, P., Finn, D., Moore, R., and Willis, P. (1984). *Schooling for the Dole?* London: Macmillan.
Bell, L. (1986). Managing to Survive in Secondary School Physical Education. In J. Evans (ed.) *Physical Education, Sport and Schooling* (95-117). Lewes: The Falmer Press.
Best, R., Jarvis, C. and Ribbins, R. (1980). *Perspectives on Pastoral Care.* London: Heineman.
Burgess, R. (1986, February). *Points and Posts: A Case Study of teacher careers in a Comprehensive School.* Paper presented to the British Educational Research Association Conference, Comprehensive Education in the 1980s, King's College, University of London.
Corbishley, P. & Evans, J. (1980). Teachers and Pastoral Care on Empirical Comment. In Best, R., Jarvis, C. and Ribbins, P. *Perspectives on Pastoral Care* (201-225). London: Heineman.
Davies, B. (1986). Halting Progress. Some comments on recent British educational policy and practice. *Journal of Education Policy, Vol. 4,* 340-366.
Deem, R. (1978). *Women and Schooling.* London: Routledge and Kegan Paul.
Department of Education and Science (1982). *The Secondary School Staffing Survey. Statistical Bulletin.* Elizabeth House: London.
Evans, J. (ed.) (1988). *Teachers, Teaching and Control in Physical Education.* Lewes: The Falmer Press.
Evans, J. & Davies, B. (1988). Sociology, Schooling and Physical Education. In J. Evans (ed.). *Physical Education, Sport and Schooling* (11-41). Lewes: The Falmer Press.
Evans, J. & Davies, B. (1988). Teachers, Teaching and Control in Physical Education. In J. Evans (ed.). *Teacher, Teaching and Control in Physical Education.* Lewes: The Falmer Press.
Evett, J. (1988, January). *Assessment and appraisal of primary teaching; the consequence for primary teachers' careers.* Paper presented at the conference, Assessment, Appraisal and Accountability; the Politics of Educational Control, Westhill College, Birmingham, England.
Greene, M. (1985). Teaching as Project: Choice Perspective, and the Public Space. In M. M. Carnes (ed.), *Proceedings of the Fourth Conference on Curriculum Theory in Physical Education* (1-13). (Available from A. E. Jewett. Division of Health, Physical Recreation and Dance, The University of Georgia, Athens, Georgia 30602).
Giroux, H. (1983). *Theory and Resistance in Education.* South Haddley, MA: Bergin and Garvey.
Hilsum, S. & Start, K. R. (1974). *Promotion and Careers in Teaching.* Windsor: National Foundation for Educational Research.
Kirk, D., McKay, J. & George, L. F. (1986). All Work and No Play? Hegemony In The Physical Education Curriculum. *Proceedings of the VIII Commonwealth and International Conference on Sport, Physical Education, Dance, Recreation and Health,* 170-178.
Lawn, M. & Grace, G. (eds) (1987). *Teachers: The Culture and Politics of Work.* Lewes: The Falmer Press.
Ozga, J. (1988). *Schoolwork. Approaches to the Labour Process of Teaching.* Milton Keynes: The Open University Press.
Rosenbaum, J. E. (1986). Institutional Career Structures and the Social Construction of Ability. In J. G. Richardson (ed.) *Handbook of Theory and Research for the Sociology of Education.* New York, London: Greenwood Press.
Scraton, S. (1985, September). *Losing Ground: The Implications for girls of mixed physical education.* Paper presented at the British Educational Research Association annual conference. Sheffield.
Sparkes, A. (in press). Strands of Commitment Within the Process of Teacher Initiated Innovation. *Educational Review.*
Sykes, P. (in press). Growing Old Gracefully? Age, Identity and Physical Education. In J. Evans (ed.), *Teachers, Teaching and Control in Physical Education.* Lewes: The Falmer Press.

Templin, T. J. (1988). Settling Down: An Examination of Two Women Physical Education Teachers. In J. Evans (ed.), *Teachers, Teaching and Control in Physical Education*. Lewes: The Falmer Press.

Whitehead, N. W. & Hendry, L. (1976). *Teaching Physical Education in England*. London: Lepus Books.

Wexler, P. (1988). *Social Analysis and Education*. London: Routledge and Kegan Paul.

Williams, T. (1988). *The Career Opportunities of PE teacher*. Unpublished master's thesis. Faculty of education studies, University of Southampton, Southampton, England.

13

The Social World
of High School
Athletic Coaches:
Multiple Role
Demands and Their
Consequences

GEORGE H. SAGE
University of Northern Colorado

Interscholastic sports began in the latter part of the 19th Century. Early high school teams were organized and coached by the students themselves, but this pattern of organization began to change in the first two decades of the 20th Century. Gradually, high school sports came under the jurisdiction of high school authorities (school boards and principals), and coaching of the teams was turned over to physical education teachers (Massengale, 1979; Mills, 1979; Mirel, 1982; Spring, 1974). However, as the number of sports teams sponsored by high schools increased, "classroom" teachers were increasingly recruited to coach. Currently, the typical high school organizational arrangement is one in which

251

coaches are employed to teach classes in their area of certification and are given additional pay for coaching school athletic teams.

American high school athletics is unlike any others in the world. There is a great deal of public interest in the teams, large crowds attend some of the contests, and community spirit and reputation often are linked to the teams' performances. The social climate of the school and even the social status of the student-athletes are affected by the athletic programs. Sociologist James Coleman (1961a) once observed:

> The amount of attention devoted to athletics [in American high schools] would be most striking to an innocent visitor. . . . As an impressionable stranger, this visitor might well suppose that more attention is paid to athletics by teen-agers, both as athletes and as spectators, than to scholastic matters. He might even conclude, with good reason, that the school was essentially organized around athletic contests and that scholastic matters were of lesser importance to all involved. (p. 34)

Because there is such great emphasis on athletics, high school teachers who coach athletic teams have far different career contingencies than teachers with different extracurricular assignments. They also must contend with a unique set of demands and pressures.

Over the past two decades most of the research about high school athletics has involved quantitative analyses of their effects on school climate (Coleman, 1961b), educational expectations of high school athletes, and educational achievement of the participants (Hanks, 1979; Hauser & Lueptow, 1978; Landers et al, 1978; Otto & Alwin, 1977; Rehberg & Cohen, 1975; Schafer & Armer, 1968; Spreitzer & Pugh, 1973). However, there is very little research—especially of a qualitative, field based nature—of teachers/coaches, the men and women who are the leaders of these sports teams. This is particularly curious, given that each year over 190,000 athletic teams involving over six million youths are sponsored by American high schools, and that most of these teams are coached by men and women who have the dual assignment of teacher and coach. In every high school in the country from one-third to one-half of the teaching force coach one or more sports teams (National Federation Handbook, 1987).

Teaching is a demanding occupation. Teachers instruct five or six classes each day, perform various duties around the building, serve on committees, and most have some extracurricular assignment. These professional responsibilities constitute a full-time, exhausting job (Sutton, 1984). Although athletic coaching is officially viewed as an extracurricular assignment, it differs uniquely from other extracurricular assignments. It requires intense daily work over several months of the school year. Also, teams perform in public, and coaches are judged by the performance of the teams, and sometimes the coach's job security depends upon the success of the team (Lackey, 1986). Yet, many coaches prefer the position of coach over that of teacher (Segrave, 1981).

The multiple role demands upon teachers/coaches, and their responses to them, have been the subject of some empirical inquiry in recent years in the form of research on the teacher/coach role conflict. However, most previous research on teachers/coaches has focused only on teachers of physical education who were also coaches (Bain, 1978; Bain & Wendt, 1983; Chu, 1981; Locke & Massengale, 1978), has concentrated exclusively on the conflict over the role expectations of teacher and coach, and has tended to use questionnaires and quantitative analyses. As valuable as such research is, it does not probe into the meanings and varieties of shared experiences of teachers/coaches.

I wanted to extend previous research, but I chose to use a different approach for studying teachers/coaches. I wanted to focus on the occupational contextual setting of teachers/coaches and attempt to understand how occupational attitudes, feelings, and meanings are socially constructed as they orchestrate the multiple demands of the jobs. The research reported here is part of a field study[1] of the occupational culture of high school teachers/coaches that was guided by the following general questions: what is it like being a high school teacher/coach? What are the main occupational contingencies for high school teachers/coaches? How do teachers/coaches think about themselves and their situations?

The study of work and occupations is intrinsically eclectic, drawing upon and integrating insights from various theoretical perspectives and value orientations. This study takes its direction from organizational and occupational theorists who stress the importance of attempting to understand occupational life from the worker's perspective (Katz, 1980; Smircich, 1983; Van Maanen, 1977; Van Maanen & Barley, 1984). Fine (1984) notes that organizational culture represents one "of the major recent approaches to the study of organizational life" (p. 239). According to this perspective, it is necessary to examine subjective experiences in order to understand the development of personal and professional identities; this is because self and professional roles and attitudes emerge in response to social interaction and interpretative processes within the framework of environmental variables constituting the work setting. Organizations, then, are viewed as settings not merely for instrumental actions but for expressive behavior as well (Fine, 1984).

---

[1] Several sport studies scholars have recently called for more field-based research; Harris (1981, 1983) and Park (1986) have emphasized hermeneutic perspectives, while Klein (1986) has encouraged greater attention to sport ethnography.

Insights from role theory also were employed.[2] In role theory, the social world is viewed as a network of variously interrelated positions within which individuals enact roles (Biddle, 1979; Hardy & Conway, 1978; Zurcher, 1983). Thus, there are role expectations with every position. The underlying principle behind different role expectations for each position is that a division of labor enables the goals of the organization to be accomplished. Recent years has seen an increased interest in the use of role theory for describing and explaining the stresses associated with membership in organizations (Stryker & Statham, 1985; Van Sell, Brief, & Schuler, 1981).

RESEARCH SETTING AND METHODS

The field study that provided the data base for this paper was conducted over a five-month period in 1985 during which I observed teachers/coaches in six high schools having student enrollments between 1,000 and 1,500. I did not attempt to select a representative sample of high schools, but chose these schools because they were mid-sized and similar in enrollment to the average high school. American high schools encompassing grades 10 through 12 have an average enrollment of 1,050 students (Plisko & Stern, 1985).

All the schools were located in communities with populations between 38,000 and 58,000. The schools were members of the same athletic conference, one that is considered to be among the best in the state. During the year of this study teams in this conference won the state football, basketball, and baseball championships within their classification.

There is a great deal of community interest in high school athletics in these communities. Coaches are expected to develop "competitive" teams. A comment from one high school booster typifies an attitude I often heard expressed: "A coach can't stay long if his teams are perennial losers." An athletic director corroborated this: "We begin to get a lot of community 'heat' if a team does poorly over several years."

Permission to collect data was obtained through the central administration of each school district, the school principal, the athletic director, and finally, the coaches. During a coaches meeting at three of the schools, the athletic director introduced me. I briefly explained that I was interested in studying the occupational world of high school coaches and enlisted their permission to observe and interview them. In the other three schools I contacted the coaches directly and enlisted their permission. I received permission to conduct the research at each of these levels.

---

[2] In this study, organizational culture and role theory perspectives are viewed as providing a way of looking at organizational life rather than providing specific testable propositions.

Coaches and other school personnel were assured that their conversations and responses to my questions would be confidential. Their actions in my presence and their virtual obliviousness to me indicated that I had gained their trust. After I had been in one school for about a week, one administrator said, "The coaches are acting as if you weren't even here."

I spent at least two weeks in each school.[3] Follow-up observations and interviews took up the remaining weeks. At each school I attended classes with teachers/coaches and observed them teaching and interacting with students, colleagues, and administrators; I also observed team practices and attended their athletic events. I observed coaches who taught physical education, math, social studies, industrial arts, English, business, foreign languages, and driver education. Originally, I had planned to include both male and female teachers/coaches in the study because I wanted to compare and contrast the social worlds of teachers/coaches of both sexes. Research from a variety of occupational settings suggests that organizational life and career contingencies are experienced differently by males and females in the same occupation (Bain, 1978; Berch, 1982; Reskin, 1984; Spitze & Waite, 1980). But there were so few female teachers/coaches at each school that I did not have a large enough sample of them to make sound comparative analyses; I decided to concentrate on male coaches.

Much of the data were drawn from naturally occurring observations and conversations with teachers/coaches, non-coaching teachers, and school administrators. Formal in-depth interviews of between one and two-and-one half hours also were conducted with 50 teachers/coaches. All interviews were done in the school; they were tape-recorded and later transcribed verbatim to written form.

Data described in this paper are qualitative and focus on teachers/coaches' feelings and attitudes about their profession and the occupational pressures and stresses they encounter. The focus is on an analysis of the shared concerns and subjective experiences these generate. Shared concerns are considered as social outlooks that have a bearing on current satisfactions and decisions about remaining in or moving from an organization or a career line. The emphasis is on describing teachers/coaches perspectives which, after Becker et al. (1961), may be considered "a coordinated set of ideas and actions a person uses in dealing with some problematic situation . . . patterns of thought and action which have grown up in response to a specific set of institutional processes" (p. 34).

---

[3] One decision many field researchers must make is whether to collect data at a single site or whether to use multi-site data collection. Each strategy has advantages and disadvantages, and the appropriate strategy for a given study depends primarily on the nature and purposes of the study.

MULTIPLE ROLE DEMANDS AND THE TEACHER/COACH

In American high schools, the positions of teacher and coach are clearly distinct socially. The teaching position carries with its specific role expectations, mainly the transmission of subject matter to students (see Figure 13-1 for a description of the role concepts used in this paper and their interrelationships).[4] But there are more diverse role demands. Teachers serve on committees, attend meetings, and carry out many other tasks. They are expected to devote a great deal of their time and energy to preparing for classes, developing methodological techniques for transmitting subject matter, evaluating and grading student progress, and remaining abreast of their subject field through various "professional commitments." There is typically little public evaluation of teachers or their students, and organizational evaluation tends to be sporadic and ambiguous.

The coaching position in high schools carries with it specific role prescriptions as well. The job is done after school each day. In addition, athletic contests are scheduled in the evenings and on weekends and, of course, the coach must be present for all of them. Typically, a coach will spend 30 to 40 hours per week just with coaching duties: planning and supervising practices, preparing for games, coaching during games, studying films, arranging for the team's transportation to and from contests, and so forth (Chu, 1981). The coach is expected to develop a team that will be successful (the most universal definition of which is "winning"). Public evaluation of coaches is common. That public opinion, often conveyed to school administrators, is typically based on the winning records.[5]

Given the role expectations for high school teachers/coaches one can immediately see the potential for role stress due to the demands of the two positions. Role stress encompasses several types of problems, but it is always located in the social structure of an organization and usually leads to role strain, that is, subjective feelings of frustration, tension, or anxiety for role actors (Goode, 1973). High levels of role strain are associated with low quality work, low job satisfaction, absenteeism, and job leaving (Hardy & Conway, 1978).

Teacher/Coach Role Overload

As I observed teachers/coaches in their everyday activities, it became apparent that role stress was pervasive, especially role overload and interrole conflict. The workday typically begins at 7:30 a.m., and ends

---

[4] The role theory literature is riddled with inconsistencies in the use of concepts. Concept usage in this paper draws heavily from Biddle (1979) and Hardy & Conway (1978).
[5] Stresses on coaches to produce winning teams will not be addressed in this paper.

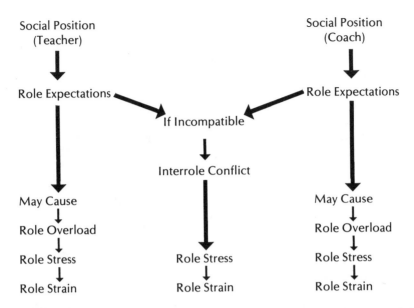

FIGURE 13-1. *Role concepts and interrelationships. A social position is a defined status in a social structure; it is an identity that designates a commonly recognized set of persons. Every position involves role expectations, which are position-specific norms that identify the attitudes, behaviors, and cognitions that are anticipated or required of a position occupant. Interrole conflict is pressure arising from incompatible role expectations associated with different positions. Role stress is a social structural condition in which role obligations are difficult, conflicting, or irritating. Role strain is the subjective state of distress experienced by a position occupant when exposed to role stress (Biddle, 1979; Hardy & Conway, 1978).*

nearly 12 hours later at 7:00 p.m. As typical high school teachers, they have five or six classes with an average of 25 students per class; thus, they will have at least 125 students each day. The time-locked schedule requires that one class follows another, with perhaps five minutes between classes. Daily teaching demands include preparing and grading examinations, planning student learning materials, meeting with students for make-up work or other academic problems, attending committee meetings, and performing numerous other activities, such as supervising the lunchroom or the parking lot. A substantial body of literature links teacher role stress to role overload (Cichon & Koff, 1980; Kyriacou & Sutcliffe, 1977; Lortie, 1975; Raphael, 1985). Sutton (1984) recently found role overload to be a significant predictor of role strain among schoolteachers.

In addition to these job demands for all teachers, teachers/coaches must, when classes end in the afternoon, conduct two to three hour practice sessions each weekday. They must attend all contests in which their team is involved, usually in the evenings or on weekends. If the game is out-of-town, an entire day may be consumed with the game and travel to and from the contest. But over and above these demands, teachers/ coaches also must schedule games for their team; arrange for buses; order, store and repair equipment; meet with coaching staffs; study game films of previous games and up-coming opponents; meet with booster groups; and counsel athletes. Finally, throughout the occupational community of coaching there is a feeling—supported by examples familiar to all coaches as well as by empirical findings (Lackey, 1986)—that if one does not produce winning teams this will irrevocably affect chances for further mobility in coaching. Therefore, the collective understanding is salient that a coach must win to maintain or improve his coaching position, and hard work is considered the surest way to develop winning teams. Coaches universally subscribe to the slogan "Workers Are Winners." It is prominently displayed in many of their offices.

The teachers/coaches I observed seemed to be in a daily struggle to keep up with the various job demands; they hurried from one task to another, often eating lunch while watching game films or holding coaching staff meetings. Their conversations were sprinkled with, "I don't have time for that," "I'm too busy," and "I'm running behind." One teacher/ coach's comments are representative:

> It's just like having two jobs instead of one to put in the same time period. . . . I always feel like I just don't have time to do what I really want to do in either [teaching or coaching].

Perceptions that teachers/coaches have a time-consuming job was shared by others around the school. During lunch one day a noncoaching teacher remarked, "I don't see how coaches have time to get everything done; I have a difficult time keeping up with my job and I don't even coach." Another time, referring to the dual responsibilities of teaching and coaching, a school principal declared, "I don't know how in the hell coaches have time to do both jobs."

There is a great deal of ambiguity about teachers/coaches' feelings about the role overload they experience. They are bothered that they are not able to devote more time and effort to teaching duties; on the other hand, they get enormous satisfaction from coaching. Perhaps what is most troubling is that they perceive that non-coaching teachers and administrators do not understand nor appreciate the role overload they experience. A comment by one football coach characterizes the attitudes of many coaches.

> I think [non-coaching] teachers have only a vague idea of the total

time we give to our jobs . . . but I don't think they have a . . . complete picture of what it takes to be a teacher/coach.

The combination of high time demands, a sense of incomplete institutional recognition, and minimal material rewards for both positions result in a kind of chronic consternation for teachers/coaches about their jobs.

Teacher/Coach Interrole Conflict

When a person occupies multiple positions, interrole conflict sometimes occurs because one position has one set of role expectations and the other position has another set of role expectations (Getzels & Guba, 1954; Kahn & Wolfe, 1964). Thus, interrole conflict results when the role expectations placed upon an individual are incompatible; the person finds it difficut to conform to both sets of expectations at the same time. My observations and interviews indicated that role expectations for the positions of teacher and coach result in a great deal of interrole conflict for the teacher/coach.

Many conversations between coaches and their colleagues concerned the pressures and stresses of teaching and coaching. In the interviews I would ask: "You have two major roles here at the school, teaching your classes during the day and coaching your (sport) team. To what extent do the demands, the expectations, the time commitment, the psychological commitment, and the responsibilities you have in carrying out the demands of these two positions cause a conflict between them?" The responses I got and some of the comments I overheard in informal discussions illustrate the meanings and variety of interrole conflict experienced by teachers/coaches.

The crush of time to meet the demands of the two positions was particularly troubling to coaches because they had to disproportionately allocate time to one position at the expense of the other; there was consistent agreement that priority was given to coaching. One coach described the conflict he routinely encountered:

The biggest conflict that I have . . . is the time . . . if I'm honest with myself, it's the classroom that gets shortchanged more than the coaching and that is I may not come prepared on a certain day, as prepared as I would if I didn't have the coaching responsibilities.

Another coach complained:

There just aren't enough hours in a day to do everything that you want. I know I want to be as innovative and creative as I can as a teacher but my role . . . as a coach really prohibits me from achieving what I want to in the classroom. . . . My role as teacher definitely does suffer because of my dual role as a coach.

Two others were more direct in their description:

> During the season your time is so limited that there is no question
> . . . that your classroom work suffers to an extent, not intentionally
> in most cases, but you just plain don't have the time to spend that you
> otherwise spend.

> You can get so wrapped up in your coaching that you don't do any
> teaching . . . you may be so wrapped up in preparing for this next
> team that you give the kids the shaft in your class.

Most of the coaches did not candidly articulate their reasons for giving priority to coaching, but there is little doubt that job security for teachers/coaches is far more contingent upon the wins and losses of their teams than their performance in the classroom. One coach was very open about his reasons, and he probably spoke for many others.

> Anytime a coach is teaching a full load he has to make decisions
> which [job he's] going to do well . . . I know why they hired me,
> [the school board] probably won't say [this] but . . . you know why
> you've been hired . . . if you do a halfway good teaching [job]
> they're not going to fire you and if you don't do a good job coaching
> they probably are.

Lackey (1986) has recently provided empirical support for this coach's definition of the situation. In a study of high school coaches, Lackey reported that "failure to win . . . was the foremost reason . . . for dismissal" from their coaching positions (p. 32). Although there are variations in the expectation that coaches of various teams develop a winner, general public attitudes imply that in order to have coached well one has to have produced a winning team.

Another reason may account for coaches giving precedence to their coaching position demands over those of teaching—commitment to the coaching position. One coach's remarks are characteristic:

> During my sports season, teaching is definitely secondary on my
> mind. . . . It becomes a burden, I guess . . . I know it doesn't
> make sense. [I'm] hired to teach and to coach second, but during the
> season teaching is a burden to me; coaching is where I like to com-
> mit my energy.

Does interrole conflict affect coaches' teaching? The statements quoted above demonstrate that teaching duties are impacted by coaching responsibilities, and, despite rationalizations or denial, that coaching does not adversely affect teaching duties, it appeared evident from my observations that commitment to teaching does suffer, especially when a coach's sport is in-season.

Coaches are bothered by their inability to devote full time and effort to their teaching duties. Younger coaches seemed to be more uneasy about this than older coaches who seemed to have come to grips with the realities of the situation. However, there is an overall resignation that there is not enough time to give full commitment to both positions, and the demands of coaching are more urgent for the allocation of work effort.

Coach/Family Interrole Conflict

Previous research on role conflict of the teacher/coach has focused only on the job-related aspects of the teacher/coach's life. It has not gone beyond the study of those two positions. But it was evident to me from coaches' remarks and behaviors that coaching role expectations conflicted with the role expectations of another social position most of them occupy, that of family man. The inability to give enough attention to one's family was a common theme. As one coach put it:

If it's not away from home doing things in your football program, it's time at home when your mind is somewhere else and you're not really relating to your wife or your children like you would if you were not . . . involved in coaching.

One basketball coach explained to me that he and his wife frequently quarreled about his commitment to coaching:

The family role becomes quite watered down and it's a difficult time as far as family time. . . . It seems like your priorities almost get twisted out of shape and out of control. . . . It does really knock into that quality time that you have with your family.

Sometimes the inability to resolve the conflicting role demands is a precipitating condition in divorce. One coach revealed:

When I first got into coaching/teaching, coaching was everything, I mean it was everything. . . . I didn't approach it right, I didn't take time for my family and I lost my wife; I was divorced, and to this day I look back on it and I should have done things differently, but I didn't realize it at the time.

No national data are available about the divorce rate among high school coaches, but there is little doubt that the demands of coaching often strain family relationships. Several coaches said that it takes a "special," understanding wife to keeping the conflict between coaching and family expectations from becoming acute.

Some of the coaches' comments concerning their children were the most poignant. A frequent complaint among them was that they were missing out on activities with their children. A biology teacher who has coached track and field and cross country for 20 years explained:

> Coaching has taken a tremendous toll on my family because there were times when I should have been there when I wasn't. One of my biggest disappointments was the year that my daughter, as a senior in high school, was one of the candidates for homecoming queen and they had the nice homecoming parade and I didn't even get to go see it; and there have been other situations in which there was a choice between doing some things where my kids were involved and where my team was involved, and because the team was what I was hired and was under contract to do that's where I went, and I cheated my family. . . . I found that conflict was a major problem for me, and to be very honest any success my children will have I credit my wife rather than myself because of the fact that I just wasn't there.

More coaches mentioned withdrawing from coaching over the role strain arising from their inattention to their children than from any other source. The following three coaches' comments are illustrative:

> As you get older and as your children get older [the conflict increases]. This is why a lot of coaches have quit . . . for me personally, I'm about at the end [as a coach] because my kids are becoming too important and they're only going to be with me another few years and then they're gone, and maybe you'd better spend more time coaching your own kids than everybody else's kids.

> That's one reason I'm going to be out of coaching real soon . . . over the years, now that we have a family, it's become real stressful because of the time.

> I have had activities that my daughters are in that I can't make because I have a coaching responsibility . . . and it really tears me apart. It's probably the one thing that will take me out of coaching.

Coakley (1986) observed, "Marriage partners may feel that coaching interferes with maintaining a satisfying husband-wife relationship, and children may feel ignored when one parent is always at school or with a sport team" (p. 309). Although no effort was made in this study to assess the attitudes and perceptions of the coaches' wives and children, comments and actions by the coaches suggested that the demands of coaching had an impact on all family members.

COPING AND RESOLUTION STRATEGIES

Substantial evidence suggests that role strain produced by role over-load and interrole conflict is related to various personal outcomes such as job-related tension and dissatisfaction, anxiety, and propensity to leave the organization, and that it is inversely related to job satisfaction (Fisher & Gitelson, 1983; Kahn et al., 1964; Miles, 1975; Rizzo et al., 1970; Tosi, 1971; Van Sell et al., 1981). The teachers/coaches in this study did not overtly exhibit the high states of tension, anxiety, and job dissatisfaction that have been reported in other organizational settings. Though the experiences of role overload and conflict were real and personally troubling to them, they seemed to have resolved their situation in various ways.

Differential Commitment

Because occupants of social positions can decide to what extent they will allocate their resources to the positions they occupy, one resolution strategy in interrole conflict is the establishment of one position as domi-nant, and the other as partial withdrawal (Bidwell, 1961; Burchard, 1954; Gross et al., 1966). This strategy takes the form of a reduced commitment, to one of the two conflicting positions. For the teacher/coach, this is usually the teaching position (Chu, 1981). While many of the coaches in this study indicated they enjoyed and valued teaching, few of them said or behaved in a way to indicate that they gave preference to the teaching position; indeed, most admitted they gave preference to the coaching position, while acknowledging that "officially" they were employed primarily as teachers.

For many teachers/coaches it is an easy decision to favor coaching, thus attenuating the conflict caused by the teaching role expectations because coaching was the original motivation for becoming a teacher/coach. This is typified by one coach's comment: "One of the main rea-sons [that I got] a teaching degree was so I could coach." Most high school coaches were once athletes themselves and, as one said, "I wanted to do something that would keep me involved with athletics." Coaching thus becomes a career choice.

Professional sports and major university athletics provide about the only opportunities for full-time coaching employment in the United States and, unfortunately, for those whose career goal is coaching, there are very few of these positions. Therefore, those who wish to earn a living while coaching must be employed somewhere in the educational system. Segrave (1981) reported that among prospective physical education teachers, 76% of the males identified coaching as the preferred position. When I asked coaches in the present study if they preferred teaching or coaching they overwhelmingly replied that they would choose coaching if they were given a choice between coaching or teaching, providing the income remained about the same.

A Coaching Identity

Social support as well as intrinsic and extrinsic rewards are important reasons for the preference of coaching over teaching. As one coach said, "No one around here knows or cares what I do in the classroom, but the community, administration, and students are behind my teams." In his theory of role-person merger, Turner (1978) enumerated several propositions concerning the social construction of the merger of person to role. One is that "the more intensely and consistently significant others identify a person on the basis of a certain role, the greater the tendency for the individual to merge that role with his person" (p. 14).

Similarly, to the extent the demands of a role are imposed on an individual in the course of social interaction, the individual is socially "constrained to be the person who corresponds to the assumptions that others are making about him" (p. 4). These propositions are confirmed for teachers/coaches. They are known around school and the community as "coach." Conversations with students in their classes, with colleagues around the school, and with persons outside the school often center around their coaching. Thus, teachers/coaches tend to define their personal selves inside the role of coach; a person-role-merger (Turner, 1978) is evidenced by their willingness to maintain their coaching role expectations in the school and community, and in the consistencies between their privately held attitudes and beliefs and those required by their coaching position

Withdrawing from Coaching

Resigning one of the positions that is causing role strain is another resolution strategy that is frequently employed in organizational settings as a means of coping (Beehr & Gupta, 1978; van de Vliert, 1981). About one-third of the teachers/coaches said they planned to leave coaching within a few years, and others had vague plans for leaving education altogether. High school coaching is often referred to as "a young person's occupation." In a study of over 150 high school football and basketball coaches, Sage (1974) reported an average age of 32 years. The average age of the coaches in the present study was 34 years. It is evident that coaches frequently exercise the option to do other things and thus resolve role stress by withdrawing from coaching. The typical high school has a number of ex-coaches on its faculty and in administrative positions.

SUMMARY AND IMPLICATIONS

In this chapter, I have attempted to develop an understanding of the occupational world of high school teachers/coaches as experienced by them. In describing and analyzing careers it is important to determine how they are subjectively perceived and experienced, so I focused on shared career concerns as they are subjectively apprehended in fulfilling the social positions of teacher/coach, and coach/family man. Data described in this paper concentrate on feelings, attitudes, and the meanings of role stress with which the high school teacher/coach must contend. The findings demonstrate quite dramatically the complexity and pervasiveness of role overload and interrole conflict in this occupational community and the role strain that results. They supplement and extend previous research on the teacher/coach.

The salience of the role stress identified here has serious implications for educational policy efforts. What can be done to reduce or eliminate teacher/coach role stress? One solution to teacher/coach role overload and conflict problems might be to employ different individuals for each position and eventually prepare individuals with the specific skills needed for each position. Preparation for teaching should perhaps not be assumed to serve as preparation for coaching, or vice versa. An accelerating trend in high school athletics over the past 10 years is the employment of what one writer calls "off-the-street" coaches, that is, coaches who do not hold teaching positions in the school (Sisley, 1985). For many years universities with large athletic programs have employed full-time coaches. One option that high schools may have to consider is the adoption of the collegiate model of employing full-time coaches.

Another solution that might be considered is to reduce the time demands on one or both of the positions. In almost every case where teachers/coaches express role overload and conflict problems, time is a major culprit. At colleges where coaches also hold a faculty appointment and teach classes, they usually receive a reduced teaching load as recognition for the time devoted to coaching. This pattern is not often found at high schools; it is not prevalent because it is about three times more expensive than paying coaches a stipend for coaching, which is the customary practice. However, if school districts want to seriously address the problem of role stress among coaches and want coaches who will remain in coaching for many years, various ways of reducing time demands must be explored.

Although these solutions sound rather simple and straightforward, there is presently little inclination for change in the teacher and coach positions in the high schools. This is because sports are an integral part of American schools, schools gets coaches cheaply, the supply of coaches outstrips demand, and teachers/coaches do not have an organized system to induce change. While there are coaches and teachers associations in every state, little is done in any of them to address teachers/coaches' interests. These associations could, however, become agents for social change on behalf of high school teachers/coaches.

Individual field studies, such as the one reported here, are not in themselves generalizing studies. But, as Giddens (1984) has argued, "they can easily become such if carried out in some numbers, so that judgments of their typicality can justifiably be made" (p. 328). This study provides considerable data that can be useful for such an agenda. Moreover, examinations of work cultures may inform the study of careers generally. For example, the role stress identified here bears considerable similarity to the role stress reported in studies of health careers (Hardy & Conway, 1978).

REFERENCES

Bain, L. L. (1978). Differences in values implicit in teaching and coaching behaviors. *Research Quarterly* 49, 5-11.
Bain, L. L. & Wendt, J. C. (1983). Undergraduate physical education majors' perception of the roles of teacher and coach. *Research Quarterly for Exercise and Sport, 54,* 112-118.
Becker, H. S., Geer, B., Hughes, E., and Strauss, A. L. (1961). *Boys in white: Student culture in medical school.* Chicago: University of Chicago Press.
Beehr, T. A. and Gupta, N. (1978). A note on the structure of employee withdrawal. *Organizational Behavior and Human Performance, 21,* 73-79.
Berch, B. (1982). *The endless day: The political economy of women and work.* New York: Harcourt Brace Jovanovich.
Biddle, B. J. (1979). *Role theory: Expectations, identities, and behaviors.* New York: Academic Press.
Bidwell, C. E. (1961). The young professional in the army: A study of occupational identity. *American Sociological Review, 26,* 360-372.
Burchard, W. W. (1954). Role conflict of military chaplains. *American Sociological Review 19,* 528-535.
Chu, D. (1981). Functional myths of education organizations: College as career training and the relationship of formal title to actual duties upon secondary school employment. In V. Crafts (Ed.), *Proceedings of the National Association for Physical Education in Higher Education, Vol. II.* Champaign, IL: Human Kinetics.
Cichon, D. J. and Koff, R. H. (1980). Stress and teaching. *National Association of Secondary School Principals Bulletin, 64,* 91-104.
Coakley, J. J. (1986). *Sport in society.* St. Louis: Mosby.
Coleman, J. S. (1961a) Athletics in high school. *Annals of the American Academy of Political Science, 338,* November, 33-43.
Coleman, J. S. (1961b). *The adolescent society.* New York: Free Press.
Fine, G. A. (1984). Negotiated orders and organizational cultures. In R. H. Turner and J. F. Short (Eds.), *Annual Review of Sociology, Vol. 10.* Palo Alto, CA: Annual Reviews.
Fisher, C. D., and Gitelson, R. (1983). A meta-analysis of the correlates of role conflict and ambiguity. *Journal of Applied Psychology, 68,* 320-333.
Getzels, J. W. and Guba, E. G. (1954). Role, role conflict, and effectiveness: An empirical study. *American Sociological Review, 19,* 164-175.
Giddens, A. (1984). *The constitution of society.* Berkeley, CA: University of California Press.
Goode, W. J. (1973). A theory of role strain. In W. J. Goode (Ed.), *Explorations in Social Theory.* London: Oxford University Press.
Gross, N., McEachern, A. and Mason, W. S. (1966). Role conflict and its resolution. In B. J. Biddle and E. J. Thomas (Eds.), *Role Theory: Concepts and Research.* New York: Wiley.
Hanks, M. (1979). Race, sexual status and athletics in the process of educational achievement. *Social Science Quarterly, 60,* 482-495.
Hardy, M. E. and Conway, M. E. (1978). *Role theory: Perspectives for health professionals.* New York: Appleton-Century-Crofts.
Harris, J. C. (1981). Hermeneutics, interpretive cultural research, and the study of sports. *Quest, 33,* 72-76.

Harris, J. C. (1983). Broadening horizons: Enterpretive cultural research, hermeneutics, and scholarly inquiry in physical education. *Quest, 35*, 82-96.

Hauser, W. J., and Lueptow, L. B. (1978). Participation in athletics and academic achievement: A replication and extension. *The Sociological Quarterly, 19*, 304-309.

Kahn, R. and Wolfe, D. (1964). Role conflict in organizations. In R. Kahn and E. Boulding (Eds.), *Power and Conflict in Organizations*. New York: Basic Books.

Kahn, R., Wolfe, D. M., Quinn, R. P., Snoek, J. D. and Rosenthal, R. A. (1964). *Organizational stress: Studies in role conflict and ambiguity*. New York: Wiley.

Katz, R. (1980). Time and work: Toward an integrative perspective. In B. M. Straw and L. L. Cummings (Eds.), *Research in Organizational Behavior*. Greenwich, CT: JAI Press.

Klein, A. M. (1986). Pumping irony: Crisis and contradiction in bodybuilding. *Sociology of Sport Journal, 3*, 112-133.

Kyriacou, C. and Sutcliffe, J. (1977). Teacher stress: A review. *Educational Review, 29*, 299-306.

Lackey, D. (1986, March). The high school coach: A pressure position. *Journal of Physical Education, Recreation, and Dance, 57*, 28-32.

Landers, D. M., Feltz, D. L., Obermeier, G. E., and Brouse, T. R. (1978). Socialization via interscholastic athletics: Its effects on educational attainment. *Research Quarterly, 49*, 475-483.

Locke, L. F. and Massengale, J. D. (1978). Role conflict in teacher/coaches. *Research Quarterly, 49*, 162-174.

Lortie, D. (1975). *Schoolteacher: A sociological study*. Chicago: University of Chicago Press.

Massengale, J. D. (1979, May). The Americanization of school sports: Historical and social consequences. *The Physical Educator, 36*, 59-69.

Miles, R. H. (1975). An empirical test of causal inference between role perceptions of conflict and ambiguity and various personal outcomes. *Journal of Applied Psychology, 60*, 334-339.

Mills, P. R. (1979). The place of interscholastic sport in American education, 1920-1939. In W. M. Ladd and A. Lumpkin (Eds.), *Sport in American Education: History and Perspective*. Washington, D.C.: AAHPERD.

Mirel, J. (1982, Winter). From student control to institutional control of high school athletics: Three Michigan cities, 1883-1905. *Journal of Social History, 16*, 83-100.

National Federation Handbook 1987-88. (1987). Kansas City, MO: National Federation of State High School Associations.

Otto, L. B., and Alwin, D. F. (1977). Athletics, aspirations and achievement. *Sociology of Education, 42*, 102-113.

Park, R. J. (1986). Hermeneutics, semiotics, and the 19th century quest for a corporeal self. *Quest, 38*, 33-49.

Plisko, V. W. and Stern, J. C. (Eds.). (1985). *The condition of education*. National Center for Educational Statistics, Washington, D. C.: U. S. Government Printing Office.

Raphael, R. (Ed.). (1985). *The teacher's voice: A sense of who we are*. Portsmouth, NY: Heinemann.

Rehberg, R. A., and Cohen, M. (1975, Number 1). Athletes and scholars: An analysis of the compositional characteristics and images of these two youth culture categories. *International Review of Sport Sociology, 10*, 91-106.

Reskin, B. (Ed.). (1984). *Sex segregation in the workplace: Trends, explanations, remedies*. Washington, D. C.: National Academy Press.

Rizzo, J. R., House, R. J., and Lirtzman, S. I. (1970). Role conflict and ambiguity in complex organizations. *Administrative Science Quarterly, 15*, 150-163.

Sage, G. H. (1974). Machiavellianism Among College and High School Coaches. In G. H. Sage (Ed.), *Sport and American Society*. Reading, MA: Addison-Wesley.

Schafer, W. E., and Armer, J. M. (1968). Athletes are not inferior students. *TransAction, 5*, 21-26, 61-62.

Segrave, J. O. (1981) Role Preferences Among Prospective Physical Education Teacher/Coaches: Its Relevance to Education. In V. Crafts (Ed.), *Proceedings of the National Association for Physical Education in Higher Education, Vol. II*. Champaign, IL: Human Kinetics.

Sisley, B. L. (1985, November/December). Off-the-street Coaches. *Journal of Physical Education, Recreation, and Dance 56*, 63-66.

Smircich, L. (1983). Concepts of culture and organizational analysis. *Administrative Science Quarterly, 28*, 339-358.

Spitze, G. E. and Waite, L. (1980). Labor force and work attitudes: Young women's early experiences. *Sociology of Work and Occupations., 7*, 3-32.

Spreitzer, E., and Pugh, M. (1973). Interscholastic athletics and educational expectations. *Sociology of Education, 46*, 171-182.

Spring, J. H. (1974). Mass culture and school sports. *History of Education Quarterly, 14*, 483-500.

Stryker, S. and Statham, A. (1985). Symbolic interaction and role theory. In C. Lindzey & E. Aronson (Eds.), *Handbook of Social Psychology, vol 1*. New York: Random.

Sutton, R. I. (1984). Job stress among primary and secondary schoolteachers. *Work and Occupations, 11*, 7-28.

Tosi, H. W. (1971). Organizational stress as a moderator of the relationship between influence and role response. *Academy of Management Journal, 14*, 7-20.

Turner, R. H. (1978). The role and the person. *American Journal of Sociology, 84,* 1-23.

Van Maanen, J. (1977). *Organizational careers: Some new perspectives.* New York: Wiley.

Van Maanen, J. and Barley, S. R. (1984). Occupational communities: culture and control in organizations. In B. M. Staw and L. L. Cummings (Eds.), *Research in Organizational Behavior, Volume 6.* Greenwich, CY: JAI Press.

van de Vliert, E. (1981). A three-step theory of role conflict resolution. *Journal of Social Psychology, 113,* 77-83.

Van Sell, M., Brief, A. P. and Schuler, R. S. (1981). Role conflict and role ambiguity: Integration of the literature and directions for future research. *Human Relations, 34,* 43-71.

Zurcher, L. A. (1983). *Social roles: Conformity, conflict, and creativity.* Beverly Hills, CA: Sage.

14

Educational Policy and Teaching

BERNARD OLIVER
St. Cloud State University

The 1980s has witnessed a spate of reports and interest in schooling in America. The much heralded report, *A Nation at Risk*, signaled the warning signs that America's educational system was in serious trouble. The high functional illiteracy rate of America's youth; the declining scores on the college board exams; the dismal performance of American students on achievement tests when compared with their foreign counterparts; and the concern over the competence and training of America's teachers has pushed education to the forefront of policy agendas for local, state, and federal legislatures.

Confronted with this grim view of schooling in America, policy makers have implemented a number of regulatory policies with the intent of defining the nature of excellence in teachers and schooling. This recent emphasis on educational policy is not new. State and federal attempts to regulate education through policy stem from the mid-1950s landmark court decision in the Brown vs. Topeka case. Given the nature of the policy process and the role of local, state and federal governments in education, it is common to ask, what are educational policies? Who makes them?

Consequently, the purpose of this chapter is to assess the role of educational policy and its impact on schooling and teaching physical education. The discussion is organized around the following: first, definitions and models of educational policy will be presented; next, a brief historical background on early federal policy; thirdly, a discussion of educational policy and teaching; and finally, implications for teachers and teaching.

DEFINITIONS OF POLICY

The term "policy," "policy analysis," etc., is an elusive term that raises more questions than it answers. A quick perusal of educational literature and jargon will reveal that "policy," "policy analysis," "educational policy," "federal policy," etc., are used in many ways. This variegated use of policy poses serious problems for educators. That is, it is the definition of policy that determines the type of questions asked, determines which data are collected and utilized and determines what course of action is taken. Examples of this are easily seen in federal policies and schooling.

Harman (1984), in response to definitional difficulty, defined policy as "the implicit or explicit specification of courses of purposive action being followed or to be followed in dealing with a recognized problem or matter of concern, and directed toward the accomplishments of some intended or desired set of goals" (p. 14-15). Harman further concludes that policy:

- is a stance developed in response to a problem
- is directed toward a particular objective
- refers to courses of action rather than desired decisions
- may be negative or positive
- may be written and unwritten
- may be substantive or procedural

Guba (1984) identified eight different definitions of policy as follows:

1. Policy is an assertion of intents or goals.
2. Policy is the accumulated standing decisions of a governing body by which it regulates, controls, promotes, services, and otherwise influences matters within its sphere of authority.
3. Policy is a guide to discretionary action.
4. Policy is a strategy undertaken to solve or ameliorate a problem.
5. Policy is sanctioned behavior, formally through authoritative decisions, or informally through expectations and acceptance established over time.
6. Policy is a norm of conduct characterized by consistency and regularity in some substantive action area.
7. Policy in the output of the policy-making system: the cumulative effect of the actions, decisions, and behaviors of millions of people who work in bureaucracies. It occurs and is made at every point in the policy cycle from agenda setting to policy impact.

8. Policy is the effect of the policy-making and policy-implementing system as it is experienced by the client.

From Guba's and Harman's points of view, one can readily see that policy can take many forms, fulfill a variety of functions, and have diverse effects. Regardless of the definition employed, educational policy can be grouped into a number of categories. In a comprehensive treatise of policy, Guba (1984) suggests three policy categories: (a) policy-in-intention or statements about policy, (b) policy-in-implementation or activities described in the implementation process, and (c) policy-in-experience, the actual experiences of the client (see Table 14-1).

Table 14-1 also illustrates how policy is determined, what the policies look like, and how far the policy making resides from the action point.

In a more general sense, policy can also be categorized by content. Mitchell (1984) suggests that educational policy usually falls under one of the following categories: equity research topics; school governance; teaching and learning; and the economics of education. Within Mitchell's framework, policies are further divided into sub-topics that are identified by the nature of the policy process associated with it and the content of policies.

It is clear from this brief discussion that defining educational policy is tricky business.

The establishment of policies pertaining to the teaching profession can be visualized in a variety of ways. However, for this discussion, the process of establishing policy related to teachers typically goes through four stages: problem identification, policy formulation, implementation, and termination or change (Harman, 1984). For example, in the teaching profession, the quality of teachers is the identifiable problem, which is followed by the trends we see in the reform movement that attempt to address the problem of teacher quality. Thus, various mandates are instituted that are geared toward changing the preparation of teachers. The last stage of the policy process would focus on evaluating the impact of the various strategies to determine if, in fact, we have improved teacher quality.

Brewer and deLeon (1983) offer a more detailed conception of the policy process in the model they posit (see table 14-2). It is clear, albeit simplified, that the two models of policy process presented here provide a useful classification for studying policy making and schooling.

Policy Makers

Who makes policy about teachers/teaching? The quality of teachers entering our schools is often controlled by state-level policy formation. In an informative study, Marshall, Mitchell, and Wirt (1986) studied this

TABLE 14-1. *Policy Types, Determiners and Appearances for Eight Definitions of Policy*

Policy Types	Policy Determiners	Definition of Policy	Proximity to Point of Action	Policy Looks Like
Policy-in-intention	CJCC: State legislature SPED: U.S. Congress HEAC: Commission on institutions of higher education of a regional accrediting association	1. Goals or intents	Distant	Ends
	CJCC: State criminal justice division and local supervisors SPED: State education agency and local supervisors HEAC: Regional association administrators	2. Standing decisions	Intermediate	Rules
		3. Guide to discretionary action	Intermediate	Guidelines

			Intermediate	Sets of tactics
		4. Problem-solving strategy		
Policy-in-action	CJCC:	Street-level bureaucrats and local supervisors		
	SPED:	Street-level bureaucrats		
	HEAC:	Street-level bureaucrats and regional association administrators		
		5. Sanctioned behavior	Close	Expectations
		6. Norms of conduct	Close	Norms
	CJCC, SPED, HEAC: All of the above	7. Output of the policy making system	NA	Effects
Policy-in-experience	CJCC, SPED, HEAC: Clients	8. Constructions based on experience	Inside	Encounters

Note. From "The Effects of Definitions of Policy on the Nature and Outcomes of Policy Analysis" by E. Guba, 1984 Educational Leadership, 42, p. 65. Copyright 1984 by ASCD. Reprinted by permission.

TABLE 14-2. *Educational Policy Research Topics*

	PROCESS ANALYSIS	CONTENT RESEARCH
EQUITY RESEARCH TOPICS:		
1. Race (Segregate/Desegregate)	How decisions to desegregate are made	What effects racial isolation has on children
2. Wealth (Aid/Finance)	Resource generation/allocation	Categorical program effects
3. Location (Rural/Urban/Suburban)	Rural/urban tension management	Effects of program differentiation
4. Language/Ethnicity (Bi-lingual/ Multicultural policy)	Mobilization and response to interest groups	How soon should English language be taught
5. Handicap (Special Education)	Political origin of court cases P.L. 94-142, etc.	Impacts of mainstreaming, IEPs, test bias, etc.
6. Gender	Politics of EBOC, Title IX, ERA, and affirmative action	Impact of sex discrimination on job opportunities and organization processes
SCHOOL GOVERNANCE TOPICS:		
1. Authority to act (fed, state, intermed, district, site	Distribution of powers and responsibilities	Effects of power or level on educational process/outcome
2. Representation/participation	Who gets access to decisions and how are they made	What difference does it make for educational processes or outcomes
3. Centralization/decentralization	Community control, vouchers, advisory committees	Implementation of innovations, mandate compliance
4. Collective bargaining	Teacher power, citizen input, impasse resolution	Organizational and teacher work role effects

	PROCESS ANALYSIS	CONTENT RESEARCH
GOVERNANCE		
5. Innovation and reform	Resource control, planning, adoption, implementation	Effect of planned variations in program
6. Public/private (parochial/religious)	Politics of aid and accreditation	Quality of private vs. public education
TEACHING AND LEARNING		
1. Curriculum	Politics of curriculum decisions	Program effects on various students
2. Testing	Adoption, publication, mandates	Construction, bias; interpretation
3. Personnel training and certification	Who trains, what criteria for certification	What effect does training or certification have on performance
4. Instructional processes	Who decides what processes to us	What difference does it make
5. Teacher work roles	Definitions, Incentives	Organization and learning effects
6. School effectiveness	Improvement strategies and incentives	Factors: Learning time, leadership, climate
ECONOMICS OF EDUCATION		
1. Manpower forecasting	Responsibility for statistics	Job opportunity and training needs
2. Human capital	Who gets access to advanced training	What are the marginal returns
3. Education production functions	What are the values or goals to be produced	What factors are responsible for results

Note. From "Educational Policy Analysis: The State of the Art" by D.E. Mitchell, 1984, *Educational Administration Quarterly, 20*, p. 145. Copyright 1984 by the University Council for Educational Administration. Printed with permission.

FIGURE 14-1. *Stages in the policy process*

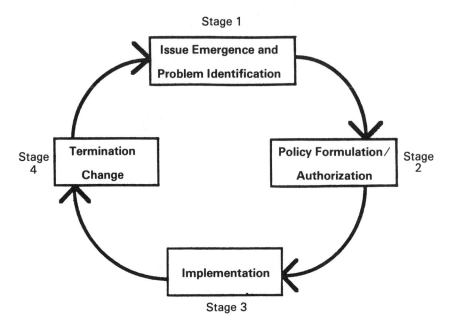

Stage 1

Issue Emergence and
Problem Identification

Stage 4 — Termination / Change

Policy Formulation / Authorization — Stage 2

Implementation

Stage 3

Note. From "Conceptual and Theoretical Issues" (p. 17) by G. Harman in *Educational Policy: An International Survey* edited by J. R. Hough, New York: St. Martin's Press. Copyright 1984, St. Martin's Press. Adapted by permission.

relative power and influence of policy groups in state education. Their study of educational policy making in six states revealed that the top five influential groups in educational policy making were: individual members of the legislature, the legislature as a whole, the chief state school officer, educational interest groups, and teacher organizations (see Table 14-3 for state comparisons). Thus, there appears to be a demonstrable relationship between policy on teachers and teaching and the actors involved in the policy process. What we can infer from the Marshall et al. (1986) study is that teachers and their constituents appear to have a say in the formation of those policies that are intended to enhance teacher quality.

Federal Involvement in Educational Policy making

For many policy researchers, Brown vs. Board of Education signaled the rise of federal involvement in educational policy making. The decade that followed is often highlighted as the period of establishing a federal presence in education, particularly in regards to improving equality of educational opportunity (Guthrie, 1979; Turnbull, 1986). The Supreme

TABLE 14-3. *Phases and Characteristics of the Policy Process*

Phase	Characteristics/uses
Initiation	Creative thinking about a problem Definition of objectives Innovative option design Tentative and preliminary exploration of concepts, claims, and possibilities
Estimation	Thorough investigation of concepts and claims Scientific examination of impacts; e.g., of continuing to do nothing for each considered intervention option Normative examination of likely consequences Development of program outlines Establishment of expected performance criteria and indicators
Selection	Debate of possible options Compromises, bargains, and accommodations Reduction of uncertainty about options Integration of ideological and other nonrational elements of decision Decisions among options Assignment of executive responsibility
Implementation	Development of rules, regulations, and guidelines to carry out decision Modification of decision to reflect operational constraints, including incentives and resources Translation of decision into operational terms Setting up program goals and standards, including schedule of operations
Evaluation	Comparison of expected and actual performance discrepancies according to established criteria Assignment of responsibility for discovered discrepancies in performance
Termination	Determination of costs, consequences, and benefits for reductions or closures Amelioration as necessary and required Specification of new problems created during termination

Note. From *The Foundations of Policy Analysis* (p. 20) by Garry Brewer and Peter deLeon, 1983, Hammond, IL: Dorsey Press. Copyright 1983 by Dorsey Press. Reprinted with permission.

Court decision in the Brown case has clearly spawned more debate and strife than any other educational policy issue.

Implicit in this early federal involvement in educational policy is the subliminal message about teachers and teaching. The fact that the courts

TABLE 14-4. *Policy Influences by State*

Policy Group	Six-state rank	AZ	WV	States CA	WI	PA	IL
Individual members of legislature	1[b]	1	3[b]	2	4[c]	1	3
State legislature as whole	2[b]	2	5	1	6	4	2
Chief State School Officer	3	4	2[a]	7	1[a]	3	12[c]
All education interest groups combined	4	9	8	3[b]	5	6	4
Teachers' organizations	5	12	6	4	2[a]	7	1[a]
Governor and executive staff	6	13[c]	9	6	3[b]	2[a]	5
Legislative staff	7	7	11	5[b]	9[d]	5[a]	6
State Board of Education[e]	8	3[a]	4[a]	16		9	14[c]
Others	9	10	7	8	13	18	7
School Board Association	10	6	15[c]	11	7[b]	11	8
State Administrators' Association	11	15	12	9[b]	8	8[b]	13[d]
Courts	12	11	1[a]	10[b]	14	12	11
Federal policy mandates	13	8[b]	10[a]	13	11	10	9
Noneducation groups	14	5[a]	13	12	10	13	10
Lay groups	15	14	16	15	12	14	15
Education research organizations	16	16	14	17	15	15	17
Referenda	17	18	18	14[b]	17	17	16
Production of education materials	18	17[b]	17	18	16	16	18

[a] Ranked much higher than in other states.
[b] Ranked higher than in other states.
[c] Ranked much lower than in other states.
[d] Ranked lower than in other states.
[e] Wisconsin has no State Board of Election.

Note. From "The Context of State-Level Policy Formation," by C. Marshall, D. Mitchell, & F. Wirt, 1986, *Educational Evaluation and Policy Analysis, 8*, p. 347. Copyright 1986 by American Education Research Association. Reprinted with permission.

ruled that segregated classrooms were harmful to children implied that now teachers would have to be prepared to deal with diversity in their classrooms—both black and white teachers. This ruling also suggested that the curriculum of teacher-preparation programs must also be responsive to the issue of equity and equality of educational opportunity.

During the 1960s, governmental presence in the policy arena was to become more established with the Elementary and Secondary Education Act of 1965. A major thrust of this act was to redirect resources and services to underserved students. Again, with the emphasis on providing services and resources to the underserved, this act had strong implications for the preparation of teachers. The amendments to the education acts of the 1960s set the tone for educational policy-makers until the 1980s (Timar & Kirp, 1988; Turnbull, 1986).

The period of the 1970s saw the development and implementation of P.L. 94-142, Title I programs and the Bilingual Education Act. The ineffectiveness of local educational agencies to adequately manage these programs resulted in increased federal policy dealing with fiscal management, program design, sanctions, etc. (Turnbull, 1986).

The educational policies of the 1960s and 1970s had a tremendous impact on teachers and teaching. At the local level, teachers altered governmental procedures and policies to simplify their work and enhance services to those students in need. For many, these classroom practices went unchecked for years, thus reaffirming what educators profess about teacher control and autonomy in the classroom.

The 1980s witnessed a shift in educational policy-making from a focus on equity to the pursuit of excellence. The much heralded report, *A Nation at Risk*, called for changing standards, increased expectations for student and teacher performance, improved competence in school personnel, and strengthening the leadership and organization of America's schools. This change in focus in educational policy-making, that is, the change from equality/social justice to the excellence movement, brought a new emphasis on school personnel and school organization (Timar & Kirp, 1988).

The states have been instrumental in the reform of educational policy; however, other constituents have assumed an active role in the reform movement. The policy initiatives instituted by these policy groups usually fall into the following areas: teachers and teaching, school organizations and environment, curriculum and student achievement, school leadership, and funding (Oliver, 1988; Timar & Kirp, 1988). As you can see in Table 14-4, there are a number of policy initiatives pertaining to teachers that have been implemented in a number of states.

EDUCATIONAL POLICY AND TEACHING

Early Warning Signs

The emergency of teacher quality and competence as a policy issue is not new. For many educators, the recent focus on teaching policy confirmed some suspicions about the quality of some graduates entering the profession. Weaver (1978), Lyons (1979), and the national press highlighted the fact that standardized test scores of students entering teaching were substantially lower than their college counterparts entering other fields. The performance of teachers on tests of basic skills in California

TABLE 14-5. *Educational Reform*

Area	Proposed Changes
I. Teachers	• teacher compensation • career ladders • merit pay • competency testing • performance evaluation • alternative credentialing • special incentives to teach
II. Students	• academic preparation for colleges • basic skills • broaden curriculum • competency tests • graduation requirements • homework emphasis • increased graduation requirements • increased time • policies on athletics/extracurricular activities
III. School Organization	• extend school year/day • reduce teaching loads • role and training of administration • community and industry partnerships • alternative schools
IV. Funding	• expanded state financial support • scholarship programs • financial incentives for school personnel • increased taxes • incentive programs for educational quality
V. Teacher Education Higher Education	• recruitment/admission to teacher education programs • scholarships for teachers • content of programs • faculty involvement in public schools • redesign of teacher education programs • establish links with public schools • greater involvement of liberal arts • alternative credential programs • minority recruitment

Note. From "Educational Reform in Physical Education," by Bernard Oliver, 1988, *Journal of Physical Education, Recreation, and Dance, 59,* p. 69. Copyright 1988 by the American Alliance for Health, Physical Education, Recreation, and Dance. Reprinted by permission.

and Texas further indicated that the quality of the nation's teachers was suspect.

Coupled with the decline in the performance of teachers on standardized tests has been the erosion of the teaching profession. The expanding job opportunities for women and brighter teacher-education students have compounded the issue of teacher quality. In addition, the workplace of teachers has been singled out repeatedly as a factor contributing to the erosion of the teaching profession. Duke's (1984) treatise of teaching as an imperiled profession further identifies job ambiguities/insecurities, financial insecurity, and violence against teachers as factors leading to the decline of the teaching profession.

Teachers and students are not alone in this quest for school improvement. The blame for teacher incompetence and poor quality is often placed on colleges of education. Most recently, research efforts on subject matter knowledge and teacher expertise further points to the importance of teacher preparation in school improvement.

The critics of teacher-preparation programs have continually held such programs in low esteem on most college campuses. The amount of time spent in education courses, the lack of change in program content, and the length of time in training continues to haunt teacher-preparation programs across the country. (Kerr, 1983).

In response to this concern over the quality of teachers and teaching, there has been the implementation of a number of educational policies and regulations relating to teacher quality. In addition, there is continuing growth of educational policies directed at schools and colleges of education.

Policy Initiatives

Resulting from the erosion of the teaching profession has been the implementation of wide-spread policies to improve the quality of teachers and teaching. Policies to this end include: strengthening entry standards, proficiency testing, career ladders, increased salaries, performanced-based pay, inservice training, scholarships for brighter students, etc. (for a fuller discussion of these policies see Chandler et al. 1988; Olivier, 1988; Timar & Kirp, 1988).

On the other side of the coin, schools and colleges of education and professional organizations are initiating policies for improving the profession. Strategies affecting the preparation of teachers in schools and colleges of education include: recruitment and admission strategies; strategies to enhance mastery of subject matter content; strategies for collaborating with local school districts; comprehensive and extended field experiences; extending the length of time in training; requiring teacher preparation faculty to participate in the schools; revising standards for the approval and evaluation of preparation programs; and providing alternative routes for entering the teaching profession (Oliver, 1988). In these latter categories, National Council Accreditation of Teacher Education and other accrediting agencies have changed the focus in program evaluation from institutional to more candidate-centered assessment.

In sum, there has been widespread implementation of educational policies geared to the improvement of teachers and schooling. Although there has not been wholesale adoption of all the policies, the intent and implementation of most have been embraced by educators and policy makers. The logical question to ask is how does this tie to physical education programs and the teaching of physical education? In the final section, educational policy and reform and teaching physical education is examined.

PHYSICAL EDUCATION AND POLICY

In a recent symposium on educational policy and physical education, a number of physical educators bemoaned the fact that this profession has not been proactive in establishing educational policy nor being involved in the process. Taylor (1986) has suggested that reform in physical education has not surfaced in the discussions about educational excellence, nor have professional organizations engaged in the reform dialogue. Despite this professional apathy, federal and local policies have had an impact on programs of physical education and teachers of physical education.

Earlier, I alluded to some of the policies implemented during the 1960s and 1970s. During this era, a number of policies had a direct impact on physical education and school desegregation, P.L. 94-142, Title IX, and in California, Proposition 13.

Educational policy aimed at desegregation of schools had a profound impact on physical education programs. Teacher-student relationships and the curriculum program changed dramatically. For example, the programs offered at racially segregated schools became more comprehensive and diversified. With this change in focus brought the need for inservice education, multicultural curriculum, expanded after-school programs, etc. There are some, however, who would suggest that desegregating schools has had a negative impact on physical education, particularly athletics (ARAPCSD, 1980).

Perhaps the most significant educational policies to have an impact on physical education were the Title IX legislation and Public Law 94-142. Each of these policies had a profound impact upon teacher preparation, teaching, curriculum, and students. P.L. 94-142 established a number of projects at the state and local levels (for example, the Adaptive Physical

Education Consortium) that were geared to alter the traditional ways of preparing physical education teachers. For many preparation programs, this meant requiring prospective teachers to enroll in adaptive physical education or other special education classes, and spending time during field experiences working with handicapped individuals. Project I Can, developed by Janet Wessel and her colleagues, provided a much needed curriculum and instructional model for beginning and experienced teachers (Wessel, 1977).

Title IX has been the most heralded of educational policies relating to physical education. The increased resources, the increased curriculum opportunities, and the increased attention to instructional behavior has probably had more impact on teaching and the profession of teaching in physical education than any other enacted policy. A quick review of the massive personnel changes in physical education as a result of Title IX would quicky lead one to believe that staffing patterns in physical education have change dramatically. The impact of these personnel changes, coupled with the changes in the school curriculum, has tremendous implications for teacher/student socialization patterns in physical education.

The impact of these three policies, albeit 10 to 20 years ago, is still being debated and discussed. As more and more reform reports indicate, these are important issues in schooling and preparation programs, and hence they subsequently impact on the day-to-day realities of teaching.

POLICIES RELATED TO TEACHERS AND TEACHING

In the last five years we have witnessed the "second wave" of educational policy directed at teachers and teaching. These policies have typically centered on admission requirements; programs, or content, changes; alternative certification routes; competency tests (in three areas—basic skills, professional knowledge, and subject matter); teacher induction programs for beginning teachers; and continuing certification requirements (Darling-Hammond & Berry, 1988).

Policy practices related to admission practices were implemented as a result of the concern over the academic quality of teachers. These requirements ultimately served as screens for lowly qualified applicants and forced early career decisions regarding entering the teaching profession. Ironically, these early admission requirements have restricted the opportunities for students to pursue subject matter knowledge during a time when more and more emphasis is being placed on subject matter expertise.

The recent debates over the content of preparation programs, spurred by the Holmes and Carnegie reports, have had an additional influence on educational policy. State after state has mandated curriculum changes in liberal studies, pedagogical courses, and subject matter. Moreover, some states have mandated that prospective teachers have coursework in human sexuality, human relations, drug education, family studies, ethnic studies, mainstreaming, and the like. Despite the seemingly widespread implementation of various policies, colleges and schools of education have not drastically changed the credit-hour requirement for the baccalaureate degree, student teaching, methods courses or subject matter requirements. (Darling-Hammond & Berry, 1988). On the other hand, teacher-preparation programs have been encouraged to explore alternative preparation routes and to alter the structure of the credentialing process.

Perhaps the most significant policy affecting teachers and the teaching profession has centered on teacher testing. As of 1988, all but four states have instituted a teacher-testing program. It is this policy that is blamed for the decline in minority applicants in teacher-education programs. In addition, the competency movement has spurred considerable debate in physical education, particularly on the question of "What is the knowledge base of physical education?" Despite the widespread implementation of competency testing policies, few researchers in physical education have explored the performance of prospective physical education teachers on test measures relative to their college age counterparts.

One other area that has spawned policy growth is in the induction or beginning teacher arena. The impetus for this line of policy came from the demonstrable relationship between attrition rates and poor supervisory practices. (Darling-Hammond, 1986; McLaughlin, 1986). Although critics of these programs often point to pitfalls in instituting these programs, for me they represent an attempt to provide a reasonable support system for the neophyte teacher.

Outside the preparation of teachers, compensation for teaching has received considerable interest and concern. Many states have already implemented statewide teaching salaries, and some have gone so far as to tie compensation to a career development model of teaching (see, for example, the Rochester Plan, Donohue, 1988). Many states have instituted different types of performance-based compensation plans (such as mentor/master teachers, career ladders, merit pay, etc.). Obviously, these performance-based pay systems have been controversial in literature and have received various criticisms from educators, teacher organizations, and researchers (Oliver et al., 1988).

Although criticisms still abound, the implementation of policies improving the compensation of teachers is viewed as a significant step in professionalizing teaching. Moreover, teacher-compensation schemes have been viewed by educational policy-makers as one avenue to attract the more academically able students into the "imperiled profession."

DOES TEACHING POLICY IMPACT
THE TEACHERS IN THE GYM?

The teacher policy activities implemented in recent years have implications for physical education teachers. The vast array of state and local policies have not excluded physical education teachers.

Licensure changes and new standards for teacher-preparation programs reflect serious efforts to control the admission and retention of prospective physical educators (Oliver, 1988). Moreover, the recent interest in the knowledge base of teacher education, particularly subject matter knowledge vs. pedagogical knowledge, suggests to some educators that the world of teaching is different than has been traditionally conceptualized. In physical education it has not been proactive in the knowledge base question, except for "ivory tower" debates. This fragmentation will have little value in improving the quality of programs and instruction in physical education, nor will it have impact upon attracting more academically able teachers to the profession who are more interested in "physical education" than coaching.

Compensation, alternative licenses, and other policy initiatives have placed us at an important crossroads; The intentions of which are in good faith, but neglect to involve teachers. The curriculum, the goals of the school, student achievement and performance are subject to the teacher's disposal. As Lightfoot (1983) states:

> Teachers must not be seen as empty vessels or mouthpieces for curriculum developers, but be intimately involved in shaping, developing, and interpreting [policy]. They have a perspective on students [gymnasiums, and playing fields] that is more subjective, more complex, and more intimate than the distance stance of policy-makers and academic specialists. (p. 258)

Educational policies affect what teachers do in the classroom. The research conducted by Schwille et al. (1983) suggests this, despite the fact that many of the educational policies in place do not have the attributes of strong policy. However, I doubt if physical educators are at the dilemma stage when it comes to policy. We are not aiming for improvement from a distance, for we have not found the targets. Fenstermacher and Amarel (1983, p. 407) portray our dilemma clearly:

> Policy and rules and regulations that flow from it are [not] for the purpose to instruct teachers on what and how to teach. Policy is neither the instrument nor the content of education. It is a temporary resolution of completing potentials and demands to optimize the attainment of the ends we seek. The ends we seek for [physical education] are the education of teachers and their students; the

purpose of policy is to enable attainment of these ends in the most equitable and excellent way. Policy that is well formulated and thoughtfully implemented fosters the creation of schools that are good places for teachers and students.

For policy to have the intended impact on what physical educators and students do in the gymnasium, we have to become aware and knowledgeable of the new policy culture. Educational policy makers look to organizations for guidance in the formulation of policy. Perhaps the time is ripe for researchers and physical educators to examine the structure of the teaching occupation of physical education teachers and initiate and refine ways that will allow us to talk about the impact of policy on becoming a teacher in the gym.

REFERENCES

Bowers, G.R. (1988, Spring). Linking research, policy and practice: state perspective. *Theory Into Practice, 27,* 132-136.
Boyd, W.L. (1988). Policy analysis educational policy and management: Through a glass darkly? In N.J. Boyan, (Ed.), *Handbook of research on educational administration* (501-523). New York: Longman.
Boyd, W.L., & Kerchner, C.T. (Eds.). (1987). *The politics of excellence and choice in education.* New York: The Falmer Press.
Brewer, G., & deLeon, P. (1983). *The foundation of policy analysis.* Homewood, IL: The Dorsey Press.
Brickell, H.M. (1988, October). Ten policies for raising student achievement. *Educational Leadership, 42,* 54-62.
Burlingame, M. (1988). The politics of education and educational policy: The local level. In N.J. Boyan (Ed.), *Handbook of research on educational administration* (439-452). New York: Longman.
Burlingame, M. (1978). Impact of policy decisions on schools. In L. Shulman (Ed.), *Review of research in education: Vol. 5* (236-272). Itasca, IL: Peacock.
Chandler, T., Lane, S., Bibik, J., & Oliver, B. (1988). The career ladder and lattice. A new look at the teaching career. *Journal of Teaching in Physical Education 7*(2), 132-141.
Clune, M. (1983). Courts and teaching. In L. Shulman & G. Sykes (Eds.), *Handbook of teaching and policy* (449-483). New York: Longman.
Clune, W.H. (1987, Summer). Institutional choice as a theoretical framework for research on educational policy. *Educational Evaluation and Policy Analysis, 9,* 117-132.
Collins, J., & Lucove, J.J. (1982, January). Proposition 2½: Lessons from Massachusetts. *Educational Leadership, 39,* 246-249.
Cronin, J.M. (1983). State regulation of teacher preparation. In L. Shulman & G. Sykes (Eds.), *Handbook of teaching and policy* (171-191). New York: Longman.
Darling-Hammond, L., & Berry, B. (1988). *The evolution of teacher policy.* Santa Monica, CA: The Rand Corporation.
Darling-Hammond, L. (1986). A proposal for evaluation in the teaching profession. *Elementary School Journal, 86,* 86-94.
Doherty, V.W., & Fenwick, J.J. (1982, January). Can budget reduction be rational. *Educational Leadership, 39,* 252-257.
Donohue, T. (1988). Rochester raises will boost teaching quality. *Instructor, 97*(7):12.
Dror, Y. (1988). *Policy making under adversity.* New Brunswick, NJ: Transaction Books.
Duke, D. (1984). *Teaching: The imperiled profession.* Albany, NY: State University of New York Press.
Eisenhart, M.A., Cuthbert, A.M., Shrum, J.L., & Harding, J.R. (1988, Spring). Teacher beliefs about their work activities: Policy implications. *Theory Into Practice, 27,* 137-144.
Fenstermacher, G.D., & Amarel, M. (1983). The interests of the student, the state and humanity in education. In L. Shulman and G. Sykes (Eds.), *Handbook of Teaching and Policy* (392-407). New York: Longman.
Guba, E. (1984, October). The effect of definitions of policy on and outcomes of policy analysis. *Educational Leadership, 42,* 63-71.
Guthrie, J.W. (1979). Educational policy research and the pursuit efficiency, and liberty. In G.L. Immegart & W.L. Boyd (Eds.), *Problem-finding in educational administration.* Massachusetts: D.L. Heath and Company.

Guthrie, J.W. (1980). *School finance policies and practices.* Cambridge, Ballinger Publishing Co.

Hannaway, J. & Lockheed, M.E. (Eds.). (1986). *The contributions of the social sciences to educational policy and practice: 1965-1985.* Berkeley, CA: McCutchan Publishing Co.

Harman, G. (1984). Conceptual and Theoretical issues. In J.R. Hough (Ed.), *Educational Policy: An international survey* (13-27). New York: St. Martin Press.

Hetrick, B., & Van Horn, C.E. (1988, Spring). Educational research information: Meeting the needs of state policy makers. *Theory Into Practice, 27,* 106-110.

Hough, J.R. (1984). *Educational policy: An international survey.* London: Croon Helm Ltd.

Jung, R.K. (1988). The federal role in elementary and secondary education: Mapping a shifting terrain. In N.J. Boyan (Ed.), *Handbook of research on educational administration* (487-500). New York: Longman.

Kerr, D. (1983). Teaching competence and teacher education in the United States. In L. Shulman & G. Sykes (Eds.), *Handbook of Teaching Policy* (126-149). New York: Longman.

Kirp, D.L., & Jensen, D.N. (Eds.). (1986). School days, rule days: *The legalization and regulating of education.* Philadelphia: The Falmer Press.

Kirst, M. (1983). Teaching policy and federal categorized programs. In L. Shulman & G. Sykes (Eds.), *Handbook of teaching and policy* (426-448). New York: Longman.

Klein, S.S. (1987, Fall). The role of public policy in the education of girls and women. *Educational Evaluation and Policy Analysis, 9,* 219-230.

Klein, S.S. (1988, Spring). Using sex equity research to improve education policies. *Theory Into Practice, 27,* 152-160.

Lieberman, A., & McLaughlin, M.W. (1982). *Policy making in education: Eighty-first yearbook of the national society for the study of education.* Chicago: The National Society for the Study of Education.

Lightfoot, S.L. (1983). The lives of teachers. In L. Shulman & G. Sykes (Eds.), *Handbook of Teaching and Policy* (pp. 241-260). New York: Longman.

Luby, R., Tobin, I., & Lewandowski, D. (1980). Effects of federal legislation on physical education programs in three big cities. *Journal of Physical Education and Recreation, 51,* 34-42.

Lutz, F.W. (1988, Spring) Policy oriented research: What constitutes good proof. *Theory Into Practice, 27,* 126-131.

Lyons, G. (1979, September). Why teachers can't teach, *Texas Monthly,* 122-130.

Malen, B., Murphy, M.J., & Geary, S. (1988, Spring). The role of evaluation information in legislative decision making: A case study of a loose cannon on deck. *Theory Into Practice, 27,* 111-125.

McLaughlin, M.W. (1986). Why teachers won't teach. *Phi Delta Kappan, 67,* 420-426.

Marshall, C. (1988, Spring). Bridging the chasm between policy makers and educators. *Theory Into Practice, 27,* 98-105.

Marshall, C., Mitchell, D., & Wirt, F. (1986, Winter) The context of statelevel policy formation. *Educational Evaluation and Policy Analysis, 8,* 347-378.

McDonald, F.J. (1976). *Designing research for policy making.* Paper presented at annual meeting of the American Educational Research Association, San Francisco, CA:

McDonnell, L.M. (1988, Spring). Can education research speak to state policy. *Theory Into Practice, 27,* 91-97.

McDonnell, L.M., & Elmore, R.F. (1987, Summer). Getting the job done: Alternative policy instruments. *Educational Evaluation and Policy Analysis, 9,* 133-152.

Mitchell, D.E. (1984, Summer) Educational policy analysis: The state of the art. *Educational Administration Quarterly, 20,* 129-160.

Michell, D.D. (1981). *Shaping legislative decisions: Education policy and the social sciences.* Massachusetts: D.C. Heath and Company.

Mitchell, D.F. (1988). Educational politics and policy: The state level. In N.J. Boyan (Ed.), *Handbook of Research on educational administration* (453-467). New York: Longman.

Murphy, J. (1988, Spring). Equity as student opportunity to learn. *Theory Into Practice, 27,* 145-151.

Odden, A. (1987, Fall). Education reform and services to poor children: Can the two policies be compatible? *Educational Evaluation and Policy Analysis, 9,* 231-243.

Oliver, B. (1988, January). Educational reform and physical education. *JOPERD, 59,* 68-72.

Oliver, B., Bibick, J., Chandler, T., & Lane, S. (1988). Teacher development and job incentives: A psychological view. *Journal of Teaching in Physical Education, 7,* 121-131.

Oliver, B. (1988, Spring). Developing standard for teacher education programs: A state agency perspective. *Physical Educator, 45,* 58-62.

Odden, F., & Odden E. (1984, October). Education reform, school improvement, and state policy. *Educational Leadership, 42,* 13-19.

Rabe, B.G., & Peterson, P.E. (1988). The evolution of a new cooperative federalism. In N.J. Boyan (Ed.), *Handbook of research on educational administration* (467-486). New York: Longman.

Rubin, L. (1984, October). Formulating education policy in the aftermath of the reports. *Educational Leadership, 42,* 7-12.

Savage, D. (1982, January). The unanticipated impact of Proposition 13. *Educational Leadership, 39,* 250-251.

Schwille, J., Porter, A., Belli, G., Floden, R., Freeman, D., Knappen, L., Kuhs, T., & Schmidt, W. (1983). Teachers as policy brokers in the content of elementary school mathematics. In L. Shulman & G. Sykes (Eds.), *Handbook of teaching and policy* (370-391). New York: Longman.

Sebring, P.A. (1987, Fall). Consequences of differential amounts of high school coursework: Will the new graduation requirements help. *Educational Evaluation and Policy Analysis, 9,* 258-273.

Sykes, G. (1983). Public policy and the problem of teacher quality: The need for screens and magnets. In L. Shulman & G. Sykes, *Handbook of teaching and policy* (97-125). New York: Longman.

Taylor, J. (1986). Surviving the challenge. *JOPERD, 57,* 69-72.

Timar, T.B., & Kirp, D.L. (1988). *Managing educational excellence.* New York: Falmer Press.

Turnbull, B.J. (1986). Federal and state policy. In J. Hannaway & M. Lockheed (Eds.), *The contributions of the social sciences to educational policy and practice 1965-1985* (99-114). Berkeley, CA: McCutchan Publishing Co.

Weaver, T.W. (1978). Educators in supply and demand: Effects on quality. *School Review, 86,* 522-593.

Weaver, T.W. (1979) In search of quality: The need for talent in teaching. *Phi Delta Kappan, 61,* 29-32.

Wessell, J.A. (1977). *Planning individualized education programs in special education.* Northbrook, IL: Hubbard Co.

Zajano, N.C., & Mitchell, B. (1988, Spring). Schoolhouse blues: Tensions among research policy and practice. *Theory Into Practice, 27,* 161-168.

15

Implicit Values in Physical Education

LINDA L. BAIN
California State University at Northridge

Most of us are familiar with the phrase, "Actions speak louder than words." In school settings, the planned curriculum is conveyed through our words—statements of philosophy, program objectives, and curriculum guides. The operational curriculum or the program as implemented is the result of our actions. It is this operational curriculum which will have an impact on our students. What we do in our day-to-day activities will be based in part on the values and beliefs explicitly stated in the planned curriculum, but our actions also will communicate other unstated or implicit values to students. The implicit values communicated by factors such as how the class is organized and how the teacher interacts with students have been called the hidden curriculum (Bain 1975, 1985a).

The term "hidden curriculum" has been used extensively in educational literature since the early 1970s to refer to "what is taught to students by the institutional regularities, by the routines and rituals of teacher/student lives" (Weis, 1982, p. 3). Dodds (1983, 1985) suggests that implicit values may be covert (planned but unstated), or hidden (unplanned and unrecognized). In this chapter, hidden curriculum will refer to all implicit values taught and learned through the process of schooling. One of the questions which will be examined is the extent to which these values, though unstated, are recognized or intended by teachers.

THEORETICAL PERSPECTIVES

Several theoretical approaches to the study of the hidden curriculum have been identified (Bain, 1985a). Some of the work has been atheoretical in that it describes events in classrooms without attempting to relate those descriptions to a theory about schooling and society. Other research related to the hidden curriculum has been based on one of four theoretical perspectives: (1) functionalism, (2) correspondence theory, (3) symbolic interactionism, and (4) critical theory.

The functionalist perspective views society as a social system composed of interrelated parts, each contributing to the maintenance of the other parts. The norms and values taught by the routines and rituals of schooling are presumed to contribute to the effective functioning of the larger society. Study of the hidden curriculum focuses on how the implicit values learned in school prepare students for participation in adult society and help to maintain that society (Dreeben, 1968).

Correspondence theory is based on a view of society characterized by conflict of interests, and held together by power and coercion. The scholar analyzes how differential distribution of power and authority are maintained by social institutions such as schools. The hidden curriculum is seen as a mechanism which contributes to the maintenance of existing social structures characterized by domination, exploitation and inequality (Bowles & Gintis, 1976).

Both the functionalist and correspondence perspectives view the school as contributing to the maintenance of society; but, they differ in their beliefs about the fundamental nature of society and whether it is just or unjust. Functionalism and correspondence theory have been criticized for their determinism which portrays students as passive recipients of the values communicated by schools. The two other theories, symbolic interactionism and critical theory, view knowledge and values not as passively received but as socially constructed.

The symbolic interactionist perspective focuses on the interactions and negotiations through which people reciprocally define expectations or rules about appropriate behavior. It also shifts attention from an analytic examination of behavior to a nonreductive understanding of human interaction; that is, the research focuses on the whole event rather than selecting specified variables for study. The emphasis in hidden curriculum research is on describing and understanding the experience of schooling from the perspective of teachers and students.

Critical theorists also are interested in how meanings are negotiated, but wish to examine schooling not in isolation but in relation to other aspects of society. They propose that meanings and values are not merely accepted but are negotiated in social settings that are characterized by both constraints and opportunities for action. Apple (1982, p. 14) suggests that "student reinterpretation, at best only partial acceptance, and often outright rejection of the planned and unplanned meanings of schools are more likely." For this reason, schools contain the potential for both reproduction and transformation of society. The goal of critical science is to understand the patterns of belief and social conditions that restrict human action and to empower those being researched, to provide them with the insight necessary to demystify and critique their own social circumstances and to choose actions to improve their lives (Lather, 1985). The critical theorist studies the hidden curriculum to analyze its relationship to the larger society and to identify opportunities to transform society.

Much of the research on the hidden curriculum in physical education has not specified the theoretical perspective underlying the work. Most of the research seems to be based on the symbolic interactionist perspective. The emphasis is on describing patterns of behavior and examining the meanings that participants attach to those experiences. Some of the studies, especially those employing quantitative research methods, appear to be derived from the functionalist perspective. A few studies have adopted a critical theory stance and have attempted to examine how physical education programs reproduce or transform society.

RESEARCH METHODS

Research on the hidden curriculum attempts to describe implicit values transmitted through the process of schooling. Regardless of theoretical perspective, the research begins with observation of "regularities" in the process of schooling. What are the day-to-day actions which characterize life in the school or, in this case, the physical education program? Some early discussions of the hidden curriculum have been criticized for treating the school as a "black box" and not providing data to support the analyses. However, recent work has been based on observations in schools.

Observations focus on three elements of the program: teacher-student interactions, organizational aspects of the instructional setting, and structural properties of class content. Teacher-student interactions are examined for patterns that might reveal implicit values. For example, does that teacher systematically treat specific categories of students or certain types of behavior in ways that send messages to students? How do students interact with each other and how does the teacher respond to those interactions? Organizational aspects such as grouping decisions, allocation of resources and grading practices also are examined. In addition, program content is examined to identify characteristics that may reveal unstated values. Although content is presumably selected because of its relationship to explicit goals, selections also may be influenced by implicit values.

Observation of regularities in the program must be followed by an interpretation of the values implied by those patterns of behavior. The interpretation can be done from either an outsider's or an insider's perspective. The functionalist and correspondence perspectives have relied predominantly on the researcher as an outside observer who describes and interprets classroom events. The symbolic and critical theorists believe that it is not the events that are important but the meanings that teachers and students attach to those events. For this reason, these researchers have examined insiders' views of the hidden curriculum and have discussed results with participants to provide for collaborative validation of the interpretation.

Most of the research on the hidden curriculum has employed naturalistic observation techniques which have the advantage of providing extensive time in the setting to gain a thorough understanding of routines and rituals. Qualitative research methods also permit the researcher to explore the participants' interpretations of classroom events. This is particularly important when the research is based on a symbolic or critical theory perspective. Some research using systematic observation or questionnaires is relevant to a discussion of implicit values even though it may not have been identified as hidden curriculum research. The research which will be reviewed in this chapter attempts to answer three questions: (1) What implicit values are communicated in the physical education setting? (2) Through what practices and procedures are these values transmitted? (3) What are the consequences of the this value transmission for the students and the teacher? Possible origins or explanations of the implicit values also will be discussed.

LIFE IN THE GYM

Research on the hidden curriculum in physical education attempts to describe life in the gym and on the playing fields. The research is conducted in naturalistic settings using observation and interview techniques. The focus of the research in on the implicit values communicated by the routines and rituals in the program.

This type of research is not easy to review. Because each research project examines a unique case, it is difficult to make generalizations. Because many projects employ qualitative methods over a period of several months and describe multifaceted, complex situations, the results are difficult to summarize in tables or lists of results. The original reports of qualitative studies include numerous quotations and examples which support their results and make them "come alive." What follows will be a brief description of the major observation and interview studies that have dealt with the hidden curriculum in physical education.

Context

Philip Jackson (1968) did some of the earliest work on the hidden curriculum, conducting intensive observations of elementary school classrooms and describing the day-to-day lives of teachers and children. He noted that life in those classrooms was hectic and fast-paced because of the constant presence of a "crowd." The situation was dominated by the power and authority of the teacher but students learned to maneuver in the setting through negotiations with the teacher and impression management. Because of their constant involvement with students, teachers were relatively isolated from other adults.

Observations of physical education programs reveal many similarities to the situation described by Jackson. However, as illustrated in a recent series of profiles of physical education teachers, the context in which physical educators work seems to differ in some respects (Locke & Griffin, 1986). First, the problem of dealing with crowds is exaggerated in physical education programs in which teachers deal with as many as five to 12 classes per day, often large classes with inadequate facilities and equipment. Second, teacher isolation is increased by the separation of physical education facilities and by what Hendry (1975) has called the marginal status of physical education within the school.

A brief visit to a physical education setting reveals several characteristics which distinguish it from the rest of the school. Classes are conducted in large, open spaces which are sometimes shared by more than one class. In contrast to the self-contained classroom, it is not uncommon for unannounced visitors to walk through and observe the class. The gym is usually noisy and full of activity. Students are sometimes separated by sex for physical education activities. The atmosphere within the class tends to be informal; students are allowed to talk to each other during most activities. In some cases, students refer to the teacher as "coach" rather than using the teacher's name. Teachers and students wear special clothing for physical education classes. Generally students, and sometimes teachers, wear uniforms. Students who do not have the prescribed uniform frequently are not permitted to participate in class activities. All these aspects of the physical education setting are part of the routines and rituals of the program. Most observers are so accustomed to these routines that they do not even notice them and few research reports include any reference to them. Nevertheless, these unique aspects of the physical education context are an integral part of the hidden curriculum.

Not only is the context of physical education unique, so is the content. Physical education content requires different instructional approaches and has different social meanings than classroom instruction. The subject matter in physical education is closely related to fundamental human dilemmas such as the definitions of and relationships between mind and body, play and work, and masculine and feminine. Because of its unique characteristics, the hidden curriculum in physical education warrants special attention.

Teacher Behaviors and Perceptions

One of the first studies of the hidden curriculum in physical education was conducted by Bain (1976). This study was an observation of 24 secondary school physical education teachers in the Chicago area. A systematic observation instrument was used to collect data about teacher verbal behavior and class organization. A questionnaire provided information about class regulations and grading procedures. Each teacher was observed three times. The information collected was used to produce scores on six predetermined value dimensions: achievement, autonomy, orderliness, privacy, specificity, and universalism. The results indicated that women teachers protected the privacy of students more than men did, the difference being greater in urban schools than in suburban schools. (None of the classes was coeducational.) Women teachers also talked more and tended to be more business-like (higher scores on specificity). Students in city schools were given less autonomy and were more likely to be treated as a member of a group rather than as an individual, despite the unexpected existence of small class sizes in the city schools.

Bain (1978) replicated this initial investigation studying 20 teachers and 20 coaches in secondary schools in the Houston area. The results were generally similar to those of the earlier study. Women scored higher than men on privacy and on instructional achievement (emphasis on teaching and learning). Coaches scored higher than teachers on privacy, instructional achievement, and specificity. Coaches were more likely to treat students as individuals than were teachers, a difference which may have been due in part to the smaller group size in athletic settings. These two studies indicated that there were patterns of behavior within the physical education setting that could be interpreted by an observer as communicating implicit values. Although differences among teachers were found, the results in general were consistent with an emphasis on order and control rather than achievement.

This emphasis on order and control also is supported by the research on teacher expectations. (See Chapter 10.) Although this work often is not associated with the hidden curriculum, it can be interpreted as the examination of how teachers' values affect their behavior and are implicitly communicated to students. The research by Martinek and his colleagues has indicated that physical attractiveness and perceived effort are impression cues that influence teacher expectations, especially their expectations related to social relations and cooperative behavior (Martinek & Johnson, 1979; Martinek 1980, 1981; Martinek & Karper, 1982, 1984). Students for whom the teacher has low expectations are treated differently than high expectancy students. The "lows" receive less attention, less praise and more criticism, and less content-related information. Martinek (1983, p. 65) suggests that "the teachers appeared to have a more positive bias toward students who were conforming, cooperative, orderly, and high-achieving."

The studies just described have focused on patterns of teacher behavior in physical education classes. Research on teachers' perceptions of life in the gym also have revealed an emphasis on order and control. Placek (1983, 1984) used observation and interviews to examine the influences on planning of four physical education teachers (two elementary, one junior high, one K-12). Two influences, student behavior and practical concerns, had the greatest impact on their planning. Three aspects of student behavior were of particular concern to teachers: student enjoyment, participation, and incidents of misbehavior. Student learning was not of much concern to the teachers. Placek (1983, p.49) suggests that the teachers "seemed to define the teaching situation in terms of keeping students busy, happy, and good."

An emphasis on student participation and enjoyment also has been found in other studies of teachers' perceptions. Earls (1981) conducted extensive interviews with 12 middle school teachers who were judged to be distinctive teachers. Each teacher also was observed for at least one day. The teachers reported that their behavior had changed over the years as they abandoned a "coaching ethos" and became more child-oriented. None of the subjects continues to emphasize skill instruction in physical education. These teachers evidenced a nonauthoritarian manner and an unconditional positive regard for children of all types. Their satisfactions of teaching related primarily to student enjoyment and success.

In a study of teachers' assessment practices, Veal (1986, 1988) found that teachers tend to evaluate participation and effort rather than achievement and skills. She observed and interviewed six middle school and seven high school teachers over a four month period. The frequency of formal assessment varied among teachers and activities, but in general the frequency was low. Five themes emerged in teachers' explanations of their assessment practices: (1) effort, (2) improvement, (3) individualization, (4) purpose/utility, and (5) efficiency. Veal suggests that while instruction tends to be aimed at a group's mean level of ability, evaluation appears to be geared to the individual's achievement interpreted in terms of effort and improvement rather than a normative standard of ability. Teachers seem to emphasize effort because they feel that they and the students have some control over effort while they are uncertain about the causes of achievement.

Another series of research studies that provide insight into teachers' perceptions of life in the gym is the "Profiles of Struggle" project (Locke & Griffin, 1986). This series provides brief profiles of five elementary and two secondary school physical education teachers developed collaboratively by the teacher and a researcher-author based on interviews and observation. The profiles revealed a number of systematic inpediments to excellence including the isolation of teachers and the acceptance of mediocrity (Griffin, 1986). Teachers responded to the systemic obstacles in varying ways including many which could be described as compromising or giving up. A few teachers were able to overcome the barriers and develop excellent programs characterized by teacher enthusiasm and student interest and learning. However, the overall picture that emerges is one of programs in which compliance and smooth operations are valued over teaching competence.

Why is an emphasis on order, compliance and control characteristic of many physical education teachers? One possible explanation is that those who choose physical education as an occupation tend to be conservative. Because occupational choice involves comparing one's abilities, interests, and aspirations with the perceived requirements of a field, occupations tend to attract recruits who share certain characteristics. Teachers in all fields generally come from middle class or lower middle class backgrounds and seem to be conformist and conservative (Lanier & Little, 1986). The evidence suggests that physical educators, especially males, are more conservative than other teachers (Hendry & Whiting, 1972; Kenyon, 1965; Sage, 1980).

The tendency toward conservatism seems closely related to identification with the coaching profession. A number of scholars have proposed an interactionist interpretation of such data arguing "that the specific social situation and role expectancies have a major effect upon those personal characteristics which are evidenced by physical educator/ coaches" (Sage, 1980, p. 118). The high visibility of athletic programs and the pressure upon coaches to win may foster development of conservative attitudes. The coaching ethos, with its emphasis on the development of elite performers, may be inherently conservative unless balanced by egalitarian and humanistic values.

The close association between physical education and athletics also may affect physical education teaching behaviors because of the conflicts experienced by those employed in the dual roles of teacher and coach (Bain, 1983; Locke & Massengale, 1978). The heavy time demands required to fulfill both roles is a major source of stress for physical educators. The solution to this problem often is to select coaching as the primary role and to spend less time and energy on teaching. The priority given to coaching seems likely since a desire to coach not to teach is often the primary motive for selecting physical education, especially for males (Bain & Wendt, 1983; Chu, 1978, Segrave, 1980). This choice is reinforced by the visibility and prestige associated with the coaching role. The resulting deemphasis of teaching may explain the lack of emphasis on instruction and achievement in physical education classes.

The emphasis on order and control rather than learning also may reflect inadequate professional socialization programs. The usual assumption of those responsible for teacher education is that prospective teachers were taught the "right" way to teach but simply fail to do so because they are overwhelmed by bureaucratic demands of schools (Zeichner & Tabachnick, 1981). An alternative view is that the professional socialization in universities does not provide physical education teachers with an adequate concept of quality physical education programs (Lawson, 1986), nor with the teaching skills needed to implement the program (Siedentop, 1986).

Each of these explanations of the implicit values communicated by physical education teachers seems to have some validity. If change in the hidden curriculum is sought, attention will need to be given to the characteristics of recruits, the nature of teacher education programs and the situational factors in schools that affect teachers' performances.

Program Structure

The studies reviewed to this point indicate that the teacher has an important role in communicating implicit values to students. What activities are included and how the program is organized also communicate messages to students.

One aspect of program structure related to the hidden curriculum is the selection of activities for inclusion in the program. Although content selection is presumed to be based on the explicit philosophy of the institution, the possibility exists that tacit assumptions have affected those choices. Dodds (1985) suggests that students receive messages both from what is taught and what is omitted from the program (the null curriculum). To identify those messages, we must examine patterns of activities offered and values associated with particular activities. Although little effort has been made to analyze what activities are taught, Bain (1979) has studied the values which students seem to associate with particular activities.

In Bain's study, a sample of 1,421 college students completed a word pair association instrument in which each subject rated one of 24 movement activities on 21 word pairs. Factor analysis procedures were used to identify seven value dimensions associated with activities. The results indicated that students evaluated the worth of activities based on aesthetic and health values. Students seemed to differentiate two types of difficulty associated with specific activities: physical demand and novelty or complexity. Both sociability and vertigo were on a continuum related to gender. At one end of the continuum were activities seen as unsociable, dangerous, and masculine and at the other end were activities seen as sociable, safe, and feminine. This study indicates that students' reactions to movement activities are complex and multidimensional.

In contrast to the survey approach used by Bain, Tindall (1975) used qualitative research methods to examine student reactions to one particular activity—basketball. He conducted a participant observation study of, physical education classes, an interclass tournament, and a community basketball program in a community with Mormon and Native American students. His analysis indicated that the game of basketball was experienced as a lesson in proper personal behavior. The premise underlying the tournament, that individuals ought to and do control other individuals, was accepted by most students but rejected by those for whom it conflicted with their Native American culture. The style of play also differed between the two cultures. In games where the players were predominantly Native Americans, the games were structures of individual performances, while Mormon games were strategic organizations of group effort. This study reinforces our understanding that the meanings attached to specific activities are culturally constrained.

What both of these studies suggest is that physical education content must be examined not only in relationship to stated program goals but also in terms of the cultural meanings associated with it. Although teachers cannot change these cultural constraints, they can consider such meanings in making content selections and can help students become more aware of cultural influences on movement participation (Bain, 1988).

The other structural feature of physical education programs that has received much attention is the way in which competition is dealt with in the program. Frequently physical education programs are compared with informal games and with organized sport. Siedentop (1987, p. 80) recently asked the question: "Why is interscholastic and youth sport so relatively exciting and school physical education so relatively dull? And why is it sometimes dull even when it is taught effectively, given teacher skills or student engagement as effectiveness criteria?" He suggests the difference in relative excitement exists because in physical education spot activities and skills are taught in isolation rather than in the context of the sport culture. His proposal is that physical education programs should be redesigned to incorporate the features of institutionalized sport: seasons, affiliation with a team, formal competition, a culminating event, and records. His suggestion seems compatible with the athletic orientation and background of many physical education teachers.

Whether or not one concurs with Siedentop's recommendation, a comparison of physical education programs with informal and formal spot programs would seem useful.

Chalip and colleagues (1984) examined the reactions of 75 high school students to sport experiences in three settings: organized sport, informal sport, and physical education class. Each respondent carried an electronic pager and a pad of self-report forms for a week. At random times the pager signalled them to fill out a self-report form indicating what activity they were doing and their feelings related to each of eight dimensions: self-consciousness, skills, challenges, mood, motivation, sense of control, how much was at stake, and difficulty in concentrating. Of 4,489 observations, 114 were related to sport: 20 organized sport, 54 informal sport, 40 physical education class. When sport was compared to non-sport experiences, higher than average challenges were found in all three sport settings. Moods were significantly above average in informal sports and PE class, while sense of skill and motivation stood out in informal sport.

When the three sport settings were compared, some differences were found. Sense of control was highest in PE class and lowest in informal sport, while sense of skill was lowest in PE and highest in informal sport. The stakes of the activity were perceived to be higher in organized sport than in either of the other two settings. The analysis also examined the flow model which defines enjoyment as a balance between the challenges of an activity and the skills of the participant (Csikszentmihalyi, 1975). In organized sport and in physical education, students report their challenges to be greater than their skills. Only in informal sport does a matching of challenge and skill appear to be common.

This balance between skill and challenge in informal sport seems to be the result of player decisions intended to maintain the flow of the experience. Coakley (1980) conducted observations of 84 informal, player-controlled games and 121 formally organized, adult-controlled games over a 12 month period. In each game, interviews were conducted with at least two of the players. Results indicated that the informal games were generally action centered while the formal games were rule centered. Children organizing their own games modified rules to maximize personal involvement in action, balanced competition, and opportunities to reaffirm friendships. Formal games were more likely to be serious and concerned with performance quality and game outcomes. Rules were enforced by adults according to universalistic criteria with no exceptions for individual abilities or characteristics.

Although performance and outcomes are more central in formal sport, action remains an important concern of participants. Harris (1983, 1984) used participant-observation and interviews to study two youth baseball teams. The player interpretations of their experiences centered on three concepts: winning and losing, paying attention, and knowing how to play the game. The team with the most successful record viewed winning and losing as very important, but both teams stressed proving their playing ability more than proving their ability to win games. Although fun did not emerge as a central issue in group ratings of concepts, it was highlighted as important in individual interviews. Players saw fun as related to involvement in action. However, coaches rarely emphasized enjoyment and players saw other aspects of the experience as more salient.

Fine (1987) conducted a three year participant observation study of five Little League baseball teams. He suggests that youth baseball has elements of both work and play. It is work-related in that it is forced, directed, and constrained by rules and regulations. It is play because of the excitement in the game and because of instances of non-serious activity.

Dubois (1986) interviewed 110 boys and girls, ages 8-10, selected from two youth soccer programs: a community-wide parent operated competitive program and an elementary school-sponsored instructional league. The two programs attracted somewhat different clienteles; participants in the competitive league were slightly older, included a higher proportion of males, and placed more importance on winning before the program began. The subjects in both groups viewed these values as most important to their involvement in sport: to improve playing skills, play fairly, have fun, display good sportsmanship, improve physical fitness, and be part of a team. Both groups' values changed from pre- to post-season with the changes generally reflecting the distinctive competitive emphasis of the leagues.

The implications of these comparisons for physical education programs are difficult to assess. Both informal play and organized sport have positive aspects that seem difficult for physical education programs to incorporate. The informal setting is playful, action centered, and accommodating of individual differences. The organized sport program is exciting, intense, and achievement oriented. Many physical education programs espouse a philosophy that emphasizes both achievement and the accommodation of individual differences. However, the observation of classes in action and interviews of students often indicates that physical education programs may not be consistent with this explicit philosophy. Physical education programs seem to be characterized by high structure and control without a clear achievement orientation.

Student Experiences

To understand the hidden curriculum in physical education programs, we must examine not only the teacher's perspective and the structural features of the program, but also the students' behaviors and perceptions. How do students react to the teacher's emphasis on order and participation? How are teachers affected by student responses? Research indicates that individual students develop different patterns of response.

Tousignant and Siedentop (1983) used qualitative methods to identify task structures and student participation patterns in four secondary school physical education classes. They identified four basic categories of student behavior: (1) task as stated by the teacher, (2) modified task, (3) deviant off-task behavior, and (4) competent bystanders or avoidance of participation without misbehaving. Different students adopted different types of behavior in different situations and frequently a student shifted from ontask behavior to a modified task to off-task behavior within a single activity. The difficulty of the task and the teacher's accountability system influenced student responses. In some classes, the students were held responsible for minimal participation or for effort, but not for reaching any particular level of skill or knowledge. The authors suggest that cooperation between teachers and students was achieved through a subtle and tacit process of negotiation.

Griffin (1983, 1984, 1985a, 1985b) conducted a three month case study examining a coeducational middle school physical education program in a white, middle-class community in New England. The major focus of her work was sex equity and gender (those results are discussed in Chapter 12). This chapter will review the work as it relates to the more general issue of implicit values in physical education. Based on observations and interviews with teachers, Griffin classified student participation patterns in gymnastics and team sports classes (see Table 15-1). Her observations revealed considerable variation in participation both within and between sexes. Participation style seemed to be affected by the nature of the activity, personal characteristics such as size and skill, and the reactions of others, many of which were gender-based. Teachers tended to accept differences in participation style as inevitable and to respond differently to the different groups of students (Griffin, 1985a).

Bain (1985b) conducted a participant-observation study of a university exercise class entitled fitness and weight control. Four patterns of student participation emerged: serious runners, serious walkers, social interactors, and absentees. In general, the more successful students were lean and fit, but the class was not effective in changing the exercise patterns of those who were less fit. Student participation patterns may be related to race; seven of eight black subjects were classified as social interactors. These students talked and joked while exercising and did not seem to exhibit the intensity about exercise and weight loss that typified many of the white students.

These studies have indicated variations in student behaviors in physical education classes, but each has produced a somewhat different list of participation patterns. One way to interpret these patterns might be to

TABLE 15-1. Participation Patterns of Middle School Students

Gymnastics[1]		Team Sports	
Boys	Girls	Boys[2]	Girls[3]
1. Serious	1. Serious	1. Machos	1. Athletes
2. Frivolous	2. Exploratory	2. Junior machos	2. JV players
3. Reluctant	3. Reluctant	3. Nice guys	3. Cheerleaders
		4. Invisible players	4. Femmes fatales
		5. Wimps	5. Lost souls
			6. System beaters

[1]Griffin, 1983
[2]Griffin, 1985
[3]Griffin, 1984

use a classification of work and play activities developed by King (1983, 1987). King (1983) studied how elementary school children define their school activities as work or play. She observed children in all their activities including physical education and interviewed them regarding the observed events. Children viewed work as associated with learning and usually requiring concentration, control, individual accomplishment, and quiet. Three categories of play emerged from the analysis. Instrumental play is incorporated within the practice of school work and enhances that work's goals and objectives. Recreational play constitutes a planned, sanctioned respite from work. Illicit play involves unsanctioned interactions that oppose the explicit rules and expectations of work; examples include whispering, poking other children, and clowning around. King suggests that instrumental play is an extension of work, recreation is compensation for work, and illicit play is resistance to the dominant social order and the demands of the work situation. King does not provide an analysis of work and play in physical education, but she does give examples which indicate that physical education activities were included in children's definitions of both work and play.

The physical education teachers' emphases on participation and enjoyment might be interpreted as a focus on play, not work. If learning objectives are incorporated into the activities, they would be instrumental play; if not, the activities would be recreational play. Emphasis on busy, happy, and good may indicate that recreational, not instrumental, play dominates many physical education programs. The student participation patterns also seemed to be characterized as play. Their responses included not only instrumental and recreational play but also numerous examples of illicit play. The presence of illicit play and of non-participatory behaviors seems to indicate resistance to the curriculum as planned and implemented by teachers. Several studies have examined differences in teacher and student perceptions of the physical education program.

Ennis (1985) used observation, interviews, questionnaires, and content analysis to study the physical education program in the sixth, seventh, and eighth grades in five elementary schools in a predominantly rural school system in Georgia. Although her focus was primarily on the explicit curriculum, multiple data sources permitted her to compare the formal curriculum as stated in the curriculum guide, the operational curriculum as witnessed by an observer, the teachers' perceptions of what is being taught, and the students' reports of their experiences. Her results revealed discrepancies between the teachers' intended curriculum and the curricuum as perceived by students or an observer. The teachers felt their programs emphasized a wide range of instrumental purposes (21 of 22 possibilities) while the students and the observer saw the purposes being emphasized as more limited (12-13 purposes).

Bain's (1985b) study of a university exercise class also revealed a difference between teacher and student perceptions. The instructional approach in the course seemed to be based on a technical-rational view which assumes that information will change behavior. In contrast, student reactions seemed to reflect a subjective-affective view that behavior is influenced by emotions and perceptions.

Teachers and students may not only have differing views of the instructional process, but they also may have different perceptions of social and moral values. Wang (1977) conducted a participant observation study of a fifth grade physical education class in a school in North Carolina that recently had been racially integrated. She discovered a teacher-sponsored curriculum and a separate, contradictory, student-imposed curriculum. The teacher-sponsored curriculum promoted an ideal of integrated, democratic living in which rules of individual worth were tempered with emphasis upon cooperation, equality, and social responsibility. The student-imposed curriculum revealed patterns of discrimination based on gender, race, social class, personality, and skills. Skillful sport performance had a property-like nature in the student society. Wang suggests that more active instruction in skills might be the most effective way to counter discrimination.

Fine (1987) also found a discrepancy between the moral themes emphasized by coaches and those emphasized by players. The four basic themes that coaches employ "to instruct their players in the moral order of sport are: (1) effort, (2) sportsmanship, (3) teamwork, and (4) coping with victory and defeat" (Fine, 1987, p. 61). Coaches particularly emphasize the importance of effort and tend to treat defeat or poor individual performance as evidence of lack of effort. The participants use the themes emphasized by coaches but transform them to emphasize self-presentation and behaving properly. The concerns of the preadolescent boys included: (1) the display of appropriate emotions, especially toughness; (2) controlling one's aggression, fears, and tears; (3) publicly displaying a desire to win (hustle); and (4) not breaking the bond of unity. These concerns became a moral code enforced by peers.

The lack of symmetry between teacher and student perceptions implies that for a complete understanding of the hidden curriculum we need to study not only patterns of behavior but also students' and teachers' interpretations of events in physical education classes. Kollen (1981, 1983) conducted a phenomenological inquiry into the perceptions of 20 high school seniors regarding their physical education classes. Based on her interviews, she concluded that the physical education environment is perceived as sterile (stressing conformity) and unsafe (characterized by embarassment and humiliation). Students respond to the environment by "withholding something of themselves through minimal compliance, lack of involvement, manipulation of the teacher, false enthusiasm, rebellion, leaving, failing class, isolation or giving up" (Kollen, 1983, p. 87). Kollen suggests that the movement standard in physical education is masculine-athletic-competitive and that it creates a fragmented rather than an integrated movement experience. This view of physical education seems derived from physical educators' close association with athletics and from the traditional definition of sport as a male domain (Theberge, 1985).

Potential embarassment is also a concern for participants in adult exercise programs. Kotarba and Bentley (1985) used interviews and participant-observation to study corporate wellness programs. They found that a strong self-concept and a sense of competence in the exercise setting were requisite for joining the program and for continuing participation. They also noted a tendency of exercise instructors to implicitly or explicitly present a moralistic perspective on the wellness movement. That is, the need to maintain one's health and fitness was presented as a moral obligation and those who were physically unfit were judged to be morally unfit.

Bain and her colleagues (in press) also found a concern about judgment by others in their study of participant perceptions of exercise programs for overweight women. The participants' shared experience of social disapproval based on body size affects their perceptions of exercise programs and their decisions about participation. The women reported experiences in previous exercise settings which made them feel judged on the basis of body size and performance ability. Although they continued to worry about social disapproval, the women responded positively to the instruction provided in the project, which they perceived as appropriately paced and non-judgmental. Discussions of the exercise sessions were included for research purposes but were perceived to be of value to the instructional process. Participants liked having this opportunity to reflect on the exercise experiences and to provide feedback to the instructors. They considered it unusual for an exercise program to provide opportunities for either reflection or input.

WHAT ARE THE MESSAGES?

Research on the hidden curriculum attempts to describe the implicit values transmitted by the routines and rituals of life in the gym. In this chapter, we have reviewed a number of studies done in a variety of settings. Many of these were case studies that cannot be generalized to other situations. However, examining the body of work does permit us to suggest possibilities and raise questions about what messages are communicated by the hidden curriculum in physical education.

One type of implicit value that is communicated to students is messages about basic human nature and desirable personal qualities. Physical educators place considerable emphasis on the importance of effort. Perceptions of student effort affect teacher expectations (Martinek, 1983). Teachers and coaches emphasize effort or hustle in their interactions with participants (Tousignant & Siedentop, 1983; Fine, 1987). Evaluation procedures tend to focus on student effort (Veal, 1986).

There are several possible explanations for this emphasis on effort. The view that hard work and persistence lead to success is central to the American value system. Physical educators, because of their conservatism and their association with athletic programs with a strong emphasis on effort and achievement, tend to believe strongly in this work ethic. In some cases, this emphasis on effort might reflect an understanding of attribution theory in which effort is the causal factor related to success or failure over which the individual is most likely to have control, in contrast to factors such as ability, task difficulty, and luck (Brawley & Roberts, 1984). Veal's research (1988) suggests that many teachers assume a connection between effort and student learning in which effort is often considered more important than skill and is used as a substitute for achievement. However, in some classes, it would appear that effort is emphasized not as a means to achievement but as an end in itself.

The emphasis on effort seems to be accompanied by mixed messages on achievement. On one hand, many K-12 physical education classes seem to place minimal emphasis on student learning and achievement. Achievement receives little attention in teacher planning (Placek, 1984), in some instructional settings (Bain, 1976, 1978; Tousignant & Siedentop, 1983) and in evaluation procedures (Veal, 1986). This seems to contrast with the greater emphasis placed on achievement in athletic and youth sport programs (Bain, 1978; Harris, 1983, 1984; Dubois, 1986; Fine, 1987). There seem to be two ways to interpret these mixed messages. One interpretation is that only the highly skilled are entitled to motor skill instruction, a position which Dodds (1986) has labelled "motor elitism." Physical education classes and athletic programs become a form of ability grouping in which instruction is provided only for the high ability group. The low ability group is not expected to learn nor provided the instruction necessary to do so.

A second interpretation is that motor skill instruction is not a legitimate responsibility of the school and that those who want such instruction must have the opportunity and resources to participate in extracurricular or non-school programs. The latter interpretation seems to reinforce an assumption of mind-body dualism. Children are being told that their minds and bodies are separate and that the business of schools is to educate their minds. While neither of these positions is likely to be explicitly endorsed by physical educators, they may be responding to the marginality of physical education programs in schools which value only intellectual activity by emphasizing athletics, the one activity which can bring them prestige (Hendry, 1975).

In the absence of an emphasis on learning, making an effort may be an overt expression of one's willingness to comply with the authority of the teacher. As discussed earlier, physical education teachers seem to value order and control. This affects the activities they choose to teach (Placek, 1984) and class organization and regulations (Bain, 1976, 1978). Students are expected to exhibit compliance by participating in the activities. But the message seems to be that participation is not enough; a successful student must demonstrate effort and enthusiasm. In some cases, students put forth effort because they enjoy the activity. In other cases, students learn impression management; that is, they learn to fake participation and perhaps even effort and enjoyment (Tousignant & Siedentop, 1983; Kollen, 1983; Griffin, 1984, 1985a).

Expectations for compliance generally are associated with work, not play. However, many physical education programs focusing on what seem to be recreational not instructional activities emphasize student compliance. Finkelstein (1987) suggests that schools may be viewed as liberating agencies which free children to play by expanding their play repertoire or as regulatory agencies which constrain and direct children's play. Physical education programs which teach skills and knowledges help children expand their repertoire. Physical education programs which emphasize compliance, participation, and effort in the absence of a focus on learning and achievement would seem to be regulatory not liberating agencies. Such regulatory programs may serve to undermine the importance of play and constrain one's tendency to play, rather than to validate play and expand the child's ability to play. Physical educators' tendencies to regulate and control play may be an effort to improve their status within the school by identifying their programs as worklike and disassociating themselves from play, an activity that may be viewed as frivolous.

Another area in which students receive messages about desirable personal qualities relates to appearance. Martinek (1983) notes that student somatotype and physical attractiveness influence teacher expectations. Students in physical education have relatively little privacy; both their bodies and their skills are visible to others (Bain, 1976, 1978). Participants in physical education classes and exercise programs report feelings of embarassment and concerns about being judged by others (Kollen, 1983; Bain et. al., in press). Judgments related to body size are sometimes justified by being framed in terms of a moral obligation to maintain one's health and fitness (Kotarba & Bentley, 1985).

Although such a moral interpretation of health is not unique to physical education, it may be embraced by physical educators because it helps to address the problem of marginality and low status. By viewing health and fitness as moral issues and by claiming special expertise in dealing with these issues, physical educators can enhance their professional status. However, concerns have been expressed about this tendency to treat health and fitness as a moral issue. Vertinsky (1985, p. 73) suggests that health promotion programs may be characterized as "imposing values packaged in scientific wrapping." Pellegrino (1981, p. 373) cautions not to confuse technical authority with moral authority, saying "experts have no special prerogatives entitling them to make value judgments for the rest of humankind."

The issue of judgments based on appearance and body size is particularly critical for women. In our society, men tend to be judged more on the basis of actions and women more on the basis of appearance (Orbach, 1978). One result is that women are preoccupied with weight regardless of actual body size (Dwyer, 1973). This preoccupation is manifested in a high incidence of eating disorders and frequent dieting (Schwartz et al. 1982). The dilemma confronting physical education teachers is how to design and conduct programs which promote health and fitness without communicating social or moral rejection of the unfit or reinforcing sexist beliefs and practices.

Programs that have an instructional focus on fitness may adopt what has been called a technical-rational view. This perspective assumes that information will change behavior and tends to ignore the subjective-affective concerns of students (Bain, 1985b). By embracing affective neutrality, this approach would seem to avoid value issues. However, Bain (1985b) notes that a dominant characteristic of patriarchal societies is a dualism which ascribes objectivity and rationality to the male-dominated, public domain and views these characteristics as superior to the female, private domain of subjectivity and emotion. Physical education programs that include a public emphasis on technical-rational information and exclude subjective-affective concerns may serve to reinforce this dualism. This may be especially true if classes on fitness and weight control, which draw mostly female students, do not acknowledge participants' emotions and perceptions regarding body size.

Another major component of the hidden curriculum is messages about social relations. Students learn how to relate to other people from the implicit values communicated by teachers and by their peers. One of the values that seems to be taught by schooling has been called universalism. This refers to learning to treat all members of a category similarly. Children learn to identify people with categories and to distinguish between the person and the social position he or she occupies. The research seems to indicate that universalistic values are communicated to students in physical education and organized sport settings (Bain, 1976, 1978; Coakley, 1980). Given the central role of universalism in the maintenance of social structures in highly developed, bureaucratic societies (Dreeben, 1968), it is not surprising that such values are endorsed by physical education teachers. The question that emerges is what categories are used to determine treatment of individuals in a physical education context.

Some of these messages deal with how to relate to particular groups of people based on gender, race, social class, or skill. Because physical education content is strongly associated with beliefs about gender, the hidden curriculum in physical education incorporates powerful messages regarding gender relations. The physical education experience differs for male and female teachers and for male and female students. Physical education programs have the potential to reinforce or to transform traditional gender relations.

Physical education programs also may communicate implicit values related to race and social class. The students may be the strongest communicators of these values. In Wang's study (1977), despite a teacher curriculum advocating cooperation and mutual support, the students ran a hidden curriculum in which children of different sex, race, skill level, and socioeconomic status were treated differentially. The issue for the teacher is how to respond to these peer interactions. Teachers may reinforce, ignore, or attempt to intervene. If differential status is seen as inevitable, teachers will probably choose to ignore such interactions unless they are disruptive. This tendency to ignore certain peer interactions may be part of the complex negotiation process by which teachers and students reach an unspoken agreement about what behavior is acceptable or tolerable in the physical education class. The unspoken agreement seems to based on the teacher's need to survive in a stressful situation and may be a response to the emphasis by administrators on compliance and control (McNeil, 1988).

Differential treatment based on skill may take many different forms in the physical education environent. As mentioned previously, the lack of emphasis on learning in many physical education classes could be interpreted as an example of motor elitism in which only highly skilled athletes are entitled to instruction. Within physical education classes, skill level may affect student participation patterns and teachers' reactions to students. A predominance of competitive activities within the curriculum also may send messages that the skillful are entitled to greater recognition and attention.

Some have argued that emphasis on competitive activities may affect students' interpersonal skills and values. However, the effects of competition may differ, depending on how the competitive action is organized. In his study of youth soccer programs, Dubois (1986) found that children who participated in a less competitive context tended to have more fun and stress affiliation and sportsmanship while those in the more competitive league seemed to value competition, winning and receiving recognition for skilled performance. In an experimental study with kindergarten children, Orlick, McNally & O'Hara (1978) found that children who participated in cooperative games exhibited more spontaneous cooperative behavior than children who participated in traditional competitive games.

Physical educators sometimes believe that participation in competitive activities develops sportsmanship and contributes to moral growth. However, research by Bredemeier & Shields (1983, 1984) indicates that sport seems to elicit lower levels of moral reasoning than do other life dilemmas. They state that "some facets of sport structure may actually discourage moral growth by making it difficult for competitors to consider the welfare of other participants or of themselves" (Bredemeier & Shields, 1983, p. 16). They suggest that in order to foster moral growth, those experiences must provide opportunity for student dialogue about the moral dilemmas involved.

This call for dialogue seems to reinforce the importance of reflection and discussion in dealing with value issues. Participants in an adult exercise project suggested that every exercise program should provide an opportunity for discussion (Bain et. al., in press). This suggestion may be appropriate not only for adults but also for children. Hellison (1985) has recommended that discussion of students' actions and beliefs is an integral part of promoting the social and moral growth of children in physical education. It is inevitable that the routines and regularities of the physical education program will communicate implicit values to students. But it is not inevitable that the hidden curriculum of the program will remain unexamined.

IMPLICATIONS AND CONCLUSIONS

Schooling is not merely an academic experience; it is an intensive experience in institutional living (Silberman, 1971). The routines and rituals of daily life in the school communicate basic principles and assumptions about the culture. The messages are powerful because they are pervasive and continuously repeated. The fact that the messages remain unspoken and unacknowledged may make them even more powerful by making them seem natural and inevitable. The initial step in evaluating and perhaps changing the hidden curriculum is a careful analysis of our programs.

Becoming aware of the values implicit in one's program is not easy. A teacher's behavior is often the expression of tacit beliefs that are so "taken-for granted" that they cannot be recognized or verbalized. Raising them to the level of awareness is a difficult process. A major value of the research on the hidden curriculum is that reading the research may provide teachers with a mirror in which they can see their own programs. To serve this function adequately, more research is needed at every level of schooling. These need to be qualitative studies conducted in naturalistic settings focusing not just on behaviors but also on the meanings of those events. The analysis also needs to examine the relationship of the observed, face-to-face interactions to the larger society in which that particular school exists. Physical educators need to see the ways in which their day-to-day behaviors reinforce or challenge cultural beliefs and practices. Teacher educators need to understand the origins of the hidden curriculum and the ways in which the socialization process can be modified to change it.

In addition to reading research describing the hidden curriculum in physical education, teachers also need to examine life in their own gyms. One strategy might be to participate in "consciousness-raising" discussions with colleagues, but the difficulty may be finding the time and willing participants. An observer can provide useful information if the person can observe long enough to see patterns of behavior and can provide feedback in a non-evaluative manner. Student perceptions can be another valuable source of information. Anonymous questionnaires are one way to get student perceptions. Another useful technique called Interpersonal Process Recall involves showing students videotapes of class sessions and having them discuss what they were thinking and feeling during those events (Trang & Caskey, 1981). The goal of all of these strategies is for teachers to increase their awareness of patterns of behavior, the meanings associated with those patterns, and the influences and values underlying the behavior.

Awareness is only a first step. The next step is to examine the consistency of the hidden curriculum with the explicit educational philosophy of the program, the school, and the society, and to deal with any contradictions that are identified. Such an examination can be a very threatening process. What if others see you differently than you see yourself? What if close scrutiny reveals patterns which you cannot justify but which are hard to change? Dodds (1986) has discussed the difficulties faced by teachers trying to work on equity issues. One implication of the research is that changing teaching patterns is complex and that teachers attempting such change require support.

Teachers beginning to look at the hidden curriculum should seek support from others. Providing such support may be an important responsibility of university physical education faculty. One advantage of collaboration between school and university faculty is that both the insider's and the outsider's perspective can be included in the discussions. To provide a balanced perspective, such groups might also examine the hidden curriculum in university teacher education and graduate programs.

Changing the hidden curriculum is a difficult task because it requires changing behavior that is habitual and that reflects deeply held beliefs. The task often involves transforming not merely the program or the school but challenging existing social conditions which contradict publicly endorsed principles of democracy and justice. This is not easy, but as Giroux (1981, p. 218) states, "While it would be naive and misleading to claim that schools alone can create the conditions for social change, it would be equally naive to argue that working in schools does not matter."

REFERENCES

Apple, M. W. (1982). *Education and power.* Boston: Routledge & Kegan Paul.
Bain, L. L. (1975). The hidden curriculum in physical education. *Quest, 24,* 92-101.
Bain, L. L. (1976). Description of the hidden curriculum in secondary physical education. *Research Quarterly, 47,* 154-160.
Bain, L. L. (1978). Differences in values implicit in teaching and coaching behaviors. *Research Quarterly, 49,* 5-11.
Bain, L. L. (1979). Perceived characteristics of selected movement activities. *Research Quarterly, 50,* 565-573.
Bain, L. (1983). Teacher/coach role conflict: Factors influencing role performance. In T. J. Templin & J. K. Olson (Eds.), *Teaching in physical education.* Champaign, IL: Human Kinetics Publishers.
Bain, L. L. (1985a). The hidden curriculum re-examined. *Quest, 37,* 145-153.
Bain, L. L. (1985b). A naturalistic study of students' responses to an exercise class. *Journal of Teaching in Physical Education, 5,* 2-12.
Bain, L. L. (1988). Curriculum for critical reflection in physical education. In Brandt, R. (Ed.) Association for Supervision and Curriculum Development, *Content of the curriculum.* Alexandria, Va.: ASCD publisher
Bain, L. L., & Wendt, J. C. (1983). Undergraduate physical education majors' perceptions of the roles of teacher and coach. *Research Quarterly for Exercise and Sport, 54,* 112-118.

Bain, L. L., Wilson, T., & Chaikind, E. (in press). Participant perceptions of exercise programs for over-weight women. *Research Quarterly for Exercise and Sport.*

Bowles, S., & Gintis, H. (1976). *Schooling in capitalist America.* New York: Basic Books.

Brawley, L. R., & Roberts, G. C. (1984). Attributions in sport: Research foundations, characteristics, and limitations. In J. M. Silva, III & R. S. Weinberg (Eds.), *Psychological Foundations of Sport.* Champaign, IL: Human Kinetics Publishers.

Bredemeier, B., & Shields, D. (1983). Body and balance: Developing moral structures through physical education. Paper presented at the annual convention of the American Alliance for Health, Physical Education, Recreation and Dance, Minneapolis.

Bredemeier, B., & Shields, D. (1984). Divergence in moral reasoning about sport and everyday life. *Sociology of Sport Journal, 1,* 348-357.

Chalip, L., Csikszentmihalyi, M., Kleiber, D., & Larson, R. (1984). Variations of experience in formal and informal sport. *Research Quarterly for Exercise and Sport, 55,* 109-116.

Chu, D. (1978). A foundational study of the occupational induction of physical education teacher-coaches as it is affected by the organizational requirements of the training institution and its environment. *Dissertation Abstracts International, 39,* 3860-A. (University Microfilms No. 78-22, 488).

Coakley, J. (1980). Play, games and sports: Developmental implications for young people. *Journal of Sport Behavior, 3*(3): 99-118.

Csikszentmihalyi, M. (1975). *Beyond Boredom and Anxiety.* San Francisco: Jossey-Bass.

Dodds, P. (1983). Consciousness raising in curriculum: A teacher's model for analysis. In A. E. Jewett, M. M. Carnes, & M. Speakman (Eds.), *Proceedings of the Third Conference on Curriculum Theory in Physical Education.* Athens: University of Georgia.

Dodds, P. (1985). Are the hunters of the function curriculum seeking quarks or snarks? *Journal of Teaching in Physical Education, 4:* 91-99.

Dodds, P. (1986). Stamp out the ugly "isms" in your gym. In M. Pieron & G. Graham (Eds.), *Sport Pedagogy.* Champaign, IL: Human Kinetics Publishers.

Dreeben, R. (1968). *On what is learned in schools.* Reading, MA: Addison-Wesley.

Dubois, P. (1986). The effect of participation in sport on the value orientations of young athletes. *Sociology of Sport Journal, 3,* 29-42.

Dwyer, J. T. (1973). Psychosexual aspects of weight control and dieting behavior in adolescents. *Medical Aspects of Human Sexuality, 7,* 82-108.

Earls, N. F. (1981). Distinctive teachers' personal qualities, perceptions of teacher education and the realities of teaching. *Journal of Teaching in Physical Education, 1:* 59-70.

Ennis, C. D. (1985). Purpose concepts in an existing physical education curriculum. *Research Quarterly for Exercise and Sport, 56,* 323-333.

Fine, G. A. (1987). *With the Boys: Little League Baseball and Preadolescent Culture.* Chicago: University of Chicago Press.

Finkelstein, B. (1987). Historical perspectives on children's play in school. In J. H. Block & N. R. King (Eds.), *School Play.* New York: Garland Publishing Co.

Giroux, H. (1981). Pedagogy, pessimism and the politics of conformity: A reply to Linda McNeil. *Curriculum Inquiry, 11*(3), 211-223.

Griffin, P. S. (1983). Gymnastics is a girls' thing: Participation and Interaction patterns in middle school gymnastics classes. In T. J. Templin & J. K. Olson (Eds.), *Teaching in physical education.* Champaign, IL: Human Kinetics.

Griffin, P. S. (1984). Girls' participation patterns in a middle school team sports unit. *Journal of Teaching in Physical Education, 4,* 30-38.

Griffin, P. S. (1985a). Boys' participation styles in a middle school physical education sports unit. *Journal of Teaching in Physical Education, 4,* 100-110.

Griffin, P. S. (1985b). Teacher perceptions of and reactions to equity problems in a middle school physical education program. *Research Quarterly for Exercise and Sport, 56*(2), 103-110.

Griffin, P. S. (1986). Analysis and discussion: What have we learned? *Journal of Physical Education, Recreation and Dance, 57*(4): 57-59.

Harris, J. C. (1983). Interpreting youth baseball: Players' understanding of attention, winning and playing the game. *Research Quarterly for Exercise and Sport, 54:* 330-339.

Harris, J. C. (1984). Interpreting youth baseball: Players' understandings of fun and excitement, danger and boredom. *Research Quarterly for Exercise and Sport, 55:* 379-382.

Hellison, D. (1985). *Goals and strategies for teaching physical education.* Champaign, IL: Human Kinetics.

Hendry, L. B. (1975). Survival in a marginal role: The professional identify of the physical education teacher. *British Journal of Sociology, 26:* 465-476.

Hendry, L. B., & Whiting, H. T. A. (1972). General course and specialist physical education student characteristics. *Educational Research, 14,* 152-156.

Jackson, P. W. (1968). *Life in classrooms.* New York: Holt, Rinehart, & Winston.

Kenyon, G. S. (1965). Psychosocial and cultural characteristics unique to prospective teachers of physical education. *Research Quarterly 36,* 105-142.

King, N. R. (1983). Play in the workplace. In M. Apple & L. Weis (Eds.), *Ideology and Practice in Schooling.* Philadelphia: Temple University Press.

King, N. R. (1987). Elementary school play: Theory and research. In J. H. Block & N. R. King (Eds.), *School Play.* New York: Garland Publishing Co.

Kollen, P. (1981). The experience of movement in physical education: A phenomenology. Unpublished doctoral dissertation, University of Michigan.

Kollen, P. (1983). Fragmentation and integration in movement. In T. J. Templin & J. K. Olson (Eds.), *Teaching in physical education.* Champaign, IL: Human Kinetics.

Kotarba, J. A., & Bentley, P. (1985, August). Social psychological factors in corporate wellness compliance. Paper presented at the annual meeting of the Society for the Study of Social Problems, Washington, D.C.

Lanier, J. E., & Little, J. W. (1986). Research on teacher education. In M. C. Wittrock (Ed.), *Third handbook of research on teaching.* New York: MacMillan.

Lather, P. (1985). *Empowering research methodologies.* Paper presented at the annual meeting of the American Educational Research Association, Chicago.

Lawson, H. A. (1986). Occupational socialization and the design of teacher education programs. *Journal of Teaching in Physical Education,* 5, 107-116.

Locke, L. F., & Griffin, P. (Eds.). (1986). Profiles of struggle. *Journal of Physical Education, Recreation and Dance,* 57(4), 32-63.

Locke, L. F., & Massengale, J. (1978). Role-conflict in teacher-coaches. *Research Quarterly,* 71, 27-40.

Martinek, T. (1980). Stability of teachers' expectations for elementary school aged children. *Perceptual and Motor Skills,* 51, 1269-1270.

Martinek, T. (1981). Physical attractiveness: Effects of teacher expectations and dyadic interactions in elementary age children. *Journal of Sport Psychology,* 3, 196-205.

Martinek, T. J. (1983). Creating Golem and Galatea effects during physical education instruction: A social psychological perspective. In T. J. Templin & J. K. Olson (Eds.), *Teaching in physical education.* Champaign, IL: Human Kinetics.

Martinek, T., & Johnson, S. (1979). Teacher expectations: Effects on dyadic interactions and self-concept in elementary age children. *Research Quarterly,* 50, 60-70.

Martinek, T., & Karper, W. (1982). Canonical relationships among motor ability, expression of effort, teacher expectations and dyadic interactions in elementary age children. *Journal of Teaching in Physical Education,* 1, 26-39.

Martinek, T. J., & Karper, W. B. (1984). Multivariate relationships of specific impression cues with teacher expectations and dyadic interactions in elementary physical education classes. *Research Quarterly for Exercise and Sport,* 55, 32-40.

McNeil, L. M. (1988). Contradiction of control, part 1: Administrators and teachers. *Phi Delta Kappan,* 69, 333-339.

Orbach, S. (1978). *Fat is a feminist issue.* New York: Berkley Books.

Orlick, T., McNally, J., & O'Hara, T. (1978). Cooperative games: Systematic analysis and cooperative impact. In F. L. Smoll and R. E. Smith (Eds.), *Psychological perspectives in youth sports.* New York: Wiley.

Pellegrino, E. D. (1981). Health promotion as public policy: The need for moral groundings. *Preventive Medicine,* 10, 371-378.

Placek, J. H. (1983). Conceptions of success in teaching: Busy, happy and good? In T. J. Templin & J. K. Olson (Eds), *Teaching in physical education.* Champaign, IL: Human Kinetics.

Placek, J. H. (1984). A multi-case study of teacher planning in physical education. *Journal of Teaching in Physical Education,* 4, 39-49.

Sage, G. H. (1980). Sociology of physical educator/coaches: Personal attributes controversy. *Research Quarterly for Exercise and Sport,* 51(1), 110-121.

Schwartz, D. M., Thompson, M. G., & Johnson, C. L. (1982). Anorexia nervosa: The socio-cultural context. *The International Journal of Eating Disorders,* 1, 20-36.

Segrave, J. O. (1980). Role preferences among prospective physical education teacher/coaches. In Virginia Crafts (Ed.), *Proceedings, national association for physical education in higher education, volume II.* Champaign, IL: Human Kinetics Publishers.

Siedentop, D. (1986). The modification of teacher behavior. In M. Pieron & G. Graham (Eds.), *Sport pedagogy.* Champaign, IL: Human Kinetics Publishers.

Siedentop, D. (1987). The theory and practice of sport education. In G. T. Barrette, R. S. Feingold, C. R. Rees, & M. Pieron (Eds.), *Myths, models, and methods in sport pedagogy.* Champaign, IL: Human Kinetics Publishers.

Silberman, M. (Ed.). (1971). *The Experience of Schooling.* New York: Holt, Rinehart, and Winston.

Theberge, N. (1985). Toward a feminist alternative to sport as a male preserve. *Quest,* 37, 193-202.

Tindall, B. A. (1975). Ethnography and the hidden curriculum in sport. *Behavioral and Social Science Teacher,* 2(2), 5-28.

Tousignant, M., & Siedentop, D. (1983). A qualitative analysis of task structures in required secondary physical education classes. *Journal of Teaching in Physical Education,* 3(1), 47-57.

Trang, M., & Caskey, O. (1981). *Improving instructional effectiveness through video recall.* Palo Alto, CA: R & E Research Associates.

Veal, M. L. (1986). A descriptive study of pupil assessment in secondary school physical education. Unpublished doctoral dissertation, Teachers College, Columbia University.

Veal, M. L. (1988). Pupil assessment: Perceptions and practices of secondary teachers. *Journal of Teaching in Physical Education, 7*(4):327-342.

Vertinsky, P. (1985). Risk benefit analysis of health promotions: Opportunities and threats for physical education. *Quest, 37*(1), 71-83.

Wang, B. (1977). An ethnography of a physical education class: An experiment in integrated living. *DAI, 38,* 1980A. (University Microfilms No. 7721750)

Weis, L. (1982). Schooling and the reproduction of aspects of structure. *Issues in education: Schooling and the reproduction of class and gender inequalities* (pp. 1-16). Occasional Paper #10, SUNY at Buffalo.

Zeichner, K. M., & Tabachnick, B. R. (1981). Are the effects of university teacher education "washed out" by school experience? *Journal of Teacher Education, 32*(3), 7-11.

16

Culture and Ideology in Physical Education

ANDREW C. SPARKES PH.D.,
Exeter University

When addressing the literature to gain a basic comprehension of the central aspects of culture and ideology, I immediately was struck by the range of intellectual frameworks that have utilized these concepts, and consequently the diversity of interpretations that are available. Gibson (1986) believes that " 'Culture' is one of the most complex and elusive concepts we possess" (p. 66), while McLellan (1986) claims that "ideology is the most elusive concept in the whole of science" (p. 1). Both are essentially *contested* concepts, that is, concepts about the very definition, and therefore application, of which there is acute controversy. This contestation needs to be born in mind throughout the following discussion which, is in part, a reflection of my own confusions concerning the nature of culture and ideology, and their influence upon physical educators in school.

As Feiman-Nemser and Floden (1986) point out, many studies that focus upon culture assume it to provide a common base of knowledge, values, and norms for action. Accordingly, Woods (1983) notes:

Cultures, in turn, develop when people come together for specific purposes, intentionally or unintentionally, willingly or unwillingly. People develop between them distinctive forms of life—ways of doing things and not doing things, forms of talk and speech patterns,

315

subjects of conversation, rules and codes of conduct and behaviour, values and beliefs, arguments and understandings. These will not be formally regulated, but heavily implicit. One's part in them may not be consciously recognised. Rather one grows into them, and may recognise them as a natural way of life (p. 8-9)

Physical educators, like anyone else, are inducted into certain cultures such as, social class, religious, ethnic, school or sporting cultures, via the ordinary processes of socialization. Through this process they come to be and to understand what it means to be a physical educator. With regard to the influence of culture upon individual behavior, it often is assumed that the culture provides a set of values that form the major link between culture and action by directing human action to some ends rather than others, but this linkage is problematic. In contrast, Swindler (1986) conceives of culture as a "tool kit" of symbols, stories, rituals and world views which people may use in numerous configurations to solve different kinds of problems. She notes:

> . . . all real cultures contain diverse, often conflicting symbols, rituals, stories and guides to action . . . A culture is not a unified system that pushes action in a consistent direction. Rather, it is more like a "tool kit" or repertoire (Hannerz, 1969: 186-188) from which actors select differing pieces of constructing lines of action. Both individuals and groups know how to do different kinds of things in different circumstances . . . People may have in readiness cultural capacities they rarely employ; and all people know more culture than they use. (p. 277)

THE TOOL KIT METAPHOR

When translating this view into the context of teaching and learning in schools, teachers may come to value ends for which their cultural equipment is well suited (cf. Mancini, 1980). In this sense, culture's causal significance is not in defining ends of action, but rather in providing cultural components that are used to construct strategies of action in the classroom[1] and the school. These strategies become persistent ways of ordering behavior through time as teachers organize both their actions and values to take advantage of cultural competencies. Hence, the apparent conservatism of many teachers, for example, in the face of change, may not simply be due to the fact that they value the outcomes of their present way of teaching; rather, they may not have been supplied with the cultural competences to teach any other way—they do not have the necessary tools at their disposal. The "tool kit" metaphor also draws our attention to some other features of culture.

---

[1] The term classroom is used throughout this chapter to cover the wide range of contexts that physical educators operate in, such as the gymnasium, swimming pool, games field, tennis courts, etc.

Teachers as creative users of culture

It suggests that teachers are skillful users of culture and are not simply "cultural dopes" (Garfinkel, 1967; Wrong, 1961). They are active and creative in "coping" (Hargreaves, 1978; Pollard, 1982) with the structural constraints of schooling that impose themselves upon them, whilst at the same time they assist in the construction, and maintenance, of these very structures that socialize and constrain them. As Giddens' (1976) theory of structuration notes, "social structures are both constituted by human agency, and yet at the same time are the very medium of this constitution" (p. 120). Therefore, teachers are not passive and unreflective vessels into which culture is "poured" but are active in defining and redefining any given culture and their circumstances within it.

Cultures and the maintenance of routine

The constant use of a given tool ensures that its application and operation becomes routinized and taken for granted. Confronted with similar problems one naturally uses the "appropriate" tool for the situation. In this sense, cultures are similar to any paradigm that people are socialized into which provide the individual with forms of "recipe knowledge" (Schultz, 1962), "tacit" understandings (Polanyi, 1978), and "preunderstandings" (Bullough et al., 1984a), that determine what is important, legitimate and reasonable. These forms of understanding allow the individual to act without the need for prolonged existential consideration, which is a strength. However, as Patton (1978) argues, this is also a weakness since the very reasons for action are hidden in the unquestioned assumptions of the paradigm (read culture). Consider for a moment the essential characteristics of preunderstanding outlined by Bullough et al. (1984a). Firstly, they are taken to be *historical*, they are situated within a culture (local to universal) and change slowly over time. Secondly, they serve as a backdrop of meanings that *enable* understanding and are, therefore, essential elements in all situations requiring understanding. Finally, preunderstandings both *limit* and *distort* meaning because they "significantly predetermine it by virtue of the world view and values inherent in a native language and a family and social context" (p. 2). Thus, culture constrains and enables us simultaneously. As an example, progressive "child-centered" teachers see the world very differently from traditional "subject-centered" teachers, and both organize their behavior accordingly. On this account, culture structures the world we perceive and the way we think.

Similarities and differences in the range of tool kits available

Different tool kits contain different combinations of tools, and various groups in society will have access to many kinds of tool kits. This suggests that rather than there being an homogenous culture in which there is uniformity of values, beliefs, orientations, and practices, within teaching as an occupational group, there can be many cultures and sub-cultures (see Hargreaves, 1984a). As Feiman-Nemser and Floden (1986) realize:

> The assumption of cultural uniformity is, however, untenable. Teachers differ in age, experience, social and cultural background, gender, marital status, subject matter, wisdom and ability. The schools in which they work also differ in many ways, as do the groups of students they teach. All these may lead to differences in teaching culture. (p. 507)

However, though it is wrong to over-homogenize, it is also inappropriate to over-heterogenize, since despite all these differences most teachers *do* engage in activities that are recognizable as "teaching" across situations, and they often *do* share similar concerns and face similar dilemmas (see Berlak and Berlak, 1981). For example, Hargreaves (1980, 1982) suggests that teachers in general are concerned about status, competence, and (social) relationships. Hoyle (1986) believes that, "As a profession, teaching is prone to status concerns, and within teaching, physical educationalists are particularly given to pondering status issues" (p. 43). Though these concerns may be common to physical educators, the responses to them can vary, but once again the strategies adopted to enhance subject status often display strong similarities. For instance many physical educators choose to promote successful school teams or link into the examination system in order to gain subject status within the school (see Carroll, 1982; Glew, 1983).

Teacher isolation also would appear to be another cultural norm in both the United Kingdom and the United States (see Copeland and Jamgochian, 1985; Denscombe, 1985; Lortie, 1975; Templin, 1986). As Hargreaves (1980) notes:

> The most startling feature of teachers in their relation with adults, including colleagues, is their sensitivity to observation whilst teaching. Like sexual activity, teaching is seen as an intimate act which is most effectively and properly conducted when shrouded in privacy. To be watched is to inhibit performance. (p. 141)

This isolation may reflect the professional's concern for autonomy but, as Locke et al. (1986) realize, the high degree of autonomy given to the PE teacher is often a reflection of an isolation linked to institutional neglect which is itself related to the low or peripheral status of the subject in schools. Such a situation means that unlike other occupations, teaching does not seem to promote, to any high degree, a shared culture based on the movement from knowledge to experience in the company of one's peers. In the classroom one fails or succeeds alone, and as Templin (1986) notes:

> The limited data we have indicate that physical educators are thrown to their own resources; that is, they must provide self-stimulation, develop their own solutions to pedagogical problems when assistance is needed, and assess their own success and failures. (p. 10)

Despite the dominance of isolation, some schools described by Little (1982) and Oldroyd (1985) do have norms of collegiality, schools where the culture supports such practices as teachers observing each others' teaching, providing suggestions for improvement, and discussing professional problems. These norms have a positive influence on the frequency of teacher interaction, the quality of teaching, the promotion of a shared technical culture among teachers, and increased pupil achievement. Unfortunately, such schools are rare, and the prevailing norm remains that of isolation.

Cultures and the construction of competent membership

Just as we learn how to use tools, so we learn how to use cultures. Similarly, just as expertise in the use of tools is displayed in the doing, the same is true for a person entering the school for the first time as a physical educator since he/she must quickly display "competent membership," which Denscombe (1980) rightly points out resides in *action* not status. He notes:

> It is how competent members interpret situations, how they use the rules, bend, neglect or invoke the official prescriptions which explains the activity of members rather than the official prescriptions themselves. (p. 283)

Therefore, what distinguishes the competent from the non-competent teacher is not knowledge of the formal structure of the individual school per se, but rather the ability to interpret it in the appropriate manner. This is defined by other competent members who, despite different personalities and biographies, share patterns of understandings which form the basis of a specific "work culture" or "subject subculture." These patterns of understandings, which the newcomer must grasp, make up the various cultures of teaching and informs a process of reality construction that enables individuals to see and understand particular events, objects, utterances or situations in *distinctive* ways. Hence, teacher cultures are *embodied* in the work-related beliefs and knowledge that they share, which includes beliefs about the appropriate ways of acting on the job, what is rewarding in teaching, and the "craft knowledge" (Zeichner et al., 1987) that enable teachers to do their work. Importantly, these patterns of understandings (part of the tool kit) also provide a basis for making the individuals' behavior meaningful, and culture should be viewed as an active living phenomenon through which teachers create and recreate the worlds in which they live. As Morgan (1986) notes:

> Just as a tribal society's values, beliefs and traditions may be embedded in kinship and other social structures, many aspects of an organization's culture are thus embedded in routine aspects of everyday practice. For these routine activities define the socially constructed stage on which the current generation of actors lend their culture living form. (p. 132)

COMING TO TERMS WITH IDEOLOGIES

As the individual is socialized into the cultures of teaching via a prolonged "apprenticeship of observation" (Lortie, 1975), (the experiences of pre-service teacher education, and the impact of school experience), so he/she is socialized into a variety of ideologies which forms part of the tool kit of cultures that can lead teachers to approach their tasks in a number of different ways (see Bell, 1980). Hence, in terms of their classroom practice, their classification of pupils, and their relationships with pupils, it is possible to find great differences between teachers of subject departments in the same school and similarly between teachers in the same department. These differences often are related to the different educational ideologies the teachers hold. Sharp and Green (1975) define a teaching ideology as follows:

> A connected set of systematically related beliefs and ideas about what are felt to be the essential features of teaching. A teaching ideology involves both cognitive and evaluative aspects, it will include general ideas and assumptions about the nature of knowledge and of human nature—the latter entailing beliefs about motivation, learning and educability. It will include some characterization of society and the role and functions of education in the wider social context. There will be assumptions about the nature of the tasks teachers have to perform, the specific skills and techniques required together with ideas about how these might be acquired and developed. Finally, the ideology will include criteria to assess adequate performance, both on the material on whom teachers "work" i.e. pupils, and for self-evaluation or the evaluation of others involved in education. In short, a teaching ideology involves a broad definition of the task and a set of prescriptions for performing it, all held at a relatively high level of abstraction. (p. 68)

Here, ideology can be located at an individual level; but, these systems of beliefs and values also can be held by a group of teachers which serve to support their interests, and are taken for granted by them. As Seaman et al. (1972) note, "Individuals have beliefs or opinions which they use to conduct their lives. Organised collections of people have ideologies" (p. 137)[2]. They go on to suggest, that the main utility of this concept derives from its ability to illustrate that this patterning of ideas and beliefs often serves the interests of groups of people *independently* of the views they hold; that is, ideology often can work behind peoples' backs without them being consciously aware of its operation. Ideologies, in turn, penetrate into the world of schools via the familiar assumptions, mundane practices, and beliefs of teachers. They are made manifest in the taken-for-granted assumptions of the classroom, staffroom, and the social relationships that prevail in school. As Gibson (1986) notes, "Ideology, thus, is a form of consciousness which pervades common-sense assumptions and everyday practices" (p. 11). He goes on to suggest that this "common-sense" can distort and conceal true interests. They may serve to maintain the interests of some groups in schools and society at the expense of others. Thus, ideologies may be identified and analyzed at various levels, such as societies as a whole, whole professions, segments of the profession against each other, teachers against parents, and teachers against pupils.

For some, such as Bullough and Gitlin (1985), the concept of ideology is central to an understanding of what happens in schools since they believe that over time school structure and ideology, interactively, combine to establish those firm patterns of action and meaning which characterize life in schools. Their analysis forms part of a movement that engages in a "cultural level of analysis" (cf. Zeichner et al., 1987) that attempts to link the actions of individual teachers at the micro level of the classroom to ideologies, practices, and material conditions at the macro level of society, such as inequalities in wealth and power. One strand of this movement takes as its starting point a proposed relationship between cultural forms and teacher socialization, which is then linked to the actions of schools and classrooms by various forms of meaning and rationality which are dominant in the wider society. Thus, Rizvi (1986) considers the widespread persistence in education of a "bureaucratic rationality"; Bullough et al. (1984a, 1984b) suggest that teachers are constrained by "technological and public-servant" ideologies; Hargreaves (1984b) com-

[2] This is not to suggest that an ideology is merely the sum total of individual opinions. By adding one opinion to another we do not get two opinions but an argument, a debate, which may lead to a qualified agreement. Thus, an ideology contains more than all the relevant opinions and beliefs of those who adhere to it, and one obvious factor will be the unrecognized assumptions underlying the beliefs of the individual adherents. See Mannheim (1960) for a more detailed analysis of this point.

ments upon the presentism, conservatism and individualism of teachers; Dale (1977a, 1977b) believes teachers to be enthused with an ideology of "liberal individualism"; Giroux (1983) claims that teachers are dominated by a "technocratic rationality"; and Popkewitz (1987) and Ginsburg (1987) see teaching as pervaded by an "ideology of professionalism."

Although these writers differ in certain ways, their central theme would appear to be this: teachers, via the socialization process, have had instilled in them a dominating form of consciousness or mode of thinking which has an emphasis upon individualism, rationality, efficiency, and objectivity. Thus, teachers become preoccupied with *means* in preference to *ends*, they become concerned with *method* and efficiency rather than with *purposes*, focus their attention on "How to do it?" questions rather than "Why do it?" The operation of this consciousness in schools is seen to perpetuate particular forms of curriculum and pedagogy which support the interests of certain powerful groups in society by leaving the status quo unchallenged, as teachers continue to socially and culturally reproduce the inequalities of the wider society based on class, gender, and race.

Following directly from this, Charles (1979) believes a technocratic ideology pervades the PE program in schools. He sees the cornerstones of this ideology as mechanisticity (child as a machine, with teachers and pupils a cog in a larger administrative machine), reproducibility (production of uniform movement patterns for all children), componentiality (the development of isolated physical skills with a lack of concern for the whole person), and measurability (performance is evaluated in terms of precise, quantifiable criteria in relation to pre-stated objectives). All these are taken to have a pervasive influence upon the curriculum, the forms of pedagogy employed, and the manner of evaluating the PE program which is characterized by a strong framing and classification of knowledge (Bernstein, 1971). In addition, the teacher is legitimated as an expert controller of knowledge which is given direct to passive pupils via a whole class teaching method where the emphasis is upon physical skills and the attention is directed towards the highly skilled performers.

Though Charles' (1979) argument is plausible at a superficial level his adoption of Bowles and Gintis' (1976) reproduction stance weakens his case considerably. "The educational system helps integrate youth into the economic system, we believe, through a structural correspondence between its social relations and those of production" (Bowles and Gintis, 1976, p. 131). In their eyes (and Charles'), schools are subordinate to the economic system, they are determined by it, and therefore they function to reproduce it. Thus, PE is simply a means of producing a compliant labor force for the wheels of industry. However, as Gibson (1986) points out, such correspondence theories adopt a stereotyped view of capitalist factory life and schools. They neglect the ability of the individual and the group to challenge and resist. In fact, the passivity of pupils and workers simply does not exist in the real life situation as any teacher will tell you. Indeed, my own experience of teaching in secondary schools is a graphic reminder that pupils are most definitely *not* passive individuals who are molded into ideal final products on the conveyor belt of the educational system.

Adopting a "critical" perspective, Kirk et al. (1986) offer a much more complex analysis of the relationship between PE and the capitalist mode of production. Again, they contend that the dominant ideology in PE is that of "instrumental rationality," and claim that attempts by physical educators to disassociate themselves from the "play" element of their subject in order to make it more "work" like, along with their quest for academic respectability by the adoption of exams has:

> ". . . simply compounded the trivialisation and marginalisation of play like activities, and physical educators have contributed to their own subordination by unconsciously accepting definitions, which are historically contingent and culturally arbitrary, as natural, obvious, and given. In other words the hegemonic order has been reproduced and strengthened. (p. 173)

Their analysis of play and work in PE suggests how present curricular practices may serve to reinforce dominant ideologies that legitimize the vested interests of powerful groups. Tinning (1987) offers a similar analysis and believes that a major problem in western culture is the prevailing ideology of competitive individualism which focuses upon the development of the individual as the principle social ethic. He is concerned that technocratic rationality is becoming increasingly absorbed into the very logic of the educational system, which leads individuals to believe in a meritocratic society and prevents them from questioning, "the hegemonic influences which work to define ability in the interest of power elites" (p. 9). In his consideration of the development of Daily Physical Education Programs (DPE Programs) in Australia, Tinning suggests that knowledge has been fragmented and a mental-manual division has been imposed upon the teaching process. The DPE Programs are seen to define curriculum development in a hierarchical manner, in which educational knowledge is devised by experts and merely implemented by teachers. He notes:

> Here is the classical technocratic separation of means from ends and the focus on the efficiency with which the means contribute to the ends. Good teaching becomes defined as the extent to which the program is faithfully implemented. (p. 4).

Consequently, teachers are placed in the role of technicians who have little control over their work process, and are expected to implement in the most efficient way possible the ideas that are devised by curriculum makers outside of the individual school. Tinning (1987) stresses that DPE Programs have the *potential* to de-skill plus trivialize the work of teachers, and warns that the DPE materials need to be considered problematic by teachers who would be involved in actively questioning the values which underpin the program itself.

In a similar vein, Hargreaves (1986) notes the part that the ideologies contained in PE can play in the reproduction of social inequality and the maintenance of the status quo. He claims:

> The aims and objectives of physical education, as annunciated in official publications and by leading members of the profession in texts and journals, not only encode, but in many cases are explicitly committed to, views concerning the nature of the social order, which find ready agreement amongst dominant groups. (p. 164)

Hargreaves' critique of PE as "schooling the body" offers challenges to the claims of several major innovations that have taken place in the U.K. in recent years, namely Health Related Fitness (HRF) and Games for Understanding (GFU)[3]. Both Evans (1987) and Evans and Clarke (1987), building on the work of Bernstein (1986), have argued that HRF and GFU have become the new *official discourse* in PE which provides images, ideas, and prescriptions for action relating to the teaching of these approaches. This constitutes an important and influential belief system upon which practitioners in PE departments now turn to in order to construct both a rationale and a guide to curriculum planning, the organization and selection of subject content, and action inside classrooms. The official discourse would appear to offer a strong challenge to the traditional elitist ideologies contained in many PE programs since it challenges the emphasis upon competitive games with its authoritarian pedagogic mode and prefers a "non-authoritarian," "non-didactic" approach to teaching (Pain, 1985, 1986). However, Evans and Clarke (1987) raise issues concerning the significant *silences* in this official discourse to question whether these innovations are as emancipatory or as radical as they would have us believe.

On closer inspection, both HRF and GFU, in terms of philosophy and content, seem radically *child* rather than *subject-centerd*, with the focus according to Pain (1985) on "individual needs rather than activities and on individual responses to exercise rather than marks of achievement" (p. 5). Such sentiments seem to echo the concerns of the "progressive movement education" teachers of the 1950s and 1960s with their emphasis on dance and educational gymnastics. These activities were seen as

---

[3] For a rationale of Games for Understanding see Thorpe et al. (1986), and for Health Related Fitness see Biddle (1987), and Pain (1985, 1986).

vital for developing in the *individual* child the qualities of flexibility and adaptability, the ability to explore and solve problems independently, and cooperate with others; those qualities, as Hargreaves (1986) notes, were required for "competent occupational role performance among the new middle class" (p. 162). If this analysis has any validity, then HRF and GFU may be just a new means of imposing middle class values on children since at the center of both initiatives lies the ideology of *individualism* which is at the very heart of contemporary radical conservatism in the U.K. (see Elliot & McCrone, 1987), and forms the bedrock of the British educational system (see Hargreaves, 1982). In this sense, HRF and GFU provide little that is radical since, as Hargreaves (1986) points out, the predominant value underpinning the discourse of PE has always been individualism which he claims:

> . . . accomplishes the virtual disappearance of the social structure, that is, social processes and social phenomena are radically individualised, reducing them to the attributes of persons and of interaction between them. The school as a social organisation, knowledge of the nature of the social context of the education process and of the cultural characteristics of the pupils forms no part of this discourse . . . It is precisely the abstraction of the individual child from its socio-cultural context that enables this discourse to construct social integration from a middle class standpoint: its silences assume that the character of society can be taken for granted. (p. 165)

This essential individualism also can be linked to the ideology of *healthism* that George and Kirk (1987) claim is central to many PE teachers. This is a belief that the attainment and maintenance of health is a self-evident good which accepts unquestioningly the obvious link between organized physical activity and health. They note, "Not only are physical activity and health believed to be unquestionably linked, but by virtue of this link the subject is seen to be rationally-based, wholesome and politically neutral" (p. 2). The combination of individualism and healthism work toward a redefinition of "health" as an individual rather than a social concern and responsibility, and rarely are the wider social and mainly economically based industrial processes that influence health called into question or challenged.

Linked to the ideology of healthism is the preoccupation that many physical education teachers have with their own physique and the physique of others. Tinning (1985) claims this forms part of the "cult of slenderness" and notes:

> Disturbingly, however, I know of some physical educators who while themselves "blessed" with the genes of slenderness, actually find fatness in others to be repugnant. Moreover, this attitude of repug-

nance is conveyed readily in both explicit and implicit ways as they interact with adults and children alike. These very individuals who should understand the relevance of somatotypes seem to condone a unidimensional cultural concept of acceptability with respect to physique. (p. 138)

This undimensional cultural concept of physique is seen to serve the vested interests of certain groups in our society who benefit directly or indirectly from the cult of slenderness. These include drug companies, owners of fitness clubs and gymnasia, owners and marketers of the sports/fitness fashion industry, the manufacturers of weight reduction equipment, the government, and the media who sell the images of fitness. Last, but not least, the physical education profession stands to gain a great deal as their "expert" services are bought by other vested interests.

Unfortunately, despite the tenuous claims made concerning the relationship between health, fitness, and fatness; and despite the unnecessary anxieties of large numbers of the population (particularly women), Tinning (1985) believes that the physical education profession has a vested interest in maintaining the cult of slenderness rather than challenging it. He suggests that due to a process of occupational preselection by physique, coupled with their professional socialization, physical education teachers find it difficult to relate to overweight pupils. As a consequence, many physical educators through their daily classroom practices (both overt and covert) may in fact play a significant part in alienating large numbers of children from their own bodies and reinforcing their feelings of inadequacy. To act against this trend, Tinning calls for the physical education profession to challenge the negative aspects of the pursuit of slenderness, and notes:

> We should be actively educating our pupils to the folly of the media portrayed stereotypes as image models for all people and of the dangers associated with various forms of weight loss (from starvation diets to excessive exercising) which are employed in an attempt to look like the media image. Moreover, we should show in our own behaviours a tolerance of different body types. It should be reflected in our teaching and in our interpersonal relationships with adults and children alike. (p. 142)

MACRO AND MICRO LINKAGES: SOME PROBLEMS

Such critiques previously addressed are a valuable aid in challenging the assumptions underlying curriculum innovations and common practice in schools, yet they tend to remain weak in their explanations of why physical educators act as they do in the immediacy of the classroom context. In addition, as Zeichner et al. (1987) note:

. . . there is currently very little, if any, empirical evidence available that substantiates these claims and that documents that individual teachers actually incorporate forms of meaning and modes of rationality into their perspectives in ways consistent with the macro-level theories. (p. 31)

There is, however, another identifiable strand within this cultural level of analysis which explores how practices and policy initiatives outside the school affect the material resources available to teachers and the character of their work. Apple (1982), Gitlin (1983), and Wise (1979) see the reactions of teachers in schools and classrooms as creative responses to the constraints, dilemmas, and opportunities that are *determined externally* at the societal level and mediated through institutional structures and processes. Here, factors in the wider culture, such as the de-skilling of labor, the cultural stereotypes of women, the bureaucratization of work, and the social division of labor, have been claimed to affect the circumstances of teachers work (see Apple, 1986; Ball & Goodson, 1985; Feiman-Nemser & Floden, 1986; Scratton, 1986, 1987).

This form of analysis clarifies that the events in school do not take place in a social vacuum, but are linked to happenings beyond the school gates. In addition, it identifies the place of institutional structures as a mediator in the enactment of ideologies in school. As Hargreaves (1986) suggests, given the limited resources and the constraints imposed upon them in school, then the response of elitism by many physical educators is not only sensible but essential for survival. He notes:

It is not simply that PE teachers share elitist values—many, no doubt do—it is that individualism and elitism are built into the system of constraints and thus they come to pervade the ethos of the PE programme. Classes are far too large for teachers to be able to give all pupils sufficient attention to raise their standards of performance significantly and facilities, in any case, do not permit it. (p. 173)

Clearly, the ecology of the classroom which Doyle and Ponder (1975) define as "that network of interconnected processes and events which impinge upon behaviour in the teaching environment" (p. 183) has important implications for teacher action. Such factors as teacher-pupil ratio, resources, and time not only act as constraints on the actions of teachers but also exert positive pressures to act in certain ways (see Denscombe, 1980, 1985; Connell, 1985). Since resources are part of the ecology of the classroom, then these conditions are themselves (in part) products of policy decisions and political actions at levels beyond the classroom.

However, just what the link is, and what form it takes between the wider societal forces and the life in the classroom, remains problematic.

As Atkinson and Delamont (1985) suggest, this cultural level of analysis has been under-used in the sociology of education and consequently it is in need of further development. Accordingly, Zeichner et al. (1987) note:

> Although many of the analyses at a macro level are very persuasive on analytical grounds and although some definite influences have been amply documented regarding the link between the cultural and institutional contexts, there is much work that remains to be done regarding empirical substantiation of theories of the influence of "cultural codes" and the material conditions of a society on the socialization of teachers . . . the links between these cultural factors and the socialization of individual teachers has not been firmly established. (p. 31)

THE SCHOOL AS A SITE OF IDEOLOGICAL STRUGGLE

It may be useful at this point to turn our attention to the school as a workplace, in order to focus on the operation of ideologies in action. Here, as Seaman et al. (1972) note, "when they are not closing the ranks to contest for resources at the inter-professional level, ideological factions within subjects often dispute amongst themselves" (p. 50). Indeed, it is important to realize that historically the development of a comprehensive[4] schooling system in the U.K. has drawn upon a teaching force socialized into and committed to a number of distinct, and often conflicting, educational traditions and occupational cultures. As Hargreaves (1980) believes, "Today the resonances are still to be felt in the staffrooms of comprehensive schools where two distinct if overlapping occupational cultures have been brought together in an uncomfortable alliance" (p. 129). Yaakobi and Sharan (1985) indicate that different subject subcultures may be socialized into different beliefs and practices with differing professional identities via their university training. Hence, the school can contain numerous ideologies, and several ideologies may be in operation within a subject subculture or department where there may be little agreement on subject paradigm or subject pedagogy (Ball & Lacey, 1980). The former refers to the appropriate content of the subject; the latter refers to the system of ideas and procedures for the organization of learning in the classroom under specific conditions, that is, appropriate method.

---

[4] It is usual to take 1965 as the most significant date in the history of comprehensive education in the U.K. In this year, Harold Wilson's Labor Government issued Circular 10/65 requesting local authorities to submit plans for comprehensive reorganization. The "ideal" of the comprehensive school was a nonselective intake of children of *all* abilities. Prior to this, following the 1944 Education Act, a tripartite system operated which was selective in nature and depended upon success in the national "11 plus" examination. For a detailed development of comprehensive schooling and the problems involved, see Ball (1984) and Hargreaves (1982).

Not surprisingly, these differing ideologies tend to become most evident during periods of crisis and change in schools, since as Ball (1987) realizes, "Innovations are rarely neutral. They tend to advance or enhance the position of certain groups and disadvantage or damage the position of others" (p. 32). Indeed, Ball's (1981, 1985) work indicates clearly how attempts to introduce mixed-ability grouping into a school produced conflict between those subject subcultures which held a progressive ideology and those which held a traditional ideology. Work on innovations in PE involving mixed-ability and mixed-gender grouping illustrates similar conflicts *within individual* PE departments (Evans, 1985; Evans et al., 1987; Sparkes, 1986, 1987a, 1988a, 1988b). These studies strongly suggest that schools are sites of ideological struggle involving competition and contestation over material advantage and vested interest. Thus, if we are to understand the limits and possibilities of educational change, then it is necessary to consider schools and departments as "arenas of struggle," contexts in which power is unevenly distributed amongst members and in which there are likely to be ideological differences and conflicts of interest.

A CASE STUDY OF STRUGGLE

To illustrate the above points, my own work on teacher initiated innovation will be briefly considered[5]. This involved a three year case study (1983-1986) of a PE department of seven specialists at a large co-educational, comprehensive school in England named Branstown. Up until April 1983 this department was bound together by an elitist ideology which was subject-centered, meritocratic, traditional, and with an emphasis on the teaching of skill acquisition, fitness, sporting success, and achievement. According to Whitehead and Hendry (1976) this is the dominant ideology in British PE, and at Branstown School it was expressed in a curriculum where both boys and girls were streamed by ability in games lessons, with the most able pupil (and potential school team players) forming a top-group which was taken by the PE specialist. In contrast, the less able were allocated to non-specialist helpers who varied a great deal in their ability to teach games. In addition, the boys curriculum, in particular, was heavily "skewed" (Glew, 1983) toward the major team games of rugby, football, and cricket at the expense of individual activities such as educational gymnastics.

At the beginning of the summer term in 1983 Alex arrived as the newly appointed Head of Department, and he held an ideology whereby his paradigmatic and pedagogic values ran counter to the rest of the department. His progressive ideology was child-centred, egalitarian, with

---

[5] This work is considered in more detail in Sparkes (1986, 1987a, 1987b, 1988a, 1988b).

the emphasis on individualized learning, cooperation, and collaboration rather than intense competition, together with a concern for self-expression and fulfillment via such activities as educational gymnastics and swimming. During this summer term the two ideologies co-existed together in the same department (see Sparkes, 1986), but by the Autumn term 1983, for a complex variety of reasons including vested interests, ideological interests, and self-interests, Alex began to conceive of changing the extant curriculum. The essential change he proposed to make was that of abolishing streaming by ability in games lessons for all pupils, and to make these *mixed-ability*. In addition, he proposed that PE specialists only taught in year 1-3, that more individual activities, such as educational gymnastics, were included in the boys' curriculum. Overall he made great efforts to convert those within his department to his own teacher ideology.

Once these proposals were out in the open, the two ideologies collided; the academic year 1983-1984 (the adoption phase of the innovations) was a period of great tension, anxiety, confusion, and at times, simply open conflict as those holding the elitist ideology battled to protect their own vested, ideological and self-interests in the face of change. Of great importance for our present discussion is the fact that these conflicts were never made public, that is, in the staffroom and at staff meetings the whole department acted as a "performance team" (Goffman, 1959) in their quest for enhanced subject and individual *status*. For *all* those in the department, the perceived marginal status of their subject in the school was a burning issue since they realized that the higher the status of the subject then the higher the resources, and the better prospects for the teachers involved in terms of staffing ratios, higher salaries, higher capitation allowances, more graded posts, and better career prospects. Therefore, their battle for status was, above all, a battle over the material resources and career prospects of each subject teacher and subject community (see Goodson, 1984; Pollard, 1982).

An essential feature of this innovation, for our purposes, was the manner in which those holding an elitist ideology developed a "strategic rhetoric" (Sparkes, 1987a) which allowed them to create the impression of holding a *progressive* ideology during their interactions with "significant publics" (Reid, 1984), such as, senior teachers, the Headteacher, Heads of Department, and interview panels for promotion. These interactions took place in the "educational" context of the school, for example, the staffroom and staff meeting, which Keddie (1971) defines as those arenas of debate where teachers discuss school politics and draw selectively and consciously upon educational theory and research. Here, teachers operate predominantly in the "discursive" mode of consciousness (see Cole, 1985) which involves them using knowledge they are able to express at the level of discourse. To emphasize the point, those holding an elitist ideology learned a language form from their new Head of Department involving key phrases, such as "relevant life skills" and "individual learning styles," and then presented themselves as "informed educators," espousing a *progressive* ideology in the educational context of the school to enhance subject and individual status.

Phenomenologically distinct from the educational context is the classroom context, which Keddie (1971) claims involves the world of *is* rather than *ought*, a pragmatic world focused upon deeds not words, practice not theory. In this context, Cole (1985) suggests that the "practical" mode of consciousness is dominant in which teachers draw upon their tacit common-sense knowledge to survive in the classroom. Concerning this private classroom arena of practice, Ball (1987) notes:

> The simple arguments of the debate are invariably overwhelmed by the complexities and messy realities of classroom life. The language employed here is the everyday discourse of pragmatism. The high flown rhetoric must be adapted to the immediate physical and material constraints of survival at the chalk face. (p. 39)

Once back in the classroom, the "progressive ideologists" of the staffroom returned to their elitist practice which bore no relationship to the content of their strategic rhetoric. Indeed, even when the innovations were implemented in 1984, those holding a strong elitist ideology still did not consider changing their teaching practice. As an example, the men in the department now had to teach *educational* gymnastics, but several of them simply transformed these into *formal Olympic* gymnastics lessons where they utilized a whole-class teaching method and grouped pupils in the lesson by ability. In contrast, Alex (the new Head of Department) in the same lessons used open tasks, mixed-ability, and was much more individually oriented and rarely addressed the class as a whole. Thus, for Alex there was some degree of congruence between ideologies as expressed in the educational context and their articulation in the classroom context, but for the rest of the department there was incongruence. In this sense, Alex had succeeded in introducing mixed-ability *grouping*, but not mixed-ability *teaching* and there was innovation without change. In such situations, Evans (1985) notes:

> Stratification, social division, inequality of educational opportunity stand largely unscathed, despite the hustle and bustle of curricular activity which on the surface suggests that substantial educational innovation is afoot. (p. 147)

Similar findings have been reported in relation to attempts to introduce mixed-sex grouping (see Evans et al. 1987), and this suggests that there are important sub-cultural variations between PE teachers (often gender specific), in which different groups are supplied with contrasting sets of paradigmatic and pedagogic views plus abilities as part of their tool kit on induction into a particular PE subculture. Thus, it may well be that some physical educators simply have not been culturally equipped to teach mixed-ability or mixed sex groupings and in the face of change, quite rightly for them, hold onto the practices which their own particular tool kit allows them to perform with relative ease and competence. A major shift in practice would call for a major re-tooling which has a high cost for the individual and may be rejected as a high risk operation (Sparkes, 1986, 1988b). Therefore, the subcultural differences in the tool kit of physical educators can severely inhibit the development of innovations, often leading to forms of curricular change which tamper only with the surface of educational practice. Within this process of superficial change, teacher ideologies remain untouched and unchallenged, allowing the practices of the classroom to remain static. These subcultural differences also ensure that conflict and tension within PE departments is an inevitable and inescapable feature of organizational change.

PROBLEMS OF RESEARCHING TEACHER CULTURES AND IDEOLOGIES

The concepts of "culture" and "ideology" defy simple definition; they are utilized within a variety of theoretical frameworks which ascribe different meanings to them and provide analyses at different levels of operation. With such a state of confusion prevailing, it is hardly surprising that Feiman-Nemser and Floden (1986) comment, "Two striking things about research on the cultures of teaching is how little there is and how hard it is to do" (p. 523). They also note, "While all educational research is difficult, research on the cultures of teaching has special difficulties because of its elusive subject matter and the diversity of the teaching population" (p. 506). In particular, any focus on cultures and ideologies implies inferences about knowledge, beliefs, values, and norms, *none of which are directly observable.* In addition, as earlier sections have indicated, there is a range of teaching cultures and ideologies available within the occupational culture and subject subcultures of teaching which can be in operation within the same school or department. Also, does one address the *formal* culture of the school, or does one move behind the scenes to examine the ethos and tradition in a school or department that is communicated via the *informal* teacher, pupil, and school cultures present in each setting? There may well be one formal school culture but as indicated earlier there may be several contrasting and often conflicting versions of the informal school culture within a given school. Therefore, what methodologies are more appropriate for studying this informal culture? As Zeichner et al. (1987) realize:

Informal school cultures are often tacit rather than explicit. Even when explicit, the informal culture was less visible than the formal culture, being expressed in private conversations between teachers, casual remarks not intended for wide distribution, interpretations of the publicly acknowledged formal culture expressed not in words but in teacher, principal, and pupil actions. (p. 54)

This statement suggests prolonged periods of fieldwork are needed, involving observation and interviews in a school or department, in order to gain access to this micropolitical matrix of informal culture. Then, there are the problems of documenting similarities and differences between and within cultures, plus the ethics of reporting "insider" information given in confidence. Last, but not least, research on teaching cultures tends to be labor intensive, observations and interviews take considerable time to conduct and analyze. Therefore, the lone researcher or small research group operating on a small budget cannot be expected to go beyond a small sample of teachers, and this linked to the variations in teaching cultures has implications for the generality of conclusions from such studies.

The material presented earlier in this chapter also suggests other important problems in researching teacher ideologies. Teachers may express significantly differing ideologies depending upon the circumstances they find themselves in; ideologies may be *context specific*. Indeed, the ability to articulate different ideologies, depending upon the context and to facilitate impression management may well be a critical aspect of competent membership in marginal subjects such as PE, where subject survival is often at stake in a school. In such situations physical educators illustrate their skillful use of culture by creatively manipulating the cellular structure of the school. Several writers have noted the "structural looseness" and "loose coupling" of the school as a social system (see Bidwell, 1965; Weick, 1988) in which structure is disconnected from technical (work) activity, and activity is disconnected from its effects (cf. Meyer & Rowan, 1978). This is taken to be a basic property of educational organizations and means that there is little (if any) direct supervision of teachers in the "closed" classroom (Denscombe, 1985) where they retain a relatively high degree of autonomy as to their method of teaching.

Therefore, ideologies expressed in one context of the school may not be articulated in another, and both Hammersley (1981) and Woods (1984) have illustrated that the use of sexist and racist humor form part of a *staffroom* ideology which ends at the staffroom door; it carries no essential implications for actions and beliefs *outside of that particular situation*. As one moves from the staffroom to the classroom one enters a phenomenologically different world involving different dilemmas and interests-at-hand. Here, the ecology of the classroom may further mediate the influence of any ideology upon practice as teachers react to the multidimensionality, simultaneity, immediacy, unpredictability, and history of classroom life. In this context, *pupils* rather than colleagues exert a strong pressure, and Doyle (1979) has noted how teachers adjust their general approach, language, as well as type and frequency of specific teaching methods in relation to pupils. Thus, declared opinions and beliefs (ideologies) may differ greatly from observed classroom behavior. As Hoy (1968) realizes:

> Perfect congruence between the role ideology and role behavior is not expected in the school situation; contemporary social system pressures as well as interpersonal processes probably intervene to reduce the congruence. (p. 264)

Other studies have commented upon the problematic relationship between ideologies and action. As Keddie (1971), and Sharp and Green (1975) have indicated, teacher ideologies tend to be held at relatively *high levels of abstraction* which may not correspond to classroom practice. Hence, there exists contradictions and inconsistencies between the two levels of operation. Woods (1983) notes:

> We cannot assume, for example, that such beliefs are necessarily a reflection of basic attitudes or that they form a platform for action. They may rather be the product of particular circumstances. (p. 63)

Others, like Zeichner and Grant (1981), question whether a focus on ideologies is appropriate in attempting to explain teacher classroom behavior, and comment upon the lack of attention given to how ideologies are expressed in this particular context. They suggest that ideology only refers to a connected set of beliefs, assumptions, and ideas about what are *thought to be* the essential features of teaching in general; as such, it is not tied to specific situations and *does not include an action component*. To assist researchers in transcending the abstract level of ideology, they propose the heuristic tool of teacher perspectives. According to Becker et al. (1961), perspectives are a "co-ordinated set of actions and ideas a person uses in dealing with some problematic situation" (p. 34). These thoughts and actions are coordinated in the sense that the actions flow reasonably, according to the actor's point of view, from the idea contained within the perspective. Thus, perspectives are taken to contain an action component. Hammersley (1977) believes that in the individual's perspective are the initial clues to the immediate motives for action. To study perspective implies a focus not only on what the teachers think about their work (purposes, values, beliefs, and goals) but also on the way in which they give meaning to those beliefs and actions in the classroom. In addition, there is some evidence (see Zeichner et al., 1987) that perspectives are not situation specific and that they influence styles of pedagogy across situations, regardless of institutional demands.

These are but a few of the problems that bedevil attempts to investigate teacher cultures and ideologies, and they will need to be faced by researchers in the near future. Importantly, there is a need for conceptual clarity, and distinctions need to be made between ideology and perspectives. Though their influence may be interactive, they wuld appear to be analytically distinct for research purposes. The common practice of using them interchangably only serves to add to the confusion that prevails in this area. In addition, there is a need to move away from an either-or stance in which some studies argue that individual teacher characteristics, dispositions, and capabilities are more influential in determining teacher behavior than are institutional characteristics. Others argue for the primacy of institutional factors and ignore the influence of individual and biographical factors. Such a polarized stance can only lead to a fragmentary and partial understanding of cultures and ideologies. A more holistic approach is required, as exemplified by Lacey (1977) and Pollard (1982) in England; Zeichner & Tabachnick (1985) and Zeichner et al. (1987) in the United States; and Connell (1985) in Australia, all of whom emphasize in their studies the *interactive* nature of individual, biographical, and institutional factors upon teachers.

These studies indicate the need for more information concerning the *same* group of teachers in different settings, in order to get some sense of the contextual variability of teachers' conduct and the sources of that variation. It also would seem appropriate to bring a variety of research methods to bear upon the questions of culture and ideology and to promote multidisciplinary inquiry where possible. At present, the research community is high on speculation but low on evidence concerning the influence of teaching cultures and ideologies in the process of schooling. This trend needs to be reversed as soon as possible.

REFERENCES

Apple, M. (1986). *Teachers and Texts.* London: Routledge and Kegan Paul.
Apple, M. (1982). *Education and Power.* London: ARK Paperbacks.
Atkinson, P., and Delamont, S. (1985). Socialization into teaching: The research which lost its way. *British Journal of Sociology of Education, 6,* 307-322.
Ball, S. (1981). *Beachside Comprehensive.* Cambridge: Cambridge: Cambridge University Press.
Ball, S. (Ed) (1984). *Comprehensive Schooling: A Reader.* Lewes: Falmer Press.
Ball, S. (1985). School politics, teachers' careers and educational change: A case study of becoming a comprehensive school. In L. Barton and S. Walker (Eds). *Education and Social Change.* London: Croom Helm.
Ball, S. (1987). *The Micro-Politics of the School.* London: Methuen.
Ball, S., and Goodson, I. (1985). Understanding Teachers: Concepts and Contexts. In S. Ball and I. Goodson (Eds). *Teachers' Lives and Careers.* Lewes: Falmer Press.
Ball, S., and Lacey, C. (1980). Subject disciplines and the opportunity for group action: A measured critique of subject subcultures. In P. Woods (Ed). *Teacher Strategies.* London: Croom Helm.

Becker, H., Greer, B., Hughes, E., and Strauss, A. (1961). *Boys in White.* Chicago: University of Chicago Press.

Bell, L. (1980). The school as an organization: A reappraisal. *British Journal of Sociology of Education, 1,* 183-192.

Berlak, A., and Berlak, H. (1981). *Dilemmas of Schooling: Teaching and Social Change.* London: Methuen.

Bernstein, B. (1971). *Class, Codes and Control.* London: Routledge and Kegan Paul.

Bernstein, B. (1986). On Pedagogic Discourse. In J. Richardson (Ed). *Handbook for Theory and Research in Sociology of Education.* London: Greenwood Press.

Biddle, S. (Ed) (1987). *Foundations of Health Related Fitness in Physical Education.* London: Ling Publications.

Bidwell, C. (1965). The School as a Formal Organization. In J. March (Ed). *Handbook of Organizations.* Chicago: Rand McNally.

Bowles, S., and Gintis, H. (1976). *Schooling in Capitalist America.* New York: Basic Books.

Bullough, R., and Gitlin, A., (1985). Beyond Control: Rethinking Teacher Resistance. *Education and Society, 3,* 65-73.

Bullough, R., Gitlin, A., and Goldstein, S. (1984). Ideology, teacher role and resistance. *Teachers College Record, 86,* 339-358.

Bullough, R., Goldstein, S., and Holt, L. (1984). *Human Interests in the Curriculum: Teaching and Learning in a Technological Society.* New York: Teachers College Press.

Carroll, R. (1982). Examinations and curriculum change in physical education. *Physical Education Review, 5,* 26-26.

Charles, J. (1979). Technocratic Ideology in Physical Education. *Quest, 31,* 277-284.

Cole, M. (1985). "The Tender Trap?" Commitment and Consciousness in Entrants to Teaching. In S. Ball and I. Goodson (Eds). *Teachers' Lives and Careers.* Lewes: Falmer Press.

Connell, R. (1985). *Teachers Work.* Sydney: Allen and Unwin.

Copeland, W., and Jamgochian, R. (1985). Colleague training and peer review. *Journal of Teacher Education, 36,* 18-21.

Dale, R. (1977a). Implications of the Rediscovery of the Hidden Curriculum for the Sociology of Teaching. In D. Gleason (Ed). *Identity and Structure: Issues in the Sociology of Education.* Driffield, Yorks: Nafferton.

Dale, R. (1977b). *The Structural Context of Teaching.* Milton Keynes: Open University Press.

Denscombe, M. (1980). The work context of teaching: An analytical framework for the study of teachers in classrooms. *British Journal of Sociology of Education, 1,* 279-292.

Denscombe, M. (1985). *Classroom Control.* London: Allen and Unwin.

Doyle, W. (1979). Classroom Effects. *Theory into Practice, 18,* 138-144.

Doyle, W., and Ponder, G. (1975). Classroom ecology: Some concerns about a neglected dimension of research on teaching. *Contemporary Education, 46,* 183-188.

Elliot, B., and McCrone, D. (1987). Class, culture and morality: A sociological analysis of neo-conservatism. *Sociological Review, 35,* 485-515.

Evans, J. (1985). *Teaching in Transition: The Challenge of Mixed Ability Grouping.* Milton Keynes: Open University Press.

Evans, J. (1987). Teaching for Equality in Physical Education? Paper presented to the conference, Ethnography and Inequality, St. Hilda's College, Oxford, September.

Evans, J., and Clarke, G. (1987). Changing the Face of Physical Education. Paper presented to the conference, Ethnography and Inequality, St. Hilda's College, Oxford, September.

Evans, J., Lopez, S., Duncan, M., and Evans, M. (1987). Some thought on the political and pedagogical implications of mixed sex grouping in the physical education curriculum. *British Educational Research Journal, 13,* 59-71.

Feiman-Nemser, S., and Floden, R. (1986). The Cultures of Teaching. In M. C. Wittrock (Ed). *Handbook of Research on Teaching.* London: Collier Macmillan.

Garfinkel, H. (1967). *Studies in Ethnomethodology.* Englewood Cliffs, New Jersey: Prentice Hall.

George, L., and Kirk, D. (1987). Barriers to Change in Physical Education: The Influence of Teachers Biography and Ideology. Paper presented at the British Educational Research Association Annual Conference, Manchester, September.

Gibson, R. (1986). *Critical Theory and Education.* London: Hodder and Stoughton.

Giddens, A. (1976). *New Rules of the Sociological Method.* London: MacMillan.

Ginsburg, M. (1987). Reproduction, Contradiction and Conceptions of Professionalism: The Case of Pre-service Teachers. In T. Popkewitz (Ed). *Critical Studies in Teacher Education: Its Folklore, Theory and Practice.* Lewes: Falmer Press.

Giroux, H. (1983). *Theory and Resistance in Education: A Pedagogy for the Opposition.* London: Heinemann.

Gitlin, A. (1983). School Structure and Teachers' Work. In M. Apple, and L. Weis (Eds). *Ideology and Practice in Education.* Philadelphia: Temple University Press.

Glew, P. (1983). Are your fixtures really necessary? *British Journal of Physical Education, 14,* 126-128.

Goffman, E. (1959). *The Presentation of Self in Everyday Life.* New York: Anchor Books.

Goodson, I. (1984). Beyond the Subject Monolith: Subject Traditions and Subcultures. In P. Harling (Ed) *New Directions in Educational Leadership*. Lewes: Falmer Press.

Hammersley, M. (1977). Teacher Perspectives. Open University Course E202, *School and Society*. Milton Keynes: Open University Press.

Hammersley, M. (1981). Ideology in the staffroom? A critique of false consciousness. In L. Barton and S. Walker (Eds). *Schools, Teachers and Teaching*. Lewes: Falmer Press.

Hannerz, V. (1969). *Soulside: Inquiry into Ghetto Culture and Community*. New York: Columbia University Press.

Hargreaves, A. (1978). Towards a theory of classroom coping strategies. In L. Barton and R. Meighan (Eds). *Sociological Interpretations of Schools and Classrooms: A Reappraisal*. Driffield: Nafferton.

Hargreaves, A. (1984a). Experience counts, theory doesn't: How teachers talk about their work. *Sociology of Education, 57*, 244-254.

Hargreaves, A. (1984b). Educational Policy and the Culture of Teaching: Some Prospects for the Future. Paper presented at the American Educational Research Association meeting, New Orleans, Louisianna, April.

Hargreaves, D. (1980). The Occupational Culture of Teachers. In P. Woods (Ed). *Teacher Strategies*. London: Croom Helm.

Hargreaves, D. (1982). *The Challenge of the Comprehensive School*. London: Routledge and Kegan Paul.

Hargreaves, J. (1986). *Sport, Power and Culture*. Cambridge: Polity Press.

Hoy, W. (1968). The Influence of Experience on the Beginning Teacher. *School Review, 76*, 312-323.

Hoyle, E. (1986). Curriculum development in physical education 1966-1985. In, *Trends and Developments in Physical Education*. Proceedings of the VIII Commonwealth and International Conference on Sport, Physical Education, Dance, Recreation and Health. London: E. and F. N. Spon.

Keddie, N. (1971). Classroom Knowledge. In M. Young (Ed). *Knowledge and Control*. London: Collier-MacMillan.

Kirk, D., McKay, J., and George, L. (1986). All work and no play? Hegemony in the PE curriculum. In, *Trends and Developments in Physical Education*. Proceedings of the VIII Commonwealth and International Conference on Sport, Physical Education, Dance, Recreation and Health. London: E. and F. N. Spon.

Lacey, C. (1977). *The Socialization of Teachers*. London: Methuen.

Little, J. (1982). Norms of collegiality and experimentation: Workplace conditions of school success. *American Educational Research Journal, 19*, 325-340.

Locke, L., Griffen, P., and Templin, T. (Eds) (1986). Profiles in Struggles. *Journal of Physical Education, Recreation and Dance, 57*, 32-63.

Lortie, D. (1975). *Schoolteacher*. Chicago: University of Chicago Press.

Mancini, J. (1980). *Strategic Styles: Coping in the Inner City*. Hanover: University Press of New England.

Mannheim, K. (1960). *Ideology and Utopia*. London: Routledge and Kegan Paul.

McLellan, D. (1986). *Ideology*. Milton Keynes: Open University Press.

Meyer, J., and Rowan, B. (1978). The structure of educational organizations. In J. Meyer and W. Marshall (Eds). *Environments and Organizations*. San Francisco: Jossey Bass.

Morgan, G. (1986). *Images of Organization*. London: Sage.

Oldroyd, D. (1985). The management of school-based staff development at Priory School. *British Journal of In-Service Teaching, 11*, 82-90.

Pain, S. (1985). *Physical Education and Health in the United Kingdom*. British Journal of Physical Education, *17*, 4-9.

Pain, S. (1986). Current Issues in Physical Education and Health in Schools in the United Kingdom. In, *Trends and Developments in Physical Education*. Proceedings of the VIII Commonwealth and International Conference on Sport, Physical Education, Dance, Recreation and Health. London: E. and F. N. Spon.

Patton, M. (1978). *Utilization-focused evaluation*. Beverly Hills: Sage.

Polanyi, M. (1978). *The Tacit Dimension*. New York: Anchor Press.

Pollard, A. (1982). A model of classroom coping strategies. *British Journal of Sociology of Education, 3*, 19-37.

Popkewitz, T. (1987). Ideology and Social Formation in Teacher Education. In T. Popkewitz (Ed). *Critical Studies in Teacher Education: Its Folklore, Theory and Practice*. Lewes: Falmer Press.

Reid, W. (1984). Curriculum topics as institutional categories: Implications for theory and research in the history and sociology of school subjects. In I. Goodson and S. Ball (Eds). *Defining the Curriculum: Histories and Ethnographies*. Lewes: Falmer Press.

Rizvi, F. (1986). Bureaucratic rationality and the democratic community as a social ideal. Paper presented at the Annual Meeting of the American Educational Research Association, San Francisco, April.

Schutz, A. (1962). *The Problem of Social Reality*. The Hague: Martinus Nijhoff.

Scratton, S. (1986). Images of Femininity and the Teaching of Girls' Physical Education. In J. Evans (Ed). *Physical education, Sport and Schooling: Studies in the Sociology of Physical Education*. Lewes: Falmer Press.

Scratton, S. (1987). Boys muscle in where angels fear to tread—girls sub-cultures and physical activities. In

J. Horne, D. Jary, and A. Tomlinson (Eds). *Sport, Leisure and Social Relations*. London: Routledge and Kegan Paul.

Seaman, P., Esland, G., and Cosin, B. (1972). Innovation and Ideology. Open University Press.

Sharp, R., and Green, A. (1975). *Education and Social Control*. London: Routledge and Kegan Paul.

Sparkes, A. (1986). Strangers and Structures in the Process of Innovation. In J. Evans (Ed). *Physical Education, Sport and Schooling: Studies in the Sociology of Physical Education*. Lewes: Falmer Press.

Sparkes, A. (1987a). Strategic Rhetoric: A Constraint in Changing the Practice of Teachers. *British Journal of Sociology of Education, 8*, 37-54.

Sparkes, A. (1987b). The Genesis of an Innovation: A Case Study of Emergent Concerns and Micropolitical Solutions. Unpublished Ph.D. Thesis, Loughborough University of Technology, England.

Sparkes, A. (1988a). Strands of Commitment within the Process of Teacher Initiated Innovation. *Educational Review*. (in press).

Sparkes, A. (1988b). The Micropolitics of Innovation in the Physical Education Curriculum. In J. Evans (Ed). *Teachers, Teaching and Control in the Physical Education Curriculum: Studies in the Sociology of Physical Education*. Lewes: Falmer Press (in press).

Swindler, A. (1986). Culture in action: Symbols and strategies. *American Sociological Review, 51*, 273-286.

Templin, T. (1986). Teacher Isolation: A Case for Collegiality. Keynote Address, World Conference of the International Association for Physical Education in Higher Education, Heidelberg, West Germany, August.

Thorpe, R., Bunker, D. J., and Almond, L. (1986) *Rethinking Games Teaching*. Loughborough University. Northants: Nene Litho

Tinning, R. (1985). Physical education and the cult of slenderness: A critique. *ACHPER National Journal, 107*, 10-14.

Tinning, R. (1987). The 'Good Ship Physical Education'—A View from the Crows Nest. *Plenary Papers, ACHPER 17th National Bennial Conference*, 9-17 January. Canberra: A.C.T.

Weick, K. (1988). Educational organizations as loosely coupled systems. In A. Westoby (Ed). *Culture and Power in Educational Organizations*. Milton Keynes: Open University Press.

Whitehead, N., and Hendry, L. (1976). *Teaching Physical Education in England*. London: Lepus Books.

Wise, A. (1979). *Legislated Learning: The Bureaucratization of the American Classroom*. Berkeley, California: University of California Press.

Woods, P. (1984). The Meaning of Staffroom Humour. In A. Hargreaves and P. Woods. *Classrooms and Staffrooms*. Milton Keynes: Open University Press.

Woods, P. (1983). *Sociology and the School*. London: Routledge and Kegan Paul.

Wrong, D. (1961). The Oversocialized Conception of Man in Modern Sociology. *American Sociological Review, 26*, 183-193.

Yaakobi, D., and Sharan, S. (1985). Teacher beliefs and practices: the discipline carries the message. *Journal of Education for Teaching, 11*, 187-199.

Zeichner, K., and Grant, C. (1981). Biography and Social Structure in the Socialization of Student Teachers. *Journal of Education for Teaching, 1*, 298-314.

Zeichner, K., and Tabachnick, B. (1985). The Development of Teacher Perspectives: Social Strategies and Institutional Control in the Socialization of Beginning Teachers. *Journal of Education for Teaching, 11*, 1-25.

Zeichner, K., Tabachnick, B., and Densmore, K. (1987). Individual, Institutional, and Cultural Influences on the Development of Teachers' Craft Knowledge. In J. Calderhead (Ed). *Exploring Teachers' Thinking*. London: Cassell Educational Ltd.

INDEX